Contents

DOCUMENTS AND RESOURCES

WOMEN'S STUDIES: A WORLD VIEW

Pioneers: Programs Founded in the 1970s

Breaking Ground: Programs Founded in the 1980s

New Voices: Programs Founded in the 1990s

NEWSBRIEFS

Editorial

This extra-large double issue of *Women's Studies Quarterly* combines two themes, related but distinct: a report on the largest United Nations–sponsored gatherings of women in history—at Beijing and Huairou—and a series of national reports on women's studies. What does women's studies have to do with the United Nations? With the Platform for Action? And what does the United Nations have to do with women's studies? In the course of answering these questions, of connecting these two themes, this editorial will also respond to a third—the future work, in the twenty-first century, of the women's movement and the relationship of women's studies to it. In sum, then, the first purpose of this volume is to offer firsthand accounts of the United Nations Fourth World Conference on Women, as well as useful materials that will illuminate the dimensions of the document that emerged from its deliberations. That document, the Platform for Action, can be described, as Australian law professor Judith Grbich did in Huairou, as a women's studies curriculum. Thus, one connection: we see women's studies as a key strategy for implementing the Platform for Action. As the national reports indicate, furthermore, in many economically developing countries around the world, women's studies is the strategically located venue for the production of scholars and activists, both of whom are essential to carrying the women's movement into the twenty-first century.

How We Got to Beijing—and Huairou

Two chronologies provided the contexts for personal experiences, political expectations, and the documents that follow. First, we have included a chronology of the United Nations conferences and preparatory meetings held between 1975 and 1995. Second, with appreciation for the work of those who produced them, we have reprinted generous sections from the Global FaxNet Bulletins issued by the International Women's Tribune Centre between April 3 and September 25, 1995. These were at first occasioned by the news that the Chinese had changed the location of the forum from Beijing, where government leaders would meet, to a small town about sixty kilometers north of Beijing that did not have the essential facilities for an NGO Forum that might grow to include 36,000 participants.

Since 1975 and the United Nations First World Conference on Women, such events have really been two closely linked conferences: the official meeting of governments to debate the situation of the world's women and the associated meeting of nongovernmental organizations (known as NGOs). Ten years ago, at the Third World Conference on Women, 300 of these NGOs were formally recognized by the United Nations and thus could name delegates formally credentialed to attend the governmental meetings, both to advise their own national leaders and to lobby their agendas more generally to leaders of other countries. By the time of the meeting in China, the United Nations had credentialed 2,000 NGOs, including Women's Studies International: A Network, organized by the Feminist Press at the City University of New York. While the governmental meetings have remained stable in size, at under 5,000, the meetings of NGOs have grown—from 6,000 in Copenhagen, to 14,000 in Nairobi, to 30,000 in Huairou. Hence, the consternation indicated in the Global FaxNet Bulletins, the outpouring of support requesting (and demanding) that China provide adequate space and facilities for the forum, and in Beijing, close to the governmental meetings, for the NGOs that were credentialed to be able to do their work responsibly in both places, since the meetings, once scheduled sequentially, now overlapped significantly.

We need not summarize the day-to-day accounts that faithfully render the plot of this memorable drama. Anne Walker, the director of the International Women's Tribune Centre, continues the firsthand narrative even through the garbage hauling, the rain, and the mud in Huairou. We cheer her and we expect you will as well.

Women's Studies International Goes to China

Like *Women's Studies Quarterly* itself, Women's Studies International is an educational project of the Feminist Press. Conceived by Vina Mazumdar, emerita director of New Delhi's Center for Women's Development Studies, Women's Studies International: A Network and

Educational Program began at the United Nations Second World Conference on Women, held in 1980 in Copenhagen. At the end of two
weeks of plenaries, workshops, and roundtables on women's studies,
attended by some 1,500 people, Women's Studies International was
voted into existence—with headquarters at the Feminist Press—at a
meeting of some 400 women from fifty-five countries. Several publications followed and were distributed to network participants, but the
main function of Women's Studies International eventually became
planning for similar plenaries and workshops at the Third World
Conference on Women, held five years later, in 1985, in Nairobi.

During the years between 1985 and 1995, Women's Studies International began to plan events at other international conferences, the
most ambitious of which was held in Costa Rica early in 1993. There,
building on *Women's Studies in Europe*, a collection of essays published in *WSQ* (Volume XX, Fall/Winter 1992) and edited by Angelika
Köster-Lossack and Tobe Levin, we envisioned a series of meetings at
which some twenty-five national reports would be presented by pioneers representing all the continents and organized chronologically
rather than geographically. These highly successful sessions were
chronicled—and the national reports published—in *WSQ* (Volume
XXII, Fall/Winter 1994). They became the model for our major work at
the forum we expected to be held in Beijing.

Thus, our plans for the Beijing forum began with an effort to invite
new pioneers, especially in Africa and Eastern Europe, as well as in
Latin America and Asia, to write and present national reports. In
addition, we had hoped we could repeat the very successful resource
center that we had organized for Copenhagen, as a place not only
to register interest in Women's Studies International and to meet
others working in women's studies but this time as a place where we
would *give books* to women's studies faculty for the libraries of their
institutions.

Once the forum was moved to Huairou, more than an hour's ride
from Beijing, and with insufficient space for the more than 40,000
women who had registered, even for the 30,000 who arrived, our
resource center fell victim to the space problem, as did the scheduling
of some of our major women's studies sessions. Nevertheless, we
managed, with the generous help of the International Women's Tribune Centre, to organize an area of tables and bookshelves from which
we proceeded to distribute—free of charge—some 1,500 copies of
Women's Studies Quarterly (Volume XXII, Spring/Summer 1994); 1,500
copies of *Re-Visioning Feminism Around the World*, our twenty-fifth-
anniversary journal; 500 copies of *A Rising Public Voice: Women in*

Politics Worldwide, edited by Alida Brill; 400 copies of *Seeds 2: Supporting Women's Work Around the World*; and 400 other feminist press books and *WSQ*s, as well as 1,000 catalogs.

While we gave copies of our catalog, the journal, and *WSQ* to everyone we could, we reserved the books for women from economically developing countries. The responses were heartwarming, often disbelieving as well. "You mean you are *giving* these books away?" was a familiar refrain. Some people asked, occasionally with suspicion, *why* we were doing this. "Why do you want us to 'register'?" When we said we'd like to know about their need for books more generally, we sometimes heard more expressions of disbelief.

With support from several foundations, we expect to send a copy of this volume, along with a more explicit questionnaire, to all who registered with us from Africa, Asia, Latin America, and Eastern Europe. And we expect that Women's Studies International will continue to work on the question of distributing books to women's studies programs and other educational institutions overseas.

The Forum at Huairou

The Global FaxNets, Robin Morgan's essays, and Laura Hershey's essay describe the chaos, the failure to provide for the disabled, the extraordinary discomfort, and the even more extraordinary spirit of the thousands of women who trudged through rain and mud, up hills and down again, to stand at the back of tents, holding their umbrellas over the heads of the hapless standing with them, or seeking temporary shelter in unfinished, cold, damp, wall-less, or windowless buildings. The few hot, sticky days provided, if not relief, then at least sharp contrast. Looking back, one remembers with awe the resilience of women, undaunted by such obstacles as the Chinese security checks or their own conference organizers' unexpected and sometimes unannounced changes in times or locations of sessions, or by the difficulties of announcing new sessions that had been called into existence right then and there. No one was going to let the expense and spirit that had brought them thousands of miles to this unfamiliar shore go to waste. They were going to make the best of it, and leave regrets for later on.

The United Nations Fourth World Conference on Women: Background

As a result of a worldwide women's movement, and on the recommendation of the Commission on the Status of Women, the United Nations designated 1975 as International Women's Year, a step designed to remind the international community that discrimination against women was a persistent problem throughout the world. As part of International Women's Year, a global Conference on Women was held in Mexico City in 1975 that brought together 2,000 delegates from 133 member states. In a parallel gathering called the International Women's Year Tribune, some 6,000 representatives of nongovernmental organizations (NGOs) met in panel discussions and workshops to share experiences and perspectives and to bring these perspectives to bear on the official conference.

The Mexico City conference set in motion a long-term campaign for the advancement of women, giving particular attention to women in economically developing countries. Delegates adopted the World Plan of Action for the Implementation of the Objectives of International Women's Year. The conference also urged the United Nations to proclaim the period from 1976 to 1985 as the United Nations Decade for Women. Immediately following the conference, the proclamation was put into effect.

The Decade for Women spawned a variety of national and international programs, as well as activities on behalf of women by nongovernmental organizations (NGOs), some of which were newly formed grassroots organizations. A mid-decade conference was held in Copenhagen in 1980 to review the progress of these efforts, and a third conference was held in Nairobi at the end of the decade to assess achievements. The Nairobi conference was also charged to identify obstacles to further improvement in the status of women and to recommend measures to overcome these obstacles. The outcome of the conference was a document titled "Nairobi Forward-Looking Strategies for the Advancement of Women," which offered guidelines for national and international measures to achieve equality for women in all spheres of society. At this stage it was clear that, while some progress had been made, much remained to be done.

The first review and appraisal of the implementation of the forward-looking strategies was conducted by the Commission on the Status of Women in 1990, and in 1991 the United Nations published a landmark volume titled *The World's Women, 1970–1990*, providing for the first time trends and statistics on the situation of women. Data were provided in specific key categories: family life, leadership and decision making, health and childbearing, education, and economic participation. These statistics and indicators confirmed and clarified the slow rate of progress toward full equality with men. The need for a Fourth World Conference on Women was growing increasingly apparent.

Meanwhile, a series of world conferences and summit meetings sponsored by the United Nations after 1990 addressed various aspects of development—the environment, human rights, population, and social development. In each case, the achievement of these develop-ment goals was dependent on the advancement of women. The 1992 United Nations Conference on Environment and Development, known as the Earth Summit, that was held in Rio de Janeiro, reflected a consensus on the vital participation of women in promoting sustain-able development. The World Conference on Human Rights held in Vienna in 1993 stressed the importance of women's rights as human rights. The International Conference on Population and Development, held in Cairo in 1994, affirmed that essential to any program of population and development were gender equality for women and women's ability to control their own fertility. The World Summit on Social Development, held in Copenhagen in March 1995, proclaimed the central function of women in fighting poverty and securing social and economic development. The Copenhagen Declaration also af-firmed the importance of the relationship between the Social Summit and the Beijing conference and the need for collaboration on the achievement of common objectives.

The year 1995 was not only the year of the United Nations Fourth World Conference on Women; it also marked the fiftieth anniversary of the United Nations Charter, which proclaimed "the equal rights of men and women." The United Nations Charter was the first interna-tional agreement to proclaim gender equality as a fundamental hu-man right. It was followed by the creation of the Commission on the Status of Women with a mandate to prepare recommendations and reports on promoting women's rights in the political, economic, civil, social, and educational fields, a mandate that was later expanded to include advocacy on behalf of women, monitoring the implementa-tion of internationally agreed-upon measures for the advancement of women, and reviewing and appraising progress at the national, re-gional, and global levels.

Thus, the United Nations Fourth World Conference on Women came into being after twenty years of preliminary meetings, documents, and examinations and reexaminations of the status of women. It was uniquely organized through a complex series of regional and interna-tional preparatory meetings, held during the eighteen months preced-ing September 1995. The purpose of these preparatory conferences was to write regional versions of the draft Platform for Action, which would be amended or accepted by the Commission on the Status of Women, meeting in March 1994 and again in March 1995 in New York.

The Making of the Platform for Action

The United Nations conferences described above, as well as the regional and international preparatory meetings during 1994 and 1995, were all part of the process leading to the adoption of the Platform. Robin Morgan's essay offers an account of the process in Beijing itself, where scores of caucuses met, sometimes all day and into the night, on their particular sections of the Platform and where, each morning, the Linkage Caucus (organized by Bella Abzug's WEDO) provided a briefing and the U.S. governmental delegation provided a briefing each afternoon—in each case organized by topic or theme and with key persons reporting on progress or impasse in agreement on specific language of the document.

We include in this section a brilliantly analytical essay by Gloria Bonder, mother of Argentine women's studies and founder of the Center for Women's Studies in Buenos Aires. She describes the movement from an emphasis on educational access in the 1985 Nairobi Forward-Looking Strategies to an emphasis on educational quality in the 1995 Platform for Action. Her essay summarizes the accomplishments of twenty years of feminist work in education and suggests the still more difficult, but strategically hopeful, work ahead.

We also selected for this volume a representative sample of interesting, often feisty, speeches offered by heads of governmental delegations or representatives of nongovernmental organizations. They range from the fiery defense of women of Islam by Pakistan's Benazir Bhutto and the strong declaration of women's rights as human rights by the U.S.'s Hillary Clinton to the more specific targets of Indian Nandini Azad, representing GROOTS, an international organization of grassroots women, and South African Palesa Beverly Ditsie, representing the International Gay and Lesbian Human Rights Commission. Most of these are hopeful expressions. Significantly, they come from every sector of the world.

Documents and Resources: The Platform for Action

We include here not only the documents surrounding the Platform for Action, but Mariam Chamberlain's review of five volumes that the United Nations caused to be produced directly for the Fourth World Conference on Women, as well as two other volumes published for that purpose by others. We also include a Guide to On-line Information and Resources connected to the Beijing conference.

Because we are convinced of the importance of the Platform for Action, we present it not only in summary and through commentary but in its entirety. It is available on-line and from the United Nations, but it is not easily accessible to the general public in a bookstore—and within a generous context. After two years of national, regional, and international meetings, 187 countries debated the document in Beijing, meeting sometimes around the clock, and ultimately voted the Platform for Action into existence.

There are many ways of describing the Platform for Action: most of its language is bureaucratic; occasionally a phrase or a sentence soars with a writer's touch. More important, its diction has had to suit the cultures of the world, in which the words "the family" and "families," for example, carry different meanings, in which the right to be homosexual rather than heterosexual is still strongly contested.

In a seminar at Huairou on teaching about women and the law, Australian law professor Judith Grbich said, "The Platform for Action reads like a women's studies course." What she meant was that it covered every topic or theme of women's lives, from education and work, to marriage, health, politics, violence, to the legal right to inherit and to own land, and even to the right to sexuality. In many countries, the work of moving the Platform forward will need to be done by those who understand this women's studies curriculum, whether or not they are faculty members or students learning about the history and contemporary lives of women in their countries and the world over.

From long years in the women's movement, we have all learned that, while it is important to have a document, the document does not ensure changed behavior or conditions. The document names problems and proposes potential solutions. It urges governments and other institutions to act to solve these problems, to adopt its suggested solutions. But unless the world's women understand the terms of both the problems and the solutions and join together in smaller and larger groups—in streets, villages, cities, states, and nations, and in further international meetings—to continue to press for the adoption of these solutions, we will not move forward.

Toward the Twenty-First Century of Women

We include here several visions of the potential significance of the Platform for Action in the century to come. Gertrude Mongella, secretary general of the United Nations Fourth World Conference on Women, declared at its opening session, "A revolution has begun." Bella Abzug, co-chair of WEDO and a tireless activist on behalf of women, envisions "a global movement for democracy" and announces, for the

United States, a Contract with American Women. Madeleine K. Al-
bright, head of the U.S. delegation to the United Nations, announces
the U.S. commitments to the Platform for Action. Gro Harlem Brundtland, prime minister of Norway, sees "women power as a formidable
force." Finally, Leticia Ramos-Shahani, a Philippine senator and the
leader of the Group of 77—the powerful caucus of economically
developing countries, speaks the words that we have chosen to use for
this section of the volume and for the volume itself: "Toward the
Twenty-First Century of Women: From Commitment to Action."

Women's Studies As One Key Strategy for Action: National Reports

While the national reports we offer in this volume are meant to
continue the process established in previous issues, they appear here
in a fresh context: as potential agents for carrying through the Platform for Action. Certainly, the curriculum described in Makerere
University's women's studies program mirrors the Platform's topics
directly.

Other connections may be even more important. While we in the
West understand that women's studies grew out of the women's movement that preceded it, and while some of us decry the alleged aban-
donment of the women's movement by young members of academe,
even by some of those who currently teach in or lead women's studies
programs, the newer patterns of women's studies in Africa, Asia, and
Eastern Europe are quite different. In many of these countries, women's studies pioneers *are* the women's movement—or are consciously
teaching those they expect to become future women's studies faculty,
future women-centered government officials, or future leaders of
women's movements in their countries. Women's studies practitioners
are often called upon by governments to provide statistics, studies, and
other intellectual expertise. In some cases, especially in Eastern Europe, women's studies pioneers have successfully fought conservative
efforts to end abortion rights or to send women back into wifely
dependence. In some countries—especially in Northern Europe, for
example, women's studies scholars work more closely with the government on women's issues than they do with their male academic colleagues. In sum, if one follows the national histories and current status
of women's studies in a variety of countries around the world, one will
find the essential elements for knowledge about the contents of the
Platform for Action and, just as important, strategies for moving it
forward.

Can a Book Make a Difference?

If you believe in the power of the word, spoken and written, then you may believe also that this volume, in the hands of as many thousands as possible, will make a difference. Will it get into those hands? We will work to see that that happens, and we appreciate the assistance of those foundations that have made this much of our work thus far possible: the Ford Foundation, the AT&T Foundation, the Shaler-Adams Foundation, and the Rockefeller Foundation. We wish to thank as well the staff of the Feminist Press, all of whom worked long-past-inhuman hours and over weekends to see that this book appeared in a timely fashion, despite blizzards, computer breakdowns, and virulent influenzas. We appreciate also the editorial assistance of Mariam K. Chamberlain, who read and commented on the entire manuscript, as well as Tobe Levin, our European coordinator, and Gloria Bonder, our Latin American coordinator. Finally, we thank all the contributors to the volume, whose payment will be in copies that will help us to distribute the power of the word.

Florence Howe *is director of The Feminist Press at The City University of New York and professor of English at City College and the Graduate School and University Center, CUNY.*

Women's Studies Quarterly is pleased to announce the appointment of a new general editor, Liza Fiol-Matta. Liza Fiol-Matta is assistant professor of English at LaGuardia Community College, CUNY, and has served on The Feminist Press's Publication and Policy Committee and its Board of Directors for several years. With Liza Fiol-Matta's appointment *Women's Studies Quarterly* renews its commitment to publishing feminist theory, literature, and scholarship affecting the curriculum. *WSQ* also renews its commitment to publishing work that explores the intersections of race, class, and gender, and encourages original work from a wide range of multicultural and multidisciplinary perspectives, including international perspectives and student voices.

Women's Studies Quarterly also congratulates the contributors to the Working-Class Studies issue edited by Janet Zandy (*Women's Studies Quarterly* 23:1–2, Spring/Summer, 1995). The issue was awarded a Best Special Issue prize by the Council of Editors of Learned Journals. The CELJ judges wrote:

> [B]y publishing essays and narratives authored by working-class women, this issue gives voice to those who comprise its topic. . . . This particular issue is likely to become not only an important resource but also a model for other journals. . . . [A] study of the working class is emerging as the next, and perhaps last, marginalized group for academic study. . .

A special issue of *Women's Studies Quarterly*, focusing on working-class studies, will expand upon the Spring/Summer 1995 issue of *WSQ*. The editors are seeking submissions that explore the intersections of gender, race, ethnicity, sexual preference, and class, and are particularly interested in including works by writers of color as well as lesbian/bisexual writers. Please send submissions by August 1, 1996, to one of the following addresses: Renny Christopher, Department of English, California State University—Stanislaus, 801 West Monte Vista, Turlock, CA 95382; Lisa Orr, Department of English, University of California—Los Angeles, 225 Rolfe Hall, Box 951530, Los Angeles, CA 90095-1530; Linda Strom, Department of English, Youngstown State University, Youngstown, OH 44555-3415.

The Road to Huairou and Beijing

Chronology, 1975–1995

1975. Mexico City, Mexico. International Women's Year. United Nations First World Conference on Women and International Women's Year Tribune (the first "Forum"). 1976–85 is declared the UN Decade for Women.

1979. Convention on the Elimination of All Forms of Discrimination Against Women (CEDAW) is adopted by the UN. To date, 139 member states have ratified.

1980. Copenhagen, Denmark. Second World Conference on Women and NGO Forum emphasize education, employment, and the participation of women in the development process.

1985. Nairobi, Kenya. Third World Conference on Women and NGO Forum support three goals of the UN Decade for Women—equality, development, and peace. The Conference adopts the Nairobi Forward-Looking Strategies for the Advancement of Women Towards the Year 2000.

1992. Rio de Janeiro, Brazil. UN Conference on Environment and Development. Agenda 21, the Program of Action for environment issues in the 21st century, includes a chapter on women.

1993. Vienna, Austria. World Conference on Human Rights. Recognizes that women's rights are human rights. UN Special Rapporteur on Violence Against Women is appointed. The UN Declaration on the Elimination of Violence Against Women is adopted.

Manila, The Philippines. November 16–20. Asia-Pacific NGO Symposium, a regional pre-preparatory conference. Approximately 600 women attend.

1994. New York City, U.S. March. NGO Consultation prior to the 38th session of the UN Commission on the Status of Women (CSW), the Preparatory Committee for the Fourth World Conference on Women.

Jakarta, Indonesia. June 7–14. Preparatory Conference for Asia. Economic and Social Commission of Asia and the Pacific (ESCAP) develops its regional plan of action around three major themes: women in economic development, women in social development, and women and empowerment.

Cairo, Egypt. September 5–13. International Conference on Population and Development affirms that reproductive rights are basic rights for couples and individuals; that women have a right to safe motherhood and full and timely knowledge about reproductive health and sexuality; that women's empowerment is the key to population and development.

Mar del Plata, Argentina. September 20–24. Preparatory Conference for Latin America and the Caribbean. 1,200 participants from 41 countries develop a regional plan around the themes of structural adjustment, democracy and citizenship, and violence against women.

Vienna, Austria. October 13–15. Preparatory conference for North America and Europe. 54 countries represented.

Amman, Jordan. November 4–6. Preparatory conference for Western Asia. Over 800 women from 16 countries.

Dakar, Senegal. November 12–15. Preparatory conference for Africa. 4,000 delegates from 52 countries.

1995. Copenhagen, Denmark. March. World Summit on Social Development and NGO Forum pursue an agenda to eradicate poverty, increase employment, and halt social disintegration.

New York City, U.S. March 15–April 5. Final Preparatory Committee reports on regional meetings and develops an NGO-written draft of the Platform for Action based on regional documents. 39th session of the UN Commission on the Status of Women writes its final draft of the Platform for Action in preparation for Beijing.

Huairou, China. August 30–September 8. NGO Forum on Women. Approximately 30,000 participants.

Beijing, China. September 4–15. Fourth World Conference on Women adopts the Platform for Action: 189 countries vote by consensus.

How It Happened—From Day to Day

Excerpts from Global FaxNet Bulletins, April 3–September 25, 1995

International Women's Tribune Centre

The Global FaxNet/GlobalNet is coordinated by the International Women's Tribune Centre (IWTC). The project aims to alert women to issues related to the Fourth World Conference on Women and to mobilize action at the local, national, regional and international levels. The Global FaxNet builds upon the original WOMENET fax network of 28 regional women's media networks and has added many others in the worldwide mobilization effort around the NGO Forum site change. The Global FaxNet/Global Net currently reaches over 450 groups or information multipliers via fax and E-mail.

Global FaxNet 1, April 3, NGO Forum Site Changed!

The Chinese Organizing Committee has informed Supatra Masdit, Convenor of the NGO Forum on Women '95, that the NGO Forum can no longer be accommodated at the Beijing Workers Stadium Complex. According to an official letter received on Friday, March 31, the Gymnasium at the Workers Stadium Complex has been deemed structurally unsound and unable to support the number of participants expected. Chinese officials are therefore changing the location of the Forum to another site which appears to have two major drawbacks: (1) it is twice as far from the official conference (i.e. about 45 minutes by bus) and (2) it does not include a meeting place that can accommodate plenaries of more than 1700 at a time—a far cry from the plenary space for 15,000 that had been formerly available at the Gymnasium! An additional site has been suggested for the opening and closing ceremonies.

The NGO Forum Office has informed the China Organizing Committee that this situation is not acceptable and asked for more details. In addition, Forum officials will be going to China for face-to-face talks. We will keep you in touch with further developments as they happen.

Global FaxNet 2, April 4, Petition/Appeal to the UN!

To all WOMENET members:

Attached you will find the following:

Petition/Appeal to the United Nations. The UN Commission on the Status of Women/Preparatory Committee for the UN Fourth World Conference on Women (PrepCom) has been extended to Friday, April 7, 1995. It would be great if we could get a first round of signatures on this petition before then, to hand out to delegates before they go home. Please make copies of the petition and get them circulating as widely as possible. . . .

An Urgent Appeal from Women's Groups to the UN

We, the undersigned, urge the Member States of the United Nations to support NGO efforts to have adequate access and input into the preparatory processes for the Fourth World Conference on Women in Beijing. We are concerned that many of the gains made by and for women at recent conferences in Rio, Vienna, Cairo, and Copenhagen are being seriously eroded.

We also urge governments to speak out against any efforts to place the NGO Forum on Women far away from the World Conference, on a site that does not have a meeting space that will hold more than 1700 people. This fact alone will mean that the plenaries cannot be held each day as previously planned, except in the open air without interpretation or amplification facilities.

We appeal to Member States of the United Nations to stand behind NGOs in their efforts to have a real voice in these deliberations, and not to allow last minute attempts to shut out what has been an extremely effective lobby on behalf of women's rights in recent UN conferences.

Global FaxNet 3, April 10, Great Response to Petition Against NGO Forum Site Change!

What a great response to the Petition! Some 111 organizations from 40 countries in 8 world regions had responded by April 7, when the third PrepCom for the Fourth World Conference on Women ended. Some of you sent signatures, others used the petition and turned it into a letter to FWCW Secretary General Gertrude Mongella. We packaged all responses received into a large "book" with a simple cover explaining what they were, and handed them to Gertrude Mongella, Irene Santiago, and Supatra Masdit of the NGO Forum Office, and delegates from every world region. Delegates from China were specifically targeted. Your efforts were greatly appreciated by NGO representatives whose spirits and energies were lifted by this timely reminder that they are not alone; by sympathetic delegations who had something concrete with which to take China to task; by the NGO Forum Office leadership who will now have a stronger voice when they go to Beijing this weekend to argue our case with the Chinese. Responses are continu- ing to come in. We shall continue to package and disseminate them. In the meantime; please let us know of any further action being taken or being planned at national and regional levels—for example some groups are lobbying their governments to make direct contact with the Chinese Government through their embassies in China. . . .

Global FaxNet 4, April 12, Appeal to Governments, United States and China

The campaign to stop China from moving the NGO Forum on Women 1995 out of Beijing to Huairou is taking on a life of its own. The number of responses to the first petition we sent out to you last week has now passed the 200 mark and they are still coming in thick and fast.

With this fax we are sending you an Appeal to the United Nations and to the Government of China addressed to the UN Secretary Gen- eral Boutros Boutros-Ghali and to the Chair of the China Organizing Committee Madame Peng Peiyun. We've also prepared a separate information sheet which brings you up-to-date on happenings so far, and can be copied and handed out to government personnel, media, ambassadors, and other opinion makers at local, national and regional levels. . . .

Appeal to The United Nations and to The Government of China

We, the undersigned, strongly protest the proposed move of the NGO Forum on Women from its present site in the city of Beijing to a new site in the suburbs of Beijing.

The NGO Forum on Women will be attended by more than 20,000 women and men from every corner of the world. Participants will be deeply involved in the issues before the Fourth World Conference on Women, and must be close to the World Conference site in order to maintain contact with the proceedings.

Additionally, government delegates attending the World Confer- ence will want to take part in many of the Forum activities. This will not be possible if the site is far removed. The travel distance from the

World Conference to the proposed site in Huairou is estimated at being from one hour to two hours in length. This is unacceptable.

Added to the very real problem of distance is the fact that the proposed site is in no way suitable as the site for a major international event of this nature. The area contains a scattered number of buildings, including hotels, villas, and training centers. There is not one large meeting place that seats more than 1700. Large daily plenaries would be out of the question. Communications are almost non-existent. For the media, the situation couldn't be more lacking in basic needs. Journalists would stay away, thereby limiting enormously the message coming out of Beijing. Participants would be bused from Beijing and spend a good part of each day traveling.

Given these facts, it would be impossible for a productive, substantive Forum on Women to take place. We therefore demand that you take strong, supportive action to make sure that a suitable site, close to the World Conference and within Beijing City itself, be found for the NGO Forum on Women. We need urgent personal attention to this matter.

Signed:

Fax to: Madam Peng Peiyun, Member, State Council, Chair/China Organizing Committee, In care of Mr Arthur Holcombe, Resident Representative, UNDP, Beijing, Fax: (86-1) 532-2567; Boutros Boutros-Ghali, Secretary General, United Nations, New York, Fax: (1-212) 963-4879

Urgent Appeal Concerning NGO Forum Site, April 11 1995

Please contact your government, the United Nations, the Government of China, the media, and—if possible—your Ambassador to the UN about the proposed change of the NGO Forum on Women from its current site to a new site in the suburbs of Beijing. Such a shift would represent a complete breakdown of previous agreements reached between the Government of China, the China Organizing Committee, the United Nations, and the NGO Forum on Women Facilitating Committee.

Background

On March 31, 1995, just five months before the opening day of the NGO Forum on Women, word was received by the NGO Forum Convenor, Supatra Masdit, that China was moving the site for the Forum to the suburbs of Beijing. The reason given was that "structural problems have been found."

Initial information on the new site given by the China Organizing Committee indicated that it was 45 minutes away from the official conference, was close to the airport, and included a large room that seats 1700 and other meeting rooms that seat from 50 to 1000. The opening and closing ceremonies would be held at the National Olympic Center that seats 20,000. Almost 6,000 hotel beds were said to be close to the new site, known as the Huairou Scenic Tourist Area; other Forum participants would be transported to and from each day in shuttle buses.

New Information

Since receiving this news, further information has come from independent contacts in Beijing who have traveled to the site.

Most importantly, the Huairou Scenic Tourist Area is very far from the official conference site, with varying estimates given of an hour to two hours travel time on a crowded highway. There is only one public bus traveling the route from Beijing. Participants would be dependent on shuttle buses provided by the China Organizing Committee. Entrance to the site is by a narrow unsealed road.

Of equal importance is the fact that the meeting spaces at the new site are scattered amongst various training centers, hotels, and villas. The China Organizing group is planning to build a makeshift covered space over a school playground area, to hold 10,000, without interpretation facilities. This does not in any way replace the modern, well-equipped covered gymnasium that seated 13,000 at the previous site, nor the Workers Stadium itself that seated 72,000.

Telecommunications facilities at the new site are minimal at best. There are limited IDD lines in the few hotels. Coverage of the NGO Forum on Women by media would suffer badly, even if journalists covering the World Conference went to the trouble of finding their way into the suburbs of Beijing, which—in most cases—would be doubtful.

Global FaxNet 7, April 27, Update on Petition and Appeal Regarding Forum Site Change

The response to the petition and appeal continues to be tremendous! Because of all your wonderful efforts, there are at least 1000 organizations representing 60 countries in all 5 world regions that are supporting the call for China not to change the Forum venue. And we are still receiving dozens of faxes every day!

We expect to hear more definite news from Beijing over the coming weekend when the NGO Forum inspection team (Supatra Masdit, Irene

Santiago, and others) send their recommendations to the NGO Facilitating Committee. The FC will make decisions about the site by the 3rd of May. . . .

Global FaxNet 8, May 2, Update on Petition and Appeal Regarding Forum Site Change

We have to marvel at what a wonderful job of mobilizing women of the world you have all done! To date, IWTC has received petitions and appeals from 1,625 organizations in 64 countries. A few are still coming in, but we all seem to know instinctively that this first phase has come to an end (further testimony of mass global team-work?!). The latest news we have comes via the accompanying *Washington Post* article received today. We should get details in the next couple of days when Irene Santiago returns from Beijing, but we do have confirmation that the article is essentially correct as far as the stand being taken by China is concerned. So! Guess it's on to the second phase! Please let us know what you are all doing locally, nationally, and regionally to get governments to take a stand. In the meantime we will keep you up to date with all the news as we get it.

Registration closed last weekend (April 30) but the NGO Forum Office will continue to accept registration forms as long as they are postmarked by April 29. We understand that they were coming in at rate of approximately 2000 a day up until yesterday! . . .

Global FaxNet 9, May 4, Follow-Up Action to Forum Site Change

To WOMENET members and petition signing groups:

With this fax we are sending you:

1. An extract from the report of the NGO Forum delegation to the NGO Facilitating Committee (FC) regarding alternative sites and

2. Proposed follow-up strategies from the New York/New Jersey Women's Human Rights Working Group (of which IWTC is a member). . . .

For Urgent Action!—NGO Forum Site Update

The report of the NGO Forum delegation to China confirms that the proposed NGO Forum site at the 'scenic tourist area' of Huairou is not suitable for the type of meeting that NGOs have been preparing for. In addition to what we already know, the delegation reported that the journey between Huairou and Beijing took 50 minutes with a police escort. The 71 meeting rooms and tents are spread out over a radius of six kilometers and can only hold a total of 9,430 persons. Only 16,000 hotel beds are available. There are no facilities for the disabled. The Chinese propose also allowing NGOs the use of the Beijing Recreation Center, which is near the site of the UN conference, but this only holds 2,000 people.

We understand that the Olympic Site and other sites in Beijing offer viable options to the Worker's Stadium. Indeed we understand that it is only the Worker's Gymnasium which suffers from structural problems thus leaving other parts of the Worker's Sport Service Center as options for our meeting. The obstacles to use any combination of these sites do not appear as impossible to overcome as the obstacles to making Huairou an appropriate site.

We also understand that approximately 40,000 women have registered so far to attend the Forum and that the Chinese government has put a cap on attendance at 20,000.

Despite all of the above, however, some members of the delegation appear ready to accept the proposed site. NGOs need to act now and present a united front to demand a site that meets the criteria for holding an effective NGO Forum. A meeting last night of the NY/NJ Human Rights Working Group, of which IWTC is a part, proposed the following strategies:

1. Lobbying the NGO Facilitating Committee not to accept the proposed alternative from the Chinese and to continue examining other sites. (A list of members of this committee is attached.)

2. Lobbying your government to make a strong statement to the Chinese that either a suitable alternative site be found for the NGO Forum or the UN conference and the NGO Forum should be moved elsewhere. The Chinese may not be meeting the needs of the UN conference either. We are trying to get more information about this from the Secretariat here and suggest that you also question your national committees or delegates.

3. Lobbying members of the special advisory group to the Secretary General to follow the same position. Members of the special advisory group need to know how the NGO movement feels. The group is scheduled to meet in Amman, Jordan on May 18. We've passed out the list of members separately by E-mail. Boutros Boutros-Ghali is scheduled to be in Russia next week. When he was in Fiji recently, women were not allowed a meeting with him and so took out a full page ad in the *Fiji Times* protesting the site change.

Global FaxNet 10, May 11, NGO Facilitating Committee Rejects Huairou Site

The NGO Facilitating Committee has rejected the China Organizing Committee (COC) offer of the controversial Huairou site for the NGO Forum in August and given the COC until May 24 to come up with an alternative that meets the needs of the 40,000 participants and jour-nalists expected to take part in the event.

The decision came late yesterday during a conference call across 13 countries and six continents between the 19 members of the commit-tee. All but four FC members mandated the NGO Forum Negotiating Team headed by NGO Forum Convenor Khunying Supatra Masdit to continue talking with the COC about two alternative sites in Beijing— the Olympic Stadium or the former Workers Stadium with satellite sites to make up for the loss of the Gymnasium which China says has "structural problems." In terms of ongoing mobilization, the FC sug-gested that efforts be put into lobbying governments to make official complaints to the UN Secretary General, Boutros Boutros-Ghali.

The Negotiating Team and the FC have the backing of thousands of women and men worldwide who have been making their voices heard on the controversial bid to change the Forum site since it was first mooted by the COC some six weeks ago.

You have all been taking incredible action! Hundreds of petitions and appeals are still pouring into the UN and the COC. You all took those first IWTC initiatives and made them your own. You spread them across your own networks; you rewrote them to suit your own local flavor; you turned them into full page newspaper ads, press releases, and the bases of radio programs and call-ins, and we have been feeding information to the mainstream media in all our countries in order to galvanize wider public support. Here at IWTC we have had responses from some 2,500 local, national, regional, and international groups, organizations and networks in over 70 countries in all regions of the world and we are still counting as the faxes and mail keep pouring in.

In addition to the ongoing signature collection campaign, we have been expressing our outrage at this attempt to sideline the Forum in letters to heads of governments and in formal and informal discussions with members of our national delegations to the FWCW. We have been lobbying our government ministers, members of parliament, and parliaments; we have been holding community meetings to explain the facts and making links at national and regional levels for more impact; and, in fraternal messages and discussions, we have urged FC members to stand their ground.

As you have informed us of your actions, we have fed them to the NGO Forum Office and to UN officials here in New York. We have also brought them to the attention of the media as the controversy attracts more and more of their attention. Of great importance too was the strength and confidence that the members of the NGO Forum Office Negotiating Team could draw from you and take with them into their talks with the COC. It's just been a great effort, and we should all keep it going—stronger and wider! We will continue to keep you in touch with any news as we get it and to spread your news as we hear it.

You should all know that we're getting sounds that governments are beginning to take issue with China. The European Union has sent a strong letter of protest to the Chinese government on behalf of the European governments and we've received petitions signed by members of parliament in several countries, so there's a strong basis for women to step up lobbying efforts with their own governments.

Global FaxNet 10a, May 12, NGO Forum Convenor Asks for Help from UN Secretary General

1. On May 9, 1995, the NGO Forum Convenor, Khunying Supatra Masdit, wrote to the United Nations Secretary General Boutros Boutros-Ghali, requesting his assistance in finding a more appropriate site for the NGO Forum on Women '95. With this fax you will find a copy of the letter to the Secretary General.

We have heard through the NGO Forum Office that countries in the North have been very sympathetic and supportive to actions being undertaken to keep the NGO Forum in Beijing, but that countries in the South are holding back. How do you all see this? If it's true, can we step up action at national level? Keep us in touch. . . .

Dear Mr. Boutros Boutros-Ghali,

On behalf of the NGO Forum on Women, I ask your support in our negotiations for an appropriate site in Beijing. As you are aware, the NGOs, as of this late date, have not agreed upon a site for their August–September Forum. A delegation from the NGO Forum went to

Beijing from April 24 to 28, 1995, to visit possible sites. A copy of that report has been forwarded to your office.

The report has met with deep disappointment from the global community of women and the larger international community. There is distress and anger, and it is mounting. Today, the Facilitating Committee of the NGO Forum (list of members attached) unanimously decided to seek your good offices to propose to the government of China that other sites be considered in this order of priority: (1) National Olympic Sports Center, (2) the Beijing Workers Sports Service Center without the gymnasium but with satellite locations in the Agricultural Exhibition Center and nearby hotels. In conjunction with (1) and (2), we would also wish to use the Beijing Recreation Center, which—fortunately—the government of China has already offered.

The distance between the UN Conference and the NGO Forum will seriouly compromise the concern stated in CSW Resolution 36/8, which "emphasizes the importance of close proximity between the Forum and the Fourth World Conference on Women." I may also point out that this is not an issue of NGO access to the UN Conference alone. It is a matter of governments' access to the Conference as well, since the Forum has traditionally been the source of some of the most far-reaching and ground-breaking ideas on development.

The time has come for the UN and your office to demand that women no longer have to "make do" with whatever is handed to them. Women have participated effectively in all of the past UN conferences and the regional preparatory meetings for the Fourth World Conference on Women. It is the interconnectedness and interdependence of the UN and NGO meetings that we must continue to support and reinforce. We acknowledge the role you and member states have played in helping to make this possible.

Mr. Secretary General, we know that your action on this matter will enable us to find a solution that meets the concerns of the UN, our Chinese hosts, and the global community of NGOs. We are prepared to work with you in true partnership.

1995 is a significant year for women as well as for the UN. The whole world will be looking to your leadership on this issue to ensure the success not only of the Women's Conference and the NGO Forum but also of the fiftieth anniversary celebration of the United Nations. Indeed, how can we have a celebration if the UN Conference in Beijing serves to disenfranchise the representatives of half of humanity?

With kind regards

Sincerely yours,

Khunying Supatra Masdit
Convenor

Mr. Boutros Boutros-Ghali
Secretary General, United Nations
New York

cc: Gertrude Mongella, Secretary General Fourth World Conference
on Women, Facilitating Committee of the NGO Forum on Women

Global FaxNet 11, May 11, Secretary General's
Advisory Group to Meet in Amman

On May 18, 1995, the Secretary General of the United Nations, Mr.
Boutros Boutros-Ghali will convene a meeting of his Advisory Group on
the Fourth World Conference on Women, Beijing, September 4–15,
1995. The Advisory Group will meet in Amman, Jordan from May 18–20,
at the invitation of a member of the group, Princess Basma of Jordan.

On May 24, the China Organizing Committee for the NGO Forum on
Women will report to the NGO Forum on Women Facilitating Committee as to whether they are able to make available a larger, better-
equipped meeting site in central Beijing for the NGO Forum on
Women. . . .

Women everywhere are urged to contact their governments and
request their assistance in the search for an appropriate site for the
NGO Forum on Women. You can contact the Advisory Group in Amman by faxing them c/o Princess Basma Bint Talal at fax # (96-26)
82-73-50. . . .

Global FaxNet 12, May 19, Government's Rally Behind
NGOS . . . But US May Not Be Going to Beijing

1. From various regions of the world, governments have been protesting the actions of the government of China in placing the NGO
Forum on Women far away from the World Conference on Women on a
site that is woefully inadequate for an event of such magnitude. In
addition, governments have joined with NGOs in protesting efforts to
exclude certain categories of NGOs, e.g. Tibetan and Taiwanese women,
human rights groups, lesbian groups, local Chinese groups etc. . . .

3. Options for action should the Chinese government not come
forward with an appropriate offer on May 24th include the following:

- NGOs should lobby/picket Chinese Embassies in every country;
- Member States of the UN should be lobbied both in-country and
through their Missions to the UN;

■ The United Nations should be strongly pressured to move the Fourth World Conference on Women out of China, in which case the NGO Forum on Women would move with it.

If there are more options for action, please let us know and we will pass the suggestions on through the Global FaxNet and to the NGO Facilitating Committee, which will be meeting after May 24 to consider all options. . . .

Global FaxNet 13, May 25, Call to the UN Secretary General to Take a Stand on Behalf of NGOs and Their Search for an Appropriate Site for the NGO Forum in Beijing

. . . On May 22nd, the China Organizing Committee replied that the decision to move the site to Huairou could not possibly be changed. However, NGOs consider negotiations to be still open and have been informed by the Secretary General that he will have a response to his negotiations with the Chinese host country "in the next couple of days." . . .

Statement by Irene Santiago, Executive Director NGO Forum on Women, May 25

Like all of you, hundreds of thousands of women around the world are waiting to hear the United Nations's response to our request for help in negotiating with the Chinese government to secure a suitable site for the NGO Forum on Women. We have received a letter from our NGO counterpart in China, the All China Women's Federation, which I believe most of you have seen. We have not received a response from the Chinese government, and I regret to inform you that, as of this meeting, we have not received an official written response from the office of the Secretary General of the United Nations. Late yesterday afternoon however, a member of the Secetary General's staff called "requesting one or two more days" of additional time to continue discussions with China. In a letter to the Advisory Group to the Secretary General on the UN Women's Conference, Mr. Boutros Boutros-Ghali said: "I have been engaged for several weeks in quiet diplomacy to find a solution. . . I cannot be more specific at this stage, but I can assure you that I am making every effort to reach a solution acceptable to all concerned."

So far, this "quiet diplomacy" that we understand is being employed at the United Nations is, in fact, so quiet that the world's women can't hear it. . . .

We are not calling for a boycott. The NGO Forum belongs to the world's women. It is our meeting. Our voices must be heard. Therefore, we are continuing negotiations with the United Nations and the

Chinese govenment. We all share the goal of a successful UN Conference and NGO Forum on Women.

The world's women want access, openness, and the inclusion of all
women who have registered. The decisions we have made thus far
have been through a democratic process. This will continue. Based
on the information we currently have as well as the request from the
Secretary General's office for additional time, the Facilitating Committee of the NGO Forum will meet by teleconference early next week
to discuss options.

This is not just a women's issue; it's not just an NGO issue. The
integrity of the United Nations is at stake. As the UN prepares to
celebrate its fiftieth anniversary, it must not fail to properly represent 50 percent of the world's citizens.

Global FaxNet 15, June 2, UN Under-Secretary
General Goes to China for Last-Minute Negotiations
over Site

On Sunday, June 4, 1995, Mr. Ismat Kittani, Under-Secretary General
and Special Adviser to the Secretary General of the United Nations
Boutros Boutros-Ghali, is traveling to Beijing to attempt last-minute
negotiations with the Chinese authorities to move the NGO Forum on
Women from Huairou Tourist Scenic Area to a more appropriate site
in Beijing city. During the two months since, news was received of the
site change for the NGO Forum on Women due to "structural problems" at the Workers Gymnasium in Beijing. Thousands of women and
supporters worldwide have flooded the offices of the Secretary General and the China Organizing Committee (COC) with letters of
protest.

The overwhelming response from women worldwide has clearly
shown the seriousness with which women have planned for the Beijing
meetings. Mr Kittani, in looking for a win-win situation for NGOs,
China, and the UN, will bring the following issues to Beijing:

1. The need for accessibility to the World Conference so that NGOs,
particularly those without accreditation, can take part in the dialogue
and negotiation process that occurs between delegates and their NGO
constituencies—a process that is especially significant if the follow-up
and implementation activities are to be successful.

2. The adequacy of the facilities in view of the substantive, far-
reaching and important activities and events NGOs have been planning
for years.

3. The adequacy of the housing and transport arrangements, as no one wants to spend long hours traveling from their hotels to the Forum site or from the Forum site to the World Conference.

4. The adequacy of the communications structure, facilities, and access not only for the world's press but also for women's media networks, radio, and television programs and all participants.

This week the NGO Forum Office has mailed out confirmation notices to about 35,000 registrants. Acknowledgment postcards have been mailed to about 5,000 NGOs that have requested time and space for activities. Planning for the Forum is proceeding on the basis that the above requirements will be met so that women worldwide can meet to network, consolidate gains, and plan our agenda for the twenty-first century.

Wherever the final site is located, women have put the world on notice. It's possible to see the Forum as a part of a larger process well underway that is working towards women taking their rightful place as decision-makers and planners for the future. As part of this process, women have greatly influenced the development of regional plans of action that speak more clearly to our issues and concerns than the troubled Platform for Action. It is likely that implementation of these regional plans will be a focus of activities after Beijing.

We expect the United Nations to take the concerns of women seriously in its negotiations with China. Please continue to raise your concerns with your government until the successful resolution of this issue. . . .

Global FaxNet 16, June 8, Organizers Gain "Major Concessions" for NGO Forum

Irene Santiago, Executive Director of the NGO Forum on Women, announced today that major concessions had been made by the China Organizing Committee. Irene's announcement is as follows:

> I am pleased to inform you of the successful resolution of most of the outstanding issues surrounding the site for the NGO Forum on Women. After meetings in Beijing among Mr. Ismat Kittani, UN Under Secretary General and Special Adviser to the UN Secretary General, officials of the China Organizing Committee, Khunying Supatra Masdit, NGO Forum Convenor, and Sylvia Ordonez, NGO Forum Logistics, an agreement was concluded on June 8, 1995. We sincerely believe that the terms of the agreement will enable the holding of a substantive and celebratory Forum such as women worldwide have

been planning for years. It will also preserve the integrity of the UN process by enabling both accredited and non-accredited NGOs to have easy access to their delegations to the UN Fourth World Conference on Women.

The major points of the agreement are as follows:

1. NGO Forum site and NGO satellite site in Beijing. The Forum will be held in what has become a very different site than the one we originally saw in Huairou last April. Additionally, a satellite site in Beijing near to the UN World Conference site has been made available. This satellite site will enable both accredited and non-accredited NGOs to be close to the UN site for meetings with government delegates, consultations, and briefings. This satellite site is in addition to the Beijing Recreation Centre which will be the base for accredited NGOs to lobby the World Conference.

2. Acceptance of *All* registered participants. This was a major concession, achieved after extensive dialogue. All participants registered as of April 30, 1995—a total of 36,000—will be able to participate in the Forum.

3. Visas. *All* registered participants will be granted visas.

4. Contiguous Area. Buildings are now situated in one contiguous area on the 42-hectare site in Huairou. Many additional structures have been made available to cope with the much larger crowd than China originally expected. The one defined area will enable participants to network and have easy access to all activities.

5. Facilities for *All* Activities. The China Organizing Committee (COC) and the NGO Forum Office will work together to ensure that all 5,000 requests for activities will be accommodated.

6. Choice of Hotels. Registered participants will have a choice of staying in either Beijing or Huairou hotels. However, the COC will try its best to provide the majority of the accommodations in Huairou and to encourage participants to stay there and avoid commuting to the Forum site. A specially erected outdoor stage will make evening events possible at Huairou.

7. Transportation. The COC will provide shuttle bus services to and from Huairou and within Huairou.

8. Communications. The COC agreed to provide as many international direct distance dialing lines as needed for the press and NGOs.

At the conclusion of the negotiations, Supatra Masdit acknowledged the extraordinary contribution made by women worldwide in bring-

ing a resolution to the site issue. She also thanked the China Organizing Committee for their efforts in making the Forum a viable one. In
her letter to the members of the NGO Facilitating Committee, Supatra
Masdit expressed the hope that "We can all move forward and make
our Forum a success." . . .

Global FaxNet 17, June 15, Mixed Feelings over Site Decision

We are hearing from women and groups from all over the world, and
so far, most seem to have accepted the change of site . . . but not
without some feelings of regret that China missed out on this opportunity to host women of the world in downtown Beijing. . . . Women
showed enormous solidarity and momentum during these past two
months of lobbying and campaigning for a more appropriate site,
resulting no doubt in a number of concessions (including visas for all,
acceptance of the total number registered, provision of additional
buildings/tents/spaces in Huairou so that all activities requested could
be accommodated, provision of a second "satellite" site in Beijing,
etc.). But the main stumbling block remains: removal to a far-away
location where close contact among delegates, NGOs, media, and Forum activities will be difficult. NGOs will try to overcome these difficulties. We will have our Forum and get on with the business of
organizing, mobilizing, lobbying, and making change.

Global FaxNet 25, July 24, NGO Forum Office Begins Regular Postings On-Line

. . . Who Is Coming to Beijing? The following are the numbers, by
region, of registered participants to the NGO Forum on Women: Africa,
3,245; Europe and North America, 14,833; Latin America and the
Caribbean, 2,020; Asia and the Pacific, 12,336; Western Asia, 819. (This
adds up to 33,233, with 18,400 from the Global South and 14,833 from
the Global North.) . . .

Global FaxNet 30, August 10, Where We Will Be Staying . . . Those Who Will Not Be Going . . . And a New Publication from IWTC

. . . Individuals and groups who will not be in Beijing. There are many
people and groups who, for various reasons, will not be making it to
Beijing. Some cannot go because of lack of funds. In one instance, it
has been reported to IWTC that five Bahai International women from
Malaysia were informed by the COC that "there was not enough space"

for them. Other groups cannot go because they did not receive accreditation for the World Conference or because they are not permitted to
travel to China on other than a China passport (e.g. women from Tibet
and Taiwan). Some individuals and groups are boycotting both the
World Conference and the NGO Forum on Women because they are
angered by human rights abuses.

In recognition of all these individuals and groups, it is suggested
that we should all gather the names and photographs of individuals
and groups within our own regions who planned to participate but
will not be with us in Beijing and have T-shirts made with the photo
and name imprinted on the front. These would be worn in Beijing to
give a visible presence to those who are absent. . . .

Global FaxNet 32, August 22, Worldwide Visa Crisis. Women in Every Region Denied Entry to China

1. Visas. Based on faxes, phone calls, e-mail, letters, and personal
visits we have received, it has been a week of problems and frustrations
for women from every world region as more and more have found that
they cannot get visas to go to Beijing. The lack of Hotel Confirmation
Letters (HCLS), Registration Confirmation Letters (RCLS) or names not
appearing on the data base supplied to Embassies and Consulates by
the China Organizing Committee are all causing major obstacles. One
problem with the data base is that the COC is slow in updating it. . . .

Then there are the women who have sent in complete visa applications, i.e. applications containing an RCL and an HCL and whose names
are on the data base, and who are still told they cannot have a
visa. . . . When questioned why, many have been told: "We don't have to
tell you. China has the final say on who gets visas." In Central America,
hundreds of women have been told that they cannot process their visas
until 20 days, i.e. after the Forum is over. Visas have been denied to
representatives of the United States–based Taiwan International Alliance, Tibetan women carrying legal identity passports from India,
Tibetan–Canadians and Iranian–Canadians. They are amongst what
is beginning to look like thousands of women who will not be able to
participate in the Forum because they cannot get visas.

At this point in time, it is hard not to conclude that these "technical
difficulties" for denying visas, and the seemingly random way in which
percentages of women in each region are being denied visas for no
apparent reason, is an effort to limit the numbers of NGOs going to
Beijing. Whether this is being done for political reasons or simply to
control numbers, or both, we cannot say. There clearly is a problem

with accommodations and space out at Huairou, and the hotels in
Beijing are filling up.

IWTC has been actively involved in attempting to support the efforts
of women in every region to overcome the hurdles they are facing
obtaining visas. We strongly suggest that you keep fighting this travesty
of justice and make very sure that your name and Forum registration
number is faxed to the COC in Beijing. Alert your government delegations to this problem. We think it is important to fight this at every
level and to hold China to its commitment to host the NGO Forum on
Women, a working forum of 36,000 registered participants. There is a
definite role to be played by NGOs, governments, the UN and the world's
media. . . .

Global FaxNet 34, August 31, First FaxNet
from Beijing/Huairou!

. . . Yesterday was the Opening Ceremony at the Olympic Stadium in
Beijing. A fleet of buses transported Forum women the 50 miles from
Huairou to Beijing, and all other traffic on the highway was forbidden.
No buses ran the other way either, which was difficult for all those
women staying in Beijing or in the airport area hotels. . . . They had to
scramble to find taxis, those taxis that are permitted to enter Huairou.
Those of us not at the Opening Ceremony watched it on Chinese
television last evening. It was much like an Olympic Opening and
Closing Ceremony all in one, a real extravaganza with a cast of
thousands. A blimp floated above taking aerial shots. It had equality,
development, and peace banners fluttering on both sides.

From the beginning it has been a logistical nightmare for those who
have planned events and activities around an issue area. The Forum
site is closed off like a military encampment, with security gates at
every entrance, and areas within the site fenced off. To go from one
area of the site to another, one must leave through one security gate
and re-enter through another security gate. In the space of one day, it's
possible to be searched, have bags gone through, and have everything
X-rayed a dozen times. We may all be glowing on our return! It is the
inability to cross from one area to another within the site that is
making things very difficult. Renting of vans, cars, or bikes is impossible. We have bought some bikes just to be able to get books and things
from one area to another. But transporting equipment and supplies is
backbreaking, and we finish each day totally wiped out!

The building set aside for the Once and Future Pavilion, the
Women's Alternative Media Space, and the Women, Ink. Women's

Bookstore (all events that IWTC is part of, along with dozens of groups worldwide) was garbage to the ceiling when we arrived last week. It has been physically exhausting getting the place in shape for setting up, and setting up is only now under way. We are still awaiting the delivery of the Women, Ink. books from the China National Publications Import and Export Corporation. . . . The trucks bringing the shelves had an odd last number on the registration plate and yesterday was an even date. . . .

A major theme on the Forum site is the buying and selling of merchandise, and much money has been spent by the Chinese hosts in decking out all market areas with banners, flags, and enormous air balloons. It's a festive scene, much like a circus compound, and the arrival today of thousands of women has added to the festivities. Workshops and plenaries started today and women are wandering this vast area trying to find classrooms, hotel conference rooms, auditoriums, and tents. It will be some time before anyone can find their way around. Unfortunately, to add to the confusion, it seems that the police and military personnel are mostly from Beijing and have never been to Huairou before; so no one can give directions. Many major sites, such as the Pass Distribution Building, are not on the official map. But hey! That's how to meet people! Gather on corners, at security gates, under a parasol (though you have to go through another security gate to get to the parasol area) and toss around ideas with perfect strangers on which direction to walk! . . .

Global FaxNet 35, September 3, Second FaxNet from Beijing/Huairou!

It's been a chaotic week here at the NGO Forum on Women in Huairou, with high moments and low moments and lots in between. Each morning begins with a plenary session, but one has to be on site very early to get in as the Plenary Hall holds only 1,500. The promised Plenary Hall—to seat 3,000 with 3,000 on the second floor watching closed circuit television—is but a shell looming against the skyline! In fact, local entrepreneurs have turned the empty space within the skeleton building into a "Free Bar," i.e. a restaurant for soft drinks and noodles. Each day, more food begins to appear on the Forum site as people realize that we need to eat and are in fact having a problem finding food!

There have been problems these last couple of days, mostly to do with the continuing tight security on the site and the surveillance and disruptive tactics of Chinese security agents. A Tibetan workshop was raided yesterday morning and an attempt made to confiscate a video being shown. A scuffle ensued as participants stopped the agents getting hold of the tape, and they finally left the room. A similar situation developed at an Amnesty International meeting, and also at an Australian meeting in Beijing, where the microphone and the VCR were removed during a Women's Speakout that is held every evening in the Kunlun Hotel.

Yesterday, Saturday, September 2, things reached a head when the NGO Facilitating Committee called a press conference to protest these and other actions of Chinese security agents. The NGO Forum Convenor, Khunying Supatra Masdit, said that if they received any written reports of violations of the agreements reached between the NGO Forum and the China Organizing Committee, they would go to their constituents and consult them on what action to take. Actions mentioned included cancellation of the Forum and demonstrations. Foremost among the agreements previously reached was that within the Forum site "people would be totally free to carry on any activity" and that there would be "no security actions, no surveillance, no censorship" of these activities. Members of the FC said they had detected a pattern of surveillance of Forum participants. They had received reports about incidents taking place within the Forum area, such as meetings, even friendly gatherings, in the parasol area, being broken up and the people asked to disperse; of attempts to confiscate audio-visual materials or the disappearance of materials during a presentation; and of women being questioned about the contents of a song in a cassette to be played at a workshop.

An ultimatum was given by the NGO Facilitating Committee to the COC to see that such activities ceased and desisted before 12 noon today. It would appear that there has been some response, as there was a noticeable difference at security gates today, and women passed through the metal detectors without taking bags off their shoulders. A large and noisy anti-nuclear demonstration in front of the Plenary Hall was allowed to take place, even though much of the anger was directed towards Chinese nuclear testing, particularly by Korean and Japanese protestors. South Pacific participants took an active role also, protesting the recommencement of French nuclear testing at 'Muroroa Atoll today. Other demonstrations in the last 24 hours have included those organized by Bosnian women, Indian grassroots women, Laotian, and Muslim women. All have been allowed to continue without harassment from security agents.

One last comment. We have had torrential rain this week, turning the site into a quagmire reminiscent of Woodstock 1969 and 1994! The scenes have been memorable, as women in costumes from all parts of the world slipped and slithered through the mud and over the newly laid, tenuously placed pavement blocks. Tents collapsed on workshops in progress, and more than one woman gave up attempting the stone stairs that lead to the regional tents, the newly erected MacDonald's tent, or the parasol area. Our Once and Future Pavilion held up well, though many activities such as the paper-making and permaculture demonstrations had to be moved inside. A lake developed at the entrance, and we had to route everyone through the Women's Book-store. But we survived and have been hosting bigger and more respon-sive crowds each day. Today the sun was shining again, Rigoberta Menchu came to visit, and all's well with the world!

Global FaxNet 36, September 25, Safely Back from Huairou and Beijing!

. . . What did we achieve at the NGO Forum? Every participant will have a different answer to that question. It was a chaotic, colorful, intense, exciting, difficult, delightful, exhausting, stimulating, frustrating, en-couraging, thoughtful event that will take many months to absorb and evaluate. Many participants believe, as do we, that we must assess this most recent experience carefully, so that the next time around, we do some things differently, including not accepting a site so spread out and so lacking in basic facilities. An NGO Forum needs plenary space that will hold an adequate number of participants; an abundance of clean toilets; appropriate food (prawn chips, noodles and bottles of water will only go so far in assuaging real hunger); secure, dry shelter for booths, workshops, and events; and proximity to the World Confer-ence itself. Accommodation for participants must be carefully in-spected so that groups and individuals do not find themselves in unfinished structures with power lines running through shower stalls, wet concrete under foot, and no telephones for miles. For those who had requested budget accommodation at Huairou and were prepared for basic facilities, these conditions may have been understood. But for the many who had expected hotel standards and services, this was another factor that made life uncomfortable at the NGO Forum.

How many participants were there at the NGO Forum? Frankly, we don't know. Various figures were given by the three available publi-cations—*World Women* (a subsidiary of *China Daily*), *NGO Forum*, and *Earth Times*—ranging from 20,000 to 40,000. Probably the figure was closer to 20,000, though 39,000 women had pre-registered. In the second week, many Chinese women came on site to look around, and this built up the numbers somewhat. On the other hand, in the second week many of the NGOs staying at Beijing hotels stopped coming out to Huairou, a combination no doubt of fatigue, the length of the journey (an hour to an hour and a half each way), and the fact that the Fourth World Conference on Women had started. Many accredited NGOs switched their activities from Huairou to the Beijing International Convention Centre where the FWCW was held, to hold daily caucuses, lobby delegates, participate in special events organized by United Nations departments and agencies, and generally get their feet dry from the mud of Huairou.

From information provided by the United Nations Information Centre in Sydney, Australia, over 30,000 people attended the NGO Forum, which with the 17,000 registered participants at the FWCW made the occasion the largest number of women and men ever to gather in connection with a United Nations global conference. Statistics on the World Conference itself were released by the UN Office of Protocol on September 15, 1995, and showed that the total number of people registered for the FWCW was 16,921, including 4,995 delegates, 3,250 media, 4,035 NGO representatives, 446 UN staff, and 363 VIPs. The number of UN Member States attending the Conference was 181, and only two Member States, Grenada and Saudi Arabia, did not register for the Conference. Two UN Member States, Somalia and the Federal Republic of Yugoslavia (Serbia and Montenegro) were not invited. Another eight countries, which are either associate members of the UN or of its specialized agencies, also participated in the World Conference as Observers. These countries were mainly from the South Pacific (Cook Islands, Kiribati, Nauru, Niue, Tonga, and Tuvalu) plus Switzerland and the Holy See. . . .

Reprinted, with permission, by Anne S. Walker and Joan Ross Frankson, International Women's Tribune Centre, 777 United Nations Plaza, New York, New York 10017; phone: 212-687-8633; fax: 212-661-2704; e-mail: iwtc@IGc.apc.org.

Action Is the Only Way Forward

Excerpts, Opening Address, Plenary Session,
4 September 1995

Gertrude Mongella, Secretary General, UN Fourth World Conference on Women

At long last, we are here in Beijing participating in the Fourth World Conference on Women—a conference which is phenomenal in several aspects. It has generated much interest and debate globally, among men and women, old and young, from country to country. It has brought together the largest gathering of persons ever to attend any United Nations Conference on any subject. All the indications point to a social revolution in the making! . . .

. . . I wish to appeal to each woman participating in this conference and in the NGO Forum not only to serve as representatives of their governments and NGOs but also to become committed crusaders in the struggle in which we have been engaged for many, many years. As I noted at the opening of the NGO Forum 1995, "Millions have placed their trust in us. We must not fail them."

I would like to highlight a few salient features that became obvious during the process and planning for this conference. First, there is the need to look at women's issues in a holistic manner and to address them as part of overall societal and developmental concerns. It will not be possible to attain sustainable development without cementing the partnership of women and men in all aspects of life. Women have all along struggled with their men-folk for the abolition of slavery, the liberation of countries from colonialism, the dismantling of apartheid, and the struggle for peace. It is now the turn of men to join women in their struggle for equality. Second, because of the cross-cutting nature of women's issues, it is imperative that each issue is given due weight and consideration. Third, there is the need to recognize the intergenerational link, a link which is unique among women, as well as the need to consider issues cumulatively. . . . Finally, since the United Nations First World Conference on Women in Mexico in 1975, some twenty years ago, women have learned that achieving equality depends on themselves. Necessary actions will not be taken on behalf of women based on some theoretical principle of equality.

Women have researched and they have been the subject of research. The statistics are much too gloomy in several key sectors such as poverty, education and illiteracy, health, violence against women, governance and politics, and human rights. With the statistics and facts now well documented, there is no denying that women fare badly relative to men. Only last month, the 1995 edition of *The World's Women: 1990–1995 Trends and Statistics* showed irrefutably the changes that had occurred and the remaining obstacles. We are at the crucial last decade of the twentieth century and the solidarity that binds us in our common experiences, irrespective of race, color, and religion should become the instrument to propel us into the twenty-first century—armed with vision, imagination, and the potential to create difference in our own lives, those of our children, and those of our grandchildren. We have been saying all along that women and men must work together if we are to bring this world safely and successfully into the coming century; so too, must we ensure the participation of the youth. They are our hope and future. . . .

Our agenda must address the need to eradicate illiteracy, ill-health, poverty, unemployment, and violence as well as the need to promote decision-making and empowerment. It must focus on actions that will eliminate discrimination, marginalization, and social exclusion. The basis for change is here; what is lacking is the commitment which will ensure actions that could bring about change. When the facts and statistics are disaggregated, the undeniable fact is that action is required to change the status quo. Action is the only way forward. There is no substitute. The Fourth World Conference on Women must elicit commitment to action coupled with commitment of resources, nationally and internationally. This is the mission of Beijing. Each government must now set priorities, specify the resources it will contribute, and declare what steps it will take to hold itself accountable to the world's women. This conference must preserve the achievements and the agreements reached in earlier Conferences and move beyond the rhetoric to work toward genuine change. . . .

I must conclude now by raising some questions that are close to my heart and the hearts of many women. How long will women toil to contribute to the purchase of arms? How long will women continue to give life just to see it taken away by the use of arms? And how long will the world continue to ignore women's tears during armed conflicts?

This platform will not see light until the issue of peace is properly addressed.

I thank you for your attention.

Words to Break the Silence

Excerpts, Remarks to the NGO Forum,
6 September 1995

Hillary Rodham Clinton, First Lady, United States

. . . I have come here, to Huairou, to salute you for your dedication to a cause greater than all of us. I know that many of you went to great efforts to be here. I know many were kept from attending this forum. I know that for many of you who did get here, getting here was far from easy. Many of you did not even know until the last minute that you would be permitted to travel here, and others bore great personal expense in order to come.

I know that, in addition to the weather, which is not in anyone's control and is always unpredictable, you have had to endure severe frustrations here as you have pursued your work. And I also want to say a special word on behalf of women with disabilities, who have faced particular challenges.

But I mostly want to thank you for your perseverance, because you did not give up, you did not stay away. You are here, and the fact that you are will make a difference in the days and months and years to come. Because even though you may not be physically present in Beijing at the conference during these ten days, the wisdom that is accumulated here, the experience, the energy, the ideas are on full display.

. . . [T]he faces of the women who are here mirror the faces of the millions and millions who are not. It is our responsibility, those of us who have been able to attend this conference and this NGO Forum, to make sure that the voices that have gone unheard will be heard. This conference is about making sure that women, their children, their families, have the opportunities for health care and education, for jobs and political participation, for lives free of violence, for basic legal protections, and yes, for internationally recognized human rights no matter where they are or where they live.

Time and time again we have seen that it is NGOs that are responsible for making progress in any society. Some of us never knew we were NGOs twenty and twenty-five and thirty years ago. That was not even a phrase that any of us had ever heard. We were people working together on behalf of all of those rights that we care about and hold dear. But when one looks at the progress that has been made throughout the world, it is clear that it is the NGOs that have charted real advances for women and children.

It is the NGOs that have pressured governments and have led governments down the path to economic, social, and political progress, often in the face of overwhelming hostility. Again, NGOs have persevered, just as you have by coming here and staying here and participating in this forum.

What will be important as we end the forum and the conference at the end of this week is that it will be NGOs that will hold governments to the commitments that they make. And it is important that the final Platform for Action that is adopted be distilled into words that every woman, no matter where she lives, or how much education she has, can understand. I think we should want every woman, no matter where she is, to believe that there are women all over the world who care about her health, who want her children to be educated, who want her to have the dignity and respect that she deserves to have.

When I think of the faces that I have seen in my own country, when I think of the women who did not have health care because they could not afford it in the United States of America, I think particularly of a woman I met in New Orleans, Louisiana, who told me that because she did not have enough money she was told by physicians there in our country that they would not do anything about the lump in her breast but would merely wait and watch, while if she had had insurance she would have been sent to a surgeon. I think about the woman I met in a village outside Lahore, Pakistan, who had ten children, five boys and five girls, and was struggling as hard as she could to make sure her girls were educated and wanted help to get that job done.

I think of the faces of the beautiful women I met at SEWA, the Self-Employed Women's Association, in India. All of them had walked miles and miles, some of them for twelve and fifteen hours, to get to our meeting together, and I listened as they stood up and told me what it had meant that for the first time in their lives, they had a little money of their own. They could buy their own vegetable carts. They could buy their own thread and materials so that they could make income for themselves and their families.

I think of the women in a village in Bangladesh, a village of untouchables—the women were Hindus—who invited to their village for my visit Muslim women from the neighboring village. I think of how those women sat together under a lean-to—Hindus and Muslims together in one of the poorest countries of the world—but so many of those women telling me how their lives had been changed because they had become borrowers and were now part of the Grameen Bank microenterprise effort.

I think particularly of the play that their children put on for me to see, a play in which the children acted out the refusal by a family to let a girl child go to school. And then further down the road from that village, I stood and watched families coming to receive food supplements in return for keeping their girl children in school.

Those are the kinds of women and experiences that one sees throughout the world, whether one talks about my country or any country. Women are looking for the support and encouragement they need to do what they can for their own lives and the lives of their children and the lives of their families. The only way this conference will make a difference to these women is if the results of the conference are taken and distilled to a minimal number of easily read pages that state the basic principles. When that is done, the message can be carried into every corner of the world, where women will recognize and exchange shared experiences.

When I came home from Bangladesh, I visited in Denver, Colorado, a program that is modeled on the Grameen Bank, helping American women who are welfare recipients get the dignity and the skills that they need to take care of themselves and their children.

So despite all of the difficulties and frustrations you have faced in coming here and being here, you are here not only on behalf of yourselves but on behalf of millions and millions of women whose lives can be changed for the better. Let us all resolve to leave this place and do what we can together to make the changes that will give respect and dignity to every woman.

I know that today at the women's conference there is a special celebration of girls. The theme is "Investing in Today's Girls, Tomorrow's Women, and the Future." We know that much of what we do, we are doing not for ourselves but for our daughters, our nieces, our granddaughters. We are doing it because we have the hope that the changes we work for will take root and flower in their lives.

When I was privileged to be in New Delhi, India, I met a young woman who I think spoke for many, many women, and someone asked me yesterday at the conference if I had a copy of the poem that this young woman wrote. I said that I did, and she asked if I could read it today, and I said that I would. This was a poem about breaking the silence, the silence that afflicts too many women's lives, the silence that keeps women from expressing themselves freely, from being full participants even in the lives of their own families. This poem written by a

young woman, I think, is particularly appropriate since we are celebrating today the future of girls. Let me read it to you:

> Too many women
> in too many countries
> speak the same language.
> Of silence.
> My grandmother was always silent—
> always aggrieved—
> only her husband had the cosmic right,
> (or so it was said)
> to speak and to be heard.
> They say it is different now.
> (After all, I am always vocal
> and my grandmother thinks
> I talk too much)
> But sometimes I wonder.
>
> When a woman gives her love, as most women do, generously—
> it is accepted. When a woman shares her thoughts,
>   as some women do, graciously—it is allowed.
> When a woman fights for power,
> as all women would like to,
> quietly or loudly,
> it is questioned.
>
> And yet, there must be freedom—if we are to speak.
> And yes, there must be power—
> if we are to be heard.
> And when we have both
> (freedom and power)
> let us not be misunderstood.
>
> We seek only to give words
> to those who cannot speak
> (too many women
> in too many countries).
> I seek only to forget
> the sorrows of my grandmother's
> silence.

That is the kind of feeling that literally millions and millions of
women feel every day. And much of what we are doing here at this
forum and at this conference is to give words to break the silence and
then to act. . . .

The NGO Forum: Good News and Bad

Robin Morgan, United States

Remember the story about conflicting definitions of an elephant, each told by someone describing a different part of the animal? It's a good analogue for the varying descriptions of the NGO (Nongovernmental Organization) Forum on Women '95. This report, as subjective as the rest (not all of which admit to it), is an unabashedly eclectic mix of facts, analysis, and personal experience, with (I hope) a little perspective. It also reflects the opinions of other women—friends and colleagues from around the world—who generously shared their reactions with me. You probably shouldn't feed it peanuts.

The good news is that with characteristic hard work and optimism, thirty thousand women "rose above it." The bad news is that we had to. The plain truth is that men would never have tolerated such treatment. Women did. And that's not necessarily something to be proud of.

A spin has emerged in postmortems about the forum, one that would please those of our mothers who believed that a "ladylike" woman should speak positively or not at all. Whether based in defensive pride at having survived wretched conditions, or in dread of appearing to carp or be godforbid "ungrateful," the spin accentuates the positive to a somewhat ludicrous—and inaccurate—degree. It claims that only feminists from northern countries criticized the forum planners, or expressed indignation at the Chinese government's patronizing ethnocentrism, stultifying bureaucracy, and attempts to control (both subtly and blatantly) thousands of grassroots activists. How convenient to forget all the equal opportunities for outrage: African women charging their Chinese hosts with racist attitudes; Pacific Island women infuriated at the Chinese press's censoring of their hottest issue, French nuclear testing (China also conducts nuclear tests, of course); South Asian, Latin American, and Middle Eastern women protesting visa delays/denials, arbitrary detentions, overcrowded and sometimes unsanitary Huairou living accommodations, and hundreds of other examples.

A critique *is* in order, and no, that's not petty. In fact, it's imperative—to ensure that we understood what happened and that it never happens again. Furthermore, it's disingenuous and an act of disre-spect to Chinese women—all the *non*government-hand-picked, non-Stepford-feminist ones we never got to meet—to pretend, as did forum executive director Irene Santiago, forum convener Khunying Supatra Masdit, and Gertrude Mongella, secretary general of the UN Confer-ence, that the Chinese government was the dandiest host conceivable, or that China's just a developing nation trying to do its best. China's also a world power, and judging from all the semipornographic bill-boards promulgating multinational corporate products, its govern-ment lusts after the worst the West offers while fearing the best, such as even a pretense of free speech. In contrast, Kenya (a small developing nation that's not a world power) hosted the 1985 UN World Conference on Women and the attendant NGO Forum and, despite some friendly chaos, did so mostly with openness and warmth. Nor did the Kenyans see fit, as the Chinese government did, to issue official warnings to its own citizens to be wary of these surly foreign radicals who were likely to run around naked and be HIV/AIDS positive.

The Chinese patriarchs *really* wanted the Olympics in 2000. Losing out because of their human rights record made them cranky, so the UN awarded them a consolation prize: us. But hordes of political women instead of teams of apolitical athletes were perhaps less their compen-satory ideal than their worst nightmare. Wistfully pretending that gold medalists, not feminists, were advancing on the Forbidden City, they based the UN conference in Beijing's Asian Games Village and staged epic ceremonies, complete with torch passing at the National Olympic Sports Stadium, flag processions, acrobats, marching bands, fashion shows (truly), martial arts teams, exemplary contented ethnic minor-ities, and battalions of tiny, heavily lipsticked children costumed as matadors dancing or releasing twenty thousand stoned doves dizzy from being repeatedly caught and released for such spectacles. (The acrobats *were* fabulous, and the all-women philharmonic impressive, although there are just so many times you can appreciate Beethoven's "Hymn to Joy" in one three-day period.)

Literal red carpets—and interpreters who actually spoke languages other than Mandarin—were reserved for the UN Conference, since the government regarded it as a "VIP assembly." No such treatment for the grassroots NGO Forum. Made uneasy by even the concept of nongovern-mental organizations, the Chinese government had first panicked and tried to reject us outright, then "solved" the problem by exiling the forum from its original site near the conference out to the boondocks, more than a ninety-minute drive—in the rain, more than two hours—from Beijing. The excuse? The planned Beijing venue was suddenly

"discovered" to be structurally unsound. Yet the same structure, un-
changed, was subsequently used to host a major commercial soccer
tournament. The move to "scenic" Huairou was an insult: NGOs
around the world threatened a boycott—which arguably should have
taken place. But forum officials Santiago and Supatra, possibly holding themselves more accountable to their diplomatic careers than to
their grassroots constituency, reassured NGOs of government guarantees: excellent accommodations and communications facilities would
be built for those staying in Huairou, and, for those forum participants
who wished to lobby conference delegates, busses would shuttle every
twenty minutes between Huairou and Beijing.

Fits of mirth.

Specially constructed buildings lacked walls and roofs. Only in the
forum's last days, after women grew blessedly "shrill and strident," did
busses appear every half hour—well, sort of. Plenary venues were
never big enough to accommodate those who wanted to attend (no
really large halls in the most populous country on earth?). Colorful
ballooney things serving as Regional Tents and Diversity (e.g., constituencies) Tents were cheerful and airy, but we had to transcend paranoia when the Disabled Tent and the Lesbian Tent kept collapsing.
"Volunteer Guides" were politely unfamiliar with both Huairou and
any non-Chinese language. Maps turned out to be (1) not to scale and
(2) lacking entire buildings, a predicament compounded by the absence of directional signs—except those pointing the way to "Ladies'
Shopping Places." This, plus arbitrarily changed venues and/or times
for the thousands of workshops and events, and especially the lack of
an index in the official Forum Schedule of Activities, helped make
finding anything or anyone a bracing challenge. Tent-area "paths"—
thin concrete squares laid without fixative on bare earth—turned
graham-crackery with rain and sank in the surrounding mud. Periodic
stoppages of water and/or electricity occurred despite government-
imposed rationing of both on the hapless residents of Huairou, who
hadn't been asked if they welcomed this foreign invasion or not but
who fought back with price gouging (neighboring peasant farmers
were totally barred from Huairou for the duration, and were hard-hit,
since they were unable to sell their fresh produce).

Draconian "security" measures were *not* exaggerated by the Western
press: there were myriad uniformed and plainclothes police and
guards (plus food vendors, who on occasion could be seen to drop
proffered spring rolls and flash security badges). There were metal
detectors, body frisks, telephone interruptions, room searches, harassment of journalists, confiscation of certain film/cameras/literature/

videos/signs (human rights, lesbian rights, and most anything Tibetan); "appointed" hotels and "designated" restaurants (for quality control or female control?), and even a "regulated protest area": a *playground.*

No, men would not have endured such treatment. Why, you may ask, did women? For each other's sake. (This is how they get us.) Because here's another montage:

A virtual city of female people. Turbans, caftans, saris, abayas, sarongs, kente cloth, blue jeans. T-shirt libraries. Banners, posters, buttons. A twenty-kilometer-long Sisterhood Ribbon initiated by Cambodian women, added to at the forum, later stretched along the Great Wall. Almost four thousand workshops—on soybeans, sexuality, paid and unpaid labor, reproductive freedom, microcredit, caste, solar stoves, networking techniques, inheritance, health, refugee/displaced women, regional priorities, you name it. There were nonstop cultural events—including a complete Women's Circus from Australia. A "Once and Future Pavilion" was rich with booths demystifying men's technology and celebrating women's alternate technologies. Near the temporary bookstore, the U.S.'s Feminist Press, celebrating its twenty-fifth anniversary, used a special funding grant to give copies of its books away free; watching an "untouchable" Dalit woman from Nepal, arms full of feminist books and eyes full of incredulous tears, was pure magic. The Women's Environment and Development Organization (WEDO), the NGO co-founded by Bella Abzug and Mim Kelber, organized what was probably the most impressive array of events, panels, and actions at the forum, carried out under the guidance of its executive director, Susan Davis. Meanwhile, Vatican groupies were busy invoking their narrow definition of "the family," to which Catholics for a Free Choice responded with a welcome petition campaign to deprive the Holy See of its absurd UN rank as a "government" with observer status. Animated bolts of cloth—pawns in other fundamentalist games—sat mostly alone, talking to themselves. (The Iranian NGOs were lodged at their embassy. So much for the *N* in "NGO.") First-timers, euphoric at the sheer numbers, finally felt part of this vast global movement. Veterans were delighted that "cultural defense" justifications from previous decades were wilting under a unifying assault against purdah, genital mutilation, sexual slavery, polygyny, prostitution.

This particular veteran also noticed a number of positive new trends. One was the presence of more powerful and authoritative feminist voices of women of the global south than ever before—and, hearteningly, media willingness to hear, interview, and publish them. This process was aided by the refreshingly lower profile maintained by women of the north, who seemed a little more sensitized to their southern sisters and less eager to dominate all discourse. Another was the greater availability of NGO materials in languages in addition to their language of authorship. An example of the apparently ravenous thirst for materials in a choice of languages was the way that almost a thousand copies of "A Woman's Creed"—made available by the Sisterhood Is Global Institute in Arabic, Chinese, (original) English, French, Persian, Russian, and Spanish—were snapped up instantly. Still another positive development was the proliferation of computer technology as demystified and used by women. Laptops slung over sari-draped shoulders were a frequent sight, and there were lines of women waiting to use the media center's computers. Patient with the computers (held hostage to erratic electricity) and with each other, women taught women how to send and receive E-mail, retrieve lost copy, download. Obviously, such technology is so far available only to a privileged relative few, a contrast intensified by 70 percent of the world's poor and 75 percent of the world's illiterates being women. Still, anytime any woman seizes access to now-essential tools of global communication, it's encouraging.

Women's studies, always a hungered-after subject, seemed even more popular than usual. I moderated the Sisterhood Is Global Institute's women's studies panel, which was cosponsored by the Feminist Press. Although we suffered a last-minute-without-notice venue change in the midst of a downpour, almost four hundred intrepid people managed to locate the new room, spilling damply into aisles and out into the hall. The panelists were Greta Hoffman Nemiroff (Canada), Vanessa Griffen (Fiji), Rokiah Talib (Malaysia), and Azar Naficy (Iran); originally scheduled additional panel members from Ethiopia, Brazil, and Palestine were unable to make it out to Huairou from Beijing because of the fierce rainstorm. The panel's theme—the reclamation of women's studies as an unashamed form of political activism integral to the development of global feminism—was addressed in dramatically different ways by the various panelists. Not surprisingly, any concept of women's studies must itself "go veiled" in Iran, disguised as, for example, a literary analysis of Jane Austen's works. Talib, who has started the first ws course in Malaysia, described now-familiar basic impediments and how, in that cultural context, she and her colleagues were combatting them. Griffen and Nemiroff, albeit from very different cultures, both spoke out of a well-established tradition of ws in their respective countries, and each delivered impassioned remarks in a related vein: that for ws to be relevant requires its "liberation" from the recent fad of "ivory tower" preoccupation with patriarchal "deconstructionist" and "postmodern" theory; that the effect of that trend, however well intentioned, becomes reactionary, especially when it takes place in a context of "normalized" conservative attacks on ws as the radical hotbed of naughty multiculturalism. The enthusiastic audience response was genuinely moving. I couldn't help but be reminded that, before the dual chilling effects of both cutbacks and careerism, ws (even once, yea, called *feminist* studies) knew itself originally as inherently political, activist, in fact, proudly subversive. I also was cheered that this is still the case in the global south where, for example, *Al-Raida: The Journal of Women's Studies in the Arab World*, somehow bravely managed to continue publishing regularly throughout the hell that Beirut, Lebanon, became during the 1980s and early 1990s. Since my sisters in the global north sometimes seem mired in the unnecessary bifurcation of intellect versus action (which requires a rather pinched definition of each), it was good to hear "both/and" thinking instead of "either/or."

And speaking of activism, special honors go to a triad that emerged in spontaneous leadership at the forum: (1) Disability NGOs, outraged at crumbly paths, workshop assignments to second-floor, no-elevator venues, and hastily assembled, steep ramps—"For ski-jumping, not chairs," quipped one Filipina feminist on wheels—who daringly staged the first demonstration outside the "designated protest area": an energetic roll-in. (2) The U.S. Women of Color coalition—a de facto microcosm of the world's women, but with a shared language and experience in alliance building—who found themselves ascendant as facilitators and coalition experts. And (3) lesbian activists, who exuberantly staged the first march (*far* from the designated playground, kiddo), chanting, "Liberté, Egalité, Homosexualité." This set the tone for other breakout demonstrations, in a wide array and on every imaginable subject—"Indigenous Women's Rights!," "Justice for Comfort Women!," "Hiroshima Survivors against French Nuclear Testing!," "Women in Bosnia/Rwanda/Somalia/Palestine-Israel for Peace!" Perhaps the most courageous was the march staged by more than a hundred women from Algeria, Afghanistan, and other Muslim countries: they wore red executioners' hoods to cover their faces and shouted "No to fundamentalism and sexual apartheid!" The cumulative result of all these—five or six a day—demos was that everyone could feed on a nourishing smorgasbord of hourly defiance, while the Chinese security police suffered indigestion, eventually learning to gaze at the distant horizon or to study their own shoes intently.

Major attention to the rights of girl children was unfortunately matched by only the usual token support for the visibility of old women and their rights. But one unifying issue was violence against women in all its forms, and more than a thousand women took part in the Women in Black vigil, organized by Asia-Pacific women's groups. (How I somehow wound up making and carrying the sign reading "Don't Forget the Women of Tiananmen Square"—and the aftermath—is another story. I'd been *trying to* be good. But authoritarian regimes bring out the 1960s in me).

Lessons? For all of us, nationally *and* internationally committed to the worldwide cross-cultural women's movement: We are more politically sophisticated than ever before. But at times we've let our new-found political savvy (plus women's chronic disease, terminal gratitude) make us too polite. It's time to resurrect our rage. It's time for the energy of audacity again.

We should *not* have settled for a conference site like Huairou, even if we did pluckily make the best of it (we're *always* having to "make the best" of something. Enough!); we must not make the same mistake next time. We must not settle for an old guard NGO leadership so out of touch with the growing importance of NGOs—to governments, to the UN system, and to UN conferences. (A sizable NGO presence *in* official country delegations themselves was in large part the reason for the emergence of such a strong document as the Platform for Action. But more about that in the conference coverage.) *We must stop settling for less than we deserve.* We've gotten this far only by aiming even farther.

A personal note. It was with frustration that I left China—the first country in all my travels where I had been unable to connect with non–officially approved women of that country (feminist independents and dissidents had been sent well out of the Beijing/Huairou area). And I was saddened, since, not even in the Gaza Strip at the height of the Occupation and the Intifada, had I encountered such authoritarian control.

Then, on my way home via Hong Kong, I finally got hold of a local English-language newspaper that was not government-controlled. (The self-congratulatory *China Daily*, along with its temporary supplement, *World Women*, had been dubious entertainment; I thanked the goddess each morning for the independent small forum papers put out in challenging circumstances, most notably those by the Women's Feature Service and the *Earth Times*). In Hong Kong, I read of a cigarette-lighter factory explosion in Sunde City, Guangdong—a tragedy that had left sixty women workers critically injured and more than twenty burned to death. Hong Kong–based unionists had appealed to the Chinese government to lift the media ban about such accidents and launch an investigation, and had sent word to the conference and the NGO Forum, trying to draw attention to the conditions mainland women factory workers face. *Not one word of this tragedy had ever reached us in Beijing or Huairou.* My anger at the government's treatment of visiting activists refocused, fittingly, onto its treatment of Chinese women, who after all constitute 20 percent of all female people on the planet.

But wait. More than 60 percent of China's population is under age twenty-five—and, despite the resurgence of female infanticide, more than half is female. The first rape crisis hot lines and battery shelters have begun. There's a growing divorce rate—it has doubled in Beijing over the past four years—and 70 percent are women-initiated divorces. The reckoning is at hand.

Since women hold up half the sky, the Chinese government would do well to read the story of Chicken Little.

Robin Morgan, an award-winning poet, political theorist, novelist, and journalist, has published fourteen books. Her most recent, The Word of a Woman: Feminist Dispatches *(W.W. Norton, 1994), has just been published in Chinese. A political activist and co-founder of the contemporary U.S. feminist movement, she has been deeply involved for twenty years in the international women's movement.*

Building a Sustainable and Equitable World for Daughters and Granddaughters

Excerpts, Statement by Development Alternatives
with Women for a New Era (DAWN),
13 September 1995

Vivienne Wee, Singapore

I am privileged to address you on behalf of DAWN, a Southern women's network that was founded in 1985 at the Third World Conference on Women in Nairobi. The Fourth World Conference on Women in Beijing marks the tenth anniversary of DAWN.

In these ten years, the women's movement has grown into a global force for change, a force working at multiple levels. Women have been powerfully present at this global level of policymaking long before the present conference. Over the last four years, at the UN Conferences in Rio, Vienna, Cairo, and Copenhagen, governments and the international community have come to a consensus that women play a key role in all development processes. It has become clear that problems of ecological sustainability, human rights, population, and poverty can be solved only by taking into account women's concerns and realities. This should not be that surprising since women do constitute half of society, and no human problem can be solved by ignoring half of society.

The Fourth World Conference on Women is thus a double landmark. Not only does it mark ten years after Nairobi, it also marks the culmination of the recent series of UN Conferences on key development issues. At this conference, the global community must consolidate the gains made at the preceding conferences and seriously commit resources for the effective implementation of the recommendations that have emerged from these conferences.

But the Fourth World Conference on Women is also a conference of women by women. Forty thousand women have come to Beijing to participate in this event. More would have come if they had been able to. We are here because this is our conference. Women's needs, women's rights, and women's realities must thus be located at the heart of the debate going on right here. What is at stake is not just women's well-being but the future of our entire human race.

As we approach the twenty-first century, we are experiencing many complex and difficult changes amounting to a global crisis. . . . The end of the Cold War has not brought global peace as we had expected. Instead, it has generated new political alignments and new patterns of war and conflict, especially large-scale violence within nation–states. About 90 percent of war casualties in recent years are not soldiers, but civilians, mostly women and children. Approximately twenty million people are refugees, of whom 75 percent are women and children. The systematic rape of women has become a prevalent war crime.

New forms of prejudice and bigotry have also arisen based on religious fanaticism, racism, and conservatism. These forms of bigotry serve to restrict women's access to economic, political, and social resources.

Since the Cold War, the world has been undergoing economic globalization. While this process has generated new economic opportunities, it has also brought about new patterns of wealth and poverty. Women now constitute 70 percent of the world's 1.3 billion absolute poor. Women earn only 10 percent of the world's income and own only 1 percent of the world's property. Economic globalization is also exacerbating our environmental crisis. As a result, women in the rural sector are losing their livelihood resources, with hardly any compensatory access to new economic opportunities. At the same time, they continue to be responsible for the care of family and community on a reduced and degraded resource base. Women's lives and livelihoods are thus seriously at risk.

Why has this happened? What are the systematic processes that have brought about a crisis of such proportions? We need to address these fundamental questions collectively as a global community. If we fail to ask and answer these questions, then we have little hope of halting the ongoing processes that are producing and reproducing crisis situations for women all over the world. Such a world is clearly unsustainable and inequitable. We cannot move into the twenty-first century with half of humanity subject to systematic violence, impoverishment, dispossession, and displacement. What kind of world is this that we bequeath to our daughters and granddaughters? We are ultimately accountable to our daughters, our granddaughters, and the generations that follow. The words and paragraphs that are being debated here so painstakingly have meanings and consequences for future generations. That is what we are addressing here at this conference. As a global community, we need to look beyond the short-term gains of particular interest groups and power blocs. As a global community, our moral responsibility is to envision and build a sustainable and equitable world where all our daughters, granddaughters, and succeeding generations can enjoy stable, peaceful, and healthy lives.

This requires collective commitment and political will. It requires a global coalition of all sectors and all levels of society, including governments, NGOs, and international organizations. Such a coalition must be responsive to the needs, rights, and realities of all women, especially the poorest women living in the most-remote communities. We need leaders and institutions that are sincerely committed to the best interests of the world's women and the future generations who follow. Ultimately, the question for us all—both women and men—is the question of commitment and accountability. At this important conference, we the women of the world seek the following commitments from the global community of nations: One, we call for a Declaration and a Platform for Action founded on women's rights, responsive to women's realities and accountable to women as global constituency. Two, we call for the effective implementation of the recommendations coming out of this conference, as well as those coming out of preceding conferences at Rio, Vienna, Cairo, and Copenhagen. Three, we call for the universal ratification of the Convention on the Elimination of All Forms of Discrimination Against Women as an international legal framework for gender equity and equality. Four, we call for the allocation of adequate and substantial resources, as well as the mobilization of new and additional resources, to make a real difference to the lives of women as half of humanity. Five, we call for the strengthening of UNIFEM as the lead United Nations agency mandated to bring about women's economic and political empowerment. Six, we call for a new development agenda that will systematically address the processes of causation that have brought about our global crisis of unsustainability and poverty. Seven, we call on all governments to work towards the elimination of all forms of violence against women and all forms of prejudice and bigotry that deprive women of their full and equal human rights. Finally, we call on the governments of the world to look beyond narrow political interests to commit themselves seriously and sincerely to the making of a better world for all, particularly all our daughters and granddaughters.

No Longer Invisible and Voiceless

Excerpts, Statement by the Network of African
Rural Women Associations, 13 September 1995

Chief Bisi Ogunleye, Nigeria

.... Truly, this is the first time rural women are seen and heard on a platform like this. We are no longer invisible and voiceless. . . .

Allow me to explain what we mean by rural women. Rural women are knowledgeable and endowed with skills, talents, and creativity. They are hard-working producers who are not poor but impoverished. . . .

- 60–70 percent of the world's poor are rural women who are mothers of more than half of the new generation.

- Rural women are primary managers of the earth's natural resources: 500 million live on eroding hillsides; 200 million in the rain forests; and another 850 million on dry land in danger of decertification.

- Over half of the world's people still live in rural areas and are responsible for more than half of the world's production from farms or from community-based enterprises or microenterprises.

Therefore, worldwide rural women, who are mostly farmers and microentrepreneurs, produce most of the food; manage most of the earth's natural resources; create most of the jobs in the rural areas; and care for most of the next generation.

Despite all this, they remain unrecognized, voiceless, invisible, powerless, and impoverished. They remain poor because of socioeconomic and cultural structures that keep them entrenched in poverty. Furthermore, they continue to suffer from the injustice of globalization, which is characterized by exploitation of the natural resources, loss of traditionally used formulae and technics through patent rights, and the use of modern insensitive approaches to rural technology.

Rural women are very much aware of the economic problems in the world. However, for those in Africa, Asia, and countries going through transition, we ask the international financial institutions such as the World Bank to respect these people's existing socioeconomic structures and to provide safety net funds to relieve the suffering of rural producers and microentrepreneurs. As a matter of urgency we would also like these financial institutions to finance directly rural technology, farm mechanization, and preservation of farm produce and initiatives. This, we believe, will lessen the burden of the Structural Adjustment Programmes (SAPS) on our rural women. . . .

At the NGO Forum held during the ongoing Fourth World Conference on Women at Huairou, rural women from all regions of the world met and strategized on how to implement the Platform for Action; determined to take responsibility for their own economic and social empowerment; and decided to place before you the follow-up program that they have adopted to execute with your support. . . .

- The rural women's bank for sustainable development has just been launched.

- A special stamp for fair trade for rural women's products is now available for all continents of the world.

- An annual prize for rural women's creativity and empowerment has also been launched.

At the First World Women's Conference in Mexico, rural women were mentioned, but never seen or heard. In Nairobi, Rio, Cairo, and Copenhagen, rural women were mentioned, seen, but never heard. At last, in Beijing, rural women are finally seen, heard, and listened to. With this opportunity therefore, along with the above Plan of Action, we have a vision of establishing October 15 as World Rural Women's Day (preceding World Food Day on the October 16) as the most practical way of recognizing and acknowledging rural women as the main food providers of the world. We are convinced that you will rally round our vision and commitment to implement the Platform for Action of the Fourth World Conference on Women. In conclusion, allow me to echo the request of the rural women all over the world who contribute 60 to 80 percent of the world's wealth and are now asking for only one percent of every annual budget as a token contribution to the implementation of the initiatives they have put before you. Indeed, the rural women are full of hope by the high number of first ladies, women prime ministers, and women ministers who are present in Beijing. The rural women are now challenging *all of you* to use your good offices and positions not only to convince your various governments, but also to lobby hard for the inclusion of the 1 percent request in the 1996–97 annual budget as well as the inclusion of the voices of rural women at every level of decision–making. Finally, we the rural women of the world are committed to the eradication of poverty and the mobilization of resources to implement the recommendations and strategies we have set before you towards achieving the goals of the Platform for Action. We further believe that from Beijing we will be able to create a new society based on justice, love, and respect for human dignity. As our strong allies in the field of action, rural women of the world now await your commitment and strategies. Thank you very much.

Pursuing an Agenda Beyond Barriers: Women with Disabilities

Laura Hershey, United States

The NGO Forum on Women, though rife with barriers that restricted the movement and participation of disabled women, nevertheless gave disability issues unprecedented exposure. We were excluded from most of the workshops and other activities because of their physical inaccessibility (from six-inch curbs to flights of stairs) and their lack of such accommodations as Braille materials and sign language inter- preters. But exclusion sparked activism: we used the barriers as a staging ground for raising awareness about a broad spectrum of disability-rights issues.

Women with disabilities have come a long way since 1985, when we met at the last NGO Forum, in Nairobi, Kenya. In dozens of countries, disabled women are moving from isolation to community, and new leaders are organizing new movements. More than two hundred of these leaders gathered just before the NGO Forum to define our agenda. A hotel meeting room in Beijing was the site of the First International Symposium on Issues of Women with Disabilities, on 29 August 1995.

Part of our strategizing involved efforts to influence the official document that would result from deliberations at the Fourth World Conference on Women. The draft Platform for Action contained pass- ing references to disabled women, but advocates were not giving up on the possibility of strengthening it. Lucy Hernandez Wong, addressing the symposium, said: "Women with disabilities have both unique obstacles to overcome and unique strengths to provide and to contrib- ute to our surrounding and international community. For us, the Platform for Action has to contain actions that will allow us to over- come the obstacles that we face each day of our lives. And it has to build on our strengths, providing us with the opportunity to use our abilities."

To that end, activists spent a full day identifying, discussing, and prioritizing the concerns of disabled women. Symposium participants formed work groups that focused on key issues, including education, health, employment/economic development, and access. Each group was charged with the task of developing three to four concise, action-oriented messages. These messages would form the basis of our advocacy during the course of the NGO Forum.

Discussion ranged wide and delved deep. Within each area, multiple layers were exposed and studied. Issues led to new issues.

For example, it was impossible to discuss any issue without noting, as advocate Harilyn Russo (United States) did in her introductory remarks, that "disabled girls and women face higher rates of all kinds of violence than nondisabled girls or disabled boys—violence from men and women in their families and communities." Russo pointed out that, in addition, reproductive freedoms available to other girls and women are often denied to those with disabilities. "Disabled girls and women face double discrimination," she reminded us.

All these factors have clear implications for the education of disabled girls and young women, who, Russo concluded, "are entitled to resist unwanted sterilization; . . . are entitled to positive role models and mentors; and . . . are entitled to become strong, healthy, proud disabled women."

The work group on educational issues put these needs into practical terms. The group emphasized the right "to have communication access to education, whatever that may be, in terms of technology, sign language, or one-to-one assistance" as well as "physical barrier-free access to education for women with disabilities." So stated Angie Allard (Canada), spokeswoman for the education work group. An equally important message was "education for the purposes of gainful employment."

Barbara Michaelson (United States) reported for the work group on health issues, which urged "that government financial support for all disabled girls and women needs to be included in all basic health care." This should cover not only prevention and treatment of the disabling condition itself but also rehabilitation, gynecological, obstetric, and general health care "throughout the lifespan of disabled girls and women."

In addition, a disabled women's health advocate from Japan elaborated the working group's concerns and recommendations in the area of reproductive health rights. "Disabled women have the right to be parents," the group statement asserted. "If they cannot be biological parents, they have the right to adopt." The group advocated providing equipment, personal assistance, and other support to make parenting possible for women with different types of disabilities. Similarly, the group determined that disabled women who experience infertility should have access to the same reproductive technologies, such as in vitro fertilization, as other women do.

The health issues group also confronted the problem of forced sterilization, which, they noted, is used both to prevent disabled women from bearing children and to stop their menstruation. (Some service providers make this choice for their own convenience.) "We think it's very important, even if [a woman does] not want to have children, [that she] keep it [her uterus] because it is important that [she] have it because of hormonal reasons. We take out the uterus, you take out the necessary hormones."

Coercive uses of technology was another concern of the health issues working group. Amniocentesis and other tests used to detect gender and/or disabilities may lead to policies promoting eugenic abortions. "And so," the spokeswoman stated, "knowledge is important that it is fine to be a female, it is fine to be a *disabled* female." Attendees applauded when she added, "Our lives are fine. [Families] can have a child with a disability and their lives will be fine."

The work group on employment and economic development emphasized the primary importance of "meaningful, integrated, equal employment opportunities for women with disabilities," as spokeswoman Meenu Sekand (Canada) said. The group "called for the provision of education, training, and reasonable accommodations necessary for disabled women to take advantage of these opportunities."

Second, the work group urged policies that would "promote healthy, sustainable economies, so that women with disabilities can access employment opportunities and community support. In addition, all programs and projects for the economic development of women should be accessible and available to women with disabilities."

Third, Sekand reported, "Women with disabilities want government to value the unwaged work we do, which we have in common with all women, and our added work load of disability." This unwaged work includes things like managing attendants, negotiating service systems, and other tasks that disabled women must accomplish in order to get their needs met.

These were some of the positions on which work groups reached consensus during the symposium. Other discussion areas included human rights, strengthening the Platform for Action, and advocating for access at the NGO Forum.

Armed with these position statements, participants worked diligently throughout the days of the forum. The prevalence of barriers, unfortunately, meant that we spent a great deal of energy merely getting around and lobbying for improvements. But that work went hand in hand with our organizing and activism.

At least eight hundred women with disabilities attended the forum, although perhaps only a quarter of them identified with the disability contingent or participated actively in disability issues.

Those who did participate were greatly rewarded by the opportunities they had to connect with disabled women from dozens of countries. Many of these women had helped to found disabled women's organizations—even whole movements—in their own countries, and their examples provided models, strategies, and encouragement to other women in other countries. An international movement of women with disabilities takes root and grows.

It has a long struggle ahead.

Laura Hershey is a writer, activist, and trainer who lives in Denver. She traveled to the Fourth World Conference on Women as a recipient of the 1995 IDEAS 2000 Fellowship (International Disabilities Exchanges and Studies) from Mobility International U.S.A. and the National Institute for Disability and Rehabilitation Research.

Youth Organizations as Partners

Excerpts, Statement by Youth NGOs Accredited at the Conference, 15 September 1995

Sara Ramamonjisoa, Madagascar

... Our presence here is unprecedented. Over the last two weeks, young women have actively participated in all caucuses, workshops, panels, and other activities as part of a strategy to mainstream our needs and issues. This can be clearly noted by the presence in particular of young women's issues in the Platform for Action. Without our participation, discussion of such areas as education, poverty, health, and access to resources as they specifically related to young women would have remained silent or at best theoretical.

Because of our presence, however, discussion of these areas became informed, passionate, and realistic. This input has been vital in creating a Platform for Action that millions of young women can identify with.

Our achievement in this conference marks the ability and readiness of young women to act as partners in implementation of the outcome of Beijing. And this stands as proof that young women need to be here to be listened to and consulted with—not because of who we will become in the future, but because of who we already are. . . .

As highlighted in the mission statement of the Platform for Action, "special measures must be taken to ensure that young women have the life skills necessary for active and effective participation in all levels of social, cultural, political, and economic leadership." We urge United Nations agencies charged with the implementation of the Platform for Action to address the special needs of young women.

The active support and participation of youth organizations as partners in implementation has been agreed upon by all governments present here. In support of these tasks, as young women, we call upon the United Nations to reactivate and strengthen its existing youth program.

We now present to you an indication of our vision for a future that will be free of today's problems: A future where every girl and young woman will have access and a right to an education free of discrimination. A future where all women—young and old—will have full access to health care, related information, and complete control of their bodies. A future where women and men will share equally in the sense of ownership of the achievements of their countries. A future where women can actively participate in determining a new world order free from armed conflict and guided by the principles upheld in the Culture of Peace. A future where a commitment to the preservation of our natural environment is reflected in all our international, national, and local development plans. A future where work done by women is recognized as an indispensable contribution to the world's economic growth.

And in this vision, we foresee a Fifth World Conference on Women where the world will gather to celebrate the equality, development, and peace achieved from actions agreed upon at this conference.

So let us begin today as full and equal partners for action.

What Will You Do?—Women's Human Rights

Excerpts, Statement by Center for Women's Global
Leadership, 13 September 1995

Alda Facio, Costa Rica

For the past five years women from around the globe have been
campaigning for the recognition of women's rights as human rights
and for the integration of a gender perspective into all areas of human
rights practice and theory. The need to incorporate a gender perspective stems from the fact that in all situations some perspective of
interpreting reality is present, and—historically—the perspective
which has dominated has been the male perspective. This is why
human rights theory and practice has not adequately taken women's
views and experiences into account, rendering the everyday violations
of women's human rights invisible.

This male bias has contributed to a narrow definition of such basic
human rights as peace and development. Incorporating a gender
perspective into human rights theory and practice would not only
ensure that women's human rights violations will no longer remain
invisible, but also that the way we understand issues such as health,
bodily integrity, and economic justice will include the needs, experiences, and desires of the entire human race.

The success of this movement was reflected in the Vienna Declaration and Programme of Action, which stated unequivocally that "the
human rights of women and of the girl child are an inalienable,
integral and indivisible part of universal human rights." It can also be
seen in the recognition by key bodies within the UN system of the need
to incorporate the gender dimension into all their activities and
deliberations. It has culminated in the acceptance of the idea of
women's rights as human rights at this conference.

In fact, this entire conference is a conference about the human
rights of women. Whether addressing poverty, sexist educational systems, inadequate health care, gender-based violence, or male bias in
the definition of what constitutes peace, all the issues of the platform
are about the inequality of human rights in the economic, political,
and cultural spheres and women's lack of equal access to the funda-

mental conditions that make the exercise of political and civil rights viable. The issue of insufficient mechanisms at all levels to promote the advancement of women is a question of justice, and justice is at the heart of human rights.

Women's human rights activists have been involved in both the NGO Forum and preparations for this conference at the local, national, regional, and global levels for over two years. This has included not only many meetings but also the collection of over one million signatures for a petition calling upon the UN to promote and protect the human rights of women and to implement the promises of the Vienna Declaration.

During the NGO Forum at Huairou, we held tribunals, hearings, panels, and workshops delineating the many violations that women suffer and how these violations might be addressed. These activities covered a wide range of areas including: violence against women in war and conflict; militarism and the arms industry; violence against women in the family; violations of bodily integrity and women's health rights; economic discrimination and exploitation (including the negative impact of structural adjustment policies); political persecution, issues pertaining to migrant, refugee, and displaced women as well as to indigenous peoples; and the rights of marginalized women, lesbians, disabled women, older women, and others. In addition women exchanged strategies and methods for documenting violations of women's human rights as well as for training and educating on these issues.

All human rights violations demand accountability from states and the UN as well as other parties. The challenge then, to this conference, is not simply to recognize that women's rights are human rights but to demonstrate how the conference will concretely realize the promotion and protection of human rights. Today we ask of the delegates to the Fourth World Conference on Women, What will you do to make the words become a reality?

What will you do after you leave Beijing to eliminate poverty for women and ensure their fundamental right to food and housing? What will you do to guarantee that every girl child becomes literate and that all boys and girls receive a nonsexist education? What will you do to implement the UN Decade on Human Rights Education (1995–2005) and guarantee that it not fall back on sexist concepts and methods of understanding human rights? What will you do to assure women the right to control their physical, mental, and social well being?

In every region there was agreement that one of the fundamental obstacles to women's enjoyment of their human rights is violence against women. While a few states have taken some steps to address this global problem, a great deal more must be done to demonstrate seriousness about ending this widespread violation of human rights. Therefore we specifically call upon all governments, UN agencies, and international organizations to join the campaign to eradicate violence against women by making concrete plans—in consultation with NGOs—at both the national and international level. We urge you not to lose this opportunity to make this a "Conference of Commitments" to realize the human rights of women.

Photo Essay: Images from the NGO Forum for Women

Joan Roth, United States

Saroja Madurai Hari of India, en route to the Peace Tent, participates in a demonstration by the Women of South Asia for Peace and Solidarity.

Top. African women outside the overcrowded assembly hall during Hillary Rodham Clinton's address to the NGO Forum. *Bottom.* Chinese women with umbrellas.

The Disability Tent.

Bella Abzug, Susan Davis, Wangari Maathai, and others gather outside the opening ceremony for the UN Fourth World Conference on Women at the Great Hall of the People, Tiananmen Square.

Top and bottom. The linkage caucus, the commitment scoreboards.

Top. Two women from Women Weaving the World Together display a peace banner that was later placed on The Great Wall. *Bottom.* Women in Black demonstration. Silent meditation for worldwide human rights abuses.

Members of Women of South Asia for Peace and Solidarity demonstrate and organize in the Peace Tent.

Members of Women Weaving the World Together demonstrate with banner at The Great Wall.

Joan Roth is an award-winning photographer who lives in New York. Her work has been the subject of several individual and group shows both in the United States and throughout the world.

The UN Conference:
Out of the Holy Brackets and
into the Policy Mainstream

Robin Morgan, United States

However varied the reactions to the conference itself, most people would agree that the Platform for Action emerging from it is remarkable—a document that even with its flaws is simply the strongest official statement on women internationally to date.

This was no overnight success. It was a triumph at least twenty years in the making. Momentum had built during the 1976–85 UN Decade for Women (the Mexico City, Copenhagen, and Nairobi World Conferences on Women), and women declined to disperse obediently at the decade's end; instead, we intensified both grassroots organizing efforts and NGO pressure on governments. Furthermore, women broke out of the ghetto and mobilized regarding the UN *general* conferences: the Conference on Environment and Development (Rio de Janeiro, 1992), the World Conference on Human Rights (Vienna, 1993), the International Conference on Population and Development (Cairo, 1994), and the World Summit for Social Development (Copenhagen, 1995) all witnessed the growing presence—and clout—of women. At each of these conferences, a daily women's caucus was superbly organized for NGOs by former U.S. Congresswoman and activist Bella Abzug and her NGO, the Women's Environment and Development Organization (WEDO); these caucuses directed, focused, and steered NGOs through sophisticated on-site lobbying efforts so that government delegations were forced to realize that *all* issues are "women's issues." Meanwhile, women were painstakingly learning the complex ways of the UN and how to make an impact on its policies. Groups went through the process of application for accredited NGO status; activists dragged themselves to the numerous regional preparatory meetings that precede each conference, where the real work of affecting content and agendas takes place and from which the draft document emerges. They learned that by the time that draft actually gets to the conference for which it's intended, it's not likely to be substantively changed, and so the time for lobbying governments with new input is by then past.

They also learned to push hard for the inclusion of NGO representatives *on* government delegations. They unlearned naïveté.

It was the most organized international effort to date. And the most
organized challenge to date came in Beijing. But the payoff came
there, too, in terms of the document.

The conference (4–14 September) began a week after the forum's
opening—and was not without its own "security" incursions (largely
against journalists, although Winnie Mandela gave as good as she got
in one scuffle) into what was, supposedly, temporarily inviolate UN
"territory." Here, however, the UN intervened and the Chinese police
withdrew.

What did remain omnipresent, ironically, was an epidemic of first
ladies. Hillary Rodham Clinton (who received a press blackout in
China for her apt criticisms regarding both the conference and the
forum) certainly deserves credit for facing down the U.S. right wing
by going to China and speaking substantively in both Beijing and
Huairou. Still, as she all too well knows, the "first lady" role is a
constrained one, of ceremony or, at best, influence. The first ladies in
attendance pledged to work "toward peace," and there was a feeling
that the Africans in the group meant it seriously. Still, more than one
delegate (names tactfully withheld) conveyed to me feelings of discomfort that the drive toward women gaining and holding power in our
own right was being subtly undermined by the overabundance of these
distinguished spouses, including first ladies from Benin, Brazil,
Djibouti, Ecuador, El Salvador, Egypt, Equatorial Guinea, Gambia,
Ghana, Republic of Korea, Lebanon, Nigeria, Panama, and Suriname.
In 1985, when she was secretary general of the Nairobi conference,
Letitia Shahani, now president pro tem of the Philippine Senate, had
firmly but diplomatically discouraged rampant displays of first-
ladyhood; this time, Secretary General Mongella was apparently unable or unwilling to do the same. Consequently, female "spouses of"
were far more abundant than female heads of state or government.

But in that latter, select group, feminism is at least no longer evaded
or denied. Whether wittily articulated by Ireland's President Mary
Robinson, or metaphysically invoked in a videotaped message (sent to
the NGO Forum) by Burma's/Myanmar's Aung San Suu Kyi, feminism
finally seems acceptable for affirmation (at least in lip service) by a
female head of state or government.

The Norwegian and Pakistani prime ministers Gro Haarlem
Brundtland and Benazir Bhutto delivered especially strong speeches,
with Norway following its own uncompromisingly pro-choice prece-
dent from the UN's 1994 Cairo International Conference on Population

and Development. Bhutto's speech was a virtuoso juggling act that managed (1) to decry fundamentalist interpretations of the Koran while defending Islam from accusations of misogyny, (2) to affirm the "traditional family as the bedrock of society" while attacking female infanticide as causing the current sex imbalance in more than fifteen Asian countries, and (3) to defend "cultural values" while announcing that Pakistan would become a signatory to CEDAW (the UN Convention on the Elimination of All Forms of Discrimination against Women). Her visual subtext provided one of my favorite conference moments: Bhutto wore her usual elegantly draped headscarf—a chic gesture to the *hijab*—unsecured over her sleek hair so that it slipped slowly backward as she dislodged it, a millimeter at a time, with each nod of her head. This double message to the mullahs back home also magnetized every gaze present. The suspense was riveting: *would* she catch it in time? Always at the last possible moment, with a riddle of a smile, she would lift and resettle her chiffon banner—only to have it promptly begin its slippage all over again.

Of the mountains of paper (alas, poor trees)—statements, positions, press releases—being proffered, my favorite was the leaflet signed by Marye Kat and Meike Keldenich (ages twelve and eleven). They established themselves as members of the Netherlands delegation ("We are here because we are the women of tomorrow"), and cited UN suggested procedure that countries include youth representatives on their official delegations to all international meetings: "Most of you promised to do so . . . Now, as far as we know, we are again the only ones. If you don't do what you have promised, how can we believe you do what you are promising now at this conference? . . . When you are included in the delegation you are able to talk to important persons, which is difficult when you are only allowed to go to the NGO Forum." These girls have a political future. So does the Netherlands.

The general terminology reflected a conceptual shift. Language once used only by radical feminists has entered the so-called policy mainstream. I can remember being criticized for decrying women's "oppression" and invoking "liberation" and "power"—as opposed to using less-threatening words, like "discrimination" and "equality"; Benazir Bhutto's speech embraced all five of those words. I can remember our first buttons reading "All Women Are Working Women" (for a welfare-rights demonstration in the early 1970s) and how we had to keep explaining just what that shocking concept meant. Now, there it was, in bold letters, on the front of the ILO (International Labour Organisation) press packet. We have a long journey ahead in terms of action, but the words and ideas—lovely, seductive, dangerous—have arrived.

As for action, a high percentage of NGOs included in government delegations helped fuel the resolve not to let the clock be turned back; such resolve, together with careful strategizing, would turn out to be critical. This determination showed itself in a variety of ways. One example was the courageous lesbian disruption of a plenary session, a silent protest against excluding the words "sexual orientation" from rights named in the Platform for Action: about twenty women hung a banner proclaiming "Lesbian Rights Are Human Rights" from a balcony rail, before being hustled off and detained for a few hours by UN security guards. Another example—less dramatic but probably the most crucial—involved the document, the Platform for Action, itself.

The draft document was powerful; activist women in NGOs had helped write it at five different regional preparatory conferences around the world for well over a year preceding this conference. But even as the fundamentalist Christian-Islamist-Vatican coalition lost, it availed itself of UN procedure, inserting brackets around any text it deemed controversial. Consequently, the document went to Beijing with a record almost 40 percent of the text enclosed in what came to be called the Holy Brackets.

The process of closed-session arm-twisting, negotiated trade-offs, and hard-won compromise language left many NGOs that were new to UN processes bewildered: how could they lobby delegates if the deliberations were closed? Yet the first brackets seemed to fall away without too much difficulty, and it was only as the conference drew toward a close that reactionary forces reasserted themselves through intense backroom pressure, especially via proxy votes by Latin American (Roman Catholic) and Middle East (Muslim) states. All-night sessions became imperative, under the admirable guidance of Patricia Licuanan (chair of the UN Commission on the Status of Women), who had the thankless task of chairing the somewhat hellish final draft meetings. Finally, three forces working in tandem pulled the document free: the European Union, the Scandinavian countries (decried in fundamentalist leaflets as the "Satanic Nordic Group"), and especially the Nonaligned Movement, also known as Group of 77, the major coalition from the south, skillfully chaired by the Philippines' Senator Shahani. The United States worked creatively and quietly behind the scenes, for once keeping a low profile—a wise decision.

Some feminists have expressed disappointment that this conference had not been elevated to the status of a UN summit, like the 1992 Earth Summit on the environment in Rio or the 1995 World Summit on Social Development in Copenhagen. On the other hand, it could be said fairly that this meeting wound up as a conference of commitment, producing a final document—the Platform for Action and its shorter preamble, the Beijing Declaration—that, even with all its flaws, is historic. And 189 countries adopted it by consensus.

There *are* major flaws. The Platform contains too much abstract UN-ese language. There's too little on allocation of resources, institutional reform, and implementation—although ninety governments committed themselves to specific action. There are precious few time lines—although paragraph 297 specifies that by the end of 1996 governments *in consultation with* NGOs should have developed implementation strategies and plans of action for their countries, *with time-bound targets.* The wording is vague or bland on many issues, including the right to inheritance. We lost out on retaining the phrases "sexual orientation" and "sexual rights." (The right to freedom from discrimination for sexual orientation had been cited four times in the draft document—thanks to support from Australia, Canada, Denmark, Israel, Netherlands, Norway, South Africa, and Sweden—but was bracketed in each case.) But many countries said they would voluntarily interpret lesbian rights to be covered under paragraph 46, which recognizes that women face additional barriers to full equality such as race, age, ethnicity, religion, culture, disability, because they are indigenous, or "because of other status." Not good enough—but a great stagger forward.

Furthermore, we consolidated previous gains, and even broadened them, sometimes with implicit phraseology. Look closely at this carefully hammered-out wording, from paragraph 97: "The human rights of women include their right to have control over and decide freely and responsibly on matters relating to their sexuality, including sexual and reproductive health, free of coercion, discrimination, and violence." Paragraph 96 states, "Equal relationships between women and men in matters of sexual relations and reproduction, including full respect for the integrity of the person, require mutual respect, consent and shared responsibility for sexual behaviour and its consequences."

This is also a document that criticizes structural adjustment programs; advises cuts in military spending in favor of social spending; urges women's participation at all peace talks and in all decision making that affects development planning and environment issues; confronts violence against women—and specifies that sexual harassment, battery, dowry attacks, female genital mutilation, and rape (as well as rape as a war crime) are violations of human rights; calls for the measuring of women's unpaid work; affirms and broadens the rights of female children and adolescents; recommends the adoption of a protocol (e.g., a process for enforcement) for CEDAW; and refers to "the family in its various forms." It also establishes a new UN post—a high-level adviser to the secretary general for "women's issues"—although women worldwide have begun to mobilize for the job itself: it's time we had a secretary general who is a female human being. This is especially significant now. Women's vision and energy could rescue the weary, beleaguered institution that the UN has become, as well as honor the to-date continually reshattered promises that the UN makes about better-ing the treatment—from sexual harassment to promotions—of wo-men within its own ranks. And a woman SG might more likely put muscle into the Platform for Action, and its preamble, the Beijing Declaration.

Because if this terrific document is not enforceable, you well may ask, what use is it?

"It's essentially a contract with the world's women," explains the inimitable Bella Abzug, noting that the Platform for Action is virtually a point-by-point mirror opposite of Newt Gingrich's Contract with America. (Bella, who had been a major presence on the U.S. delegation to the Cairo conference, was noticeably and shockingly absent from the delegation to Beijing; Jesse Helms had threatened to block her if the White House named her to the delegation. But her presence and work were undeniable—at previous UN conferences [see above] and at all the preparatory meetings for this conference. Her effectiveness was so admirably irritating to the right wing that both Bob Dole and George Bush felt compelled to denounce her. Naturally, they both got their facts wrong, providing the press with much-needed laughter: Bush tastelessly denounced Bella for "running around China" when she actually was in a wheelchair; Dole, in a seizure of paranoia, referred to her as co-chairing the entire UN conference—the one decent idea the man's ever had.)

But back to this "contract with the world's women." Women in the United States should know that the U.S. government has announced eight steps, primarily interagency, to advance women's status. (1) The White House will establish a Council on Women, to plan the imple-mentation of the Platform of Action in the United States; (2) the Department of Justice will launch a six-year, $1.6 billion initiative against domestic violence and other crimes against women; (3) the Department of Health and Human Services will lead a comprehensive assault on threats to women's health (specifically targeting cigarette smoking, HIV/AIDS, and the breast cancer epidemic), and HHS will also reaffirm its commitment to the Cairo Conference positions on repro-ductive health; (4) the Department of Labor will conduct a grassroots campaign and will work with corporations to improve conditions for

women in the workplace, with special focus on equal pay and promotion policies; (5) the Department of the Treasury will take new steps for
women's access to credit and economic empowerment; (6) the Department of Education will work to remove all remaining impediments to
female students' attaining equality in education, at all levels; (7) USAID
(Agency for International Development) will encourage a greater role
for women in development planning and decision making and for
increased female participation in political processes; and (8) the
Clinton administration will continue to speak out on behalf of women's rights as human rights and will work to promote the way-
overdue U.S. ratification of CEDAW (now is the time to write your
congressional representative and senators about that!).

As for the rest of us, we women all over the world—those who went
to Beijing and those who didn't—know that the real organizing work
ultimately is done back in our own communities, countries, regions.
But this Platform for Action is a shiny new tool in our hands. That—
and the refreshed sense of international solidarity, of possibility, and
indeed of necessity inherent in our political vision—made it all
worthwhile. Friends had teased me for being quixotic in calling feminism "the politics of the twenty-first century." But the women—in
person, in spirit, and in preparation—who turned Beijing into a
victory have proved that global feminism can be called precisely that.

> Use the Platform for Action as a tool for change in real life. Be sure to *read*
> the complete document, which is reprinted in this issue. Join a women's
> NGO of your liking, if you haven't already done so—or join more than one.
> Work with other women locally to translate the rights named in the
> Platform into the particular conditions in your area, into what you know
> is needed at home, whether that's Kathmandu or Kansas. Investigate what
> your state/province/federal government is planning to do with regard to
> the Platform—its commitment, its allocated resources, its time line (if
> any)—and then push it to honor its commitment and to go further. *Let*
> *them know you're watching.* Unenforceable in a strict legal sense, the docu-
> ment still carries the weight of precedent-setting stated goals and can act
> as a powerful lever. If we use it.

***Robin Morgan**, an award-winning poet, political theorist, novelist, and journalist,
has published fourteen books. Her most recent,* The Word of a Woman: Feminist
Dispatches *(W. W. Norton, 1994), has just been published in Chinese. A political
activist and co-founder of the contemporary U.S. feminist movement, she has been
deeply involved for twenty years in the international women's movement.*

From Quantity to Quality: Women and Education in the Platform for Action

Gloria Bonder, Argentina

As I look back at the Beijing conference, I come to several conclusions about the state of the international women's movement as well as the advancements achieved by that movement over the past twenty years. I see that the stage we are now in might be described as "turbulent," for the following reasons. On the one hand, it is undeniable that the women's movement has become increasingly capable of solving problems efficiently, of organizing and establishing powerful networks that, at the international level, can intervene and influence decision-making. The women's movement has come of age as a political force that knows the rules of the game and is willing to play it. Furthermore, women demonstrated in Beijing that they are one of the very few social groups with a significant vision of and for the future, despite the fact that uncertainties about that future loom larger than ever.

At the same time, the Beijing conference made it clear that we are immersed in certain problems, the coordinates of which we are still unable to glimpse fully. One of these coordinates is a global economy that marginalizes broad sectors of the world's population, the majority of whom are women. Another is the growth of conservatism and fundamentalism—both religious and lay—whose influence again affects women most radically. Finally, the speed of new technological changes and the globalization of communications insist that we rethink our strategies and practices, since such changes can increase the gap between women from different social sectors and countries, thus undercutting the achievements of the women's movement.

Despite these currents, Beijing did not offer an apocalyptic vision of the future. Rather, it seemed to me that the women's movement exists in a dynamic transitional phase, in which past debts and future threats coexist with an important number of creative and strong, but also fragmentary, solutions.

As at past United Nations World Conferences on Women, educational topics were central in all governmental speeches as one of the main strategic tools for the improvement of women's social condition.

The "hot" debates on this topic within the official delegations were focused on predictable issues. They include, among other matters, the function of the school in sexual and reproductive education, the need to invest in women's higher education coupled with the current deficiencies in basic education for women, respect for freedom of conscience and religious expression in educational contexts, and the general funding of education.

But especially notable was the significant presence of educational topics during the forum. Everything leading up to Beijing had made us believe that the main attention of the forum would be focused on reproductive health, poverty, and access to power, while education, a traditional topic within any analysis of discrimination against women, would be less important, especially after two decades of international conferences on women. Surprisingly, however, education commanded the third largest number of workshops, lectures, and other activities, placing ahead of politics, health, and the environment. Of more significance still, on the subject of education, the Platform for Action, produced by the Beijing conference, moves far beyond—in concept and strategy—the Nairobi Forward-Looking Strategies, produced a decade ago.

Undoubtedly, to comprehend the differences between these documents one also needs an understanding of the contexts in which each was produced. Two of these contexts are "practical," referring to the context of education and politics today and in the recent past. Two are "theoretical," referring to the general intellectual environment within which the documents are embedded, and, in particular, the development of feminist theory during the past decade.

As we look back at the Nairobi Forward-Looking Strategies, we can agree that the document was written in an abstract style, based on global principles and with very few specifically stated goals. As a whole, it displays more wishful thinking than definite proposals for action. In relation to education, the document uses an approach "in between" functionalist perspectives—in particular, theories of human capital and development—and the early theoretical contributions of feminists who analyzed the discrimination against women in society and schools.

The chapter on education states this perspective very clearly: "It is required to take special measures to review women's education and adapt it to the realities of a world in development." While using an adaptive approach, the document at the same time uses the diagnosis of discrimination against women to base several of its recommendations on the research findings of early feminists in the field, specifically on studies of school texts, teacher-student interactions, and the curriculum, especially from the perspective of the theory of sex-role socialization. Hence the document advises governments "to eliminate from education any discriminatory stereotyped conception based on sex."

By 1985 and Nairobi, various forms of "militant" research had been executed in almost all countries, moved by the need to gather evidence on the universal phenomenon of sexism in education that would allow one to recommend changes in educational policies and practices. Undoubtedly, the "denouncing" of attitudes, values, and models that transmitted "sex-role stereotypes"—to use the language of the time— needs to be viewed as an incredible achievement, especially when compared to previous international documents. Furthermore, the use of this language testifies to the influence of feminist knowledge that challenged the orthodox views of sociology of education and the dominant theories of developmental psychology.

Thus female illiteracy rates, the deep inequality of educational opportunities between men and women (particularly in developing countries), and the interest in integrating women into scientific and technical fields as a possible "solution" to their lack of participation in these fields—all were significant elements of focus in Nairobi. These elements explain why, even though the Nairobi document highlights several important dimensions of educational processes (such as sexism in texts and curriculum), the eradication of female illiteracy was seen as the main political goal, an indicator of "successful" integration of women in development. This document says explicitly, "The increase in women's educational level is important to the general welfare of societies, since it is closely linked to the survival of the child and the spacing between newborns."

Ten years later, in the Platform for Action, the understanding of women's education has significantly changed. A new language, written first into the document during the Vienna Preparatory Conference in 1994, embeds education within the international concept of women's rights as human rights. The Platform clearly affirms, "Education is a human right and an essential tool for achieving the goals of equality, development, and peace." In this manner, the Platform positions the debate on women's education within an ethical and political perspective, shifting it, at least in some sense, away from the pragmatic functionalist approaches that were dominant earlier.

Without deleting the problems of illiteracy and access from the agenda of "pending topics," the Platform for Action treats them from a different perspective. One can recognize in the Platform the influence of recent developments in gender theory and its applications to the field of educational research. The principles that guide a great number of current educational reforms—particularly in Latin America, for example—identify gender equity with women's empowerment and their full participation in the construction of a new democratic citizenry.

While the language in the Nairobi document focuses on sex-role stereotypes and on changing education so as to eliminate discrimination against women, Beijing's Platform, in using the gender approach, challenged not only traditional definitions and prescriptions of femininity but also those of masculinity, and it clearly redefines the orientation and goals of educational change: to promote or create what some call "coeducation" and others "nonsexist" or "gender-sensitive" education—that is, nondiscriminatory teaching and learning contexts and processes for both women and men of all ages. In the same manner, the Platform proposes to educate new generations to develop more equitable relationships, in both the public and the private spheres. In that sense, it is important to note that education for the working life and for social participation are placed within the same framework as the preparation of men and women for sharing family and domestic responsibilities.

Apart from changes related directly to issues of gender, Beijing's Platform for Action testifies to the influence of new educational theories that take into account the complexities of social, ethnic, and cultural diversity in most societies; the technological revolution; the importance of the media; the need to link schools and education with the democratization process; and advancements in the understanding of human rights. In this respect, therefore, an important achievement of this document is its attention to the quality of education as a basic condition essential "to obtain knowledge, develop skills and ethical values necessary to fully participate in the social and political development." Interest in the quality of women's education is, in this sense, a reaction against former recommendations that focused only on the access of girls to school. Policies that promote only universal access serve to standardize the white male cultural model and to deepen the divisions between good- and poor-quality schools, between students who learn and those who fail, between those who fit into schools and those who do not. In emphasizing the importance of the quality of education, Beijing's Platform introduces an important change that echoes a key topic in current theory and educational practice.

On the one hand, concerns about the quality of education open the doors to renewed reflections about basic learning needs for tomorrow's world, in which the diversity of human experience is vital. Around this idea, new voices are insisting that gender equity is an intrinsic premise of the quality of education, that in a world in which power grows daily more concentrated in a few hands, teaching students about their rights as citizens, about democracy, social participation, and critical judg-ment is as important as—or even more important than—training young people in new information technologies or strategic planning.

But on the other hand, in several developing countries, under the guise of improving quality, governments are carrying out policies aimed only at increasing efficiency. Such policies, in fact, implicitly promote the privatization of educational services, while their dereg-ulation costs them the governmental guarantee of adequate funds, professional teacher training, and adequate working conditions. This model frequently includes the intervention of the business sector in the elaboration of educational policies, and gives business an impor-tant function in the definition and adaptation of the school's curricu-lum to meet the needs of private economic production. Thus it promotes several risks, of both medium- and long-range impact. Among them are the devaluation or exclusion from the curriculum of knowledge and skills that are central to the cultural patrimony of such marginalized peoples as women, as well as fundamental "tools" for improving social life and personal relationships in all spheres of society. The Beijing Platform does not explicitly make a point about these issues, even though it opens the possibility of debate between governments and such funding agencies as the World Bank about indicators and methodologies to be used when evaluating the quality of education in various countries, and whether those methodologies have incorporated gender equity and other ethical considerations.

Another achievement of the Beijing Platform is its articulation of specific recommendations that emphasize the need to develop media literacy programs for all levels of education. Rather than the usual "blaming the media" approach, the Platform recommends basic train-ing to improve analytical ability and critical judgment for assessing and selecting information. The Platform also does more than make the usual recommendation to stimulate women's access to scientific and technical fields. Rather, it strongly affirms the importance of women's participation in the design, application, and evaluation of technological change.

In short, the general portrait that emerges from these two state-ments clarifies important theoretical changes since Nairobi. At that time, the consensus centered mainly on the need to integrate women into an existing educational order, perhaps transforming some pieces of it in the process. But in the Beijing Platform, one can "hear" the claim that women have the right to revise and transform models, institutions, and "accepted practices." Other remarkable aspects of the Beijing Platform include the addressing of teachers as active agents in the educational process and the suggestion that girls and boys should be taught to solve conflicts peacefully. It also includes a specific recommendation to UNESCO regarding the development of an international campaign to acknowledge women's and girls' rights to education. Only in one educational area is the Platform weak: while sex education is mentioned, recommendations are muted and the language indicates major international disagreement here.

Despite all the positive aspects we have mentioned, it is also interesting to note the coexistence in the Platform of two clearly different conceptions about the function of women in society. On the one hand, for the most part, and especially in one of its central paragraphs, women are seen as autonomous, active, social persons, with rights and opportunities equal to men as participants in political and social decisions. Nevertheless, in the same paragraph, only a few lines above, women are—as in the Nairobi document—considered a resource for maintaining or "improving" a family or social order, in their lives as mothers and wives. When using the first perspective, the document indicates that the education of women attempts to "empower women to participate in decision-making in society," but with the second view, women's education trains them for "improving health, nutrition, and education in the family."

How to explain this contradiction or ambiguity? For an explanation, we need to look at the political intention behind each perspective. When the explicit or implicit goal is to motivate governments or justify to them the need to invest in women's education, human rights or ethical principles are set aside. Instead, the economic and social benefits are emphasized, and the language becomes, "Investing in formal and non-formal education and training for girls and women, with its exceptionally high social and economical return, has proved to be one of the best means of achieving sustainable development and economic growth that is both sustained and sustainable." Perhaps this is a realistic or pragmatic posture that we cannot ignore. Nevertheless, it poses challenging questions regarding the viability of developing educational innovations that are "written" into the document and that do not bring about an economic return of this nature, particularly at a time when many countries are cutting their educational budgets.

At the same time, this same argument is false. Enough evidence is available to establish that an increase in the level of a country's population does not necessarily lead to economic development—and certainly not to a more equal redistribution of wealth or greater social mobility. Moreover, it cannot be demonstrated that investment in the sort of women's education that reproduces their traditional status contributes to economic development or to their own personal development. Such economic logic, which evaluates results in terms of the ultimate employment of students, ignores the phenomenon of structural unemployment and thus the problem of how to create new jobs in the future. The fact that women reach higher levels of education every day, and that in some countries some of these levels surpass men's, does not assure in any way that women's participation in the labor market or in political and economic decision making will improve as well. In fact, the high rates of unemployment that threaten some countries have opened the doors to the old speeches that subtly "advise" women to go back home.

In sum, we need to rethink some of these contexts in order to avoid falling either into wishful thinking or into extreme practicality. The section on education, as well as the whole Platform for Action, place before us the evidence of two realities. It is undeniable that feminism has produced a considerable impact on culture, consciousness, and lifestyles. In the past few years, it has also emphasized women's will and skills for political decision making and access to power. But these achievements are embedded within a neoconservative context that subordinates political projects to the needs of the market, and within which women do not have power. The rise of a more conscious, organized citizenry, capable of posing its own demands, questioning political power, and participating in decision-making processes, including economic issues, appears now to be the best possible alternative before us. The Platform for Action challenges all of us to get on with the work.

Gloria Bonder *is director of the Postgraduate Interdisciplinary Women's Studies Program at the University of Buenos Aires, a consultant on gender and education for the Bolivian government, and the founding director and consultant for the Centro de Estudios de la Mujer. Formerly she was secretary of state on women's issues and public policies in the Ministry of Education, Argentina, and the general coordinator of the National Program for Women's Educational Equal Opportunity in the Ministry of Culture and Education.*

The Fight for the Liberation of Women

Excerpts, Remarks, 4 September 1995

Mohtarma Benazir Bhutto, Prime Minister, Islamic Republic of Pakistan

... There is a moral crisis engulfing the world as we speak—a crisis of injustice and inaction, a crisis of silence and acquiescence.

The crisis is caused by centuries and generations of oppression and repression.

This conference, therefore, transcends politics and economics. We are dealing with a fundamental moral issue.

This is a truly historic occasion. Some 40,000 women have assembled here to demand their rights; to secure a better future for their daughters; to put an end to the prejudices that still deny so many of us our rightful place in society.

On this solemn occasion I stand before you not only as a prime minister but also as a woman and a mother: A woman proud of her cultural and religious heritage, a woman sensitive to the obstacles to justice and full participation that still stand before women in almost every society on earth.

As the first woman ever elected to head an Islamic nation, I feel a special responsibility towards women's issues and towards all women. And as a Muslim woman, I feel a special responsibility to counter the propaganda of a handful that Islam gives women a second-class status. This is not true. Today the Muslim world boasts three women prime ministers, elected by male and female voters for our abilities as people, as persons, not as women. Our election has destroyed the myth built by social taboo that a woman's place is in the house—that it is shameful or dishonorable or socially unacceptable for a Muslim woman to work. Our election has given women all over the Muslim world moral strength to declare that it is socially correct for a woman to work and to follow in our footsteps as working women and working mothers. Muslim women have a special responsibility to help distinguish between Islamic teachings and social taboos spun by the traditions of a patriarchal society. This is a distinction that obscurantists would not like to see. For obscurantists believe in discrimination. Discrimination is the first step to dictatorship and the usurpation of power.

A month ago, Pakistan hosted the first ever conference of Women Parliamentarians of the Muslim world. Never in the history of Islam had so many working women and elected representatives gathered together at one place to speak in one voice. As over one hundred delegates from 35 Muslim countries gathered together, I felt an enor-mous sense of pride that we women had each other for strength and support, across the globe and across the continents, to face and oppose those who would not allow the empowerment of women. Today I feel that same sense of pride, that we women have gathered together at Beijing, at this ancient capital of an ancient civilization, to declare: We are not alone in our search for empowerment. Women across conti-nents are together in the search for self-esteem, self-worth, self-respect, and respect in society itself.

In distinguishing between Islamic teachings and social taboos, we must remember that Islam forbids injustice—injustice against people, against nations, against women. It shuns race, color, and gender as bases of distinction among fellowmen. It enshrines piety as the sole criteria for judging humankind. It treats women as human beings in their own right, not as chattel. A woman can inherit, divorce, receive alimony and child custody. Women were intellectuals, poets, jurists, and even took part in war. The Holy Book of the Muslims refers to the rule of a woman, the Queen of Sabah. The Holy Book alludes to her wisdom and to her country being a land of plenty. The Holy Prophet (peace be upon him) himself married a working woman. And the first convert to Islam was a woman, Bibi Khadija. Prophet Muhammad (peace be upon him) emphatically condemned and put an end to the practice of female infanticide in pre-Islamic Arabia. The Holy Qu'ran reads:

> When news is brought to one of them, of the birth of a female (child), his face darkens and he is filled with inward grief. What shame does he hide himself from his people because of the bad news he has had. Shall he retain it on sufferance and contempt, or bury it in the dust. Ah! what an evil choice they decide on. (Surah Al-Nahl, Ayat-57, 58, 59)

How true these words ring even today. How many women are still "retained" in their families "on sufferance and contempt," growing up with emotional scars and burdens? How tragic it is that the pre-Islamic practice of female infanticide still haunts a world we regard as modern and civilized.

Girl children are often abandoned or aborted. Statistics show that men now increasingly outnumber women in more than fifteen Asian nations. Boys are wanted. Boys are wanted because their worth is considered more than that of the girl. Boys are wanted to satisfy the ego; they carry on the father's name in this world.

Yet too often we forget that for Muslims, on the Day of Judgement, each person will be called not by their father's name but by their mother's name. To please her husband, a woman wants a son. To keep her husband from abandoning her, a woman wants a son. And, too often, when a woman expects a girl, she abets her husband by abandoning or aborting that innocent, perfectly formed child.

As we gather here today, the cries of the girl child reach out to us. This conference needs to chart a course that can create a climate where the girl child is as welcome and valued as a boy child. . . .

When I was chairperson of the South Asian Association of Regional Countries, SAARC declared 1989 as the Year of the Girl Child. Six years later, the girl child's vulnerability continues. And it continues not because of religion in the case of Pakistan, but because of social prejudice. The rights Islam gave Muslim women have too often been denied. And women are denied rights all over the world, whether developed or developing.

All over the world women are subjected to domestic violence. Often a woman does not walk out for she has nowhere to go. Or she stays and puts up with the domestic violence for the sake of her children. We in Pakistan have started a public awareness campaign against domestic violence through the mass media to inform women that domestic violence is a crime and to alert men that they can be punished for it. Often women . . . are tortured, not only by men, but also by women in-laws for financial benefits from the woman's family. Sometimes a wife is killed by her husband or in-laws so that they can gain another wife and more dowry. The dowry system is a social ill against which we must raise our voices and create greater awareness.

Women are not only victims of physical abuse, they are also victims of verbal abuse. Often men, in anger and frustration, indulge in the uncivilized behavior of rude and vulgar language against women. Unfortunately, women at times also use vulgar language to denigrate another woman. So we have to work together to change not only the attitudes of men but the attitudes of men and women.

Women have become the victims of a culture of exclusion and male dominance. Today more women than men suffer from poverty, deprivation, and discrimination. Half a billion women are illiterate. Seventy percent of the children who are denied elementary education are girls. In Pakistan we are concentrating on primary education for girls to rectify this imbalance. We are concentrating on training women teachers and opening up employment avenues for women.

It is my firm conviction that a woman cannot ultimately control her own life and make her own choices unless she has financial independence. A woman cannot have financial independence if she cannot work. The discrimination against women can only begin to erode when women are educated and when women are employed. If my father had not educated me or left me with independent financial means, I would not have been able to sustain myself, to struggle against tyranny, or to stand here before you today as a special guest speaker.

If the girl child is to be valued, if the wife is to say "No" to domestic violence, then we owe a special obligation to creating jobs for women. That is why we in Pakistan set up in 1989 the Women's Bank. A bank run by women for women to aid and to assist women in setting up their own enterprises to gain financial independence and—with it—the freedom to make one's own choices. Today 23 branches of the Women's Bank in Pakistan help working women. Our major cities are marked by enterprises set up by women: bakeries, restaurants, boutiques, interior decoration.

We have lifted the ban on Pakistani women taking part in international sporting events. In 1997 we host the Second Muslim Women's Olympics. Special sporting facilities are being set up to encourage participation by Pakistani women in sports.

And Pakistani women are playing a significant role in defusing the population bomb in Pakistan. One hundred thousand women are to be trained to reduce Pakistan's population growth levels and its infant mortality levels. When I visit poverty stricken villages with no access to clean drinking water, it gladdens my heart to see a lady health visitor— to see a working woman amidst the unfortunate surroundings. For it is my conviction that we can only conquer poverty, squalor, illiteracy, and superstition when we invest in our women, and when our women begin working. When we begin working in our far-flung villages where time seems to have stood still and where the bullock, not the tractor, is still used for cultivation; where women are too weak from bearing too many children; where the daughters are more malnourished than the sons, for the daughters get to eat the leftovers; where villagers work night and day with their women and children, to eke out an existence; where floods and rain wash out crops and destroy homes; where poverty stalks the land with an appetite that cannot be controlled until we wake up to the twin reality of population control and women's empowerment. And it is here that the United Nations and its Secretary General have played a critical role.

Some cynics argue about the utility of holding this conference. Let me disagree with them. The holding of this conference demonstrates that women are not forgotten, that the world cares. The holding of this conference demonstrates solidarity with women. The holding of this conference makes us determined to contribute each in our own way, in any manner we can, to lessen the oppression, repression, and discrimination against women. And while much needs to be done, each decade has brought with it its own small improvement.

When I was growing up, women in my extended family remained behind closed walls in village homes. Now we all travel to cities or abroad.

When I was growing up, women in my extended family all covered ourselves with the Burqa, or veil, from head to foot when we visited each other for weddings or funerals, the only two items for which we were allowed out. Now most women restrict themselves to the Duppatta or Chadar and are free to leave the house.

When I was growing up, no girl in my extended family was allowed to marry if a boy cousin was not available for fear of the property leaving the family. Now girls do marry outside the family.

When I was growing up, the boy cousin inevitably took a second wife. Now girls do not expect their husbands to marry again. From the norm, it has become the exception to the norm.

When I was growing up, women were not educated. I was the first girl in my family to go to university and to go abroad for my studies. Now it has become the norm for girls to be educated at university and abroad when the families can afford it.

I have seen a lot of changes in my lifetime. But I hope to see many more changes.

And some of these changes I hope will flow from the Universal Declaration of Human Rights calling for the elimination of discrimination against women. I hope some of these changes will flow from the Convention for the Elimination of all forms of Discrimination which Pakistan signed last month. Of course there was resistance from many quarters. But we are determined to move forward in fulfilling our dream of a Pakistan where women contribute their full potential.

As women, we draw satisfaction from the Beijing Platform for Action, which encompasses a comprehensive approach towards the empowerment of women. But women cannot be expected to struggle alone against the forces of discrimination and exploitation. I recall the words of Dante who reminded us that: "The hottest place in Hell is reserved for those who remain neutral in times of moral crisis." Today in this world, in the fight for the liberation of women, there can be no neutrality. But my dear sisters, we have learned that democracy alone is not enough. Freedom of choice alone does not guarantee justice. Equal rights are not defined only by political values. Social justice is a triad of freedom, of equality, of liberty: Justice is political liberty. Justice is economic independence. Justice is social equality.

Empowerment is not only a right to have political freedom. Empowerment is the right to be independent, to be educated, to have choices in life. Empowerment is the right to have the opportunity to select a productive career, to own property, to participate in business, to flourish in the marketplace.

Pakistan is satisfied that the draft Platform for Action of the Fourth World Conference on Women negotiated so far focuses on the critical areas of concern for women and outlines an action-oriented strategy for the solution of their problems. However, we believe that the Platform needs to address the questions of new and additional resources, external debt, structural adjustment programs, human rights of women, protection of women entrapped in armed conflicts, and the realization of the right of self-determination for territories still under foreign occupation and alien domination.

The Platform for Action must also seek to strengthen the role of the traditional family as the bedrock of the society. Disintegration of the family generates moral decay. This must be arrested. The Platform is disturbingly weak on the role of the traditional family. This weakness can lead to misinterpretation, and even distortion, by opponents of the women's agenda.

We have seen much progress. The very fact that we convene in Beijing today is a giant step forward. But new clouds darken the horizon. The end of the Cold War should have ushered in peace and an era of progress of women. Regrettably, the proliferation of regional tensions and conflicts have belied our aspirations. As in the past, women and girls have again been the most direct victims of these conflicts. They are the most helpless and thus the most abused.

The use of rape as a weapon of war and as an instrument of "ethnic cleansing" is as depraved as it is reprehensible. The unfolding of this saga in different parts of the world, including Jammu, Kashmir, and Bosnia Herzegovina has shaken the conscience of the entire international community. The enormity of the tragedy dwarfs our other issues, urgent though they are. This conference must, therefore, express its complete solidarity with our sisters and daughters who are victims of armed conflict, oppression, and brutality. Their misfortunes must be our first priority.

I come before you to speak of the forces that must shape the new decade, the new century, the new millennium. We must shape a world free from exploitation and maltreatment of women: A world in which women have opportunities to rise to the highest level in politics, business, diplomacy, and other spheres of life. A world where there are no battered women. Where honor and dignity are protected in war and conflict. Where we have economic freedom and independence. Where we are equal partners in peace and development. A world equally committed to economic development and political development. A world as committed to free markets as to women's emancipation.

And even as we catalogue, organize, and reach our goals, step by step by step, let us be ever vigilant. Repressive forces always will stand ready to exploit the moment and push us back into the past. Let us remember the words of the German writer Goethe, "Freedom has to be re-made and re-earned in every generation." We must do much more than decry the past. We must change the future.

Remembering the words of a sister parliamentarian, Senator Barbara Mikulski, that "demography is destiny," I believe time, justice, and the forces of history are on our side. We are here in Beijing to proclaim a new vision of equality and partnership.

Let us translate this vision into reality in the shortest possible time.

Women's Rights Are Human Rights

Excerpts, Remarks, 5 September 1995

Hillary Rodham Clinton, First Lady, United States

... Those of us who have the opportunity to be here have the responsibility to speak for those who could not.

As an American, I want to speak up for women in my own country—women who are raising children on the minimum wage, women who can't afford health care or child care, women whose lives are threatened by violence, including violence in their own homes.

I want to speak up for mothers who are fighting for good schools, safe neighborhoods, clean air, and clean airwaves; for older women, some of them widows, who have raised their families and now find that their skills and life experiences are not valued in the workplace; for women who are working all night as nurses, hotel clerks, and fast food cooks so that they can be at home during the day with their kids; and for women everywhere who simply don't have time to do everything they are called upon to do each day.

Speaking to you today, I speak for them, just as each of us speaks for women around the world who are denied the chance to go to school, or see a doctor, or own property, or have a say about the direction of their lives, simply because they are women. The truth is that most women around the world work both inside and outside the home, usually by necessity.

We need to understand that there is no formula for how women should lead their lives. That is why we must respect the choices that each woman makes for herself and her family. Every woman deserves the chance to realize her God-given potential.

We also must recognize that women will never gain full dignity until their human rights are respected and protected.

Our goals for this conference, to strengthen families and societies by empowering women to take greater control over their own destinies, cannot be fully achieved unless all governments—here and around the world—accept their responsibility to protect and promote internationally recognized human rights.

The international community has long acknowledged—and recently affirmed at Vienna—that both women and men are entitled to a range of protections and personal freedoms, from the right of personal security to the right to determine freely the number and spacing of the children they bear.

No one should be forced to remain silent for fear of religious or political persecution, arrest, abuse, or torture. But tragically, women are most often the ones whose human rights are violated.

Even in the late twentieth century, the rape of women continues to be used as an instrument of armed conflict. Women and children make up a large majority of the world's refugees. When women are excluded from the political process, they become even more vulnerable to abuse.

I believe that, on the eve of a new millennium, it is time to break our silence. It is time for us to say here in Beijing, and for the world to hear, that it is no longer acceptable to discuss women's rights as separate from human rights. These abuses have continued because, for too long, the history of women has been a history of silence. Even today, there are those who are trying to silence our words.

The voices of this conference and of the women at Huairou must be heard loud and clear:

It is a violation of human rights when babies are denied food, or drowned, or suffocated, or their spines broken, simply because they are born girls.

It is a violation of human rights when women and girls are sold into the slavery of prostitution.

It is a violation of human rights when women are doused with gasoline, set on fire, and burned to death because their marriage dowries are deemed too small.

It is a violation of human rights when individual women are raped in their own communities and when thousands of women are subjected to rape as a tactic or prize of war.

It is a violation of human rights when a leading cause of death worldwide among women aged fourteen to forty-four is the violence they are subjected to in their own homes.

It is a violation of human rights when young girls are brutalized by the painful and degrading practice of genital mutilation.

It is a violation of human rights when women are denied the right to plan their own families, and that includes being forced to have abortions or being sterilized against their will.

If there is one message that echoes forth from this conference, it is that human rights are women's rights and women's rights are human rights. Let us not forget that among those rights is the right to speak freely—and the right to be heard.

Women must enjoy the right to participate fully in the social and political lives of their countries if freedom and democracy are to thrive and endure.

It is indefensible that many women in nongovernmental organizations who wished to participate in this conference have not been able to attend—or have been prohibited from fully taking part.

Let me be clear. Freedom means the right of people to assemble, organize, and debate openly. It means respecting the views of those who may disagree with the views of their governments. It means not taking citizens away from their loved ones and jailing them, mistreating them, or denying them their freedom or dignity because of the peaceful expression of their ideas and opinions.

In my country, we recently celebrated the seventy-fifth anniversary of women's suffrage. It took 150 years after the signing of our Declaration of Independence for women to win the right to vote.

It took seventy-five years of organized struggle on the part of many courageous women and men. It was one of America's most divisive philosophical wars. But it was also a bloodless war. Suffrage was achieved without a shot being fired.

We have also been reminded, in V-J Day observances last weekend, of the good that comes when men and women join together to combat the forces of tyranny and build a better world.

We have seen peace prevail in most places for half a century. We have avoided another world war.

But we have not solved older, deeply rooted problems that continue to diminish the potential of half the world's population.

Now it is time to act on behalf of women everywhere.

If we take bold steps to better the lives of women, we will be taking bold steps to better the lives of children and families too.

Families rely on mothers and wives for emotional support and care; families rely on women for labor in the home; and increasingly, families rely on women for income needed to raise healthy children and to care for other relatives.

As long as discrimination and inequities remain so commonplace around the world—as long as girls and women are valued less, fed less, fed last, overworked, underpaid, not schooled, and subjected to violence in and out of their homes—the potential of the human family to create a peaceful, prosperous world will not be realized.

Let this conference be our—and the world's—call to action.

And let us heed the call so that we can create a world in which every woman is treated with respect and dignity, every boy and girl is loved and cared for equally, and every family has the hope of a strong and stable future.

Thank you very much.

God's blessings on you, your work, and all who will benefit from it.

The Planet Earth Is Our Common Home

Excerpts, Statement by The Commission on
Global Governance, 11 September 1995

Wangari Maathai, Kenya

I am speaking on behalf of the Commission on Global Governance. . . . The Commission's report is called "Our Global Neighborhood," in recognition that—despite our diversity and distances—the
planet Earth is our common home and that the electronic media and
the capacity to cover long distances within hours has truly made us
neighbors. The report addresses itself to a wide range of global issues
and explores new possibilities for international cooperation. The
report is about "global governance," rather than "global government,"
and it is about the collective management of our common affairs. The
report calls for putting women at the center of global governance. It
emphasizes that gender sensitivity must be introduced into the conceptual, decision-making, and operational stages of all multilateral
and government agencies.

Many of the issues that have been a concern to women at the just-
concluded NGO Forum and at this official conference are symptoms of
economic, political, and social forces operating at local, regional, and
global levels. These forces include the globalization of the economy;
the increasing impoverishment and marginalization of millions of
people, especially women; the militarization and the growing trade in
small arms and land mines; the fear and the culture of violence which
is exemplified by racism, xenophobia, and rising ethnic nationalism;
and the degradation of the environment due to population pressure,
overconsumption, and pollution. The Commission's report addresses
itself to the causes of these symptoms. It recognizes that many of these
symptoms will best be addressed by getting to the root causes through
genuine worldwide cooperation among governments, a reformed
United Nations, and members of civil society. This cooperation demands political will from governments and a collective commitment
from all humanity.

The report calls for a more representative United Nations concerned not only with military security, but also with the economic

security of people as promised by the charter in 1945. This security should include the security of people within their own borders, notwithstanding the principle of sovereignty. People's security ought to be paramount.

The continuing phenomenon and dynamism of people's movements as represented at this Conference and by the thousands of NGOs at the Forum bears testimony to the collective will of the people, and here, in particular, of the women of the world, to participate in shaping their destiny and safeguarding their rights and those of future generations. "Our Global Neighborhood" recognizes the force of civil society as being an irreversible catalytic agent of change. It further recognizes the need to formally institutionalize and to provide space for these non-state actors within the United Nations system. Only then can the charter's vision of "We, the people" be seen to be fully realized.

The report further acknowledges that some states are economically and politically very powerful, while others are at the other end of the spectrum.... "Our Global Neighborhood" recognizes the interdependence of states and people and therefore sees the need for humanity to find common ground, where shared values could provide the basis for genuine partnership and cooperation. Such values include respect for basic human rights, justice, equality and equity, nonviolence, caring, and integrity. A neighborhood with such values would seek liberty for all, would promote mutual respect and tolerance, and would demand that rights go hand in hand with responsibilities. Such a neighborhood would also require that the strong as well as the weak subscribe to a rule of law. It would combat the corrupted as well as the corrupting, and would encourage participatory and legitimate democratic governance within all relevant institutions.

Such is the neighborhood that women worldwide are trying to build. Indeed many of these values are reflected by many women in their own daily lives. These values ought to be shared not only by men and women in general, but also by the institutions and mechanisms of governance, such as the United Nations, sovereign governments, Bretton Woods institutions, and transnational corporations. A free press can play a vital role in promoting these values so that they become the common heritage of humanity everywhere.

With this in mind, and noting that this is the Fourth World Conference on Women, we wish to emphasize that it is necessary to ensure that there is a follow-up not only within the United Nations but also with respect to national commitments.

In the coming months and years, it will be important to integrate gender into General Assembly debates, monitor the application of

General Assembly decisions, and stimulate political and diplomatic thinking towards advancing the cause of women. Therefore, the report recommends, *inter alia*, that a senior adviser on women's issues be appointed in the office of the UN Secretary General to act as the principal advocate of the interests of women.

"Our Global Neighborhood" reinforces the vision of the world through women's eyes as we enter the twenty-first century. As the Secretary General of this conference, Gertrude Mongella, said at the opening ceremony, "There is no turning back."

Remove the Brackets from Sexual Orientation

Excerpts, Statement by International Gay and
Lesbian Human Rights Commission,
13 September 1995

Palesa Beverley Ditsie, South Africa

It is a great honor to have the opportunity to address this distinguished body on behalf of the International Gay and Lesbian Human
Rights Commission, the International Lesbian Information Service,
the International Lesbian and Gay Association, and over fifty other
organizations. My name is Palesa Beverley Ditsie and I am from
Soweto, South Africa, where I have lived all my life and experienced
both tremendous joy and pain within my community. I come from a
country that has recently had an opportunity to start afresh—an
opportunity to strive for a true democracy where the people govern
and where emphasis is placed on the human rights of all people. The
Constitution of South Africa prohibits discrimination on the basis of
race, gender, ethnic or social origin, color, sexual orientation, age,
disability, religion, conscience, belief, culture, or language. In his
opening parliamentary speech in Cape Town on 9 April 1994, His
Excellency Nelson Rolihlahla Mandela, State President of South Africa, received resounding applause when he declared that never again
would anyone be discriminated against on the basis of sexual
orientation.

The Universal Declaration of Human Rights recognizes the "inherent dignity and . . . the equal and inalienable rights of all members of
the human family," and guarantees the protection of the fundamental
rights and freedoms of all people "without distinction of any kind,
such as race, color, sex, language . . . or other status" (article 2). Yet
every day, in countries around the world, lesbians suffer violence,
harassment, and discrimination because of their sexual orientation.
Their basic human rights—such as the right to life, to bodily integrity,
to freedom of association and expression—are violated. Women who
love women are fired from their jobs, forced into marriages, beaten
and murdered in their homes and on the streets, and have their
children taken away by hostile courts. Some commit suicide due to the

isolation and stigma that they experience within their families, religious institutions, and the broader community. These and other abuses are documented in a recently released report by the International Gay and Lesbian Human Rights Commission on sexual orientation and women's human rights, as well as in reports by Amnesty International. Yet the majority of these abuses have been difficult to document because—although lesbians exist everywhere in the world, including Africa—we have been marginalized and silenced and remain invisible in most of the world. In 1994, the United Nations Human Rights Committee declared that discrimination based on sexual orientation violates the right to non-discrimination and the right to privacy guaranteed in the International Covenant of Civil and Political Rights. Several countries have passed legislation prohibiting discrimination based on sexual orientation. If the Fourth World Conference on Women is to address the concerns of all women, it must similarly recognize that discrimination based on sexual orientation is a violation of basic human rights. Paragraphs 48 and 226 of the [draft] Platform for Action recognize that women face particular barriers in their lives because of many factors, including sexual orientation. However, the term "sexual orientation" is currently in brackets. If these words are omitted from the relevant paragraphs, the Platform for Action will stand as one more symbol of the discrimination that lesbians face and of the lack of recognition of our very existence.

No woman can determine the direction of her own life without the ability to determine her sexuality. Sexuality is an integral, deeply ingrained part of every human being's life and should not be subject to debate or coercion. Anyone who is truly committed to women's human rights must recognize that every woman has the right to determine her sexuality free of discrimination and oppression.

I urge you to make this a conference for all women, regardless of their sexual orientation, and to recognize in the Platform for Action that lesbian rights are women's rights and that women's rights are universal, inalienable, and indivisible human rights. I urge you to remove the brackets from sexual orientation. Thank you.

Grassroots Women: A Response to Global Poverty

Excerpts, Statement by Grassroots Organizations Operating Together in Sisterhood (GROOTS), 9 September 1995

Nandini Azad, India

... GROOTS consists of organizations like the Working Women's Forum (India), Organization of Rural Associations for Progress, Aliens de Mujeras Costarricanses, National Congress of Neighborhood Women (USA), Sistrene Theater Collective (Jamaica), etc. GROOTS is unique in its diversity and in some cases difference of opinion and priorities. Although common in many elements, models of development differ by region in their economic, social, cultural, and political specifics and require a range of alternative forms and methods for outreach to indigenous grassroots women and their organizations.

Our view is that grassroots women are neither weak nor defenseless but are constantly confronted by structures that compartmentalize/fragment their lives and multiple roles. What they need therefore is self-initiated, integrative, and gender-equitable planning. ... Resources have to be used differently ... [to] increase the return on social investment.

GROOTS believes in linking grassroots women to the global agenda. Thus in terms of multinational institutions, we need to create transparent, democratic processes for discussing terms of foreign loans and debt. To the extent adjustment involves making decisions about how to mortgage a country's future, grassroots women that are the largest in number must evaluate which risks are the safest and most dangerous. Structural adjustment policies in the developing countries increase prices, remove subsidies to vulnerable groups, erode accumulation and livelihoods; they cannot "make the grassroots fodder" for the elites of some countries.

Although all grassroots groups believe that pro-poor strategies are needed and governments must guarantee a commitment to certain basic needs, we challenge the way these support programs are structured and the scapegoating of poor women that usually accompanies them.

Thus policymakers should study poor women's initiatives to pinpoint what kinds of resources and types of solidarity make these models work. Allowing the micro to redirect the macro will help clarify common and distinct objectives and contribute to policymakers understanding of how measurements of efficiency, productivity, and value adding should be adapted to reflect micro realities. . . .

I come from the land of Mahatma Gandhi, whose contribution to volunteerism and social movements has been legendary. Yet in countries like India where traditional values are strong, our patriarchal cultures often negate the little progress we have achieved in this direction. This is very evident in the treatment of girl children, the occurrence of female foeticide and infanticide, dowry deaths, and many other forms of discrimination that women and children undergo in powerless communities.

The position of 600 million women workers is still despicable in the informal sector. Women form over 89 percent of India's and 90 percent of world's working population, and yet they are excluded from the labor market. Policy options, protective measures, and welfare benefits are all denied to them, since there is little solidarity with the male-dominated central trade unions. Consequently there is no recognition from respective national governments. The combined result is ignoring women's valuable economic roles and excluding them from the labor market.

In contrast, the Working Women's Forum, the South Asia focal point of GROOTS that I come from, has reversed the pillars of Indian culture on their heads. 3,400,000 poor women from the Working Women's Forum have challenged class exploitation, caste inferiority, male dominance, isolation, and physical weakness through small groups of ten members with leaders that are counter-cultural agents. WWF's strategies are successful: poor women's priorities come first; leadership from below is promoted; working exclusively with the poor and exercising clout to claim the poor their rights is valued. WWF has provided credit loans worth 140 million rupees through its Indian Cooperative Network For Women, an alternative banking system. . . . [T]he cooperatives reach a population of nearly one million. The end result is a mammoth social platform of 30,000 aware groups inroading the local self-governments, challenging power structures, and spearheading social action. Women have assumed leadership in the family and community; accumulated capital, savings, and assets have insured household food security and are vanguards of social integration through this new model of development based on gender and equity and created and managed by poor women. Finally as part of the new generation that learned feminism in the womb and having been born to an admirable feminist, I believe, as do million others like me around the world, that the Platform for Action will herald a new era wherein grassroots women that are on the periphery will march to the center stage and the last will finally be the first.

Invest in the Education of Women

Excerpts, Remarks, 4 September 1995

Nguyen Thi Binh, Vice President, Socialist Republic of Vietnam

Like many other countries, my country, Vietnam, has lived through long years of wars which have ravaged this already-poor land and left behind millions of orphans, widows, disabled, and missing-in-action. Vietnamese women . . . have been tested by harsh trials and countless hardships. They have derived from these trials and hardships their exceptional endurance and tenacity, their ability to survive and to persist in their full identity through the storms of life, just like the Vietnamese bamboo tree, which is supple but unbreakable, which bends under the wind but does not break, and which afterwards, stands again as straight and proud as before.

However, what Vietnamese women have achieved along and together with men in the past could not be explained if one did not point to the other source of strength drawn from their unique experience of the past; namely their outstanding ability to take their fate in their own hands . . . to show initiative and creativeness under all circumstances, even the most difficult. . . .

Today Vietnamese women are tackling the task of rebuilding and developing their country. . . . [T]hey have brought into full play the two strengths which they had displayed during the war. Moreover, they have had to make new and additional efforts to overcome, step by step, the legacies of war and cope with the challenges of the fight against poverty and underdevelopment. Consequently, they are . . . active agents in the reform and renovation process in Vietnam, which is known as Doi Moi.

From my previous experience as Minister of Education and Training and my experiences with international conferences and symposia as well as studies and surveys at the national, regional, and international levels, I have the conviction that the two above-mentioned strengths of Vietnamese women cannot be fully enhanced unless due attention is paid to the catalytic and multiplying role of education.

We should therefore invest in the education of women, and especially of girls. Quite a few developing countries, particularly in our own region, seem to have reached the same conclusion. Consequently, we do hope that the international community and each developing country will give the necessary priority to the objective of universal education for all women as a decisive factor for development, equality, and social justice.

I am fully confident that once Vietnamese women as a whole have been equipped with knowledge and know-how, they will actively participate in . . . the socio-economic development of their country and will be . . . in a position to make a worthy contribution to building a bright future for Vietnam.

Making Commitments a Reality

Excerpts, Remarks, 7 September 1995

Joan Yuelle-Williams, Minister of Community Development, Culture, and Women's Affairs, Republic of Trinidad and Tobago

... The Government of Trinidad and Tobago has identified four areas in which it will commit itself to priority action to remove the remaining obstacles to the advancement of women: (a) alleviating poverty among women; (b) valuing the unwaged work of women; (c) providing affordable health care; and (d) eliminating violence against women.

Poverty

Over the past decade or so, the Caribbean has found itself beset by growing economic hardship. Circumstances dictated that urgent adjustments be made not only in our spending habits but also, in a more general sense, in our overall fiscal management policies. In such a climate of adjustment, it has become sadly evident that the more economically disadvantaged among us have been the most adversely affected, and it has become painfully obvious that women make up a significant percentage of the disadvantaged poor.

When women are poor, the cycle of negatives and deprivations that accompany it are passed on to future generations. The existence of poor women within a country stultifies the growth of that country, for it inhibits the maximum contribution of a vital section of its human resources. My government supports the view of the ILO that poverty anywhere constitutes a threat to prosperity everywhere.

With this in mind, and in keeping with the spirit of our commitment made at the World Summit for Social Development, my country has initiated an integrated and multi-pronged approach towards the eradication of poverty, recognizing that its ill-effects are disproportionately experienced by women.

At the macro-economic level, we are alert to developments and trends in the global economy and are pursuing policies that would encourage growth and expansion of the economy and generate employment. In my country's Medium-Term Policy Framework for 1995–1997, we have also established a number of measures which impact on the poor. These include: (a) protection of socially disadvantaged and vulnerable groups; (b) improved and increased access to quality educational services and training; (c) enhancement of health services; (d) an improved social security system; and (e) rationalization and expansion of housing services.

Unwaged Work

The measure and value of the unpaid work of women, in particular domestic or household work, was recognized in principle two decades ago at the First World Conference on Women in Mexico City. Unfortunately, many countries still have not put in place the policies needed to recognize this valuable contribution to the economy.

Permit me to report with pleasure that on June 25, 1995, a Bill for Counting Unremunerated Work was passed in the Senate of Trinidad and Tobago. This event represented the successful culmination of two decades of consultation and collaboration among a wide cross-section of individuals, NGOs, and public and private sector agencies.

My country recognizes that evaluating unremunerated work in the home and community is a strategy for equity as well as for increasing the self-worth and self-esteem of a large section of the society. A major feature of our legislation is that it provides for the recognition of all unremunerated work, including work performed in and around dwelling places; care for children, the handicapped, elderly and other care services; agricultural work; work related to food production; family businesses; and volunteer and community work in the formal and informal sectors of society. Additionally, the legislation is deliberately non-prejudicial in that it is designed to recognize the unremunerated work of both women and men.

The passage of this legislation is by no means the end of the road as far as this issue goes. Indeed, it can be said to be just the tip of the process of giving dignity and value to a much neglected area of committed effort and service. We expect that the Platform for Action will address this issue with very specific recommendations, and I call upon all countries to incorporate enabling measures to recognize these contributions to the well-being of society in their public accounts.

Health Care

Health is defined by the World Health Organization as "the state of complete mental and social well-being and not merely the absence of disease or infirmity."

We have found that factors that affect women's health in Trinidad and Tobago include lifestyles, attitudes, and behavior. We are committed to addressing the full range of health care requirements of women throughout their life cycles.

At the recently concluded United Nations International Conference on Population and Development . . . Trinidad and Tobago agreed to participate in a broad range of initiatives with respect to reproductive rights and the provision of reproductive health care services. We have not come here to join in any movement to weaken the commitments of Cairo and will resist any attempts to do so.

Violence Against Women

The Government of Trinidad and Tobago is deeply concerned with the level of gender-based violence within our society and has been actively engaged in its eradication. We recognize that violence is perpetrated against women of every class, race, income level, culture, level of education, age, or religion. We affirm that violence against women constitutes a violation of women's human rights and their fundamental freedoms and is an offense against human dignity.

The Sexual Offences Act of 1986 sets protection for women and children from sexual exploitation and sexual violence and provides for closed-court cases for rape, sexual assault, and any offenses involving children. The Domestic Violence Act of 1991 was among several pieces of legislation enacted by the government in pursuit of its commitment to protect the rights of women and to provide them with swift due process. In addition, a Juvenile Branch and Counseling Unit has been established within the police service.

We are committed to a multi-sectoral approach to the prevention and elimination of violence against women—an approach that emphasizes the prevention of violence and the criminal nature of the act. To this end, the Government of Trinidad and Tobago has decided to ratify the Inter-American Convention on the Prevention, Punishment and Eradication of Violence Against Women and will shortly deposit its instrument of ratification with the Organization of American States.

Widespread public education programs will be instituted to encourage non-violent forms of conflict resolution. This will run simultaneously with the promotion of stable family units in the society, the prosecution of offenders, and the institution of appropriate measures to ensure the protection of women subjected to violence.

I am proud to come from the Caribbean where we have a long history of commitment to the defense of human rights, the advancement of women, and the recognition of their intrinsic worth as human beings. The people of Trinidad and Tobago stand ready to join with the rest of the international community in making these commitments a reality for the women of the world. We can do no less, and they expect no less.

Our unity of purpose should be our main strength, buttressed by the women from all walks of life who join us here. We will need to draw on that strength to do our part to ensure that the Fourth World Conference on Women lives up to the expectations of women, and that it produces a Platform for Action and Commitment that will be meaningful to those millions of women who demand what is their birthright: the right to live free of violence, the right to equality, and the right to participate fully in the shaping of their own destinies.

A Revolution Has Begun

Excerpts, Welcoming Ceremony,
4 September 1995

Gertrude Mongella, Secretary General of the Fourth World Conference on Women

... We are all witnessing a historic moment, a moment which is charac-terized by unprecedented solidarity. This solidarity is reflected in one principle, which is not to be compromised. This is the principle of equality between human beings: equality between men and women.

The aim of the Beijing Conference is to capitalize on the strength and resourcefulness of women, to share it, and act upon it. This historic conference is not about business as usual. It is about changing the status quo, which is characterized by inequality. Not only do women represent 50 percent of the world's population, they also contribute substantially to the world's richness. It is not by chance that the time has come for women to receive their rightful place in all societies. . . . This planet belongs to them too.

Change towards the betterment of women is not only inevitable, it is right and essential if we are to move the world towards a better life for all individuals—men, women, and children in all nations. We must apply concrete solutions to the obstacles and constraints that women continue to experience in the political, economic, social, and cultural spheres. . . .

May I conclude by saying that a revolution has begun. There is no going back. There will be no unraveling of commitments; neither today's, nor last year's, and certainly not this decade's commitments. This revolution is too just, too important, and certainly long overdue.

A Global Movement for Democracy

Plenary Statement, 12 September 1995

Bella Abzug, Co-chair, Women's Environment and Development Organization (WEDO)

In this room is the history of civil society. In this room are the people who have been the standbys in the process of bringing people into the UN. And in this room are many people who have, for a long time, been the only voice that NGOs have had. I came to salute you and to appreciate the fact that this meeting is taking place.

Beijing has given birth to a global movement for democracy. As Gertrude Mongella said in her opening statement, "In the great hall of the people is a revolution of new partnerships between men and women based on real equality." The Beijing Platform for Action—though not perfect—is the strongest statement of consensus on women's equality, empowerment, and justice ever produced by governments. The Beijing Platform is a consolidation of the previous UN conference agreements, in the unique context of seeing it all through women's eyes. It is an agenda for change, fueled by the momentum of civil society, based on a transformational vision of a better world for all. We are essentially bringing women into politics to change the nature of politics, to change the vision, to change the institutions. Women are not wedded to the policies of the past. We didn't craft them; they didn't let us.

As women, we know that we must always find ways to change the process because the present institutions want to hold on to power and keep the status quo. Just five short years ago we developed the women's caucus methodology to influence the global agenda at the UN for the Earth Summit. The Women's Environment and Development Organization, which I co-chair with nine other co-chairs from every region of the world, and countless other NGOs have carried this work forward, linking the gains made at each conference, trying to prevent collective amnesia by governments.

Now that we have left Beijing, women will not stop. It's like jet propulsion—the fact that so many women made such an effort to participate in this historic conference. Never in the history of the

United Nations have that many women—30,000 or more—come to a conference. (This number represents only members of NGOs. Besides them, there were countless numbers of journalists and governments represented by women.) It's a historic conference, and it's a testament to the seriousness of the agenda. Now that women around the world own this agenda, women will ensure that others know about the provisions agreed to, about the commitments made, and the millions will press for their governments to follow through.

In fact, the most significant thing about this conference was that the NGOs were determined to make this a "conference of commitments," to have governments for the first time make specific commitments in their speeches to aspects of the Platform for Action. We sought this because we have cried and tried for many years in all of the agreements entered into by our government representatives, to implement, to monitor, to make sure that action came out of these agreements. Often not enough action has resulted.

We've had a lot of words on equality, but we wanted the music—the music was the action. So we pressed hard to support the "conference of commitments" that the great nation of Australia projected as the way this conference should go. Sixty-five countries in their speeches made various commitments to specific actions they would take. And we look forward to actions taken by governments together with NGOs in every single country to develop a national plan of action based upon the Beijing plan before the end of 1996.

The idea of a commitment conference started with the women's caucus at the World Summit on Social Development in Copenhagen. There, only about fourteen countries made commitments. But the conference itself is a statement that civil society has won. That civil society has made the kind of impact on the agenda and on the Platform for Action that will serve women and men for many years to come. Key provisions were passed in Beijing that went beyond the previous conferences, provisions affecting the right of women to decide freely all matters related to their sexuality and to childbearing. There were commitments specifically advanced on the question of the girl child. There were major commitments made on the position in society of the elderly, who too often are neglected in UN documents. Commitments were made to the economic power of women; access to credit was considered a critical aspect of the empowerment of women. Governments were under great pressure to provide for a guarantee of women's equal rights to inherit. And although the family was recognized as a basic unit of society, there was also recognition that there are various forms of family. For the first time in the history of the

United Nations, the question of the right of all women to be free from discrimination and to share in the rights that should be available to both men and women was thoroughly discussed on the floor of the convention—particularly with respect to a provision on sexual orientation. The point that was being made was that all women have a right to be free from discrimination, that we have to recognize the diversity among women—age, religion, sexual orientation, class, ability, disability. All of that was very strongly instilled during this conference and in the document known as the Platform for Action.

I think it's important that we were there speaking—30,000 or more women—not only for ourselves but also for the many millions who were not there, the women who had had few choices in life, the women who never had the chance to go to school or to stay in school, for those who go through life never having enough to feed themselves or their families. We were there for those forced to work in difficult circumstances, being underpaid or not being paid at all, for the women who have not been able to cut through the glass ceiling. And also for the millions who have been prevented from controlling their minds and bodies or freely expressing their sexuality, for the hundreds of thousands who die in childbirth or from unsafe abortion. For the silent suffering of women and girls who have endured the abuse of power in the family, in the community, in war. It is for these women who have been victims of land mines, nuclear testing, and toxic dumping; who have been sexually abused, raped, tortured, and even killed; and those who have been exported in sex trade or have experienced genital mutilation, that we organized in Beijing. And for the millions of women who have been silenced or persecuted because of their race, religion, or sexual orientation; and the millions who have been subject to the perpetuating gender stereotypes that crop the flights of fancy and imagination of girls and women.

It's important to understand that what we determined in China was that women *can* transform the world. And although it may seem utopian, idealistic, or just simpleminded, change always seems to happen. And it's not inconceivable that humans, and especially female humans, can participate in and influence the direction of that change. But as always, women's work is never done. And when we return home, as we have, we must be prepared to inform, organize, and press governments to deliver on their promises. Our task is also to absorb into our hearts, minds, and consciousness our responsibility to the women around the world who sent us there to represent them. We had to, and we are making our own personal commitments to them.

The decade of women is what this flowed from. As you recall, we used to have a day; it was called International Women's Day. Then in 1975 the United Nations declared it to be International Women's Year. That year they gave us a year. Then in 1975 to 1985 they declared it to be the Decade of Women. At that time, having participated in all of those conferences, both as a congressional adviser and subsequently as an NGO, I said, "Who knows? If we behave, they may let us into the whole thing." However, we did not behave.

And that is an important lesson for us to learn: that civil society has not only an obligation but a responsibility and a right to be deeply involved in the agenda, in the development of social philosophy, and in the actions taken by a universal public authority like the United Nations. The UN cannot truly call itself a universal public authority unless and until it has even greater input from the civil society than it now has. And as we consider, as we are doing, UN reform, I very much support the suggestion that has been made by the Commission on Global Governance, that there should be a People's Assembly prior to the General Assembly that takes place each year, in which the civil society has direct input into what the agenda should be for the entire United Nations. And who knows? Sometime maybe we will even have a right to say something at the General Assembly. And maybe the civil society would very much improve what goes on in terms of world peace if it had something to say in the Security Council. I realize that some of these ideas are not exactly agreed to by everyone, but all good ideas are not agreed to in the beginning, and I've had some experience with that.

So I think that civil society has won here. It came out of an interesting struggle. The NGOs and consults of status were the forerunners of an important voice of civil society. The insistence that some of us, particularly my organization, had in having a women's caucus at the Earth Summit after we read the first documents in Rio (which had only two mentions of women) has played a role for all NGOs. We have had a direct impact in the documents, and the thinking of the documents, of the United Nations at all international conferences. We have played a parallel, side-by-side partnership role with the governments since the Earth Summit, since Rio. We have made our voices heard by having a daily caucus every time the UN met in its preparatory meetings, in its informal meetings to solve problems, by being there side by side with governments, going over the documents, making suggestions line by line as to what improvements could be made, what deletions, what suggestions and additions should be made. And we have made an impact. The Earth Summit originally had about two or three mentions of women in its first document. By the time we finished with four preparatory meetings we had about 120 provisions affecting women, in a separate chapter on women.

The Vienna World Conference on Human Rights in 1993 was another significant example of the way in which NGOs and consults of status played a major role in UN deliberations. We succeeded in convincing the governments to finally state that women's rights are human rights. I mean, the fact that they had to have a whole conference to say that is sad; however, it's very hard at times to move bureaucracy. Even though we have wonderful governments, wonderful representatives, and all that, it is still a pretty heavy bureaucracy. We are very proud to have had the opportunity to move it, and to get it to move, and to get it to move even further in the future.

I think it's also important to recognize that the effective work by the women's caucus, in which many thousands of international and national NGOs from all over the world participated, had a significant impact on changing the thinking with respect to population. Thinking on the subject moved from a concern with population control and demographics to an understanding that what was involved was women's right to reproductive and sexual health, the empowerment of women, and the need for women to change the actual social conditions under which they live.

I think that the Social Summit that was held in Copenhagen and that dealt with the issues of poverty, unemployment, and social disintegration likewise was significantly influenced by the women's caucus that existed there. And in fact, during the women's conference in China, the Linkage Caucus—which is what we called ourselves—linked all of the gains that had been made in the previous conferences and demanded even more, moving beyond the scope of all other platforms.

I very seriously believe, and I know that I have said this before, that women have been trained to speak softly (that is, some of us) and to carry a lipstick. Women came out to demand a bigger stick at the international conference in China. We are no longer content to sit only at the kitchen table—women must be at *all* the tables where decisions of life and death are made: the peace table, the trade table, at every table in the parliaments and the cabinets, as ambassadors to the United Nations, in missions, in UN agencies and at the tables in the Bretton Woods and other financial institutions that are globalizing our economy.

Security is what we all seek, but security also comes from within, from inner strength. It emanates from our ability to love and treasure the peoples of the earth, especially those with whom we may not necessarily agree or those who are different from us. Each of us is a powerful creature. When we talk of the empowerment of women we are simply talking about releasing what is inside each of us, women as well as men—not only what we are but what we can become. And as we contemplate these things, the bloodiest century of human history, which dawned at Sarajevo with an incident that launched a world war followed by hundreds of other large and small wars, is ending in Sarajevo with brutal murders of children, women, and men, and mass rape and violence spurred on by age-old ethnic rivalries, and greed, with the genocide of the civilian population of Bosnia, of Herzegovina, Somalia, and the wars in the Rwandas and the Chechnyas of the world. Is it now time to admit—I hope you're not going to get mad when I say this, however, I'm going to say it regardless—that the present dominant style and conduct of male leadership has been a disaster?

We, as women, just want to share the political space. We're not going to take anything from anybody, that is, except for half of everything— half of the political space, half of the economic resources, half of the commitment to gender balance in all institutions in society. And I believe that the United Nations, through its conferences and through its own actions or its failure of action, has to be put on record as supporting this, as indeed it has done in this conference that we just came back from.

Of course, it was very sad that even as we were deliberating progress in Beijing the world continued in its destructive ways. While governments were removing the brackets from the document over the last two weeks and thereby removing the brackets on the lives of women and children, the French tested another nuclear weapon in the Pacific, NATO bombed Bosnia, and the Serbs shelled Sarajevo; refugee camps overflowed in too many places around this globe, conditions for women on factory floors did not change, women died in childbirth and in their homes, hunger gnawed at the bellies of millions—the world went on in the downward spiral that we all know too well.

In the face of so much pain, I personally remain an incurable optimist. I'm fueled by the passion of the women, especially those in the South with whom I have been privileged to work and meet, buoyed by their hope for peace, justice, and democracy. I'm strengthened by each of them, and to them and each government delegate who pushed the boundaries of progress, I say thank you. I thank the United Nations and my sisters and brothers in the NGO community for your good humor and hard work. I wish each of you well and sustainable optimism for the days ahead. Never underestimate, and we do not, the importance of what we are doing here, never hesitate to tell the truth, and never ever give in—or give up.

United States Commitments

Remarks, 6 September 1995

Madeleine K. Albright, U.S. Permanent Representative to the United Nations

Honored guests, fellow delegates, and observers, I am pleased and proud to address this historic conference on behalf of the United States of America.

My government congratulates the thousands who have helped to organize the conference, to draft the Platform for Action, to inform the world about the subjects under discussion here, and to encourage wide participation both by governments and NGOs.

We have come here from all over the world to carry forward an age-old struggle: the pursuit of economic and social progress for all people, based on respect for the dignity and value of each.

We are here to promote and protect human rights and to stress that women's rights are neither separable nor different from those of men.

We are here to stop sexual crimes and other violence against women; to protect refugees, so many of whom are women; and to end the despicable notion—in this era of conflicts—that rape is just another tactic of war.

We are here to empower women by enlarging their role in making economic and political decisions, an idea some find radical, but which my government believes is essential to economic and social progress around the world; because no country can develop if half its human resources are devalued or repressed.

We are here because we want to strengthen families, the heart and soul of any society. We believe that girls must be valued to the same degree as boys. We believe, with Pope John Paul II, in the "equality of spouses with respect to family rights." We think women and men should be able to make informed judgments as they plan their families. And we want to see forces that weaken families—including pornography, domestic violence, and the sexual exploitation of children—condemned and curtailed.

Finally, we have come to this conference to assure for women equal access to education and health care, to help women protect against infection by HIV, to recognize the special needs and strengths of women with disabilities, and to attack the root causes of poverty, in which so many women, children, and men are entrapped. We have come to Beijing to make further progress towards each of these goals. But real progress will depend not on what we say here, but on what we do after we leave here. The Fourth World Conference on Women is not about conversations; it is about commitments.

For decades, my nation has led efforts to promote equal rights for women. Women in their varied roles—as mothers, farm laborers, factory workers, organizers, and community leaders—helped build America. My government is based on principles that recognize the right of every person to equal rights and equal opportunity. Our laws forbid discrimination on the basis of sex, and we work hard to enforce those laws. A rich network of nongovernmental organizations has blossomed within our borders, reaching out to women and girls from all segments of society, educating, counseling, and advocating change.

The United States is a leader, but leaders cannot stand still. Barriers to the equal participation of women persist in my country. The Clinton Administration is determined to bring those barriers down.

Today, in the spirit of this conference, and in the knowledge that concrete steps to advance the status of women are required in every nation, I am pleased to announce the new commitments my government will undertake:

First, President Clinton will establish a White House Council on Women to plan for the effective implementation within the United States of the Platform for Action. That council will build on the commitments made today and will work every day with the nongovernmental community.

Second, in accordance with recently approved law, the Department of Justice will launch a six-year, 1.6 billion dollar initiative to fight domestic violence and other crimes against women. Funds will be used for specialized police and prosecution units and to train police, prosecutors, and judicial personnel.

Third, our Department of Health and Human Services will lead a comprehensive assault on threats to the health and security of women—promoting healthy behavior, increasing awareness about AIDS, discouraging the use of cigarettes, and striving to win the battle against breast cancer. And, as Mrs. Clinton made clear yesterday, the United States remains firmly committed to the reproductive health rights gains made in Cairo.

Fourth, our Department of Labor will conduct a grassroots campaign to improve conditions for women in the workplace. The campaign will work with employers to develop more equitable pay and

promotion policies and to help employees balance the twin responsibilities of family and work.

Fifth, our Department of the Treasury will take new steps to promote access to financial credit for women. Outstanding U.S. microenterprise lending organizations will be honored through special
residential awards; and we will improve coordination of federal efforts
to encourage growth in this field of central importance to the economic empowerment of women.

Sixth, the Agency for International Development will continue to
lead in promoting and recognizing the vital role of women in development. Today, we announce important initiatives to increase women's
participation in political processes and to promote the enforcement
of women's legal rights.

There is a seventh and final commitment my country is making
today. We, the people and government of the United States of America,
will continue to speak out openly and without hesitation on behalf of
the human rights of all people.

My country is proud that, nearly a half century ago, Eleanor Roo-
sevelt, a former First Lady of the United States, helped draft the
Universal Declaration of Human Rights. We are proud that, yesterday
afternoon, in this very hall, our current First Lady—Hillary Rodham
Clinton—restated with memorable eloquence our national commitment to that declaration.

The Universal Declaration reflects spiritual and moral tenets which
are central to all cultures, encompassing both the wondrous diversity
that defines us and the common humanity that binds us. It obliges
each government to strive in law and practice to protect the rights of
those under its jurisdiction. Whether a government fulfills that obligation is a matter not simply of domestic, but of universal, concern. For it
is a founding principle of the United Nations that no government can
hide its human rights record from the world.

At the heart of the Universal Declaration is a fundamental distinction between coercion and choice.

No woman—whether in Birmingham, Bombay, Beirut or Beijing—
should be forcibly sterilized or forced to have an abortion.

No mother should feel compelled to abandon her daughter because
of a societal preference for males.

No woman should be forced to undergo genital mutilation, or to
become a prostitute, or to enter into marriage, or to have sex.

No one should be forced to remain silent for fear of religious or
political persecution, arrest, abuse, or torture.

All of us should be able to exercise control over the course of our own lives and be able to help shape the destiny of our communities and countries.

Let us be clear. Freedom to participate in the political process of our countries is the inalienable right of every woman and man. Deny that right, and you deny everything.

It is unconscionable, therefore, that the right to free expression has been called into question right here, at a conference conducted under the auspices of the UN and whose very purpose is the free and open discussion of women's rights.

And it is a challenge to us all that so many countries in so many parts of the world—north, south, west, and east—fall far short of the noble objectives outlined in the Platform for Action.

Every nation, including my own, must do better and do more—to make equal rights a fundamental principle of law; to enforce those rights; and to remove barriers to the exercise of those rights.

That is why President Clinton has made favorable action on the Convention to Eliminate Discrimination Against Women a top priority. The United States should be a party to that Convention.

And it is why we will continue to seek a dialogue with governments—here and elsewhere—that deny to their citizens the rights enumerated in the Universal Declaration.

In preparing for this conference, I came across an old Chinese poem that is worth recalling, especially today, as we observe the Day of the Girl Child. In the poem, a father says to his daughter:

> We keep a dog to watch the house,
> A pig is useful, too,
> We keep a cat to catch a mouse,
> But what can we do with a girl like you?

Fellow delegates, let us make sure that question never needs to be asked again—in China or anywhere else around the world.

Let us strive for the day when every young girl, in every village and metropolis, can look ahead with confidence that their lives will be valued, their individuality recognized, their rights protected, and their futures determined by their own abilities and character.

Let us reject outright the forces of repression and ignorance that have held us back; and act with the strength and optimism unity can provide.

Let us honor the legacy of the heroines, famous and unknown, who struggled in years past to build the platform upon which we now stand.

And let us heed the instruction of our own lives. Look around this hall, and you will see women who have reached positions of power and authority. Go to Huairou, and you will see an explosion of energy and intelligence devoted to every phase of this struggle. Enter any community in any country, and you will find women insisting—often at great risk—on their right to an equal voice and equal access to the levers of power.

This past week, on video at the NGO Forum, Aung San Suu Kyi said that "it is time to apply in the arena of the world the wisdom and experience" women have gained.

Let us all agree; it is time. It is time to turn bold talk into concrete action.

It is time to unleash the full capacity for production, accomplishment, and the enrichment of life that is inherent in us—the women of the world.

Contract with Women of the USA

Women's Environment Development Organization (WEDO) and Center for Women Policy Studies (CWPS)

As public officials, advocates for women's rights, policy-makers, organizations, and individuals, we sign this Contract with Women of the USA to implement the Platform for Action adopted September 1995 at the United Nations Fourth World Conference on Women by consensus of 189 governments, including the United States of America.

We pledge our mutual commitment to the goal of equality and empowerment for American women, who are the continuing majority of our nations and states.

We pledge to work together to overcome discrimination based on sex, race, class, age, immigration status, sexual orientation, religion, and disability. We seek to end social, economic, and political inequities, violence, and the human rights abuses that still confront millions of women and girls in our country.

Looking to the twenty-first century, we enter into this Contract with Women of the USA for ourselves and for future generations to achieve our vision of a healthy planet and healthy nations, states, and communities, with peace, equality, and justice for all.

Empowerment of Women

We pledge to work for empowerment of women in all their diversity through their equal participation in decision-making and equal access to shared power in government, in all spheres and at every level of society.

Sharing Family Responsibilities

We pledge to work for equal sharing of family responsibilities, recognition and respect for the diversity of families, and for practices and

Women's Studies Quarterly kindly thanks WEDO and CWPS for providing us with an advance copy of this document. The Contract with Women of the USA was released on the eve of International Women's Day, 8 March 1995, to begin a national grassroots mobilization campaign to make women's concerns a central issue in policy-making and elections at the local, state, and federal levels.

policies that enhance the multiple roles, security, and well-being of women and girls, men and boys.

Ending the Burden of Poverty

We pledge to work for economic justice and to end the increasing burden of poverty on women and their children, who are a majority of the poor. Recognizing the value of women's unpaid and underpaid labor to our families, communities, and economy, we support a living wage for all workers and adequate funding for welfare and other social safety nets, child care, education and job training, and access to collateral-free credit for women-owned small businesses.

High Quality, Affordable Health Care

We pledge to work to reaffirm the rights of women and girls, regardless of income or where they live, to high quality, accessible, affordable, and respectful physical and mental health care, based on sound women-focused research.

Sexual and Reproductive Rights

We pledge to work to reaffirm and uphold sexual and reproductive rights of all women, including their right to control their own reproductive lives free of coercion, violence, and harassment.

Workplace Rights

We pledge to work for guarantees of equal pay for work of comparable value and an end to discriminatory hiring and sexual harassment. We support family-friendly workplace practices, job training and opportunities programs, strengthening of affirmative action, employees' rights to organize unions and to work in safe, healthy working environments.

Educational Equity

We pledge to work for educational equity for women and girls, including creation and strengthening of gender-fair multicultural curricula and teaching techniques, equal opportunities and access for girls and women throughout their lives to education, career development, training and scholarships, educational administration, and policy-making.

Ending Violence

We pledge to work for policies and programs to end violence against women and children in every form and to ensure that violence against women and children is understood as a violation of their human rights and civil rights.

Protecting a Healthy Environment

We pledge to work to end environmental degradation and eliminate toxic chemicals, nuclear wastes, and other pollutants that threaten our health, our communities, country, and planet. We uphold active roles by government at all levels and public and private sectors to continue and expand environmental protection programs.

Women as Peace Makers

We salute women's leading roles in peace movements and conflict resolution and pledge to work for their inclusion in policy-making at all levels aimed at preventing wars, halting the international arms trade, and eliminating all nuclear testing. We seek reductions in military spending and conversion of military facilities to socially productive purposes.

Honor Commitments and Ratify CEDAW

We pledge to support the commitments made by the United States government to implement the UN Platform for Action, which constitutes a contract with the world's women. We call on the United States Senate to ratify the Convention to Eliminate Discrimination Against Women (CEDAW), which the United States has signed.

A Long-Term Plan to Achieve Equality

We who are state and federal policy makers pledge to work in partnership with women's organizations to develop and enforce a long-term plan to achieve our goals of equality and empowerment for women. We support the re-establishment of a national Advisory Panel on Women, and the creation or strengthening of similar panels or commissions in each state, to ensure that governments at every level take the necessary steps to implement this Contract.

Reprinted, with permission, by WEDO and CWPS.

Women's Power Is a Formidable Force

Closing Address, 15 September 1995

Gro Haarlem Brundtland, Prime Minister, Norway

We came here to answer the call of billions of women who have lived and of billions of women who will live. We now need a tidal change. Women will no longer accept the role as second-rate citizens.

Our generation must answer that call. Undoubtedly, we have moved forward. But the measure of our success cannot be fully assessed today. It will depend on the will of us all to fulfill what we have promised.

The views expressed here, and the news which escaped from here, will irrevocably shape world opinion. The story of Beijing cannot be untold. What will be remembered? Zealous security? The palms of policemen? Visas not granted? Yes, but such practices cannot, and will not, long endure. Let us today count our strategic victories, not the tactical defeats. What we have achieved is to unbracket the lives of girls and women.

Now we must move on. All history of liberation struggles tells us that life, freedom, equality, and opportunity have never been given. They have always been taken. We cannot maintain the illusion that someone else is going to do the job and establish equality. Women and men working with us, men who understand, we all must fight for that freedom.

Today we know that women's contributions to the economy are decisive for growth and social development. We know that countries will continue to live in poverty if women remain under the heel of oppression. We know the costs of a continuing genderized apartheid.

Today, there isn't a single country in the world—not one—where men and women enjoy equal opportunities. So we must go back from Beijing, go back to the shanty towns of third world mega-cities, go back to the croplands at the desert's edge in Africa, go back to the indigenous communities of Latin American rain forests, go home to change values and attitudes. But not only there. No, we must go the boardrooms, to the suburbia of Europe and North America, to all of our local communities, to our governments, and to the United Nations's headquarters. This is where change is required—both in the north and in the south.

What must be done to fulfill the hopes and aspirations of generations living and yet unborn? Not only must women become free and equal to make choices about their own lives. Not only must women have the right, the formal and protected right, to take part in the shaping of society. No, far more, women must make use of that right. Women's power is a formidable force. Women's values have a lot to give.

We need women at all levels of management and government—local as well as national government. We all agree that women must have education, not only experience—but we still are far from a world that makes use of it. To take one example from the political field: There are cabinets and parliaments in the world with few or even no women. This situation cannot and will not last. And if the transition towards more real political representation is sluggish, affirmative action will work. It did, in Scandinavia.

When I first became prime minister 15 years ago, it was a cultural shock to many Norwegians. Today, four-year-old children ask their mommies: "But can a man be prime minister?"

We are adopting a comprehensive Platform for Action. All of its elements are important in this agenda for change. Let me focus on some of its most compelling thrusts.

We agree that women's education is essential. This year's Human Development Report makes it emphatically clear: The economic returns of investing in women's education are fully comparable to those for men. But the social returns from educating women far exceed those of educating men. Schooling of girls is one of the unlocking keys to development. There has been a difficult debate on how Beijing should define the human rights of women. As if there could be one set of human rights for men and another, more restricted one, for women.

I even have heard the following allegation from a country not to be named: "The West, to be frank, is attempting to impose its cultural pattern as an international model." Wrong. Most countries are today strongly defending their own cultures. And there is more respect and mutual understanding of the value of other cultures and religions than ever before.

But the point is a different one: There are limits to the practices that countries can expect the international community to accept, or con-done, even when such practices have deep cultural roots. This is where human rights enter the picture.

Violence against women, also domestic violence, can be said to be part of a "cultural pattern," in most countries including my own. We receive too many appalling reports of plain wife beating. And clearly, freedom from violence and coercion must apply also in the sexual sphere of life. This conference has rightly made clear what the existing human rights must mean in practice. The state becomes an accomplice if violence against women is seen as a separate cultural category of behavior, extraneous to the realm of justice and law enforcement.

There are stains on the world map of girl-child maltreatment. Genital mutilation of girls is just that. It does not become sacrosanct, or elevated beyond the realm of politics, just because that practice can be said to be part of a "cultural pattern." We are familiar with the terrible discrimination against girls, even before birth. What has been obscurely described as "pre-natal sex selection" and the fatal neglect of infant girls are tragic testimonies. There are often ancient roots of such practices, but they are committed by people who live today. Why are there astonishingly more boys than girls in certain countries? The question may be unpleasant for governments, which do not encourage these crimes, but we will all be found guilty if we close our eyes.

Why are girl children given less and poorer food than their brothers? Why do they receive less health care and less education? Why are they subjected to the horrible tradition of sexual exploitation?

Ingrained, centuries-old attitudes are not easily changed, but these that I have mentioned must be. The task requires vigorous action on the part of governments, religious groups, and private, nongovernmental organizations.

Greater equality in the family is for the good of men, women, and children. The allegation that this conference is against motherhood and family is plainly absurd.

Today we recognize that poverty has a gender bias. Increasingly, poverty discriminates between men and women. The myth that men are the economic providers and women are mainly mothers and care-givers in the family has now been thoroughly refuted. This family pattern has never been the norm, except in a narrow middle-class segment.

Women have always worked, in all societies and at all times. As a rule they have worked harder than men, and—as a rule—without pay and acknowledgment. Their contribution has been essential for national economies as well as to their families, where women have been the breadwinners. . . . As defined by statistics, societies have often kept women at arm's length. Women who work 10–12 hours a day in subsistence agriculture may be registered as "housewives" in the national censuses.

But overlooking women's contribution to the economy has had more severe, damaging effects. Often women cannot even obtain a modest loan to become more independent and productive. In many countries, women own nothing, inherit nothing, and are unable to offer security. On top of this, laws often work against women.

No, women will not become more empowered merely because we want them to be, but through change of legislation, increased information, and by redirecting resources.

Faced with what Beijing says about the economic role of women, ministers of finance and planning may rue their former practice. Unleashing women from the chains of poverty is not only a question of justice. It is also a question of sound economic growth and improved welfare for everyone. It is high time that we genderize development plans and government budgets.

The 20/20 concept is a promising path forward. It requires mutual commitment, the solidarity of the international community, and the responsibility of each national government to provide basic social services. It is not possible to meet the aspirations of our people or to fulfill our commitments without allocating at least 20 percent of national budgets to basic social services, and those 20 percent need to be genderized.

We learned a lesson at the Population Conference in Cairo last year. Improving the status of women and sound family planning is the key to lower fertility rates. The risky pattern of "too many, too soon, too late, and too close" is also strongly detrimental to the survival of infants and children. There is no morality in condemning women to a life of perpetual childbearing and fatigue. Where appeals for justice for women have not been listened to, perhaps the necessity of a sounder economy and sounder population trends may.

Fortunately, we managed to erect a dyke against the stormy waves threatening the Cairo consensus. But here in Beijing we managed more than just a defense of past achievements. When I said at the Cairo conference that, at the very least, we should decriminalize women who had seen no other solution than to go through an abortion, it caused an uproar. And I fail to understand, why also here in Beijing, why those who most vocally speak for what many of us favor—a caring society where all women can safely have their children—why they have held so strongly that these most dramatically difficult decisions should be cause for public prosecution. We should focus on human suffering, not on recrimination against the weakest and most vulnerable.

Every second a baby boy and baby girl are born into this world of diversity and inequality. They all deserve love and care, a future and opportunities. There is nothing so thoroughly, so unconditionally trusting as the look in the eyes of a newborn girl or boy child. From that privilege, we must depart and make ourselves worthy of the look in those eyes.

Toward the Twenty-First Century of Women: From Commitment to Action

Excerpts, Remarks, 5 September 1995

Leticia Ramos-Shahani, Senator, Philippines

Introduction

We bring to you the warm greetings of our President Fidel V. Ramos and the Filipino people. They are with us in spirit at this momentous and historic meeting as we renew our commitment to the women's cause and as we celebrate and rejoice over the gains won....

A Conference of Commitment

This is a defining moment for all of us, positioned as we are at the threshold of the twenty-first century which, in the view of the Philippine delegation, should become the Century of Women.

Women of the world: Behold, our time has come!

We are gathered here to participate in a Conference of Commitment, a conference that should go beyond empty rhetoric, a conference where delegates should have their feet firmly planted on the ground and yet have their eyes sharply focused on the beckoning stars. We seek a global consensus which could empower women to widen their choices throughout the various stages of their lives.

The 1995 Human Development Report, a most important document on gender, produced by the UNDP, makes the startling revelation that the undervalued and unpaid work of women total 11 trillion U.S. dollars annually. This staggering amount is unaccounted for because so much of women's work is not part of the national system of accounts. Experience has shown us that poor women are reliable borrowers, yet they have inadequate access to credit. Violence against women continues to destroy women's lives, but too few women are in positions of power and authority to do anything about it. And regrettably, there are few societies in the world today where women enjoy the same social, economic, and political opportunities as men.

Enough of Inequality

To these and other forms of inequality and marginalization which continue to be inflicted on women, we say: enough is enough! We said this loud and clear in Nairobi, ten years ago, when we adopted the Nairobi Forward-Looking Strategies for the Advancement of Women, which demonstrated the inseparability of equality, development, and peace. These strategies have shaped and influenced the world's agenda on concerns and challenges confronting women. But progress has been slow because the world is still dominated by man-made structures.

The Philippines and Women's Concerns

We have gone a long way since the Third World Conference on Women was held in 1985 in Nairobi . . . I was very much a part of in my capacity as Secretary General of that Conference. Permit me to say that my country has always been at the forefront of world action for women. In fact, the Philippine delegation at this conference includes three women members who served as chairs of the Commission on the Status of Women in various years: former Senator Helena Benitez, who chaired the Commission in the 1960s; myself in the 1970s; and Ambassador Rosario Manalo in the 1980s. The present chair of the Commission is another Filipina, Dr. Patricia Licuanan.

This continuity of service and commitment of Filipino women illustrates the degree of seriousness we . . . attach to educating and empowering women. In 1986, a year after Nairobi, my country showed the world that a non-violent revolution was possible and that change can—and does—come from the people themselves. This peaceful, home-grown revolution—made possible not by use of military might but by people power—was led by a woman, a courageous and determined housewife, who became our first woman President, Corazon C. Aquino. She restored democracy and respect for human rights in our country after years of authoritarian rule and economic pillage and mismanagement by the government. Within the democratic space thus provided, Filipino women consciously resumed our journey towards equality, development, and peace.

Status of Women in the Philippines

The principle of the fundamental equality between women and men is enshrined in the Philippine Constitution. This is the basis for the adoption of legislation, policies, and other types of affirmative action that seek to raise the status of Filipino women.

To illustrate, a landmark legislation is the Philippine law on Women in Development and Nation Building. This law mandates the government to ensure that women benefit and participate on an equal basis with men in all government programs and to allocate a portion of official development assistance it receives from donor countries for women projects. Another precedent-shattering piece of legislation adopted is the anti-sexual harassment law, which protects women from sexual harassment in the workplace and in learning institutions and punishes offenders. A bill which reclassifies rape as a crime against the person and not against chastity has been filed in our legislature.

The implementation of laws, policies, and programs that would close the gender gap represents a serious commitment by our government and by the dynamic and articulate NGO community of our country. This is reflected in the 1995 Human Development Report which ranked the Philippines as 28th out of 116 countries in its Gender Empowerment Measure, which examines the extent to which women are able to actively participate in the economic and political life in their countries. The same report ranked our country 64th out of 130 countries in its Gender Development Index, which gauged how countries are able to address gender inequality in terms of life expectancy, educational attainment, and real income. These are modest yet significant gains.

Engendering the Philippine Development Process

We fully believe that for the Filipino nation to move forward, full and equal partnership between women and men must be achieved: without equality, there can be no development. Accordingly, in 1989, we formulated and implemented the Philippine Development Plan for Women (1989–1992); we have just finalized the Perspective Plan for Gender-Responsive Development, a thirty-year plan that identifies gender concerns that the government must address.... Plans have been approved by President Fidel V. Ramos to engender the major programs of the government with the assistance of the National Commission on the Role of Filipino Women.

We have instituted the Women's Budget Statement in our 1995 national budget to continue annually thereafter; ... [the budget] instructs government offices to allocate a portion of their annual budget to gender-oriented programs. Already, we have allocated more than 35 percent of our national budget to social programs and services since these are central to women's concerns and everyday lives.

In all these activities, the Philippine Government fully acknowledges the catalytic role of our NGOs without whose commitment and organizational skills our country would not enjoy the many advances we have made on behalf of women. We fully support the multi-faceted, mega-NGO Forum at Huairou.

Additional Resources and Programs

In the view of our delegation, without budgetary resources, the objectives contained in the Beijing Platform for Action will again remain unimplemented, dead on official paper. In this connection, the Philippine Government will increase its annual contribution to UNIFEM by 700 percent. We hope that other countries will increase support for UNIFEM, which will play a crucial role in the post-Beijing period, so that UNIFEM's current capacity of 16 million U.S. dollars can be doubled by 1996.

South–South Cooperation

Our government also commits itself to forge stronger collaboration with developing countries . . . under the existing technical assistance program of the Philippines on South-South cooperation: We believe that it pays to invest in women. But side by side with our gains and advances are deep problems and contradictions.

Three Major Philippine Concerns

Let me therefore turn to the three key issues that the Philippine Government gives the highest priority. This concerns the plight of our rural women, our women overseas workers, and women and children who are victims of trafficking.

Our rural women, both peasants and fisherfolk, comprise 80 percent of our female population and are marginalized and neglected. Yet it is the rural women, with the men, who produce our food and provide food security. Indeed, they are the unsung heroines of the good earth. My government will intensify the training of rural women and give them more access to credit. . . .

Our migrant workers, the majority of whom are women, are among the best of our country's globally shared resources. We call on the receiving countries to forge bilateral agreements with our government and to ratify all relevant international instruments such as the International Convention on the Protection of All Migrant Workers and Their Families. We reiterate our willingness to host an international conference on migration and development.

The other area of concern for our country deals with the trafficking of women and children. The government is committed to impose more stringent penalties for those who engage in trafficking.

Concerns of the Group of 77 and China

May I now turn to the concerns of the Group of 77 and China. The Group of 77 and China are united in the aspiration to advance the rights and welfare of women. Women are important agents of healing, reform, and change; their empowerment could provide the cutting edge in the kind of development we want to see in the twenty-first century.

What follows is a brief summary of the concerns of the Group of 77 and China.

1. Poverty is the single continuing heaviest burden on women. Truly, poverty has a woman's face. Among the world's 1.6 billion poor people, 70 percent are women, a cruel condition which should not be tolerated.

2. Acts of violence against women destroy the dignity and individual worth of women. The world should not sanction, much less condone, this depraved behavior still so widespread throughout the world.

3. Human development means people-centered development, and this necessarily calls for investing in people, including women. While most of the funding in support of human development will have to come mainly from national budgets, we call on the industrialized countries to be forthcoming and lead in giving women what is long overdue.

4. As called for in the Copenhagen Programme of Action, the Member States of the United Nations should set up an International Fund for Social Development for education and other programs which will empower women. We also call for a reaffirmation on the part of developed and developing countries to allocate the 20/20 formula in their national budgets directed to social growth and progress to include gender-related programs.

5. The Group of 77 and China remind industrialized countries to stand by their pledge to allocate 0.7 of their GNP to development assistance, with 0.15 percent directed to the least-developed countries. There must be a sharing of resources: The world cannot survive three-fourths poor and one-fourth rich.

6. The call made in Copenhagen is reiterated for durable and effective solutions to the external debt problem of many Member States. This demand can be concretized through the immediate implementation of the various debt-forgiveness schemes agreed upon in 1994. at the Paris Club. The possibility of coming up with schemes as debt swaps for women's programs and other innovative measures must be explored.

7. Women in developing countries are disproportionately subjected to the adverse and hostile effects of the world's economic crisis. It is imperative that international cooperation and assistance be directed at correcting these economic imbalances, including burdens arising from external debts.

8. The Group of 77 and China give the highest priority to the mobilization of new and additional resources on the part of international financial institutions and other bilateral and multilateral development agencies to support economic and social programs linked with the strategies in the Platform for Action.

9. The existing institutions for women at the national, regional, and international levels should be strengthened in terms of budget and mandate. At the United Nations, the Committee on the Elimination of Discrimination against Women, the Division for the Advancement of Women, UNIFEM, and INSTRAW should be given the necessary financial and human resources that will strengthen their roles in implementing the provisions of the Beijing Platform for Action.

10. The United Nations system and other international organizations, male-dominated as they are, should take effective measures to eliminate barriers to the advancement of women within their respective organizations. In sum, the Group of 77 and China call upon all governments and civil society, men and women, to create in partnership sustained economic growth and sustainable development within a culture of peace and respect for human rights.

Conclusion

May I now conclude. Let the Beijing Platform for Action be the launching pad for women to enter, in partnership with men, the twenty-first century—the Century of Women. But we, women, must first transform ourselves if we want to transform the world into a better world. Empowerment must come from within and without. We must lead, not only follow. We must be the doctor who can heal and cure, and not just the patient. We must be catalysts and initiators of change, and not just seekers of the status quo. Then there will be hope and happiness for our daughters and sons and future generations, for they will be able to live—because of women—in a more humane, more caring, and less violent society and will be able to become part of a more just and a more democratic world order.

BRINGING

BEIJING

HOME

~~~

THE
PLATFORM
FOR ACTION
AND YOU

Reprinted, with permission, by the International Women's Tribune Centre.
Illustrations by Anne S. Walker.

#1 WOMEN AND POVERTY

The Platform for Action says that Governments should:

Review, adopt and maintain macroeconomic policies and development strategies that address the needs and efforts of women in poverty *(Strategic Objective A.1)*.

Revise laws and administrative practices to ensure women's equal rights and access to economic resources *(Strategic Objective A.2)*.

Provide women with access to savings and credit mechanisms and institutions *(Strategic Objective A.3)*.

Develop gender-based methodologies and conduct research to address the feminization of poverty *(Strategic Objective A.4)*.

U.S. Facts

97% of the 14.1 million people receiving Assistance to Families with Dependent Children (AFDC) are women.

Families that receive food stamps in New York, many female-headed, can't make the coupons last the entire month because benefits amount to only 70 cents a meal per person.

#2 EDUCATION AND TRAINING OF WOMEN

The Platform for Action says that Governments should:

Ensure equal access to education
(Strategic Objective B.1).

Eradicate illiteracy among women
(Strategic Objective B.2).

Improve women's access to vocational training, science and technology, and continuing education
(Strategic Objective B.3).

Develop non-discriminatory education and training *(Strategic Objective B.4).*

Allocate sufficient resources for and monitor the implementation of educational reforms *(Strategic Objective B.5).*

#3   WOMEN AND HEALTH

The Platform for Action says that Governments should:

Increase women's access throughout the life cycle to appropriate, affordable and quality health care, information and related services *(Strategic Objective C.1)*.

Strengthen preventative programmes that promote women's health *(Strategic Objective C.2)*.

Undertake gender-sensitive initiatives that address sexually transmitted diseases, HIV/AIDS, and sexual and reproductive health issues *(Strategic Objective C.3)*.

Promote research and disseminate information on women's health *(Strategic Objective C.4)*.

Increase resources and monitor follow-up for women's health *(Strategic Objective C.5)*.

U.S. Fact:
1 in 3 adults with no health insurance is a women of child bearing age–a total of 37 million women.

#4 VIOLENCE AGAINST WOMEN

The Platform for Action says Governments should:

Take integrated measures to prevent and eliminate violence against women *(Strategic Objective D.1)*.

Create, fund, and improve or develop training programmes for judicial, legal, medical, social, educational and police and immigrant personnel that increase awareness of the nature of gender-based acts and threats of violence *(para.124 (n))*;

Provide well-funded shelters and relief support for girls and women subjected to violence *(para 125 (a))*;

Support initiatives of women's organizations and NGOs all over the world to raise awareness on the issue of violence against women *(para 125 (d)*.

Develop programmes and procedures to eliminate sexual harassment and other forms of violence against women in all educational institutions, workplaces and elsewhere
(para 126 (a));

Study the causes and consequences of violence against women and the effectiveness of preventive measures *(Strategic Objective D.2)*.

#5 WOMEN AND ARMED CONFLICT

The Platform for Action says Governments should:

Increase the participation of women in conflict resolution at decision-making levels and protect women living in situations of armed and other conflicts or under foreign control *(Strategic Objective E.1).*

Reduce excessive military expenditures and control the availability of armaments *(Strategic Objective E.2).*

Recognize that women and children are particularly affected by the indiscriminate use of anti-personnel land-mines: (iii) Undertake to promote assistance in mine clearance *(para 143 (e));*

Promote non-violent forms of conflict resolution and reduce the incidence of human rights abuse in conflict situations *(Strategic Objective E.3).*

Promote women's contribution to fostering a culture of peace *(Strategic Objective E.4).*

Provide protection, assistance and training to refugee women in need of international protection and internally displaced women *(Strategic Objective E.5).*

Provide assistance to the women of the colonies and non-self-governing territories *(Strategic Objective E.6).*

#6 WOMEN AND THE ECONOMY

The Platform for Action says that Governments should:

Promote women's economic rights and independence, including access to employment, apropriate working conditions and control over economic resources *(Strategic Objective F.1)*.

Facilitate women's equal access to resources, employment, markets and trade *(Strategic Objective F2)*.

Provide business services, training and access to markets, information and technology, particularly to low-income women *(Strategic Objective F3)*.

Strengthen women's economic capacity and commercial networks *(Strategic Objective F4)*.

Eliminate occupational segregation and all forms of employment discrimination *(Strategic Objective F5)*.

Promote harmonization of work and family responsibilities for women and men *(Strategic Objective F6)*.

#7 WOMEN IN POWER AND DECISION-MAKING

The Platform for Action says Governments should:

Take measures to ensure women's equal access to and full participation in power structures and decision-making *(Strategic Objective G.1)*.

Take positive action to build a critical mass of women leaders, executives and managers in strategic decision-making positions *(para 192 (a))*;

Restructure recruitment and career-development programmes to ensure that all women have equal access to managerial, entrepreneurial, technical and leadership training, including on-the-job training *(para 192 (f))*;

Increase women's capacity to participate in decision-making and leadership *(Strategic Objective G.2.)*.

1995   2000 & Beyond!

#8 INSTITUTIONAL MECHANISMS FOR THE ADVANCEMENT OF WOMEN

The Platform for Action says that Governments should:

Create or strengthen national machineries and other governmental bodies *(Strategic Objective H.1).*

Ensure that responsibility for the advancement of women is vested in the highest possible level of government; in many cases, this could be at the level of a Cabinet minister *(para 203 (a));*

Integrate gender perspectives in legislation, public policies, programmes and projects *(Strategic Objective H.2).*

Generate and disseminate gender-disaggregated data and information for planning and evaluation *(Strategic Objective H.3).*

#9   HUMAN RIGHTS OF WOMEN

The Platform for Action says that Governments should:

Promote and protect the human rights of women, through the full imple-
mentation of all human rights instruments, especially the Convention on the
Elimination of All Forms of Discrimination Against Women *(Strategic
Objective I.1)*.

Ensure equality and non-discrimination under the law and in practice
(Strategic Objective I.2).

Achieve legal literacy *(Strategic Objective I.3)*.

Translate into local languages and appropriate formats all human rights documents pertaining to women's
human rights *(para 233 (a))*.

U.S. Fact:

**147 governments have rati-
fied CEDAW.**

The United States has not.

#10 WOMEN AND THE MEDIA

The Platform for Action says that Governments should:

Increase the participation and access of women to expression and decision-making in and through the media and new technologies of communication *(Strategic Objective J.1).*

Promote women's full and equal participation in the media, including management, programming, education, training and research *(para 239(c));*

Encourage and recognize women's media networks, including electronic networks and other new technologies of communication, as a means for dissemination of information and exchange of views...
(para 239 (f));

Encourage the media industry and education and media training institutions to develop traditional, indigenous and other ethnic forms of media, such as story-telling, drama, poetry and song, reflecting their cultures, and utilize these forms of communication to disseminate information on development and social issues *(para 242 (d));*

Promote a balanced and non-stereotyped portrayal of women in the media *(Strategic Objective J.2).*

#11   WOMEN AND THE ENVIRONMENT

The Platform For Action says that Governments should:

Involve women actively in environmental decision-making at all levels *(Strategic Objective K.1).*

Reduce the risks to women from identified environmental hazards at home, at work and in other environments *(para 253(d));*

Increase the proportion of women, particularly at grass-roots levels, involved as decision makers, planners, managers, scientists, and technical advisers and as beneficiaries in the design, development and implementation of policies and programmes for natural resource management and environmental protection and conservation *(para 254 (d));*

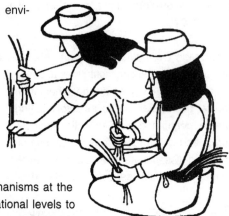

Integrate gender concerns and perspectives in policies and programmes for sustainable development *(Strategic Objective K.2).*

Strengthen or establish mechanisms at the national, regional and international levels to assess the impact of development and environmental policies on women *(Strategic Objective K.3).*

#12 THE GIRL CHILD

The Platform For Action says that Governments should:

Eliminate all forms of discrimination against the girl child *(Strategic Objective L.1)*

Eliminate negative cultural attitudes and practices against girls *(Strategic Objective L.2)*.

Promote and protect the rights of the girl child and increase awareness of her needs and potential *(Strategic Objective L.3)*.

Eliminate discrimination against girls in education, skills development and training *(Strategic Objective L.4)*.

Eliminate discrimination against girls in health and nutrition *(Strategic Objective L.5)*.

Eliminate the economic exploitation of child labour and protect young girls at work. *(Strategic Objective L.6.)*

Eradicate violence against the girl child. *(Strategic Objective L.7)*.

Promote the girl child's awareness of and participation in social, economic and political life *(Strategic Objective L.8)*.

Beijing Declaration

1. We, the Governments participating in the Fourth World Conference on Women,

2. Gathered here in Beijing in September 1995, the year of the fiftieth anniversary of the founding of the United Nations,

3. Determined to advance the goals of equality, development and peace for all women everywhere in the interest of all humanity,

4. Acknowledging the voices of all women everywhere and taking note of the diversity of women and their roles and circumstances, honouring the women who paved the way and inspired by the hope present in the world's youth,

5. Recognize that the status of women has advanced in some important respects in the past decade but that progress has been uneven, inequalities between women and men have persisted and major obstacles remain, with serious consequences for the well-being of all people,

6. Also recognize that this situation is exacerbated by the increasing poverty that is affecting the lives of the majority of the world's people, in particular women and children, with origins in both the national and international domains,

7. Dedicate ourselves unreservedly to addressing these constraints and obstacles and thus enhancing further the advancement and empowerment of women all over the world, and agree that this requires urgent action in the spirit of determination, hope, cooperation and solidarity, now and to carry us forward into the next century.

We reaffirm our commitment to:

8. The equal rights and inherent human dignity of women and men and other purposes and principles enshrined in the Charter of the

United Nations, to the Universal Declaration of Human Rights and other international human rights instruments, in particular the Convention on the Elimination of All Forms of Discrimination against Women and the Convention on the Rights of the Child, as well as the Declaration on the Elimination of Violence against Women and the Declaration on the Right to Development;

9. Ensure the full implementation of the human rights of women and of the girl child as an inalienable, integral and indivisible part of all human rights and fundamental freedoms;

10. Build on consensus and progress made at previous United Nations conferences and summits—on women in Nairobi in 1985, on children in New York in 1990, on environment and development in Rio de Janeiro in 1992, on human rights in Vienna in 1993, on population and development in Cairo in 1994, and on social development in Copenhagen in 1995 with the objective of achieving equality, development and peace;

11. Achieve the full and effective implementation of the Nairobi Forward-looking Strategies for the Advancement of Women;

12. The empowerment and advancement of women, including the right to freedom of thought, conscience, religion and belief, thus contributing to the moral, ethical, spiritual and intellectual needs of women and men, individually or in community with others and thereby guaranteeing them the possibility of realizing their full potential in society and shaping their lives in accordance with their own aspirations.

We are convinced that:

13. Women's empowerment and their full participation on the basis of equality in all spheres of society, including participation in the decision-making process and access to power, are fundamental for the achievement of equality, development and peace;

14. Women's rights are human rights;

15. Equal rights, opportunities and access to resources, equal sharing of responsibilities for the family by men and women, and a harmonious partnership between them are critical to their well-being and that of their families as well as to the consolidation of democracy;

16. Eradication of poverty based on sustained economic growth, social development, environmental protection and social justice requires the involvement of women in economic and social development, equal opportunities and the full and equal participation of women and men as agents and beneficiaries of people-centred sustainable development;

17. The explicit recognition and reaffirmation of the right of all women to control all aspects of their health, in particular their own fertility, is basic to their empowerment;

18. Local, national, regional and global peace is attainable and is inextricably linked with the advancement of women, who are a fundamental force for leadership, conflict resolution and the promotion of lasting peace at all levels;

19. It is essential to design, implement and monitor, with the full participation of women, effective, efficient and mutually reinforcing gender-sensitive policies and programmes, including development policies and programmes, at all levels that will foster the empowerment and advancement of women;

20. The participation and contribution of all actors of civil society, particularly women's groups and networks and other non-governmental organizations and community-based organizations, with full respect for their autonomy, in cooperation with Governments, are important to the effective implementation and follow-up of the Platform for Action;

21. The implementation of the Platform for Action requires commitment from Governments and the international community. By making national and international commitments for action, including those made at the Conference, Governments and the international community recognize the need to take priority action for the empowerment and advancement of women.

We are determined to:

22. Intensify efforts and actions to achieve the goals of the Nairobi Forward-looking Strategies for the Advancement of Women by the end of this century;

23. Ensure the full enjoyment by women and the girl child of all human rights and fundamental freedoms and take effective action against violations of these rights and freedoms;

24. Take all necessary measures to eliminate all forms of discrimination against women and the girl child and remove all obstacles to gender equality and the advancement and empowerment of women;

25. Encourage men to participate fully in all actions towards equality;

26. Promote women's economic independence, including employment, and eradicate the persistent and increasing burden of poverty on women by addressing the structural causes of poverty through changes in economic structures, ensuring equal access for all women, including those in rural areas, as vital development agents, to productive resources, opportunities and public services;

27. Promote people-centred sustainable development, including sustained economic growth, through the provision of basic education, lifelong education, literacy and training, and primary health care for girls and women;

28. Take positive steps to ensure peace for the advancement of women and, recognizing the leading role that women have played in the peace movement, work actively towards general and complete disarmament under strict and effective international control, and support negotiations on the conclusion, without delay, of a universal and multilaterally and effectively verifiable comprehensive nuclear-test-ban treaty which contributes to nuclear disarmament and the prevention of the proliferation of nuclear weapons in all its aspects;

29. Prevent and eliminate all forms of violence against women and girls;

30. Ensure equal access to and equal treatment of women and men in education and health care and enhance women's sexual and reproductive health as well as education;

31. Promote and protect all human rights of women and girls;

32. Intensify efforts to ensure equal enjoyment of all human rights and fundamental freedoms for all women and girls who face multiple barriers to their empowerment and advancement because of such factors as their race, age, language, ethnicity, culture, religion, or disability, or because they are indigenous people;

33. Ensure respect for international law, including humanitarian law, in order to protect women and girls in particular;

34. Develop the fullest potential of girls and women of all ages, ensure their full and equal participation in building a better world for all and enhance their role in the development process.

We are determined to:

35. Ensure women's equal access to economic resources, including land, credit, science and technology, vocational training, information, communication and markets, as a means to further the advancement and empowerment of women and girls, including through the enhancement of their capacities to enjoy the benefits of equal access to these resources, *inter alia*, by means of international cooperation;

36. Ensure the success of the Platform for Action, which will require a strong commitment on the part of Governments, international organizations and institutions at all levels. We are deeply convinced that economic development, social development and environmental protection are interdependent and mutually reinforcing components of sustainable development, which is the framework for our efforts to achieve a higher quality of life for all people. Equitable social development that recognizes empowering the poor, particularly women living in poverty, to utilize environmental resources sustainably is a necessary foundation for sustainable development. We also recognize that broad-based and sustained economic growth in the context of sustainable development is necessary to sustain social development and social justice. The success of the Platform for Action will also require adequate mobilization of resources at the national and international levels as well as new and additional resources to the developing countries from all available funding mechanisms, including multilateral, bilateral and private sources for the advancement of women; financial resources to strengthen the capacity of national, subregional, regional and international institutions; a commitment to equal rights, equal responsibilities and equal opportunities and to the equal participation of women and men in all national, regional and international bodies and policy-making processes; and the establishment or strengthening of mechanisms at all levels for accountability to the world's women;

37. Ensure also the success of the Platform for Action in countries with economies in transition, which will require continued international cooperation and assistance;

38. We hereby adopt and commit ourselves as Governments to implement the following Platform for Action, ensuring that a gender perspective is reflected in all our policies and programmes. We urge the United Nations system, regional and international financial institutions, other relevant regional and international institutions and all women and men, as well as non-governmental organizations, with full respect for their autonomy, and all sectors of civil society, in cooperation with Governments, to fully commit themselves and contribute to the implementation of this Platform for Action.

The Beijing Declaration was originally disseminated by The United Nations Department for Policy Coordination and Sustainable Development (DPCSD). Reproduction and dissemination of this document, in print or electronic format, is encouraged.

Platform for Action

Contents

Chapter I

MISSION STATEMENT

1. The Platform for Action is an agenda for women's empowerment. It aims at accelerating the implementation of the Nairobi Forward-looking Strategies for the Advancement of Women[1] and at removing all the obstacles to women's active participation in all spheres of public and private life through a full and equal share in economic, social, cultural and political decision-making. This means that the principle of shared power and responsibility should be established between women and men at home, in the workplace and in the wider national and international communities. Equality between women and men is a matter of human rights and a condition for social justice and is also a necessary and fundamental prerequisite for equality, development and peace. A transformed partnership based on equality between women and men is a condition for people-centred sustainable development. A sustained and long-term commitment is essential, so that women and men can work together for themselves, for their children and for society to meet the challenges of the twenty-first century.

2. The Platform for Action reaffirms the fundamental principle set forth in the Vienna Declaration and Programme of Action,[2] adopted by the World Conference on Human Rights, that the human rights of women and of the girl child are an inalienable, integral and indivisible part of universal human rights. As an agenda for action, the Platform seeks to promote and protect the full enjoyment of all human rights and the fundamental freedoms of all women throughout their life cycle.

3. The Platform for Action emphasizes that women share common concerns that can be addressed only by working together and in partnership with men towards the common goal of gender equality around the world. It respects and values the full diversity of women's situations and conditions and recognizes that some women face particular barriers to their empowerment.

4. The Platform for Action requires immediate and concerted action by all to create a peaceful, just and humane world based on human rights and fundamental freedoms, including the principle of equality for all people of all ages and from all walks of life, and to this end, recognizes that broad-based and sustained economic growth in the context of sustainable development is necessary to sustain social development and social justice.

5. The success of the Platform for Action will require a strong commitment on the part of Governments, international organizations and institutions at all levels. It will also require adequate mobilization of resources at the national and international levels as well as new and additional resources to the developing countries from all available funding mechanisms, including multilateral, bilateral and private sources for the advancement of women; financial resources to strengthen the capacity of national, subregional, regional and international institutions; a commitment to equal rights, equal responsibilities and equal opportunities and to the equal participation of women and men in all national, regional and international bodies and policy-making processes; and the establishment or strengthening of mechanisms at all levels for accountability to the world's women.

Chapter II

GLOBAL FRAMEWORK

6. The Fourth World Conference on Women is taking place as the world stands poised on the threshold of a new millennium.

7. The Platform for Action upholds the Convention on the Elimination of All Forms of Discrimination against Women[3] and builds upon the Nairobi Forward-looking Strategies for the Advancement of Women, as well as relevant resolutions adopted by the Economic and Social Council and the General Assembly. The formulation of the Platform for Action is aimed at establishing a basic group of priority actions that should be carried out during the next five years.

8. The Platform for Action recognizes the importance of the agreements reached at the World Summit for Children, the United Nations Conference on Environment and Development, the World Conference on Human Rights, the International Conference on Population and Development and the World Summit for Social Development, which set out specific approaches and commitments to fostering sustainable development and international cooperation and to strengthening the role of the United Nations to that end. Similarly, the Global Conference on the Sustainable Development of Small Island Developing States, the International Conference on Nutrition, the International Conference on Primary Health Care and the World Conference on Education for All have addressed the various facets of development and human rights, within their specific perspectives, paying significant attention to the role of women and girls. In addition, the International Year for the World's Indigenous People,[4] the International Year of the Family,[5] the United Nations Year for Tolerance,[6] the Geneva Declaration for Rural Women,[7] and the Declaration on the Elimination of Violence against Women[8] have also emphasized the issues of women's empowerment and equality.

9. The objective of the Platform for Action, which is in full conformity with the purposes and principles of the Charter of the United Nations and international law, is the empowerment of all women. The full realization of all human rights and fundamental freedoms of all women is essential for the empowerment of women. While the significance of national and regional particularities and various historical, cultural and religious backgrounds must be borne in mind, it is the duty of States, regardless of their political, economic and cultural systems, to promote and protect all human rights and fundamental freedoms.[9] The implementation of this Platform, including through national laws and the formulation of strategies, policies, programmes and development priorities, is the sovereign responsibility of each State, in conformity with all human rights and fundamental freedoms, and the significance of and full respect for various religious and ethical values, cultural backgrounds and philosophical convictions of individuals and their communities should contribute to the full enjoyment by women of their human rights in order to achieve equality, development and peace.

10. Since the World Conference to Review and Appraise the Achievements of the United Nations Decade for Women: Equality, Development and Peace, held at Nairobi in 1985, and the adoption of the Nairobi Forward-looking Strategies for the Advancement of Women, the world has experienced profound political, economic, social and cultural changes, which have had both positive and negative effects on women. The World Conference on Human Rights recognized that the human rights of women and the girl child are an inalienable, integral and indivisible part of universal human rights. The full and equal participation of women in political, civil, economic, social and cultural life at the national, regional and international levels, and the eradication of all forms of discrimination on the grounds of sex are priority objectives of the international community. The World Conference on Human Rights reaffirmed the solemn commitment of all States to fulfil their obligations to promote universal respect for, and observance and protection of, all human rights and fundamental freedoms for all in accordance with the Charter of the United Nations, other instruments related to human rights and international law. The universal nature of these rights and freedoms is beyond question.

11. The end of the cold war has resulted in international changes and diminished competition between the super-Powers. The threat of a global armed conflict has diminished, while international relations have improved and prospects for peace among nations have increased. Although the threat of global conflict has been reduced, wars of aggression, armed conflicts, colonial or other forms of alien domination and foreign occupation, civil wars, and terrorism continue to plague many parts of the world. Grave violations of the human rights of women occur, particularly in times of armed conflict, and include murder, torture, systematic rape, forced pregnancy and forced abortion, in particular under policies of ethnic cleansing.

12. The maintenance of peace and security at the global, regional and local levels, together with the prevention of policies of aggression and ethnic cleansing and the resolution of armed conflict, is crucial for the protection of the human rights of women and girl children, as well as for the elimination of all forms of violence against them and of their use as a weapon of war.

13. Excessive military expenditures, including global military expenditures and arms trade or trafficking, and investments for arms production and acquisition have reduced the resources available for social development. As a result of the debt burden and other economic difficulties, many developing countries have undertaken structural adjustment policies. Moreover, there are structural adjustment programmes that have been poorly designed and implemented, with resulting detrimental effects on social development. The number of people living in poverty has increased disproportionately in most developing countries, particularly the heavily indebted countries, during the past decade.

14. In this context, the social dimension of development should be emphasized. Accelerated economic growth, although necessary for social development, does not by itself improve the quality of life of the population. In some cases, conditions can arise which can aggravate social inequality and marginalization. Hence, it is indispensable to search for new alternatives that ensure that all members of society benefit from economic growth based on a holistic approach to all aspects of development: growth, equality between women and men, social justice, conservation and protection of the environment, sustainability, solidarity, participation, peace and respect for human rights.

15. A world-wide movement towards democratization has opened up the political process in many nations, but the popular participation of women in key decision-making as full and equal partners with men, particularly in politics, has not yet been achieved. South Africa's policy of institutionalized racism—apartheid—has been dismantled and a peaceful and democratic transfer of power has occurred. In Central and Eastern Europe the transition to parliamentary democracy has been rapid and has given rise to a variety of experiences, depending on the specific circumstances of each country. While the transition has been mostly peaceful, in some countries this process has been hindered by armed conflict that has resulted in grave violations of human rights.

16. Widespread economic recession, as well as political instability in some regions, has been responsible for setting back development goals in many countries. This has led to the expansion of unspeakable poverty. Of the more than 1 billion people living in abject poverty, women are an overwhelming majority. The rapid process of change and adjustment in all sectors has also led to increased unemployment and underemployment, with particular impact on women. In many cases, structural adjustment programmes have not been designed to minimize their negative effects on vulnerable and disadvantaged groups or on women, nor have they been designed to assure positive effects on those groups by preventing their marginalization in economic and social activities. The Final Act of the Uruguay Round of multilateral trade negotiations[10] underscored the increasing interdependence of national economies, as well as the importance of trade liberalization and access to open, dynamic markets. There has also been heavy military spending in some regions. Despite increases in official development assistance (ODA) by some countries, ODA has recently declined overall.

17. Absolute poverty and the feminization of poverty, unemployment, the increasing fragility of the environment, continued violence against women and the widespread exclusion of half of humanity from institutions of power and governance underscore the need to continue the search for development, peace and security and for ways of assuring people-centred sustainable development. The participation and leadership of the half of humanity that is female is essential to the success of that search. Therefore, only a new era of international cooperation among Governments and peoples based on a spirit of partnership, an equitable, international social and economic environment, and a radical transformation of the relationship between women and men to one of full and equal partnership will enable the world to meet the challenges of the twenty-first century.

18. Recent international economic developments have had in many cases a disproportionate impact on women and children, the majority of whom live in developing countries. For those States that have carried a large burden of foreign debt, structural adjustment programmes and measures, though beneficial in the long term, have led to a reduction in social expenditures, thereby adversely affecting women, particularly in Africa and the least developed countries. This is exacerbated when responsibilities for basic social services have shifted from Governments to women.

19. Economic recession in many developed and developing countries, as well as ongoing restructuring in countries with economies in transition, have had a disproportionately negative impact on women's employment. Women often have no choice but to take employment that lacks long-term job security or involves dangerous working conditions, to work in unprotected home-based production or to be unemployed. Many women enter the labour market in under-remunerated and undervalued jobs, seeking to improve their household income; others decide to migrate for the same purpose. Without any reduction in their other responsibilities, this has increased the total burden of work for women.

20. Macro and micro-economic policies and programmes, including structural adjustment, have not always been designed to take account of their impact on women and girl children, especially those living in poverty. Poverty has increased in both absolute and relative terms, and the number of women living in poverty has increased in most regions. There are many urban women living in poverty; however, the plight of women living in rural and remote areas deserves special attention given the stagnation of development in such areas. In developing countries, even those in which national indicators have shown improvement, the majority of rural women continue to live in conditions of economic underdevelopment and social marginalization.

21. Women are key contributors to the economy and to combating poverty through both remunerated and unremunerated work at home, in the community and in the workplace. Growing numbers of women have achieved economic independence through gainful employment.

22. One fourth of all households world-wide are headed by women and many other households are dependent on female income even where men are present. Female-maintained households are very often among the poorest because of wage discrimination, occupational segregation patterns in the labour market and other gender-based barriers. Family disintegration, population movements between urban and rural areas within countries, international migration, war and internal displacements are factors contributing to the rise of female-headed households.

23. Recognizing that the achievement and maintenance of peace and security are a precondition for economic and social progress, women are increasingly establishing themselves as central actors in a variety of capacities in the movement of humanity for peace. Their full participation in decision-making, conflict prevention and resolution and all other peace initiatives is essential to the realization of lasting peace.

24. Religion, spirituality and belief play a central role in the lives of millions of women and men, in the way they live and in the aspirations they have for the future. The right to freedom of thought, conscience and religion is inalienable and must be universally enjoyed. This right includes the freedom to have or to adopt the religion or belief of their choice either individually or in community with others, in public or in private, and to manifest their religion or belief in worship, observance, practice and teaching. In order to realize equality, development and peace, there is a need to respect these rights and freedoms fully. Religion, thought, conscience and belief may, and can, contribute to fulfilling women's and men's moral, ethical and spiritual needs and to realizing their full potential in society. However, it is acknowledged that any form of extremism may have a negative impact on women and can lead to violence and discrimination.

25. The Fourth World Conference on Women should accelerate the process that formally began in 1975, which was proclaimed International Women's Year by the United Nations General Assembly. The Year was a turning-point in that it put women's issues on the agenda. The United Nations Decade for Women (1976–1985) was a world-wide effort to examine the status and rights of women and to bring women into decision-making at all levels. In 1979, the General Assembly adopted the Convention on the Elimination of All Forms of Discrimination against Women, which entered into force in 1981 and set an international standard for what was meant by equality between women and men. In 1985, the World Conference to Review and Appraise the Achievements of the United Nations Decade for Women: Equality, Development and Peace adopted the Nairobi Forward-looking Strategies for the Advancement of Women, to be implemented by the year 2000. There has been important progress in achieving equality between women and men. Many Governments have enacted legislation to promote equality between women and men and have established national machineries to ensure the mainstreaming of gender perspectives in all spheres of society. International agencies have focused greater attention on women's status and roles.

26. The growing strength of the non-governmental sector, particularly women's organizations and feminist groups, has become a driving force for change. Non-governmental organizations have played an important advocacy role in advancing legislation or mechanisms to ensure the promotion of women. They have also become catalysts for new approaches to development. Many Governments have increasingly recognized the important role that non-governmental organizations play and the importance of working with them for progress. Yet, in some countries, Governments continue to restrict the ability of non-governmental organizations to operate freely. Women, through non-governmental organizations, have participated in and strongly influenced community, national, regional and global forums and international debates.

27. Since 1975, knowledge of the status of women and men, respectively, has increased and is contributing to further actions aimed at promoting equality between women and men. In several countries, there have been important changes in the relationships between women and men, especially where there have been major advances in education for women and significant increases in their participation in the paid labour force. The boundaries of the gender division of labour between productive and reproductive roles are gradually being crossed as women have started to enter formerly male-dominated areas of work and men have started to accept greater responsibility for domestic tasks, including child care. However, changes in women's roles have been greater and much more rapid than changes in men's roles. In many countries, the differences between women's and men's achievements and activities are still not recognized as the consequences of socially constructed gender roles rather than immutable biological differences.

28. Moreover, 10 years after the Nairobi Conference, equality between women and men has still not been achieved. On average, women represent a mere 10 percent of all elected legislators world wide and in most national and international administrative structures, both public and private, they remain underrepresented. The United Nations is no exception. Fifty years after its creation, the United Nations is continuing to deny itself the benefits of women's leadership by their underrepresentation at decision-making levels within the Secretariat and the specialized agencies.

29. Women play a critical role in the family. The family is the basic unit of society and as such should be strengthened. It is entitled to receive comprehensive protection and support. In different cultural, political and social systems, various forms of the family exist. The rights, capabilities and responsibilities of family members must be respected. Women make a great contribution to the welfare of the family and to the development of society, which is still not recognized or considered in its full importance. The social significance of maternity, motherhood and the role of parents in the family and in the upbringing of children should be acknowledged. The upbringing of children requires shared responsibility of parents, women and men and society as a whole. Maternity, motherhood, parenting and the role of women in procreation must not be a basis for discrimination nor restrict the full participation of women in society. Recognition should also be given to the important role often played by women in many countries in caring for other members of their family.

30. While the rate of growth of world population is on the decline, world population is at an all-time high in absolute numbers, with current increments approaching 86 million persons annually. Two other major demographic trends have had profound repercussions on the dependency ratio within families. In many developing countries, 45 to 50 percent of the population is less than 15 years old, while in industrialized nations both the number and proportion of elderly people are increasing. According to United Nations projections, 72 percent of the population over 60 years of age will be living in developing countries by the year 2025, and more than half of that population will be women. Care of children, the sick and the elderly is a responsibility that falls disproportionately on women, owing to lack of equality and the unbalanced distribution of remunerated and unremunerated work between women and men.

31. Many women face particular barriers because of various diverse factors in addition to their gender. Often these diverse factors isolate or marginalize such women. They are, *inter alia*, denied their human rights, they lack access or are denied access to education and vocational training, employment, housing and economic self-sufficiency and they are excluded from decision-making processes. Such women are often denied the opportunity to contribute to their communities as part of the mainstream.

32. The past decade has also witnessed a growing recognition of the distinct interests and concerns of indigenous women, whose identity, cultural traditions and forms of social organization enhance and strengthen the communities in which they live. Indigenous women often face barriers both as women and as members of indigenous communities.

33. In the past 20 years, the world has seen an explosion in the field of communications. With advances in computer technology and satellite and cable television, global access to information continues to increase and expand, creating new opportunities for the participation of women in communications and the mass media and for the dissemination of information about women. However, global communication networks have been used to spread stereotyped and demeaning images of women for narrow commercial and consumerist purposes. Until women participate equally in both the technical and decision-making areas of communications and the mass media, including the arts, they will continue to be misrepresented and awareness of the reality of women's lives will continue to be lacking. The media have a great potential to promote the advancement of women and the equality of women and men by portraying women and men in a non-stereotypical, diverse and balanced manner, and by respecting the dignity and worth of the human person.

34. The continuing environmental degradation that affects all human lives has often a more direct impact on women. Women's health and their livelihood are threatened by pollution and toxic wastes, large-scale deforestation, desertification, drought and depletion of the soil and of coastal and marine resources, with a rising incidence of environmentally related health problems and even death reported among women and girls. Those most affected are rural and indigenous women, whose livelihood and daily subsistence depend directly on sustainable ecosystems.

35. Poverty and environmental degradation are closely interrelated. While poverty results in certain kinds of environmental stress, the major cause of the continued deterioration of the global environment is the unsustainable patterns of consumption and production, particularly in industrialized countries, which are a matter of grave concern and aggravate poverty and imbalances.

36. Global trends have brought profound changes in family survival strategies and structures. Rural to urban migration has increased substantially in all regions. The global urban population is projected to reach 47 percent of the total population by the year 2000. An estimated 125 million people are migrants, refugees and displaced persons, half of whom live in developing countries. These massive movements of people have profound consequences for family structures and well-being and have unequal consequences for women and men, including in many cases the sexual exploitation of women.

37. According to World Health Organization (WHO) estimates, by the beginning of 1995 the number of cumulative cases of acquired immunodeficiency syndrome (AIDS) was 4.5 million. An estimated 19.5 million men, women and children have been infected with the human immunodeficiency virus (AIDS) since it was first diagnosed and it is projected that another 20 million will be infected by the end of the decade. Among new cases, women are twice as likely to be infected as men. In the early stage of the AIDS pandemic, women were not infected in large numbers; however, about 8 million women are now infected. Young women and adolescents are particularly vulnerable. It is estimated that by the year 2000 more than 13 million women will be infected and 4 million women will have died from AIDS-related conditions. In addition, about 250 million new cases of sexually transmitted diseases are estimated to occur every year. The rate of transmission of sexually transmitted diseases, including HIV/AIDS, is increasing at an alarming rate among women and girls, especially in developing countries.

38. Since 1975, significant knowledge and information have been generated about the status of women and the conditions in which they live. Throughout their entire life cycle, women's daily existence and long-term aspirations are restricted by discriminatory attitudes, unjust social and economic structures, and a lack of resources in most countries that prevent their full and equal participation. In a number of countries, the practice of prenatal sex selection, higher rates of mortality among very young girls and lower rates of school enrolment for girls as compared with boys suggest that son preference is curtailing the access of girl children to food, education and health care and even life itself. Discrimination against women begins at the earliest stages of life and must therefore be addressed from then onwards.

39. The girl child of today is the woman of tomorrow. The skills, ideas and energy of the girl child are vital for full attainment of the goals of equality, development and peace. For the girl child to develop her full potential she needs to be nurtured in an enabling environment, where her spiritual, intellectual and material needs for survival, protection and development are met and her equal rights safeguarded. If women are to be equal partners with men, in every aspect of life and development, now is the time to recognize the human dignity and worth of the girl child and to ensure the full enjoyment of her human rights and fundamental freedoms, including the rights assured by the Convention on the Rights of the Child,[11] universal ratification of which is strongly urged. Yet there exists world-wide evidence that discrimination and violence against girls begin at the earliest stages of life and continue unabated throughout their lives. They often have less access to nutrition, physical and mental health care and education and enjoy fewer rights, opportunities and benefits of childhood and adolescence than do boys. They are often subjected to various forms of sexual and economic exploitation, paedophilia, forced prostitution and possibly the sale of their organs and tissues, violence and harmful practices such as female infanticide and prenatal sex selection, incest, female genital mutilation and early marriage, including child marriage.

40. Half the world's population is under the age of 25 and most of the world's youth—more than 85 percent—live in developing countries. Policy makers must recognize the implications of these demographic factors. Special measures must be taken to ensure that young women have the life skills necessary for active and effective participation in all levels of social, cultural, political and economic leadership. It will be critical for the international community to demonstrate a new commitment to the future—a commitment to inspiring a new generation of women and men to work together for a more just society. This new generation of leaders must accept and promote a world in which every child is free from injustice, oppression and inequality and free to develop her/his own potential. The principle of equality of women and men must therefore be integral to the socialization process.

Chapter III

CRITICAL AREAS OF CONCERN

41. The advancement of women and the achievement of equality between women and men are a matter of human rights and a condition for social justice and should not be seen in isolation as a women's issue. They are the only way to build a sustainable, just and developed society. Empowerment of women and equality between women and men are prerequisites for achieving political, social, economic, cultural and environmental security among all peoples.

42. Most of the goals set out in the Nairobi Forward-looking Strategies for the Advancement of Women have not been achieved. Barriers to women's empowerment remain, despite the efforts of Governments, as well as non-governmental organizations and women and men everywhere. Vast political, economic and ecological crises persist in many parts of the world. Among them are wars of aggression, armed conflicts, colonial or other forms of alien domination or foreign occupation, civil wars and terrorism. These situations, combined with systematic or de facto discrimination, violations of and failure to protect all human rights and fundamental freedoms of all women, and their civil, cultural, economic, political and social rights, including the right to development and ingrained prejudicial attitudes towards women and girls are but a few of the impediments encountered since the World Conference to Review and Appraise the Achievements of the United Nations Decade for Women: Equality, Development and Peace, in 1985.

43. A review of progress since the Nairobi Conference highlights special concerns—areas of particular urgency that stand out as priorities for action. All actors should focus action and resources on the strategic objectives relating to the critical areas of concern which are, necessarily, interrelated, interdependent and of high priority. There is a need for these actors to develop and implement mechanisms of accountability for all the areas of concern.

44. To this end, Governments, the international community and civil society, including non-governmental organizations and the private sector, are called upon to take strategic action in the following critical areas of concern:

- The persistent and increasing burden of poverty on women
- Inequalities and inadequacies in and unequal access to education and training
- Inequalities and inadequacies in and unequal access to health care and related services
- Violence against women
- The effects of armed or other kinds of conflict on women, including those living under foreign occupation

- Inequality in economic structures and policies, in all forms of productive activities and in access to resources
- Inequality between men and women in the sharing of power and decision-making at all levels
- Insufficient mechanisms at all levels to promote the advancement of women
- Lack of respect for and inadequate promotion and protection of the human rights of women
- Stereotyping of women and inequality in women's access to and participation in all communication systems, especially in the media
- Gender inequalities in the management of natural resources and in the safeguarding of the environment
- Persistent discrimination against and violation of the rights of the girl child

Chapter IV

STRATEGIC OBJECTIVES AND ACTIONS

45. In each critical area of concern, the problem is diagnosed and strategic objectives are proposed with concrete actions to be taken by various actors in order to achieve those objectives. The strategic objectives are derived from the critical areas of concern and specific actions to be taken to achieve them cut across the boundaries of equality, development and peace—the goals of the Nairobi Forward-looking Strategies for the Advancement of Women—and reflect their interdependence. The objectives and actions are interlinked, of high priority and mutually reinforcing. The Platform for Action is intended to improve the situation of all women, without exception, who often face similar barriers, while special attention should be given to groups that are the most disadvantaged.

46. The Platform for Action recognizes that women face barriers to full equality and advancement because of such factors as their race, age, language, ethnicity, culture, religion or disability, because they are indigenous women or because of other status. Many women encounter specific obstacles related to their family status, particularly as single parents; and to their socio-economic status, including their living conditions in rural, isolated or impoverished areas. Additional barriers also exist for refugee women, other displaced women, including internally displaced women as well as for immigrant women and migrant women, including women migrant workers. Many women are also particularly affected by environmental disasters, serious and infectious diseases and various forms of violence against women.

A. Women and Poverty

47. More than 1 billion people in the world today, the great majority of whom are women, live in unacceptable conditions of poverty, mostly in the developing countries. Poverty has various causes, including structural ones. Poverty is a complex, multidimensional problem, with origins in both the national and international domains. The globalization of the world's economy and the deepening interdependence among nations present challenges and opportunities for sustained economic growth and development, as well as risks and uncertainties for the future of the world economy. The uncertain global economic climate has been accompanied by economic restructuring as well as, in a certain number of countries, persistent, unmanageable levels of external debt and structural adjustment programmes. In addition, all types of conflict, displacement of people and environmental degradation have under-mined the capacity of Governments to meet the basic needs of their populations. Transformations in the world economy are profoundly changing the parameters of social development in all countries. One significant trend has been the increased poverty of women, the extent of which varies from region to region. The gender disparities in economic power-sharing are also an important contributing factor to the poverty of women. Migration and consequent changes in family structures have placed additional burdens on women, especially those who provide for several dependants. Macroeconomic policies need rethinking and reformulation to address such trends. These policies focus almost exclusively on the formal sector. They also tend to impede the initiatives of women and fail to consider the differential impact on women and men. The application of gender analysis to a wide range of policies and programmes is therefore critical to poverty reduction strategies. In order to eradicate poverty and achieve sustainable development, women and men must participate fully and equally in the formulation of macroeconomic and social policies and strategies for the eradication of poverty. The eradication of poverty cannot be accomplished through anti-poverty programmes alone but will require democratic participation and changes in economic structures in order to ensure access for all women to resources, opportunities and public services. Poverty has various manifestations, including lack of income and productive resources sufficient to ensure a sustainable livelihood; hunger and malnutrition; ill health; limited or lack of access to education and other basic services; increasing morbidity and mortality from illness; homelessness and inadequate housing; unsafe environments; and social discrimination and exclusion. It is also characterized by lack of participation in decision-making and in civil, social and cultural life. It occurs in all countries—as mass poverty in many developing countries and as pockets of poverty amidst wealth in developed countries. Poverty may be caused by an economic recession that results in loss of livelihood or by disaster or conflict. There is also the poverty of low-wage workers and the utter destitution of people who fall outside family support systems, social institutions and safety nets.

48. In the past decade the number of women living in poverty has increased disproportionately to the number of men, particularly in the developing countries. The feminization of poverty has also recently become a significant problem in the countries with economies in transition as a short-term consequence of the process of political, economic and social transformation. In addition to economic factors, the rigidity of socially ascribed gender roles and women's limited access to power, education, training and productive resources as well as other emerging factors that may lead to insecurity for families are also responsible. The failure to adequately mainstream a gender perspective in all economic analysis and planning and to address the structural causes of poverty is also a contributing factor.

49. Women contribute to the economy and to combating poverty through both remunerated and unremunerated work at home, in the community and in the workplace. The empowerment of women is a critical factor in the eradication of poverty.

50. While poverty affects households as a whole, because of the gender division of labour and responsibilities for household welfare, women bear a disproportionate burden, attempting to manage household consumption and production under conditions of increasing scarcity. Poverty is particularly acute for women living in rural households.

51. Women's poverty is directly related to the absence of economic opportunities and autonomy, lack of access to economic resources, including credit, land ownership and inheritance, lack of access to education and support services and their minimal participation in the decision-making process. Poverty can also force women into situations in which they are vulnerable to sexual exploitation.

52. In too many countries, social welfare systems do not take sufficient account of the specific conditions of women living in poverty, and there is a tendency to scale back the services provided by such systems. The risk of falling into poverty is greater for women than for men, particularly in old age, where social security systems are based on the principle of continuous remunerated employment. In some cases, women do not fulfil this requirement because of interruptions in their work, due to the unbalanced distribution of remunerated and unremunerated work. Moreover, older women also face greater obstacles to labour-market re-entry.

53. In many developed countries, where the level of general education and professional training of women and men are similar and where systems of protection against discrimination are available, in some sectors the economic transformations of the past decade have strongly increased either the unemployment of women or the precarious nature of their employment. The proportion of women among the poor has consequently increased. In countries with a high level of school enrolment of girls, those who leave the educational system the earliest, without any qualification, are among the most vulnerable in the labour market.

54. In countries with economies in transition and in other countries undergoing fundamental political, economic and social transformations, these transformations have often led to a reduction in women's income or to women being deprived of income.

55. Particularly in developing countries, the productive capacity of women should be increased through access to capital, resources, credit, land, technology, information, technical assistance and training so as to raise their income and improve nutrition, education, health care and status within the household. The release of women's productive potential is pivotal to breaking the cycle of poverty so that women can share fully in the benefits of development and in the products of their own labour.

56. Sustainable development and economic growth that is both sustained and sustainable are possible only through improving the economic, social, political, legal and cultural status of women. Equitable social development that recognizes empowering the poor, particularly women, to utilize environmental resources sustainably is a necessary foundation for sustainable development.

57. The success of policies and measures aimed at supporting or strengthening the promotion of gender equality and the improvement of the status of women should be based on the integration of the gender perspective in general policies relating to all spheres of society as well as the implementation of positive measures with adequate institutional and financial support at all levels.

Strategic objective A.1. *Review, adopt and maintain macroeconomic policies and development strategies that address the needs and efforts of women in poverty*

Actions to be taken

58. By Governments:

(a) Review and modify, with the full and equal participation of women, macroeconomic and social policies with a view to achieving the objectives of the Platform for Action;

(b) Analyse, from a gender perspective, policies and programmes—including those related to macroeconomic stability, structural adjustment, external debt problems, taxation, investments, employment, markets and all relevant sectors of the economy—with respect to their impact on poverty, on inequality and particularly on women; assess their impact on family well-being and conditions and adjust them, as appropriate, to promote more equitable distribution of productive assets, wealth, opportunities, income and services;

(c) Pursue and implement sound and stable macroeconomic and sectoral policies that are designed and monitored with the full and equal participation of women, encourage broad-based sustained economic growth, address the structural causes of poverty and are geared towards eradicating poverty and reducing gender-based inequality within the overall framework of achieving people-centred sustainable development;

(d) Restructure and target the allocation of public expenditures to promote women's economic opportunities and equal access to productive resources and to address the basic social, educational and health needs of women, particularly those living in poverty;

(e) Develop agricultural and fishing sectors, where and as necessary, in order to ensure, as appropriate, household and national food security and food self-sufficiency, by allocating the necessary financial, technical and human resources;

(f) Develop policies and programmes to promote equitable distribution of food within the household;

(g) Provide adequate safety nets and strengthen State-based and community-based support systems, as an integral part of social policy, in order to enable women living in poverty to withstand adverse economic environments and preserve their livelihood, assets and revenues in times of crisis;

(h) Generate economic policies that have a positive impact on the employment and income of women workers in both the formal and informal sectors and adopt specific measures to address women's unemployment, in particular their long-term unemployment;

(i) Formulate and implement, when necessary, specific economic, social, agricultural and related policies in support of female-headed households;

(j) Develop and implement anti-poverty programmes, including employment schemes, that improve access to food for women living in poverty, including through the use of appropriate pricing and distribution mechanisms;

(k) Ensure the full realization of the human rights of all women migrants, including women migrant workers, and their protection against violence and exploitation; introduce measures for the empowerment of documented women migrants, including women migrant workers; facilitate the productive employment of documented migrant women through greater recognition of their skills, foreign education and credentials, and facilitate their full integration into the labour force;

(l) Introduce measures to integrate or reintegrate women living in poverty and socially marginalized women into productive employment and the economic mainstream; ensure that internally displaced women have full access to economic opportunities and that the qualifications and skills of immigrant and refugee women are recognized;

(m) Enable women to obtain affordable housing and access to land by, among other things, removing all obstacles to access, with special emphasis on meeting the needs of women, especially those living in poverty and female heads of household;

(n) Formulate and implement policies and programmes that enhance the access of women agricultural and fisheries producers (including subsistence farmers and producers, especially in rural areas) to financial, technical, extension and marketing services; provide access to and control of land, appropriate infrastructure and technology in order to increase women's incomes and promote household food security, especially in rural areas and, where appropriate, encourage the development of producer-owned, market-based cooperatives;

(o) Create social security systems wherever they do not exist, or review them with a view to placing individual women and men on an equal footing, at every stage of their lives;

(p) Ensure access to free or low-cost legal services, including legal literacy, especially designed to reach women living in poverty;

(q) Take particular measures to promote and strengthen policies and programmes for indigenous women with their full participation and respect for their cultural diversity, so that they have opportunities and the possibility of choice in the development process in order to eradicate the poverty that affects them.

59. By multilateral financial and development institutions, including the World Bank, the International Monetary Fund and regional development institutions, and through bilateral development cooperation:

(a) In accordance with the commitments made at the World Summit for Social Development, seek to mobilize new and additional financial resources that are both adequate and predictable and mobilized in a way that maximizes the availability of such resources and uses all available funding sources and mechanisms with a view to contributing towards the goal of poverty eradication and targeting women living in poverty;

(b) Strengthen analytical capacity in order to more systematically strengthen gender perspectives and integrate them into the design and implementation of lending programmes, including structural adjustment and economic recovery programmes;

(c) Find effective development-oriented and durable solutions to external debt problems in order to help them to finance programmes and projects targeted at development, including the advancement of women, *inter alia*, through the immediate implementation of the terms of debt forgiveness agreed upon in the Paris Club in December 1994, which encompassed debt reduction, including cancellation or other debt relief measures and develop techniques of debt conversion applied to social development programmes and projects in conformity with the priorities of the Platform for Action;

(d) Invite the international financial institutions to examine innovative approaches to assisting low-income countries with a high proportion of multilateral debt, with a view to alleviating their debt burden;

(e) Ensure that structural adjustment programmes are designed to minimize their negative effects on vulnerable and disadvantaged groups and communities and to assure their positive effects on such groups and communities by preventing their marginalization in economic and social activities and devising measures to ensure that they gain access to and control over economic resources and economic and social activities; take actions to reduce inequality and economic disparity;

(f) Review the impact of structural adjustment programmes on social development by means of gender-sensitive social impact assessments and other relevant methods, in order to develop policies to reduce their negative effects and improve their positive impact, ensuring that women do not bear a disproportionate burden of transition costs; complement adjustment lending with enhanced, targeted social development lending;

(g) Create an enabling environment that allows women to build and maintain sustainable livelihoods.

60. By national and international non-governmental organizations and women's groups:

(a) Mobilize all parties involved in the development process, including academic institutions, non-governmental organizations and grass-roots and women's groups, to improve the effectiveness of anti-poverty programmes directed towards the poorest and most disadvantaged groups of women, such as rural and indigenous women, female heads of household, young women and older women, refugees and migrant women and women with disabilities, recognizing that social development is primarily the responsibility of Governments;

(b) Engage in lobbying and establish monitoring mechanisms, as appropriate, and other relevant activities to ensure implementation of the recommendations on poverty eradication outlined in the Platform for Action and aimed at ensuring accountability and transparency from the State and private sectors;

(c) Include in their activities women with diverse needs and recognize that youth organizations are increasingly becoming effective partners in development programmes;

(d) In cooperation with the government and private sectors, participate in the development of a comprehensive national strategy for improving health, education and social services so that girls and women of all ages living in poverty have full access to such services; seek funding to secure access to services with a gender perspective and to extend those services in order to reach the rural and remote areas that are not covered by government institutions;

(e) In cooperation with Governments, employers, other social partners and relevant parties, contribute to the development of education and training and retraining policies to ensure that women can acquire a wide range of skills to meet new demands;

(f) Mobilize to protect women's right to full and equal access to economic resources, including the right to inheritance and to ownership of land and other property, credit, natural resources and appropriate technologies.

Strategic objective A.2. *Revise laws and administrative practices to ensure women's equal rights and access to economic resources*

Actions to be taken

61. By Governments:

(a) Ensure access to free or low-cost legal services, including legal literacy, especially designed to reach women living in poverty;

(b) Undertake legislative and administrative reforms to give women full and equal access to economic resources, including the right to inheritance and to ownership of land and other property, credit, natural resources and appropriate technologies;

(c) Consider ratification of Convention No. 169 of the International Labour Organization (ILO) as part of their efforts to promote and protect the rights of indigenous people.

Strategic objective A.3. *Provide women with access to savings and credit mechanisms and institutions*

Actions to be taken

62. By Governments:

(a) Enhance the access of disadvantaged women, including women entrepreneurs, in rural, remote and urban areas to financial services through strengthening links between the formal banks and intermediary lending organizations, including legislative support, training for women and institutional strengthening for intermediary institutions with a view to mobilizing capital for those institutions and increasing the availability of credit;

(b) Encourage links between financial institutions and non-governmental organizations and support innovative lending practices, including those that integrate credit with women's services and training and provide credit facilities to rural women.

63. By commercial banks, specialized financial institutions and the private sector in examining their policies:

(a) Use credit and savings methodologies that are effective in reaching women in poverty and innovative in reducing transaction costs and redefining risk;

(b) Open special windows for lending to women, including young women, who lack access to traditional sources of collateral;

(c) Simplify banking practices, for example by reducing the minimum deposit and other requirements for opening bank accounts;

(d) Ensure the participation and joint ownership, where possible, of women clients in the decision-making of institutions providing credit and financial services.

64. By multilateral and bilateral development cooperation organizations:

Support, through the provision of capital and/or resources, financial institutions that serve low-income, small-scale and micro-scale women entrepreneurs and producers, in both the formal and informal sectors.

65. By Governments and multilateral financial institutions, as appropriate:

Support institutions that meet performance standards in reaching large numbers of low-income women and men through capitalization, refinancing and institutional development support in forms that foster self-sufficiency.

66. By international organizations:

Increase funding for programmes and projects designed to promote sustainable and productive entrepreneurial activities for income-generation among disadvantaged women and women living in poverty.

Strategic objective A.4. *Develop gender-based methodologies and conduct research to address the feminization of poverty*

Actions to be taken

67. By Governments, intergovernmental organizations, academic and research institutions and the private sector:

(a) Develop conceptual and practical methodologies for incorporating gender perspectives into all aspects of economic policy-making, including structural adjustment planning and programmes;

(b) Apply these methodologies in conducting gender-impact analyses of all policies and programmes, including structural adjustment programmes, and disseminate the research findings.

68. By national and international statistical organizations:

(a) Collect gender and age-disaggregated data on poverty and all aspects of economic activity and develop qualitative and quantitative statistical indicators to facilitate the assessment of economic performance from a gender perspective;

(b) Devise suitable statistical means to recognize and make visible the full extent of the work of women and all their contributions to the national economy, including their contribution in the unremunerated and domestic sectors, and examine the relationship of women's unremunerated work to the incidence of and their vulnerability to poverty.

B. Education and Training of Women

69. Education is a human right and an essential tool for achieving the goals of equality, development and peace. Non-discriminatory education benefits both girls and boys and thus ultimately contributes to more equal relationships between women and men. Equality of access to and attainment of educational qualifications is necessary if more women are to become agents of change. Literacy of women is an important key to improving health, nutrition and education in the family and to empowering women to participate in decision-making in society. Investing in formal and non-formal education and training for girls and women, with its exceptionally high social and economic return, has proved to be one of the best means of achieving sustainable development and economic growth that is both sustained and sustainable.

70. On a regional level, girls and boys have achieved equal access to primary education, except in some parts of Africa, in particular sub-Saharan Africa, and Central Asia, where access to education facilities is still inadequate. Progress has been made in secondary education, where equal access of girls and boys has been achieved in some countries. Enrolment of girls and women in tertiary education has increased considerably. In many countries, private schools have also played an important complementary role in improving access to education at all levels. Yet, more than five years after the World Conference on Education for All (Jomtien, Thailand, 1990) adopted the World Declaration on Education for All and the Framework for Action to Meet Basic Learning Needs,[12] approximately 100 million children, including at least 60 million girls, are without access to primary schooling and more than two thirds of the world's 960 million illiterate adults are women. The high rate of illiteracy prevailing in most developing countries, in particular in sub-Saharan Africa and some Arab States, remains a severe impediment to the advancement of women and to development.

71. Discrimination in girls' access to education persists in many areas, owing to customary attitudes, early marriages and pregnancies, inadequate and gender-biased teaching and educational materials, sexual harassment and lack of adequate and physically and otherwise accessible schooling facilities. Girls undertake heavy domestic work at a very early age. Girls and young women are expected to manage both educational and domestic responsibilities, often resulting in poor scholastic performance and early drop-out from the educational system. This has long-lasting consequences for all aspects of women's lives.

72. Creation of an educational and social environment, in which women and men, girls and boys, are treated equally and encouraged to achieve their full potential, respecting their freedom of thought, conscience, religion and belief, and where educational resources promote non-stereotyped images of women and men, would be effective in the elimination of the causes of discrimination against women and inequalities between women and men.

73. Women should be enabled to benefit from an ongoing acquisition of knowledge and skills beyond those acquired during youth. This concept of lifelong learning includes knowledge and skills gained in formal education and training, as well as learning that occurs in informal ways, including volunteer activity, unremunerated work and traditional knowledge.

74. Curricula and teaching materials remain gender-biased to a large degree, and are rarely sensitive to the specific needs of girls and women. This reinforces traditional female and male roles that deny women opportunities for full and equal partnership in society. Lack of gender awareness by educators at all levels strengthens existing inequities between males and females by reinforcing discriminatory tendencies and undermining girls' self-esteem. The lack of sexual and reproductive health education has a profound impact on women and men.

75. Science curricula in particular are gender-biased. Science textbooks do not relate to women's and girls' daily experience and fail to give recognition to women scientists. Girls are often deprived of basic education in mathematics and science and technical training, which provide knowledge they could apply to improve their daily lives and enhance their employment opportunities. Advanced study in science and technology prepares women to take an active role in the technological and industrial development of their countries, thus necessitating a diverse approach to vocational and technical training. Technology is rapidly changing the world and has also affected the developing countries. It is essential that women not only benefit from technology, but also participate in the process from the design to the application, monitoring and evaluation stages.

76. Access for and retention of girls and women at all levels of education, including the higher level, and all academic areas is one of the factors of their continued progress in professional activities. Nevertheless, it can be noted that girls are still concentrated in a limited number of fields of study.

77. The mass media are a powerful means of education. As an educational tool the mass media can be an instrument for educators and governmental and non-governmental institutions for the advancement of women and for development. Computerized education and information systems are increasingly becoming an important element in learning and the dissemination of knowledge. Television especially has the greatest impact on young people and, as such, has the ability to shape values, attitudes and perceptions of women and girls in both positive and negative ways. It is therefore essential that educators teach critical judgement and analytical skills.

78. Resources allocated to education, particularly for girls and women, are in many countries insufficient and in some cases have been further diminished, including in the context of adjustment policies and programmes. Such insufficient resource allocations have a long-term adverse effect on human development, particularly on the development of women.

79. In addressing unequal access to and inadequate educational opportunities, Governments and other actors should promote an active and visible policy of mainstreaming a gender perspective into all policies and programmes, so that, before decisions are taken, an analysis is made of the effects on women and men, respectively.

Strategic objective B.1. *Ensure equal access to education*

Actions to be taken

80. By Governments:

(a) Advance the goal of equal access to education by taking measures to eliminate discrimination in education at all levels on the basis of gender, race, language, religion, national origin, age or disability, or any other form of discrimination and, as appropriate, consider establishing procedures to address grievances;

(b) By the year 2000, provide universal access to basic education and ensure completion of primary education by at least 80 percent of primary school-age children; close the gender gap in primary and secondary school education by the year 2005; provide universal primary education in all countries before the year 2015;

(c) Eliminate gender disparities in access to all areas of tertiary education by ensuring that women have equal access to career development, training, scholarships and fellowships, and by adopting positive action when appropriate;

(d) Create a gender-sensitive educational system in order to ensure equal educational and training opportunities and full and equal participation of women in educational administration and policy- and decision-making;

(e) Provide—in collaboration with parents, non-governmental organizations, including youth organizations, communities and the private sector—young women with academic and technical training, career planning, leadership and social skills and work experience to prepare them to participate fully in society;

(f) Increase enrolment and retention rates of girls by allocating appropriate budgetary resources; by enlisting the support of parents and the community, as well as through campaigns, flexible school schedules, incentives, scholarships and other means to minimize the costs of girls' education to their families and to facilitate parents' ability to choose education for the girl child; and by ensuring that the rights of women and girls to freedom of conscience and religion are respected in educational institutions through repealing any discriminatory laws or legislation based on religion, race or culture;

(g) Promote an educational setting that eliminates all barriers that impeded the schooling of pregnant adolescents and young mothers, including, as appropriate, affordable and physically accessible child-care facilities and parental education to encourage those who are responsible for the care of their children and siblings during their school years, to return to or continue with and complete schooling;

(h) Improve the quality of education and equal opportunities for women and men in terms of access in order to ensure that women of all ages can acquire the knowledge, capacities, aptitudes, skills and ethical values needed to develop and to participate fully under equal conditions in the process of social, economic and political development;

(i) Make available non-discriminatory and gender-sensitive professional school counselling and career education programmes to encourage girls to pursue academic and technical curricula in order to widen their future career opportunities;

(j) Encourage ratification of the International Covenant on Economic, Social and Cultural Rights[13] where they have not already done so.

Strategic objective B.2. *Eradicate illiteracy among women*

Actions to be taken

81. By Governments, national, regional and international bodies, bilateral and multilateral donors and non-governmental organizations:

(a) Reduce the female illiteracy rate to at least half its 1990 level, with emphasis on rural women, migrant, refugee and internally displaced women and women with disabilities;

(b) Provide universal access to, and seek to ensure gender equality in the completion of, primary education for girls by the year 2000;

(c) Eliminate the gender gap in basic and functional literacy, as recommended in the World Declaration on Education for All (Jomtien);

(d) Narrow the disparities between developed and developing countries;

(e) Encourage adult and family engagement in learning to promote total literacy for all people;

(f) Promote, together with literacy, life skills and scientific and technological knowledge and work towards an expansion of the definition of literacy, taking into account current targets and benchmarks.

Strategic objective B.3. *Improve women's access to vocational training, science and technology, and continuing education*

Actions to be taken

82. By Governments, in cooperation with employers, workers and trade unions, international and non-governmental organizations, including women's and youth organizations, and educational institutions:

(a) Develop and implement education, training and retraining policies for women, especially young women and women re-entering the labour market, to provide skills to meet the needs of a changing socio-economic context for improving their employment opportunities;

(b) Provide recognition to non-formal educational opportunities for girls and women in the educational system;

(c) Provide information to women and girls on the availability and benefits of vocational training, training programmes in science and technology and programmes of continuing education;

(d) Design educational and training programmes for women who are unemployed in order to provide them with new knowledge and skills that will enhance and broaden their employment opportunities, including self-employment, and development of their entrepreneurial skills;

(e) Diversify vocational and technical training and improve access for and retention of girls and women in education and vocational training in such fields as science, mathematics, engineering, environmental sciences and technology, information technology and high technology, as well as management training;

(f) Promote women's central role in food and agricultural research, extension and education programmes;

(g) Encourage the adaptation of curricula and teaching materials, encourage a supportive training environment and take positive measures to promote training for the full range of occupational choices of non-traditional careers for women and men, including the development of multidisciplinary courses for science and mathematics teachers to sensitize them to the relevance of science and technology to women's lives;

(h) Develop curricula and teaching materials and formulate and take positive measures to ensure women better access to and participation in technical and scientific areas, especially areas where they are not represented or are underrepresented;

(i) Develop policies and programmes to encourage women to participate in all apprenticeship programmes;

(j) Increase training in technical, managerial, agricultural extension and marketing areas for women in agriculture, fisheries, industry and business, arts and crafts, to increase income-generating opportunities, women's participation in economic decision-making, in particular through women's organizations at the grass-roots level, and their contribution to production, marketing, business, and science and technology;

(k) Ensure access to quality education and training at all appropriate levels for adult women with little or no education, for women with disabilities and for documented migrant, refugee and displaced women to improve their work opportunities.

Strategic objective B.4. *Develop non-discriminatory education and training*

Actions to be taken

83. By Governments, educational authorities and other educational and academic institutions:

(a) Elaborate recommendations and develop curricula, textbooks and teaching aids free of gender-based stereotypes for all levels of education, including teacher training, in association with all concerned—publishers, teachers, public authorities and parents' associations;

(b) Develop training programmes and materials for teachers and educators that raise awareness about the status, role and contribution of women and men in the family, as defined in paragraph 29 above, and society; in this context, promote equality, cooperation, mutual respect and shared responsibilities between girls and boys from pre-school level onward and develop, in particular, educational modules to ensure that boys have the skills necessary to take care of their own domestic needs and to share responsibility for their household and for the care of dependants;

(c) Develop training programmes and materials for teachers and educators that raise awareness of their own role in the educational process, with a view to providing them with effective strategies for gender-sensitive teaching;

(d) Take actions to ensure that female teachers and professors have the same opportunities as and equal status with male teachers and professors, in view of the importance of having female teachers at all levels and in order to attract girls to school and retain them in school;

(e) Introduce and promote training in peaceful conflict resolution;

(f) Take positive measures to increase the proportion of women gaining access to educational policy- and decision-making, particularly women teachers at all levels of education and in academic disciplines that are traditionally male-dominated, such as the scientific and technological fields;

(g) Support and develop gender studies and research at all levels of education, especially at the postgraduate level of academic institutions, and apply them in the development of curricula, including university curricula, textbooks and teaching aids, and in teacher training;

(h) Develop leadership training and opportunities for all women to encourage them to take leadership roles both as students and as adults in civil society;

(i) Develop appropriate education and information programmes with due respect for multilingualism, particularly in conjunction with the mass media, that make the public, particularly parents, aware of the importance of non-discriminatory education for children and the equal sharing of family responsibilities by girls and boys;

(j) Develop human rights education programmes that incorporate the gender dimension at all levels of education, in particular by encouraging higher education institutions, especially in their graduate and postgraduate juridical, social and political science curricula, to include the study of the human rights of women as they appear in United Nations conventions;

(k) Remove legal, regulatory and social barriers, where appropriate, to sexual and reproductive health education within formal education programmes regarding women's health issues;

(l) Encourage, with the guidance and support of their parents and in cooperation with educational staff and institutions, the elaboration of educational programmes for girls and boys and the creation of integrated services in order to raise awareness of their responsibilities and to help them to assume those responsibilities, taking into account the importance of such education and services to personal development and self-esteem, as well as the urgent need to avoid unwanted pregnancy, the spread of sexually transmitted diseases, especially HIV/AIDS, and such phenomena as sexual violence and abuse;

(m) Provide accessible recreational and sports facilities and establish and strengthen gender-sensitive programmes for girls and women of all ages in education and community institutions and support the advancement of women in all areas of athletics and physical activity, including coaching, training and administration, and as participants at the national, regional and international levels;

(n) Recognize and support the right of indigenous women and girls to education and promote a multicultural approach to education that is responsive to the needs, aspirations and cultures of indigenous women, including by developing appropriate education programmes, curricula and teaching aids, to the extent possible in the languages of indigenous people, and by providing for the participation of indigenous women in these processes;

(o) Acknowledge and respect the artistic, spiritual and cultural activities of indigenous women;

(p) Ensure that gender equality and cultural, religious and other diversity are respected in educational institutions;

(q) Promote education, training and relevant information programmes for rural and farming women through the use of affordable and appropriate technologies and the mass media—for example, radio programmes, cassettes and mobile units;

(r) Provide non-formal education, especially for rural women, in order to realize their potential with regard to health, micro-enterprise, agriculture and legal rights;

(s) Remove all barriers to access to formal education for pregnant adolescents and young mothers, and support the provision of child care and other support services where necessary.

Strategic objective B.5. *Allocate sufficient resources for and monitor the implementation of educational reforms*

Actions to be taken

84. By Governments:

(a) Provide the required budgetary resources to the educational sector, with reallocation within the educational sector to ensure increased funds for basic education, as appropriate;

(b) Establish a mechanism at appropriate levels to monitor the implementation of educational reforms and measures in relevant ministries, and establish technical assistance programmes, as appropriate, to address issues raised by the monitoring efforts.

85. By Governments and, as appropriate, private and public institutions, foundations, research institutes and non-governmental organizations:

(a) When necessary, mobilize additional funds from private and public institutions, foundations, research institutes and non-governmental organizations to enable girls and women, as well as boys and men on an equal basis, to complete their education, with particular emphasis on under-served populations;

(b) Provide funding for special programmes, such as programmes in mathematics, science and computer technology, to advance opportunities for all girls and women.

86. By multilateral development institutions, including the World Bank, regional development banks, bilateral donors and foundations:

(a) Consider increasing funding for the education and training needs of girls and women as a priority in development assistance programmes;

(b) Consider working with recipient Governments to ensure that funding for women's education is maintained or increased in structural adjustment and economic recovery programmes, including lending and stabilization programmes.

87. By international and intergovernmental organizations, especially the United Nations Educational, Scientific and Cultural Organization, at the global level:

(a) Contribute to the evaluation of progress achieved, using educational indicators generated by national, regional and international bodies, and urge Governments, in implementing measures, to eliminate differences between women and men and boys and girls with regard to opportunities in education and training and the levels achieved in all fields, particularly in primary and literacy programmes;

(b) Provide technical assistance upon request to developing countries to strengthen the capacity to monitor progress in closing the gap between women and men in education, training and research, and in levels of achievement in all fields, particularly basic education and the elimination of illiteracy;

(c) Conduct an international campaign promoting the right of women and girls to education;

(d) Allocate a substantial percentage of their resources to basic education for women and girls.

Strategic objective B.6. *Promote lifelong education and training for girls and women*

Actions to be taken

88. By Governments, educational institutions and communities:

(a) Ensure the availability of a broad range of educational and training programmes that lead to ongoing acquisition by women and girls of the knowledge and skills required for living in, contributing to and benefiting from their communities and nations;

(b) Provide support for child care and other services to enable mothers to continue their schooling;

(c) Create flexible education, training and retraining programmes for lifelong learning that facilitate transitions between women's activities at all stages of their lives.

C. Women and Health

89. Women have the right to the enjoyment of the highest attainable standard of physical and mental health. The enjoyment of this right is vital to their life and well-being and their ability to participate in all areas of public and private life. Health is a state of complete physical, mental and social well-being and not merely the absence of disease or infirmity. Women's health involves their emotional, social and physical well-being and is determined by the social, political and economic context of their lives, as well as by biology. However, health and well-being elude the majority of women. A major barrier for women to the achievement of the highest attainable standard of health is inequality, both between men and women and among women in different geographical regions, social classes and indigenous and ethnic groups. In national and international forums, women have emphasized that to attain optimal health throughout the life cycle, equality, including the sharing of family respon-sibilities, development and peace are necessary conditions.

90. Women have different and unequal access to and use of basic health resources, including primary health services for the prevention and treatment of childhood diseases, malnutrition, anaemia, diarrhoeal diseases, communicable diseases, malaria and other tropical diseases and tuberculosis, among others. Women also have different and unequal opportunities for the protection, promotion and maintenance of their health. In many developing countries, the lack of emergency obstetric services is also of particular concern. Health poli-cies and programmes often perpetuate gender stereotypes and fail to consider socio-economic disparities and other differences among women and may not fully take account of the lack of autonomy of women regarding their health. Women's health is also affected by gender bias in the health system and by the provision of inadequate and inappropriate medical services to women.

91. In many countries, especially developing countries, in particular the least developed countries, a decrease in public health spending and, in some cases, structural adjustment, contribute to the deterioration of public health systems. In addition, privatization of health-care systems without appropriate guarantees of universal access to affordable health care further reduces health-care avail-ability. This situation not only directly affects the health of girls and women, but also places disproportionate responsibilities on women, whose multiple roles, including their roles within the family and the community, are often not acknowledged; hence they do not receive the necessary social, psychological and economic support.

92. Women's right to the enjoyment of the highest standard of health must be secured throughout the whole life cycle in equality with men. Women are affected by many of the same health conditions as men, but women experience them differently. The prevalence among women of poverty and economic dependence, their experience of violence, negative attitudes towards women and girls, racial and other forms of discrimination, the limited power many women have over their sexual and reproductive lives and lack of influence in decision-making are social realities which have an adverse impact on their health. Lack of food and inequitable distribution of food for girls and women in the household, inadequate access to safe water, sanitation facilities and fuel supplies, particularly in rural and poor urban areas, and deficient housing conditions, all overburden women and their families and have a negative effect on their health. Good health is essential to leading a productive and fulfilling life, and the right of all women to control all aspects of their health, in particular their own fertility, is basic to their empowerment.

93. Discrimination against girls, often resulting from son preference, in access to nutrition and health-care services endangers their current and future health and well-being. Conditions that force girls into early marriage, pregnancy and child-bearing and subject them to harmful practices, such as female genital mutilation, pose grave health risks. Adolescent girls need, but too often do not have, access to necessary health and nutrition services as they mature. Counselling and access to sexual and reproductive health information and services for adolescents are still inadequate or lacking completely, and a young woman's right to privacy, confidentiality, respect and informed consent is often not considered. Adolescent girls are both biologically and psychosocially more vulnerable than boys to sexual abuse, violence and prostitution, and to the consequences of unprotected and premature sexual relations. The trend towards early sexual experience, combined with a lack of information and services, increases the risk of unwanted and too early pregnancy, AIDS infection and other sexually transmitted diseases, as well as unsafe abortions. Early child-bearing continues to be an impediment to improvements in the educational, economic and social status of women in all parts of the world. Overall, for young women early marriage and early motherhood can severely curtail educational and employment opportunities and are likely to have a long-term, adverse impact on the quality of their lives and the lives of their children. Young men are often not educated to respect women's self-determination and to share responsibility with women in matters of sexuality and reproduction.

94. Reproductive health is a state of complete physical, mental and social well-being and not merely the absence of disease or infirmity, in all matters relating to the reproductive system and to its functions and processes. Reproductive health therefore implies that people are able to have a satisfying and safe sex life and that they have the capability to reproduce and the freedom to decide if, when and how often to do so. Implicit in this last condition are the right of men and women to be informed and to have access to safe, effective, affordable and acceptable methods of family planning of their choice, as well as other methods of their choice for regulation of fertility which are not against the law, and the right of access to appropriate health-care services that will enable women to go safely through pregnancy and childbirth and provide couples with the best chance of having a healthy infant. In line with the above definition of reproductive health, reproductive health care is defined as the constellation of methods, techniques and services that contribute to reproductive health and well-being by preventing and solving reproductive health problems. It also includes sexual health, the purpose of which is the enhancement of life and personal relations, and not merely counselling and care related to reproduction and sexually transmitted diseases.

95. Bearing in mind the above definition, reproductive rights embrace certain human rights that are already recognized in national laws, international human rights documents and other consensus documents. These rights rest on the recognition of the basic right of all couples and individuals to decide freely and responsibly the number, spacing and timing of their children and to have the information and means to do so, and the right to attain the highest standard of sexual and reproductive health. It also includes their right to make decisions concerning reproduction free of discrimination, coercion and violence, as expressed in human rights documents. In the exercise of this right, they should take into account the needs of their living and future children and their responsibilities towards the community. The promotion of the responsible exercise of these rights for all people should be the fundamental basis for government- and community-supported policies and programmes in the area of reproductive health, including family planning. As part of their commitment, full attention should be given to the promotion of mutually respectful and equitable gender relations and particularly to meeting the educational and service needs of adolescents to enable them to deal in a positive and responsible way with their sexuality. Reproductive health eludes many of the world's people because of such factors as: inadequate levels of knowledge about human sexuality and inappropriate or poor-quality reproductive health information and services; the prevalence of high-risk sexual behaviour; discriminatory social practices; negative attitudes towards women and girls; and the limited power many women and girls have over their sexual and reproductive lives. Adolescents are particularly vulnerable because of their lack of information and access to relevant services in most countries. Older women and men have distinct reproductive and sexual health issues which are often inadequately addressed.

96. The human rights of women include their right to have control over and decide freely and responsibly on matters related to their sexuality, including sexual and reproductive health, free of coercion, discrimination and violence. Equal relationships between women and men in matters of sexual relations and reproduction, including full respect for the integrity of the person, require mutual respect, consent and shared responsibility for sexual behaviour and its consequences.

97. Further, women are subject to particular health risks due to inadequate responsiveness and lack of services to meet health needs related to sexuality and reproduction. Complications related to pregnancy and childbirth are among the leading causes of mortality and morbidity of women of reproductive age in many parts of the developing world. Similar problems exist to a certain degree in some countries with economies in transition. Unsafe abortions threaten the lives of a large number of women, representing a grave public health problem as it is primarily the poorest and youngest who take the highest risk. Most of these deaths, health problems and injuries are preventable through improved access to adequate health-care services, including safe and effective family planning methods and emergency obstetric care, recognizing the right of women and men to be informed and to have access to safe, effective, affordable and acceptable methods of family planning of their choice, as well as other methods of their choice for regulation of fertility which are not against the law, and the right of access to appropriate health-care services that will enable women to go safely through pregnancy and childbirth and provide couples with the best chance of having a healthy infant. These problems and means should be addressed on the basis of the report of the International Conference on Population and Development, with particular reference to relevant paragraphs of the Programme of Action of the Conference.[14] In most countries, the neglect of women's reproductive rights severely limits their opportunities in public and private life, including opportunities for education and economic and political empowerment. The ability of women to control their own fertility forms an important basis for the enjoyment of other rights. Shared responsibility between women and men in matters related to sexual and reproductive behaviour is also essential to improving women's health.

98. Hiv/aids and other sexually transmitted diseases, the transmission of which is sometimes a consequence of sexual violence, are having a devastating effect on women's health, particularly the health of adolescent girls and young women. They often do not have the power to insist on safe and responsible sex practices and have little access to information and services for prevention and treatment. Women, who represent half of all adults newly infected with hiv/aids and other sexually transmitted diseases, have emphasized that social vulnerability and the unequal power relationships between women and men are obstacles to safe sex, in their efforts to control the spread of sexually transmitted diseases. The consequences of hiv/aids reach beyond women's health to their role as mothers and caregivers and their contribution to the economic support of their families. The social, developmental and health consequences of hiv/aids and other sexually transmitted diseases need to be seen from a gender perspective.

99. Sexual and gender-based violence, including physical and psychological abuse, trafficking in women and girls, and other forms of abuse and sexual exploitation place girls and women at high risk of physical and mental trauma, disease and unwanted pregnancy. Such situations often deter women from using health and other services.

100. Mental disorders related to marginalization, powerlessness and poverty, along with overwork and stress and the growing incidence of domestic violence as well as substance abuse, are among other health issues of growing concern to women. Women throughout the world, especially young women, are increasing their use of tobacco with serious effects on their health and that of their children. Occupational health issues are also growing in importance, as a large number of women work in low-paid jobs in either the formal or the informal labour market under tedious and unhealthy conditions, and the number is rising. Cancers of the breast and cervix and other cancers of the reproductive system, as well as infertility affect growing numbers of women and may be preventable, or curable, if detected early.

101. With the increase in life expectancy and the growing number of older women, their health concerns require particular attention. The long-term health prospects of women are influenced by changes at menopause, which, in combination with lifelong conditions and other factors, such as poor nutrition and lack of physical activity, may increase the risk of cardiovascular disease and osteoporosis. Other diseases of ageing and the interrelationships of ageing and disability among women also need particular attention.

102. Women, like men, particularly in rural areas and poor urban areas, are increasingly exposed to environmental health hazards owing to environmental catastrophes and degradation. Women have a different susceptibility to various environmental hazards, contaminants and substances and they suffer different consequences from exposure to them.

103. The quality of women's health care is often deficient in various ways, depending on local circumstances. Women are frequently not treated with respect, nor are they guaranteed privacy and confidentiality, nor do they always receive full information about the options and services available. Furthermore, in some countries, over-medicating of women's life events is common, leading to unnecessary surgical intervention and inappropriate medication.

104. Statistical data on health are often not systematically collected, disaggregated and analysed by age, sex and socio-economic status and by established demographic criteria used to serve the interests and solve the problems of subgroups, with particular emphasis on the vulnerable and marginalized and other relevant variables. Recent and reliable data on the mortality and morbidity of women and conditions and diseases particularly affecting women are not available in many countries. Relatively little is known about how social and economic factors affect the health of girls and women of all ages, about the provision of health services to girls and women and the patterns of their use of such services, and about the value of disease prevention and health promotion programmes for women. Subjects of importance to women's health have not been adequately researched and women's health research often lacks funding. Medical research, on heart disease, for example, and epidemiological studies in many countries are often based solely on men; they are not gender specific. Clinical trials involving women to establish basic information about dosage, side-effects and effectiveness of drugs, including contraceptives, are noticeably absent and do not always conform to ethical standards for research and testing. Many drug therapy protocols and other medical treatments and interventions administered to women are based on research on men without any investigation and adjustment for gender differences.

105. In addressing inequalities in health status and unequal access to and inadequate health-care services between women and men, Governments and other actors should promote an active and visible policy of mainstreaming a gender perspective in all policies and programmes, so that, before decisions are taken, an analysis is made of the effects for women and men, respectively.

Strategic objective C.1. *Increase women's access throughout the life cycle to appropriate, affordable and quality health care, information and related services*

Actions to be taken

106. By Governments, in collaboration with non-governmental organizations and employers' and workers' organizations and with the support of international institutions:

(a) Support and implement the commitments made in the Programme of Action of the International Conference on Population and Development, as established in the report of that Conference and the Copenhagen Declaration on Social Development and Programme of Action of the World Summit for Social Development[15] and the obligations of States parties under the Convention on the Elimination of All Forms of Discrimination against Women and other relevant international agreements, to meet the health needs of girls and women of all ages;

(b) Reaffirm the right to the enjoyment of the highest attainable standards of physical and mental health, protect and promote the attainment of this right for women and girls and incorporate it in national legislation, for example; review existing legislation, including health legislation, as well as policies, where necessary, to reflect a commitment to women's health and to ensure that they meet the changing roles and responsibilities of women wherever they reside;

(c) Design and implement, in cooperation with women and community-based organizations, gender-sensitive health programmes, including decentralized health services, that address the needs of women throughout their lives and take into account their multiple roles and responsibilities, the demands on their time, the special needs of rural women and women with disabilities and the diversity of women's needs arising from age and socio-economic and cultural differences, among others; include women, especially local and indigenous women, in the identification and planning of health-care priorities and programmes; remove all barriers to women's health services and provide a broad range of health-care services;

(d) Allow women access to social security systems in equality with men throughout the whole life cycle;

(e) Provide more accessible, available and affordable primary health-care services of high quality, including sexual and reproductive health care, which includes family planning information and services, and giving particular attention to maternal and emergency obstetric care, as agreed to in the Programme of Action of the International Conference on Population and Development;

(f) Redesign health information, services and training for health workers so that they are gender-sensitive and reflect the user's perspectives with regard to interpersonal and communications skills and the user's right to privacy and confidentiality; these services, information and training should be based on a holistic approach;

(g) Ensure that all health services and workers conform to human rights and to ethical, professional and gender-sensitive standards in the delivery of women's health services aimed at ensuring responsible, voluntary and informed consent; encourage the development, implementation and dissemination of codes of ethics guided by existing international codes of medical ethics as well as ethical principles that govern other health professionals;

(h) Take all appropriate measures to eliminate harmful, medically unnecessary or coercive medical interventions, as well as inappropriate medication and over-medication of women, and ensure that all women are fully informed of their options, including likely benefits and potential side-effects, by properly trained personnel;

(i) Strengthen and reorient health services, particularly primary health care, in order to ensure universal access to quality health services for women and girls; reduce ill health and maternal morbidity and achieve world wide the agreed-upon goal of reducing maternal mortality by at least 50 percent of the 1990 levels by the year 2000 and a further one half by the year 2015; ensure that the necessary services are available at each level of the health system and make reproductive health care accessible, through the primary health-care system, to all individuals of appropriate ages as soon as possible and no later than the year 2015;

(j) Recognize and deal with the health impact of unsafe abortion as a major public health concern, as agreed in paragraph 8.25 of the Programme of Action of the International Conference on Population and Development;[14]

(k) In the light of paragraph 8.25 of the Programme of Action of the International Conference on Population and Development, which states: "In no case should abortion be promoted as a method of family planning. All Governments and relevant intergovernmental and non-governmental organizations are urged to strengthen their commitment to women's health, to deal with the health impact of unsafe abortion[16] as a major public health concern and to reduce the recourse to abortion through expanded and improved family-planning services. Prevention of unwanted pregnancies must always be given the highest priority and every attempt should be made to eliminate the need for abortion. Women who have unwanted pregnancies should have ready access to reliable information and compassionate counselling. Any measures or changes related to abortion within the health system can only be determined at the national or local level according to the national legislative process. In circumstances where abortion is not against the law, such abortion should be safe. In all cases, women should have access to quality services for the management of complications arising from abortion. Post-abortion coun-selling, education and family-planning services should be offered promptly, which will also help to avoid repeat abortions," consider reviewing laws containing punitive measures against women who have undergone illegal abortions;

(l) Give particular attention to the needs of girls, especially the promotion of healthy behaviour, including physical activities; take specific measures for closing the gender gaps in morbidity and mortality where girls are disadvan-taged, while achieving internationally approved goals for the reduction of infant and child mortality—specifically, by the year 2000, the reduction of mortality rates of infants and children under five years of age by one third of the 1990 level, or 50 to 70 per 1,000 live births, whichever is less; by the year 2015 an infant mortality rate below 35 per 1,000 live births and an under-five mortality rate below 45 per 1,000;

(m) Ensure that girls have continuing access to necessary health and nutri-tion information and services as they mature, to facilitate a healthful transi-tion from childhood to adulthood;

(n) Develop information, programmes and services to assist women to understand and adapt to changes associated with ageing and to address and treat the health needs of older women, paying particular attention to those who are physically or psychologically dependent;

(o) Ensure that girls and women of all ages with any form of disability receive supportive services;

(p) Formulate special policies, design programmes and enact the leg-islation necessary to alleviate and eliminate environmental and occupational health hazards associated with work in the home, in the workplace and elsewhere with attention to pregnant and lactating women;

(q) Integrate mental health services into primary health-care systems or other appropriate levels, develop supportive programmes and train primary health workers to recognize and care for girls and women of all ages who have experienced any form of violence especially domestic violence, sexual abuse or other abuse resulting from armed and non-armed conflict;

(r) Promote public information on the benefits of breast-feeding; examine ways and means of implementing fully the WHO/UNICEF International Code of Marketing of Breast-milk Substitutes, and enable mothers to breast-feed their infants by providing legal, economic, practical and emotional support;

(s) Establish mechanisms to support and involve non-governmental organi-zations, particularly women's organizations, professional groups and other bodies working to improve the health of girls and women, in government policy-making, programme design, as appropriate, and implementation within the health sector and related sectors at all levels;

(t) Support non-governmental organizations working on women's health and help develop networks aimed at improving coordination and collabora-tion between all sectors that affect health;

(u) Rationalize drug procurement and ensure a reliable, continuous supply of high-quality pharmaceutical, contraceptive and other supplies and equipment, using the WHO Model List of Essential Drugs as a guide, and ensure the safety of drugs and devices through national regulatory drug approval processes;

(v) Provide improved access to appropriate treatment and rehabilitation services for women substance abusers and their families;

(w) Promote and ensure household and national food security, as appropriate, and implement programmes aimed at improving the nutritional status of all girls and women by implementing the commitments made in the Plan of Action on Nutrition of the International Conference on Nutrition,[17] including a reduction world wide of severe and moderate malnutrition among children under the age of five by one half of 1990 levels by the year 2000, giving special attention to the gender gap in nutrition, and a reduction in iron deficiency anaemia in girls and women by one third of the 1990 levels by the year 2000;

(x) Ensure the availability of and universal access to safe drinking water and sanitation and put in place effective public distribution systems as soon as possible;

(y) Ensure full and equal access to health-care infrastructure and services for indigenous women.

Strategic objective C.2. *Strengthen preventive programmes that promote women's health*

Actions to be taken

107. By Governments, in cooperation with non-governmental organizations, the mass media, the private sector and relevant international organizations, including United Nations bodies, as appropriate:

(a) Give priority to both formal and informal educational programmes that support and enable women to develop self-esteem, acquire knowledge, make decisions on and take responsibility for their own health, achieve mutual respect in matters concerning sexuality and fertility and educate men regarding the importance of women's health and well-being, placing special focus on programmes for both men and women that emphasize the elimination of harmful attitudes and practices, including female genital mutilation, son preference (which results in female infanticide and prenatal sex selection), early marriage, including child marriage, violence against women, sexual exploitation, sexual abuse, which at times is conducive to infection with HIV/AIDS and other sexually transmitted diseases, drug abuse, discrimination against girls and women in food allocation and other harmful attitudes and practices related to the life, health and well-being of women, and recognizing that some of these practices can be violations of human rights and ethical medical principles;

(b) Pursue social, human development, education and employment policies to eliminate poverty among women in order to reduce their susceptibility to ill health and to improve their health;

(c) Encourage men to share equally in child care and household work and to provide their share of financial support for their families, even if they do not live with them;

(d) Reinforce laws, reform institutions and promote norms and practices that eliminate discrimination against women and encourage both women and men to take responsibility for their sexual and reproductive behaviour; ensure full respect for the integrity of the person, take action to ensure the conditions necessary for women to exercise their reproductive rights and eliminate coercive laws and practices;

(e) Prepare and disseminate accessible information, through public health campaigns, the media, reliable counselling and the education system, designed to ensure that women and men, particularly young people, can acquire knowledge about their health, especially information on sexuality and reproduction, taking into account the rights of the child to access to information, privacy, confidentiality, respect and informed consent, as well as the responsibilities, rights and duties of parents and legal guardians to provide, in a manner consistent with the evolving capacities of the child, appropriate direction and guidance in the exercise by the child of the rights recognized in the Convention on the Rights of the Child, and in conformity with the Convention on the Elimination of All Forms of Discrimination against Women; ensure that in all actions concerning children, the best interests of the child are a primary consideration;

(f) Create and support programmes in the educational system, in the workplace and in the community to make opportunities to participate in sport, physical activity and recreation available to girls and women of all ages on the same basis as they are made available to men and boys;

(g) Recognize the specific needs of adolescents and implement specific appropriate programmes, such as education and information on sexual and reproductive health issues and on sexually transmitted diseases, including HIV/AIDS, taking into account the rights of the child and the responsibilities, rights and duties of parents as stated in paragraph 107 (e) above;

(h) Develop policies that reduce the disproportionate and increasing burden on women who have multiple roles within the family and the community by providing them with adequate support and programmes from health and social services;

(i) Adopt regulations to ensure that the working conditions, including remuneration and promotion of women at all levels of the health system, are non-discriminatory and meet fair and professional standards to enable them to work effectively;

(j) Ensure that health and nutritional information and training form an integral part of all adult literacy programmes and school curricula from the primary level;

(k) Develop and undertake media campaigns and information and educational programmes that inform women and girls of the health and related risks of substance abuse and addiction and pursue strategies and programmes that discourage substance abuse and addiction and promote rehabilitation and recovery;

(l) Devise and implement comprehensive and coherent programmes for the prevention, diagnosis and treatment of osteoporosis, a condition that predominantly affects women;

(m) Establish and/or strengthen programmes and services, including media campaigns, that address the prevention, early detection and treatment of breast, cervical and other cancers of the reproductive system;

(n) Reduce environmental hazards that pose a growing threat to health, especially in poor regions and communities; apply a precautionary approach, as agreed to in the Rio Declaration on Environment and Development, adopted by the United Nations Conference on Environment and Development,[18] and include reporting on women's health risks related to the environment in monitoring the implementation of Agenda 21;[19]

(o) Create awareness among women, health professionals, policy makers and the general public about the serious but preventable health hazards stemming from tobacco consumption and the need for regulatory and education measures to reduce smoking as important health promotion and disease prevention activities;

(p) Ensure that medical school curricula and other health-care training include gender-sensitive, comprehensive and mandatory courses on women's health;

(q) Adopt specific preventive measures to protect women, youth and children from any abuse—sexual abuse, exploitation, trafficking and violence, for example—including the formulation and enforcement of laws, and provide legal protection and medical and other assistance.

Strategic objective C.3. *Undertake gender-sensitive initiatives that address sexually transmitted diseases, HIV/AIDS, and sexual and reproductive health issues*

Actions to be taken

108. By Governments, international bodies including relevant United Nations organizations, bilateral and multilateral donors and non-governmental organizations:

(a) Ensure the involvement of women, especially those infected with HIV/AIDS or other sexually transmitted diseases or affected by the HIV/AIDS pandemic, in all decision-making relating to the development, implementation, monitoring and evaluation of policies and programmes on HIV/AIDS and other sexually transmitted diseases;

(b) Review and amend laws and combat practices, as appropriate, that may contribute to women's susceptibility to AIDS infection and other sexually transmitted diseases, including enacting legislation against those sociocultural practices that contribute to it, and implement legislation, policies and practices to protect women, adolescents and young girls from discrimination related to HIV/AIDS;

(c) Encourage all sectors of society, including the public sector, as well as international organizations, to develop compassionate and supportive, non-discriminatory HIV/AIDS-related policies and practices that protect the rights of infected individuals;

(d) Recognize the extent of the HIV/AIDS pandemic in their countries, taking particularly into account its impact on women, with a view to ensuring that infected women do not suffer stigmatization and discrimination, including during travel;

(e) Develop gender-sensitive multisectoral programmes and strategies to end social subordination of women and girls and to ensure their social and economic empowerment and equality; facilitate promotion of programmes to educate and enable men to assume their responsibilities to prevent HIV/AIDS and other sexually transmitted diseases;

(f) Facilitate the development of community strategies that will protect women of all ages from AIDS and other sexually transmitted diseases; provide care and support to infected girls, women and their families and mobilize all parts of the community in response to the HIV/AIDS pandemic to exert pressure on all responsible authorities to respond in a timely, effective, sustainable and gender-sensitive manner;

(g) Support and strengthen national capacity to create and improve gender-sensitive policies and programmes on HIV/AIDS and other sexually transmitted diseases, including the provision of resources and facilities to women who find themselves the principal caregivers or economic support for those infected with HIV/AIDS or affected by the pandemic, and the survivors, particularly children and older persons;

(h) Provide workshops and specialized education and training to parents, decision makers and opinion leaders at all levels of the community, including religious and traditional authorities, on prevention of HIV/AIDS and other sexually transmitted diseases and on their repercussions on both women and men of all ages;

(i) Give all women and health workers all relevant information and education about sexually transmitted diseases including HIV/AIDS and pregnancy and the implications for the baby, including breast-feeding;

(j) Assist women and their formal and informal organizations to establish and expand effective peer education and outreach programmes and to participate in the design, implementation and monitoring of these programmes;

(k) Give full attention to the promotion of mutually respectful and equitable gender relations and, in particular, to meeting the educational and service needs of adolescents to enable them to deal in a positive and responsible way with their sexuality;

(l) Design specific programmes for men of all ages and male adolescents, recognizing the parental roles referred to in paragraph 107 (e) above, aimed at providing complete and accurate information on safe and responsible sexual and reproductive behaviour, including voluntary, appropriate and effective male methods for the prevention of HIV/AIDS and other sexually transmitted diseases through, *inter alia*, abstinence and condom use;

(m) Ensure the provision, through the primary health-care system, of universal access of couples and individuals to appropriate and affordable preventive services with respect to sexually transmitted diseases, including HIV/AIDS, and expand the provision of counselling and voluntary and confidential diagnostic and treatment services for women; ensure that high-quality condoms as well as drugs for the treatment of sexually transmitted diseases are, where possible, supplied and distributed to health services;

(n) Support programmes which acknowledge that the higher risk among women of contracting AIDS is linked to high-risk behaviour, including intravenous substance use and substance-influenced unprotected and irresponsible sexual behaviour, and take appropriate preventive measures;

(o) Support and expedite action-oriented research on affordable methods, controlled by women,0 to prevent AIDS and other sexually transmitted diseases, on strategies empowering women to protect themselves from sexually transmitted diseases, including HIV/AIDS, and on methods of care, support and treatment of women, ensuring their involvement in all aspects of such research;

(p) Support and initiate research which addresses women's needs and situations, including research on AIDS infection and other sexually transmitted diseases in women, on women-controlled methods of protection, such as non-spermicidal microbicides, and on male and female risk-taking attitudes and practices.

Strategic objective C.4. *Promote research and disseminate information on women's health*

Actions to be taken

109. By Governments, the United Nations system, health professions, research institutions, non-governmental organizations, donors, pharmaceutical industries and the mass media, as appropriate:

(a) Train researchers and introduce systems that allow for the use of data collected, analysed and disaggregated by, among other factors, sex and age, other established demographic criteria and socio-economic variables, in policy-making, as appropriate, planning, monitoring and evaluation;

(b) Promote gender-sensitive and women-centred health research, treatment and technology and link traditional and indigenous knowledge with modern medicine, making information available to women to enable them to make informed and responsible decisions;

(c) Increase the number of women in leadership positions in the health professions, including researchers and scientists, to achieve equality at the earliest possible date;

(d) Increase financial and other support from all sources for preventive, appropriate biomedical, behavioural, epidemiological and health service research on women's health issues and for research on the social, economic and political causes of women's health problems, and their consequences, including the impact of gender and age inequalities, especially with respect to chronic and non-communicable diseases, particularly cardiovascular diseases and conditions, cancers, reproductive tract infections and injuries, HIV/AIDS and other sexually transmitted diseases, domestic violence, occupational health, disabilities, environmentally related health problems, tropical diseases and health aspects of ageing;

(e) Inform women about the factors which increase the risks of developing cancers and infections of the reproductive tract, so that they can make informed decisions about their health;

(f) Support and fund social, economic, political and cultural research on how gender-based inequalities affect women's health, including etiology, epidemiology, provision and utilization of services and eventual outcome of treatment;

(g) Support health service systems and operations research to strengthen access and improve the quality of service delivery, to ensure appropriate support for women as health-care providers and to examine patterns with respect to the provision of health services to women and use of such services by women;

(h) Provide financial and institutional support for research on safe, effective, affordable and acceptable methods and technologies for the reproductive and sexual health of women and men, including more safe, effective, affordable and acceptable methods for the regulation of fertility, including natural family planning for both sexes, methods to protect against HIV/AIDS and other sexually transmitted diseases and simple and inexpensive methods of diagnosing such diseases, among others; this research needs to be guided at all stages by users and from the perspective of gender, particularly the perspective of women, and should be carried out in strict conformity with internationally accepted legal, ethical, medical and scientific standards for biomedical research;

(i) Since unsafe abortion[16] is a major threat to the health and life of women, research to understand and better address the determinants and consequences of induced abortion, including its effects on subsequent fertility, reproductive and mental health and contraceptive practice, should be promoted, as well as research on treatment of complications of abortions and post-abortion care;

(j) Acknowledge and encourage beneficial traditional health care, especially that practised by indigenous women, with a view to preserving and incorporating the value of traditional health care in the provision of health services, and support research directed towards achieving this aim;

(k) Develop mechanisms to evaluate and disseminate available data and research findings to researchers, policy makers, health professionals and women's groups, among others;

(l) Monitor human genome and related genetic research from the perspective of women's health and disseminate information and results of studies conducted in accordance with accepted ethical standards.

Strategic objective C.5. *Increase resources and monitor follow-up for women's health*

Actions to be taken

110. By Governments at all levels and, where appropriate, in cooperation with non-governmental organizations, especially women's and youth organizations:

(a) Increase budgetary allocations for primary health care and social services, with adequate support for secondary and tertiary levels, and give special attention to the reproductive and sexual health of girls and women and give priority to health programmes in rural and poor urban areas;

(b) Develop innovative approaches to funding health services through promoting community participation and local financing; increase, where necessary, budgetary allocations for community health centres and community-based programmes and services that address women's specific health needs;

(c) Develop local health services, promoting the incorporation of gender-sensitive community-based participation and self-care and specially designed preventive health programmes;

(d) Develop goals and time-frames, where appropriate, for improving women's health and for planning, implementing, monitoring and evaluating programmes, based on gender-impact assessments using qualitative and quantitative data disaggregated by sex, age, other established demographic criteria and socio-economic variables;

(e) Establish, as appropriate, ministerial and inter-ministerial mechanisms for monitoring the implementation of women's health policy and programme reforms and establish, as appropriate, high-level focal points in national planning authorities responsible for monitoring to ensure that women's health concerns are mainstreamed in all relevant government agencies and programmes.

111. By Governments, the United Nations and its specialized agencies, international financial institutions, bilateral donors and the private sector, as appropriate:

(a) Formulate policies favourable to investment in women's health and, where appropriate, increase allocations for such investment;

(b) Provide appropriate material, financial and logistical assistance to youth non-governmental organizations in order to strengthen them to address youth concerns in the area of health, including sexual and reproductive health;

(c) Give higher priority to women's health and develop mechanisms for coordinating and implementing the health objectives of the Platform for Action and relevant international agreements to ensure progress.

D. Violence against Women

112. Violence against women is an obstacle to the achievement of the objectives of equality, development and peace. Violence against women both violates and impairs or nullifies the enjoyment by women of their human rights and fundamental freedoms. The long-standing failure to protect and promote those rights and freedoms in the case of violence against women is a matter of concern to all States and should be addressed. Knowledge about its causes and consequences, as well as its incidence and measures to combat it, have been greatly expanded since the Nairobi Conference. In all societies, to a greater or lesser degree, women and girls are subjected to physical, sexual and psychological abuse that cuts across lines of income, class and culture. The low social and economic status of women can be both a cause and a consequence of violence against women.

113. The term "violence against women" means any act of gender-based violence that results in, or is likely to result in, physical, sexual or psychological harm or suffering to women, including threats of such acts, coercion or arbitrary deprivation of liberty, whether occurring in public or private life. Accordingly, violence against women encompasses but is not limited to the following:

(a) Physical, sexual and psychological violence occurring in the family, including battering, sexual abuse of female children in the household, dowry-related violence, marital rape, female genital mutilation and other traditional practices harmful to women, non-spousal violence and violence related to exploitation;

(b) Physical, sexual and psychological violence occurring within the general community, including rape, sexual abuse, sexual harassment and intimidation at work, in educational institutions and elsewhere, trafficking in women and forced prostitution;

(c) Physical, sexual and psychological violence perpetrated or condoned by the State, wherever it occurs.

114. Other acts of violence against women include violation of the human rights of women in situations of armed conflict, in particular murder, systematic rape, sexual slavery and forced pregnancy.

115. Acts of violence against women also include forced sterilization and forced abortion, coercive/forced use of contraceptives, female infanticide and prenatal sex selection.

116. Some groups of women, such as women belonging to minority groups, indigenous women, refugee women, women migrants, including women migrant workers, women in poverty living in rural or remote communities, destitute women, women in institutions or in detention, female children, women with disabilities, elderly women, displaced women, repatriated women, women living in poverty and women in situations of armed conflict, foreign occupation, wars of aggression, civil wars, terrorism, including hostage-taking, are also particularly vulnerable to violence.

117. Acts or threats of violence, whether occurring within the home or in the community, or perpetrated or condoned by the State, instil fear and insecurity in women's lives and are obstacles to the achievement of equality and for development and peace. The fear of violence, including harassment, is a permanent constraint on the mobility of women and limits their access to resources and basic activities. High social, health and economic costs to the individual and society are associated with violence against women. Violence against women is one of the crucial social mechanisms by which women are forced into a subordinate position compared with men. In many cases, violence against women and girls occurs in the family or within the home, where violence is often tolerated. The neglect, physical and sexual abuse, and rape of girl children and women by family members and other members of the household, as well as incidences of spousal and non-spousal abuse, often go unreported and are thus difficult to detect. Even when such violence is reported, there is often a failure to protect victims or punish perpetrators.

118. Violence against women is a manifestation of the historically unequal power relations between men and women, which have led to domination over and discrimination against women by men and to the prevention of women's full advancement. Violence against women throughout the life cycle derives essentially from cultural patterns, in particular the harmful effects of certain traditional or customary practices and all acts of extremism linked to race, sex, language or religion that perpetuate the lower status accorded to women in the family, the workplace, the community and society. Violence against women is exacerbated by social pressures, notably the shame of denouncing certain acts that have been perpetrated against women; women's lack of access to legal information, aid or protection; the lack of laws that effectively prohibit violence against women; failure to reform existing laws; inadequate efforts on the part of public authorities to promote awareness of and enforce existing laws; and the absence of educational and other means to address the causes and consequences of violence. Images in the media of violence against women, in particular those that depict rape or sexual slavery as well as the use of women and girls as sex objects, including pornography, are factors contributing to the continued prevalence of such violence, adversely influencing the community at large, in particular children and young people.

119. Developing a holistic and multidisciplinary approach to the challenging task of promoting families, communities and States that are free of violence against women is necessary and achievable. Equality, partnership between women and men and respect for human dignity must permeate all stages of the socialization process. Educational systems should promote self-respect, mutual respect, and cooperation between women and men.

120. The absence of adequate gender-disaggregated data and statistics on the incidence of violence makes the elaboration of programmes and monitoring of changes difficult. Lack of or inadequate documentation and research on domestic violence, sexual harassment and violence against women and girls in private and in public, including the workplace, impede efforts to design specific intervention strategies. Experience in a number of countries shows that women and men can be mobilized to overcome violence in all its forms and that effective public measures can be taken to address both the causes and the consequences of violence. Men's groups mobilizing against gender violence are necessary allies for change.

121. Women may be vulnerable to violence perpetrated by persons in positions of authority in both conflict and non-conflict situations. Training of all officials in humanitarian and human rights law and the punishment of perpetrators of violent acts against women would help to ensure that such violence does not take place at the hands of public officials in whom women should be able to place trust, including police and prison officials and security forces.

122. The effective suppression of trafficking in women and girls for the sex trade is a matter of pressing international concern. Implementation of the 1949 Convention for the Suppression of the Traffic in Persons and of the Exploitation of the Prostitution of Others,[20] as well as other relevant instruments, needs to be reviewed and strengthened. The use of women in international prostitution and trafficking networks has become a major focus of international organized crime. The Special Rapporteur of the Commission on Human Rights on violence against women, who has explored these acts as an additional cause of the violation of the human rights and fundamental freedoms of women and girls, is invited to address, within her mandate and as a matter of urgency, the issue of international trafficking for the purposes of the sex trade, as well as the issues of forced prostitution, rape, sexual abuse and sex tourism. Women and girls who are victims of this international trade are at an increased risk of further violence, as well as unwanted pregnancy and sexually transmitted infection, including infection with HIV/AIDS.

123. In addressing violence against women, Governments and other actors should promote an active and visible policy of mainstreaming a gender perspective in all policies and programmes so that before decisions are taken an analysis may be made of their effects on women and men, respectively.

Strategic objective D.1. *Take integrated measures to prevent and eliminate violence against women*

Actions to be taken

124. By Governments:

(a) Condemn violence against women and refrain from invoking any custom, tradition or religious consideration to avoid their obligations with respect to its elimination as set out in the Declaration on the Elimination of Violence against Women;

(b) Refrain from engaging in violence against women and exercise due diligence to prevent, investigate and, in accordance with national legislation, punish acts of violence against women, whether those acts are perpetrated by the State or by private persons;

(c) Enact and/or reinforce penal, civil, labour and administrative sanctions in domestic legislation to punish and redress the wrongs done to women and girls who are subjected to any form of violence, whether in the home, the workplace, the community or society;

(d) Adopt and/or implement and periodically review and analyse legislation to ensure its effectiveness in eliminating violence against women, emphasizing the prevention of violence and the prosecution of offenders; take measures to ensure the protection of women subjected to violence, access to just and effective remedies, including compensation and indemnification and healing of victims, and rehabilitation of perpetrators;

(e) Work actively to ratify and/or implement international human rights norms and instruments as they relate to violence against women, including those contained in the Universal Declaration of Human Rights,[21] the International Covenant on Civil and Political Rights,[13] the International Covenant on Economic, Social and Cultural Rights,[13] and the Convention against Torture and Other Cruel, Inhuman or Degrading Treatment or Punishment;[23]

(f) Implement the Convention on the Elimination of All Forms of Discrimination against Women, taking into account general recommendation 19, adopted by the Committee on the Elimination of Discrimination against Women at its eleventh session;[23]

(g) Promote an active and visible policy of mainstreaming a gender perspective in all policies and programmes related to violence against women; actively encourage, support and implement measures and programmes aimed at increasing the knowledge and understanding of the causes, consequences and mechanisms of violence against women among those responsible for implementing these policies, such as law enforcement officers, police personnel and judicial, medical and social workers, as well as those who deal with minority, migration and refugee issues, and develop strategies to ensure that the revictimization of women victims of violence does not occur because of gender-insensitive laws or judicial or enforcement practices;

(h) Provide women who are subjected to violence with access to the mechanisms of justice and, as provided for by national legislation, to just and effective remedies for the harm they have suffered and inform women of their rights in seeking redress through such mechanisms;

(i) Enact and enforce legislation against the perpetrators of practices and acts of violence against women, such as female genital mutilation, female infanticide, prenatal sex selection and dowry-related violence, and give vigorous support to the efforts of non-governmental and community organizations to eliminate such practices;

(j) Formulate and implement, at all appropriate levels, plans of action to eliminate violence against women;

(k) Adopt all appropriate measures, especially in the field of education, to modify the social and cultural patterns of conduct of men and women, and to eliminate prejudices, customary practices and all other practices based on the idea of the inferiority or superiority of either of the sexes and on stereotyped roles for men and women;

(l) Create or strengthen institutional mechanisms so that women and girls can report acts of violence against them in a safe and confidential environment, free from the fear of penalties or retaliation, and file charges;

(m) Ensure that women with disabilities have access to information and services in the field of violence against women;

(n) Create, improve or develop as appropriate, and fund the training programmes for judicial, legal, medical, social, educational and police and immigrant personnel, in order to avoid the abuse of power leading to violence against women and sensitize such personnel to the nature of gender-based acts and threats of violence so that fair treatment of female victims can be assured;

(o) Adopt laws, where necessary, and reinforce existing laws that punish police, security forces or any other agents of the State who engage in acts of violence against women in the course of the performance of their duties; review existing legislation and take effective measures against the perpetrators of such violence;

(p) Allocate adequate resources within the government budget and mobilize community resources for activities related to the elimination of violence against women, including resources for the implementation of plans of action at all appropriate levels;

(q) Include in reports submitted in accordance with the provisions of relevant United Nations human rights instruments, information pertaining to violence against women and measures taken to implement the Declaration on the Elimination of Violence against Women;

(r) Cooperate with and assist the Special Rapporteur of the Commission on Human Rights on violence against women in the performance of her mandate and furnish all information requested; cooperate also with other competent mechanisms, such as the Special Rapporteur of the Commission on Human Rights on torture and the Special Rapporteur of the Commission on Human Rights on summary, extrajudiciary and arbitrary executions, in relation to violence against women;

(s) Recommend that the Commission on Human Rights renew the mandate of the Special Rapporteur on violence against women when her term ends in 1997 and, if warranted, to update and strengthen it.

125. By Governments, including local governments, community organizations, non-governmental organizations, educational institutions, the public and private sectors, particularly enterprises, and the mass media, as appropriate:

(a) Provide well-funded shelters and relief support for girls and women subjected to violence, as well as medical, psychological and other counselling services and free or low-cost legal aid, where it is needed, as well as appropriate assistance to enable them to find a means of subsistence;

(b) Establish linguistically and culturally accessible services for migrant women and girls, including women migrant workers, who are victims of gender-based violence;

(c) Recognize the vulnerability to violence and other forms of abuse of women migrants, including women migrant workers, whose legal status in the host country depends on employers who may exploit their situation;

(d) Support initiatives of women's organizations and non-governmental organizations all over the world to raise awareness on the issue of violence against women and to contribute to its elimination;

(e) Organize, support and fund community-based education and training campaigns to raise awareness about violence against women as a violation of women's enjoyment of their human rights and mobilize local communities to use appropriate gender-sensitive traditional and innovative methods of conflict resolution;

(f) Recognize, support and promote the fundamental role of intermediate institutions, such as primary health-care centres, family-planning centres, existing school health services, mother and baby protection services, centres for migrant families and so forth in the field of information and education related to abuse;

(g) Organize and fund information campaigns and educational and training programmes in order to sensitize girls and boys and women and men to the personal and social detrimental effects of violence in the family, community and society; teach them how to communicate without violence and promote training for victims and potential victims so that they can protect themselves and others against such violence;

(h) Disseminate information on the assistance available to women and families who are victims of violence;

(i) Provide, fund and encourage counselling and rehabilitation programmes for the perpetrators of violence and promote research to further efforts concerning such counselling and rehabilitation so as to prevent the recurrence of such violence;

(j) Raise awareness of the responsibility of the media in promoting non-stereotyped images of women and men, as well as in eliminating patterns of media presentation that generate violence, and encourage those responsible for media content to establish professional guidelines and codes of conduct; also raise awareness of the important role of the media in informing and educating people about the causes and effects of violence against women and in stimulating public debate on the topic.

126. By Governments, employers, trade unions, community and youth organizations and non-governmental organizations, as appropriate:

(a) Develop programmes and procedures to eliminate sexual harassment and other forms of violence against women in all educational institutions, workplaces and elsewhere;

(b) Develop programmes and procedures to educate and raise awareness of acts of violence against women that constitute a crime and a violation of the human rights of women;

(c) Develop counselling, healing and support programmes for girls, adolescents and young women who have been or are involved in abusive relationships, particularly those who live in homes or institutions where abuse occurs;

(d) Take special measures to eliminate violence against women, particularly those in vulnerable situations, such as young women, refugee, displaced and internally displaced women, women with disabilities and women migrant workers, including enforcing any existing legislation and developing, as appropriate, new legislation for women migrant workers in both sending and receiving countries.

127. By the Secretary-General of the United Nations:

Provide the Special Rapporteur of the Commission on Human Rights on violence against women with all necessary assistance, in particular the staff and resources required to perform all mandated functions, especially in carrying out and following up on missions undertaken either separately or jointly with other special rapporteurs and working groups, and adequate assistance for periodic consultations with the Committee on the Elimination of Discrimination against Women and all treaty bodies.

128. By Governments, international organizations and non-governmental organizations:

Encourage the dissemination and implementation of the UNHCR Guidelines on the Protection of Refugee Women and the UNHCR Guidelines on the Prevention of and Response to Sexual Violence against Refugees.

Strategic objective D.2. *Study the causes and consequences of violence against women and the effectiveness of preventive measures*

Actions to be taken

129. By Governments, regional organizations, the United Nations, other international organizations, research institutions, women's and youth organizations and non-governmental organizations, as appropriate:

(a) Promote research, collect data and compile statistics, especially concerning domestic violence relating to the prevalence of different forms of violence against women, and encourage research into the causes, nature, seriousness and consequences of violence against women and the effectiveness of measures implemented to prevent and redress violence against women;

(b) Disseminate findings of research and studies widely;

(c) Support and initiate research on the impact of violence, such as rape, on women and girl children, and make the resulting information and statistics available to the public;

(d) Encourage the media to examine the impact of gender role stereotypes, including those perpetuated by commercial advertisements which foster gender-based violence and inequalities, and how they are transmitted during the life cycle, and take measures to eliminate these negative images with a view to promoting a violence-free society.

Strategic objective D.3. *Eliminate trafficking in women and assist victims of violence due to prostitution and trafficking*

Actions to be taken

130. By Governments of countries of origin, transit and destination, regional and international organizations, as appropriate:

(a) Consider the ratification and enforcement of international conventions on trafficking in persons and on slavery;

(b) Take appropriate measures to address the root factors, including external factors, that encourage trafficking in women and girls for prostitution and other forms of commercialized sex, forced marriages and forced labour in order to eliminate trafficking in women, including by strengthening existing legislation with a view to providing better protection of the rights of women and girls and to punishing the perpetrators, through both criminal and civil measures;

(c) Step up cooperation and concerted action by all relevant law enforcement authorities and institutions with a view to dismantling national, regional and international networks in trafficking;

(d) Allocate resources to provide comprehensive programmes designed to heal and rehabilitate into society victims of trafficking, including through job training, legal assistance and confidential health care, and take measures to cooperate with non-governmental organizations to provide for the social, medical and psychological care of the victims of trafficking;

(e) Develop educational and training programmes and policies and consider enacting legislation aimed at preventing sex tourism and trafficking, giving special emphasis to the protection of young women and children.

E. Women and armed conflict

131. An environment that maintains world peace and promotes and protects human rights, democracy and the peaceful settlement of disputes, in accordance with the principles of non-threat or use of force against territorial integrity or political independence and of respect for sovereignty as set forth in the Charter of the United Nations, is an important factor for the advancement of women. Peace is inextricably linked with equality between women and men and development. Armed and other types of conflicts and terrorism and hostage-taking still persist in many parts of the world. Aggression, foreign occupation, ethnic and other types of conflicts are an ongoing reality affecting women and men in nearly every region. Gross and systematic violations and situations that constitute serious obstacles to the full enjoyment of human rights continue to occur in different parts of the world. Such violations and obstacles include, as well as torture and cruel, inhuman and degrading treatment or punishment, summary and arbitrary executions, disappearances, arbitrary detentions, all forms of racism and racial discrimination, foreign occupation and alien domination, xenophobia, poverty, hunger and other denials of economic, social and cultural rights, religious intolerance, terrorism, discrimination against women and lack of the rule of law. International humanitarian law, prohibiting attacks on civilian populations, as such, is at times systematically ignored and human rights are often violated in connection with situations of armed conflict, affecting the civilian population, especially women, children, the elderly and the disabled. Violations of the human rights of women in situations of armed conflict are violations of the fundamental principles of international human rights and humanitarian law. Massive violations of human rights, especially in the form of genocide, ethnic cleansing as a strategy of war and its consequences, and rape, including systematic rape of women in war situations, creating a mass exodus of refugees and displaced persons, are abhorrent practices that are strongly condemned and must be stopped immediately, while perpetrators of such crimes must be punished. Some of these situations of armed conflict have their origin in the conquest or colonialization of a country by another State and the perpetuation of that colonization through state and military repression.

132. The Geneva Convention relative to the Protection of Civilian Persons in Time of War, of 1949, and the Additional Protocols of 1977[25] provide that women shall especially be protected against any attack on their honour, in particular against humiliating and degrading treatment, rape, enforced prostitution or any form of indecent assault. The Vienna Declaration and Programme of Action, adopted by the World Conference on Human Rights, states that "violations of the human rights of women in situations of armed conflict are violations of the fundamental principles of international human rights and humanitarian law."[27] All violations of this kind, including in particular murder, rape, including systematic rape, sexual slavery and forced pregnancy require a particularly effective response. Gross and systematic violations and situations that constitute serious obstacles to the full enjoyment of human rights continue to occur in different parts of the world. Such violations and obstacles include, as well as torture and cruel, inhuman and degrading treatment or summary and arbitrary detention, all forms of racism, racial discrimination, xenophobia, denial of economic, social and cultural rights and religious intolerance.

133. Violations of human rights in situations of armed conflict and military occupation are violations of the fundamental principles of international human rights and humanitarian law as embodied in international human rights instruments and in the Geneva Conventions of 1949 and the Additional Protocols thereto. Gross human rights violations and policies of ethnic cleansing in war-torn and occupied areas continue to be carried out. These practices have created, *inter alia*, a mass flow of refugees and other displaced persons in need of international protection and internally displaced persons, the majority of whom are women, adolescent girls and children. Civilian victims, mostly women and children, often outnumber casualties among combatants. In addition, women often become caregivers for injured combatants and find themselves, as a result of conflict, unexpectedly cast as sole manager of household, sole parent, and caretaker of elderly relatives.

134. In a world of continuing instability and violence, the implementation of cooperative approaches to peace and security is urgently needed. The equal access and full participation of women in power structures and their full involvement in all efforts for the prevention and resolution of conflicts are essential for the maintenance and promotion of peace and security. Although women have begun to play an important role in conflict resolution, peacekeeping and defence and foreign affairs mechanisms, they are still underrepresented in decision-making positions. If women are to play an equal part in securing and maintaining peace, they must be empowered politically and economically and represented adequately at all levels of decision-making.

135. While entire communities suffer the consequences of armed conflict and terrorism, women and girls are particularly affected because of their status in society and their sex. Parties to conflict often rape women with impunity, sometimes using systematic rape as a tactic of war and terrorism. The impact of violence against women and violation of the human rights of women in such situations is experienced by women of all ages, who suffer displacement, loss of home and property, loss or involuntary disappearance of close relatives, poverty and family separation and disintegration, and who are victims of acts of murder, terrorism, torture, involuntary disappearance, sexual slavery, rape, sexual abuse and forced pregnancy in situations of armed conflict, especially as a result of policies of ethnic cleansing and other new and emerging forms of violence. This is compounded by the lifelong social, economic and psychologically traumatic consequences of armed conflict and foreign occupation and alien domination.

136. Women and children constitute some 80 percent of the world's millions of refugees and other displaced persons, including internally displaced persons. They are threatened by deprivation of property, goods and services and deprivation of their right to return to their homes of origin as well as by violence and insecurity. Particular attention should be paid to sexual violence against uprooted women and girls employed as a method of persecution in systematic campaigns of terror and intimidation and forcing members of a particular ethnic, cultural or religious group to flee their homes. Women may also be forced to flee as a result of a well-founded fear of persecution for reasons enumerated in the 1951 Convention relating to the Status of Refugees and the 1967 Protocol, including persecution through sexual violence or other gender-related persecution, and they continue to be vulnerable to violence and exploitation while in flight, in countries of asylum and resettlement and during and after repatriation. Women often experience difficulty in some countries of asylum in being recognized as refugees when the claim is based on such persecution.

137. Refugee, displaced and migrant women in most cases display strength, endurance and resourcefulness and can contribute positively to countries of resettlement or to their country of origin on their return. They need to be appropriately involved in decisions that affect them.

138. Many women's non-governmental organizations have called for reductions in military expenditures world wide, as well as in international trade and trafficking in and the proliferation of weapons. Those affected most negatively by conflict and excessive military spending are people living in poverty, who are deprived because of the lack of investment in basic services. Women living in poverty, particularly rural women, also suffer because of the use of arms that are particularly injurious or have indiscriminate effects. There are more than 100 million anti-personnel land-mines scattered in 64 countries globally. The negative impact on development of excessive military expenditures, the arms trade, and investment for arms production and acquisition must be addressed. At the same time, maintenance of national security and peace is an important factor for economic growth and development and the empowerment of women.

139. During times of armed conflict and the collapse of communities, the role of women is crucial. They often work to preserve social order in the midst of armed and other conflicts. Women make an important but often unrecognized contribution as peace educators both in their families and in their societies.

140. Education to foster a culture of peace that upholds justice and tolerance for all nations and peoples is essential to attaining lasting peace and should be begun at an early age. It should include elements of conflict resolution, mediation, reduction of prejudice and respect for diversity.

141. In addressing armed or other conflicts, an active and visible policy of mainstreaming a gender perspective into all policies and programmes should be promoted so that before decisions are taken an analysis is made of the effects on women and men, respectively.

Strategic objective E.1. *Increase the participation of women in conflict resolution at decision-making levels and protect women living in situations of armed and other conflicts or under foreign occupation*

Actions to be taken

142. By Governments and international and regional intergovernmental institutions:

(a) Take action to promote equal participation of women and equal opportunities for women to participate in all forums and peace activities at all levels, particularly at the decision-making level, including in the United Nations Secretariat with due regard to equitable geographical distribution in accordance with Article 101 of the Charter of the United Nations;

(b) Integrate a gender perspective in the resolution of armed or other conflicts and foreign occupation and aim for gender balance when nominating or promoting candidates for judicial and other positions in all relevant international bodies, such as the United Nations International Tribunals for the former Yugoslavia and for Rwanda and the International Court of Justice, as well as in other bodies related to the peaceful settlement of disputes;

(c) Ensure that these bodies are able to address gender issues properly by providing appropriate training to prosecutors, judges and other officials in handling cases involving rape, forced pregnancy in situations of armed conflict, indecent assault and other forms of violence against women in armed conflicts, including terrorism, and integrate a gender perspective into their work.

Strategic objective E.2. *Reduce excessive military expenditures and control the availability of armaments*

Actions to be taken

143. By Governments:

(a) Increase and hasten, as appropriate, subject to national security considerations, the conversion of military resources and related industries to development and peaceful purposes;

(b) Undertake to explore new ways of generating new public and private financial resources, *inter alia*, through the appropriate reduction of excessive military expenditures, including global military expenditures, trade in arms and investment for arms production and acquisition, taking into consideration national security requirements, so as to permit the possible allocation of additional funds for social and economic development, in particular for the advancement of women;

(c) Take action to investigate and punish members of the police, security and armed forces and others who perpetrate acts of violence against women, violations of international humanitarian law and violations of the human rights of women in situations of armed conflict;

(d) While acknowledging legitimate national defence needs, recognize and address the dangers to society of armed conflict and the negative effect of excessive military expenditures, trade in arms, especially those arms that are particularly injurious or have indiscriminate effects, and excessive investment for arms production and acquisition; similarly, recognize the need to combat illicit arms trafficking, violence, crime, the production and use of and trafficking in illicit drugs, and trafficking in women and children;

(e) Recognizing that women and children are particularly affected by the indiscriminate use of anti-personnel land-mines:

(i) Undertake to work actively towards ratification, if they have not already done so, of the 1981 Convention on Prohibitions or Restrictions on the Use of Certain Conventional Weapons Which May Be Deemed to Be Excessively Injurious or to Have Indiscriminate Effects, particularly the Protocol on Prohibitions or Restrictions on the Use of Mines, Booby Traps and Other Devices (Protocol II),[26] with a view to universal ratification by the year 2000;

(ii) Undertake to strongly consider strengthening the Convention to promote a reduction in the casualties and intense suffering caused to the civilian population by the indiscriminate use of land-mines;

(iii) Undertake to promote assistance in mine clearance, notably by facilitating, in respect of the means of mine-clearing, the exchange of information, the transfer of technology and the promotion of scientific research;

(iv) Within the United Nations context, undertake to support efforts to coordinate a common response programme of assistance in de-mining without unnecessary discrimination;

(v) Adopt at the earliest possible date, if they have not already done so, a moratorium on the export of anti-personnel land-mines, including to non-governmental entities, noting with satisfaction that many States have already declared moratoriums on the export, transfer or sale of such mines;

(vi) Undertake to encourage further international efforts to seek solutions to the problems caused by antipersonnel land-mines, with a view to their eventual elimination, recognizing that States can move most effectively towards this goal as viable and humane alternatives are developed;

(f) Recognizing the leading role that women have played in the peace movement:

(i) Work actively towards general and complete disarmament under strict and effective international control;

(ii) Support negotiations on the conclusion, without delay, of a universal and multilaterally and effectively verifiable comprehensive nuclear-test-ban treaty that contributes to nuclear disarmament and the prevention of the proliferation of nuclear weapons in all its aspects;

(iii) Pending the entry into force of a comprehensive nuclear-test-ban treaty, exercise the utmost restraint in respect of nuclear testing.

Strategic objective E.3. *Promote non-violent forms of conflict resolution and reduce the incidence of human rights abuse in conflict situations*

Actions to be taken

144. By Governments:

(a) Consider the ratification of or accession to international instruments containing provisions relative to the protection of women and children in armed conflicts, including the Geneva Convention relative to the Protection of Civilian Persons in Time of War, of 1949, the Protocols Additional to the Geneva Conventions of 1949 relating to the Protection of Victims of International Armed Conflicts (Protocol I) and to the Protection of Victims of Non-International Armed Conflicts (Protocol II);[24]

(b) Respect fully the norms of international humanitarian law in armed conflicts and take all measures required for the protection of women and children, in particular against rape, forced prostitution and any other form of indecent assault;

(c) Strengthen the role of women and ensure equal representation of women at all decision-making levels in national and international institutions which may make or influence policy with regard to matters related to peace-keeping, preventive diplomacy and related activities and in all stages of peace mediation and negotiations, taking note of the specific recommendations of the Secretary-General in his strategic plan of action for the improvement of the status of women in the Secretariat (1995–2000) (A/49/587, sect. IV).

145. By Governments and international and regional organizations:

(a) Reaffirm the right of self-determination of all peoples, in particular of peoples under colonial or other forms of alien domination or foreign occupation, and the importance of the effective realization of this right, as enunciated, *inter alia*, in the Vienna Declaration and Programme of Action,[2] adopted by the World Conference on Human Rights;

(b) Encourage diplomacy, negotiation and peaceful settlement of disputes in accordance with the Charter of the United Nations, in particular Article 2, paragraphs 3 and 4 thereof;

(c) Urge the identification and condemnation of the systematic practice of rape and other forms of inhuman and degrading treatment of women as a deliberate instrument of war and ethnic cleansing and take steps to ensure that full assistance is provided to the victims of such abuse for their physical and mental rehabilitation;

(d) Reaffirm that rape in the conduct of armed conflict constitutes a war crime and under certain circumstances it constitutes a crime against humanity and an act of genocide as defined in the Convention on the Prevention and Punishment of the Crime of Genocide;[27] take all measures required for the protection of women and children from such acts and strengthen mechanisms to investigate and punish all those responsible and bring the perpetrators to justice;

(e) Uphold and reinforce standards set out in international humanitarian law and international human rights instruments to prevent all acts of violence against women in situations of armed and other conflicts; undertake a full investigation of all acts of violence against women committed during war, including rape, in particular systematic rape, forced prostitution and other forms of indecent assault and sexual slavery; prosecute all criminals responsible for war crimes against women and provide full redress to women victims;

(f) Call upon the international community to condemn and act against all forms and manifestations of terrorism;

(g) Take into account gender-sensitive concerns in developing training programmes for all relevant personnel on international humanitarian law and human rights awareness and recommend such training for those involved in United Nations peace-keeping and humanitarian aid, with a view to preventing violence against women, in particular;

(h) Discourage the adoption of and refrain from any unilateral measure not in accordance with international law and the Charter of the United Nations, that impedes the full achievement of economic and social development by the population of the affected countries, in particular women and children, that hinders their well-being and that creates obstacles to the full enjoyment of their human rights, including the right of everyone to a standard of living adequate for their health and well-being and their right to food, medical care and the necessary social services. This Conference reaffirms that food and medicine must not be used as a tool for political pressure;

(i) Take measures in accordance with international law with a view to alleviating the negative impact of economic sanctions on women and children.

Strategic objective E.4. *Promote women's contribution to fostering a culture of peace*

Actions to be taken

146. By Governments, international and regional intergovernmental institutions and non-governmental organizations:

(a) Promote peaceful conflict resolution and peace, reconciliation and tolerance through education, training, community actions and youth exchange programmes, in particular for young women;

(b) Encourage the further development of peace research, involving the participation of women, to examine the impact of armed conflict on women and children and the nature and contribution of women's participation in national, regional and international peace movements; engage in research and identify innovative mechanisms for containing violence and for conflict resolution for public dissemination and for use by women and men;

(c) Develop and disseminate research on the physical, psychological, economic and social effects of armed conflicts on women, particularly young women and girls, with a view to developing policies and programmes to address the consequences of conflicts;

(d) Consider establishing educational programmes for girls and boys to foster a culture of peace, focusing on conflict resolution by non-violent means and the promotion of tolerance.

Strategic objective E.5. *Provide protection, assistance and training to refugee women, other displaced women in need of international protection and internally displaced women*

Actions to be taken

147. By Governments, intergovernmental and non-governmental organizations and other institutions involved in providing protection, assistance and training to refugee women, other displaced women in need of international protection and internally displaced women, including the Office of the United Nations High Commissioner for Refugees and the World Food Programme, as appropriate:

(a) Take steps to ensure that women are fully involved in the planning, design, implementation, monitoring and evaluation of all short-term and long-term projects and programmes providing assistance to refugee women, other displaced women in need of international protection and internally displaced women, including the management of refugee camps and resources; ensure that refugee and displaced women and girls have direct access to the services provided;

(b) Offer adequate protection and assistance to women and children displaced within their country and find solutions to the root causes of their displacement with a view to preventing it and, when appropriate, facilitate their return or resettlement;

(c) Take steps to protect the safety and physical integrity of refugee women, other displaced women in need of international protection and internally displaced women during their displacement and upon their return to their communities of origin, including programmes of rehabilitation; take effective measures to protect from violence women who are refugees or displaced; hold an impartial and thorough investigation of any such violations and bring those responsible to justice;

(d) While fully respecting and strictly observing the principle of non-refoulement of refugees, take all the necessary steps to ensure the right of refugee and displaced women to return voluntarily to their place of origin in safety and with dignity, and their right to protection after their return;

(e) Take measures, at the national level with international cooperation, as appropriate, in accordance with the Charter of the United Nations, to find lasting solutions to questions related to internally displaced women, including their right to voluntary and safe return to their home of origin;

(f) Ensure that the international community and its international organizations provide financial and other resources for emergency relief and other longer-term assistance that takes into account the specific needs, resources and potentials of refugee women, other displaced women in need of international protection and internally displaced women; in the provision of protection and assistance, take all appropriate measures to eliminate discrimination against women and girls in order to ensure equal access to appropriate and adequate food, water and shelter, education, and social and health services, including reproductive health care and maternity care and services to combat tropical diseases;

(g) Facilitate the availability of educational materials in the appropriate language—in emergency situations also—in order to minimize disruption of schooling among refugee and displaced children;

(h) Apply international norms to ensure equal access and equal treatment of women and men in refugee determination procedures and the granting of asylum, including full respect and strict observation of the principle of non-refoulement through, *inter alia*, bringing national immigration regulations into conformity with relevant international instruments, and consider recognizing as refugees those women whose claim to refugee status is based upon the well-founded fear of persecution for reasons enumerated in the 1951 Convention[28] and the 1967 Protocol[29] relating to the Status of Refugees, including persecution through sexual violence or other gender-related persecution, and provide access to specially trained officers, including female officers, to interview women regarding sensitive or painful experiences, such as sexual assault;

(i) Support and promote efforts by States towards the development of criteria and guidelines on responses to persecution specifically aimed at women, by sharing information on States' initiatives to develop such criteria and guidelines and by monitoring to ensure their fair and consistent application;

(j) Promote the self-reliant capacities of refugee women, other displaced women in need of international protection and internally displaced women and provide programmes for women, particularly young women, in leadership and decision-making within refugee and returnee communities;

(k) Ensure that the human rights of refugee and displaced women are protected and that refugee and displaced women are made aware of these rights; ensure that the vital importance of family reunification is recognized;

(l) Provide, as appropriate, women who have been determined refugees with access to vocational/professional training programmes, including language training, small-scale enterprise development training and planning and counselling on all forms of violence against women, which should include rehabilitation programmes for victims of torture and trauma; Governments and other donors should contribute adequately to assistance programmes for refugee women, other displaced women in need of international protection and internally displaced women, taking into account in particular the effects on the host countries of the increasing requirements of large refugee populations and the need to widen the donor base and to achieve greater burden-sharing;

(m) Raise public awareness of the contribution made by refugee women to their countries of resettlement, promote understanding of their human rights and of their needs and abilities and encourage mutual understanding and acceptance through educational programmes promoting cross-cultural and interracial harmony;

(n) Provide basic and support services to women who are displaced from their place of origin as a result of terrorism, violence, drug trafficking or other reasons linked to violence situations;

(o) Develop awareness of the human rights of women and provide, as appropriate, human rights education and training to military and police personnel operating in areas of armed conflict and areas where there are refugees.

148. By Governments:

(a) Disseminate and implement the UNHCR Guidelines on the Protection of Refugee Women and the UNHCR Guidelines on Evaluation and Care of Victims of Trauma and Violence, or provide similar guidance, in close cooperation with refugee women and in all sectors of refugee programmes;

(b) Protect women and children who migrate as family members from abuse or denial of their human rights by sponsors and consider extending their stay, should the family relationship dissolve, within the limits of national legislation.

Strategic objective E.6. *Provide assistance to the women of the colonies and non-self-governing territories*

Actions to be taken

149. By Governments and intergovernmental and non-governmental organizations:

(a) Support and promote the implementation of the right of self-determination of all peoples as enunciated, *inter alia*, in the Vienna Declaration and

Programme of Action by providing special programmes in leadership and in
training for decision-making;

(b) Raise public awareness, as appropriate, through the mass media, education at all levels and special programmes to create a better understanding of
the situation of women of the colonies and non-self-governing territories.

F. Women and the economy

150. There are considerable differences in women's and men's access to and
opportunities to exert power over economic structures in their societies. In
most parts of the world, women are virtually absent from or are poorly
represented in economic decision-making, including the formulation of financial, monetary, commercial and other economic policies, as well as tax
systems and rules governing pay. Since it is often within the framework of
such policies that individual men and women make their decisions, *inter alia*,
on how to divide their time between remunerated and unremunerated work,
the actual development of these economic structures and policies has a direct
impact on women's and men's access to economic resources, their economic
power and consequently the extent of equality between them at the individual
and family levels as well as in society as a whole.

151. In many regions, women's participation in remunerated work in the
formal and non-formal labour market has increased significantly and has
changed during the past decade. While women continue to work in agriculture and fisheries, they have also become increasingly involved in micro, small
and medium-sized enterprises and, in some cases, have become more dominant in the expanding informal sector. Due to, *inter alia*, difficult economic
situations and a lack of bargaining power resulting from gender inequality,
many women have been forced to accept low pay and poor working conditions
and thus have often become preferred workers. On the other hand, women
have entered the workforce increasingly by choice when they have become
aware of and demanded their rights. Some have succeeded in entering and
advancing in the workplace and improving their pay and working conditions.
However, women have been particularly affected by the economic situation
and restructuring processes, which have changed the nature of employment
and, in some cases, have led to a loss of jobs, even for professional and skilled
women. In addition, many women have entered the informal sector owing to
the lack of other opportunities. Women's participation and gender concerns
are still largely absent from and should be integrated in the policy formulation
process of the multilateral institutions that define the terms and, in cooperation with Governments, set the goals of structural adjustment programmes,
loans and grants.

152. Discrimination in education and training, hiring and remuneration,
promotion and horizontal mobility practices, as well as inflexible working
conditions, lack of access to productive resources and inadequate sharing of
family responsibilities, combined with a lack of or insufficient services such as
child care, continue to restrict employment, economic, professional and other

opportunities and mobility for women and make their involvement stressful. Moreover, attitudinal obstacles inhibit women's participation in developing economic policy and in some regions restrict the access of women and girls to education and training for economic management.

153. Women's share in the labour force continues to rise and almost every-where women are working more outside the household, although there has not been a parallel lightening of responsibility for unremunerated work in the household and community. Women's income is becoming increasingly necessary to households of all types. In some regions, there has been a growth in women's entrepreneurship and other self-reliant activities, particularly in the informal sector. In many countries, women are the majority of workers in non-standard work, such as temporary, casual, multiple part-time, contract and home-based employment.

154. Women migrant workers, including domestic workers, contribute to the economy of the sending country through their remittances and also to the economy of the receiving country through their participation in the labour force. However, in many receiving countries, migrant women experience higher levels of unemployment compared with both non-migrant workers and male migrant workers.

155. Insufficient attention to gender analysis has meant that women's contributions and concerns remain too often ignored in economic structures, such as financial markets and institutions, labour markets, economics as an academic discipline, economic and social infrastructure, taxation and social security systems, as well as in families and households. As a result, many policies and programmes may continue to contribute to inequalities between women and men. Where progress has been made in integrating gender perspectives, programme and policy effectiveness has also been enhanced.

156. Although many women have advanced in economic structures, for the majority of women, particularly those who face additional barriers, continuing obstacles have hindered their ability to achieve economic autonomy and to ensure sustainable livelihoods for themselves and their dependants. Women are active in a variety of economic areas, which they often combine, ranging from wage labour and subsistence farming and fishing to the informal sector. However, legal and customary barriers to ownership of or access to land, natural resources, capital, credit, technology and other means of production, as well as wage differentials, contribute to impeding the economic progress of women. Women contribute to development not only through remunerated work but also through a great deal of unremunerated work. On the one hand, women participate in the production of goods and services for the market and household consumption, in agriculture, food production or family enterprises. Though included in the United Nations System of National Accounts and therefore in international standards for labour statistics, this unremunerated work—particularly that related to agriculture—is often undervalued and under-recorded. On the other hand, women still also perform the great majority of unremunerated domestic work and community work, such as caring for children and older persons, preparing food for the family, protecting the environment and providing voluntary assistance to vulnerable and disadvantaged individuals and groups. This work is often not measured in quantitative terms and is not valued in national accounts. Women's contribution to development is seriously underestimated, and thus its social recognition is limited. The full visibility of the type, extent and distribution of this unremunerated work will also contribute to a better sharing of responsibilities.

157. Although some new employment opportunities have been created for women as a result of the globalization of the economy, there are also trends that have exacerbated inequalities between women and men. At the same time, globalization, including economic integration, can create pressures on the employment situation of women to adjust to new circumstances and to find new sources of employment as patterns of trade change. More analysis needs to be done of the impact of globalization on women's economic status.

158. These trends have been characterized by low wages, little or no labour standards protection, poor working conditions, particularly with regard to women's occupational health and safety, low skill levels, and a lack of job security and social security, in both the formal and informal sectors. Women's unemployment is a serious and increasing problem in many countries and sectors. Young workers in the informal and rural sectors and migrant female workers remain the least protected by labour and immigration laws. Women, particularly those who are heads of households with young children, are limited in their employment opportunities for reasons that include inflexible working conditions and inadequate sharing, by men and by society, of family responsibilities.

159. In countries that are undergoing fundamental political, economic and social transformation, the skills of women, if better utilized, could constitute a major contribution to the economic life of their respective countries. Their input should continue to be developed and supported and their potential further realized.

160. Lack of employment in the private sector and reductions in public services and public service jobs have affected women disproportionately. In some countries, women take on more unpaid work, such as the care of children and those who are ill or elderly, compensating for lost household income, particularly when public services are not available. In many cases, employment creation strategies have not paid sufficient attention to occupations and sectors where women predominate; nor have they adequately promoted the access of women to those occupations and sectors that are traditionally male.

161. For those women in paid work, many experience obstacles that prevent them from achieving their potential. While some are increasingly found in lower levels of management, attitudinal discrimination often prevents them from being promoted further. The experience of sexual harassment is an affront to a worker's dignity and prevents women from making a contribution commensurate with their abilities. The lack of a family-friendly work environment, including a lack of appropriate and affordable child care, and inflexible working hours further prevent women from achieving their full potential.

162. In the private sector, including transnational and national enterprises, women are largely absent from management and policy levels, denoting discriminatory hiring and promotion policies and practices. The unfavourable work environment as well as the limited number of employment opportunities available have led many women to seek alternatives. Women have increasingly become self-employed and owners and managers of micro, small and medium-scale enterprises. The expansion of the informal sector, in many countries, and of self-organized and independent enterprises is in large part due to women, whose collaborative, self-help and traditional practices and initiatives in production and trade represent a vital economic resource. When they gain access to and control over capital, credit and other resources, technology and training, women can increase production, marketing and income for sustainable development.

163. Taking into account the fact that continuing inequalities and noticeable progress coexist, rethinking employment policies is necessary in order to integrate the gender perspective and to draw attention to a wider range of opportunities as well as to address any negative gender implications of current patterns of work and employment. To realize fully equality between women and men in their contribution to the economy, active efforts are required for equal recognition and appreciation of the influence that the work, experience, knowledge and values of both women and men have in society.

164. In addressing the economic potential and independence of women, Governments and other actors should promote an active and visible policy of mainstreaming a gender perspective in all policies and programmes so that before decisions are taken, an analysis is made of the effects on women and men, respectively.

Strategic objective F.1. *Promote women's economic rights and independence, including access to employment, appropriate working conditions and control over economic resources*

Actions to be taken

165. By Governments:

(a) Enact and enforce legislation to guarantee the rights of women and men to equal pay for equal work or work of equal value;

(b) Adopt and implement laws against discrimination based on sex in the labour market, especially considering older women workers, hiring and promotion, the extension of employment benefits and social security, and working conditions;

(c) Eliminate discriminatory practices by employers and take appropriate measures in consideration of women's reproductive role and functions, such as the denial of employment and dismissal due to pregnancy or breast-feeding, or requiring proof of contraceptive use, and take effective measures to ensure that pregnant women, women on maternity leave or women re-entering the labour market after childbearing are not discriminated against;

(d) Devise mechanisms and take positive action to enable women to gain access to full and equal participation in the formulation of policies and definition of structures through such bodies as ministries of finance and trade, national economic commissions, economic research institutes and other key agencies, as well as through their participation in appropriate international bodies;

(e) Undertake legislation and administrative reforms to give women equal rights with men to economic resources, including access to ownership and control over land and other forms of property, credit, inheritance, natural resources and appropriate new technology;

(f) Conduct reviews of national income and inheritance tax and social security systems to eliminate any existing bias against women;

(g) Seek to develop a more comprehensive knowledge of work and employ-ment through, *inter alia*, efforts to measure and better understand the type, extent and distribution of unremunerated work, particularly work in caring for dependants and unremunerated work done for family farms or businesses, and encourage the sharing and dissemination of information on studies and experience in this field, including the development of methods for assessing its value in quantitative terms, for possible reflection in accounts that may be produced separately from, but consistent with, core national accounts;

(h) Review and amend laws governing the operation of financial institutions to ensure that they provide services to women and men on an equal basis;

(i) Facilitate, at appropriate levels, more open and transparent budget processes;

(j) Revise and implement national policies that support the traditional savings, credit and lending mechanisms for women;

(k) Seek to ensure that national policies related to international and re-gional trade agreements do not have an adverse impact on women's new and traditional economic activities;

(l) Ensure that all corporations, including transnational corporations, com-ply with national laws and codes, social security regulations, applicable inter-national agreements, instruments and conventions, including those related to the environment, and other relevant laws;

(m) Adjust employment policies to facilitate the restructuring of work patterns in order to promote the sharing of family responsibilities;

(n) Establish mechanisms and other forums to enable women entrepreneurs and women workers to contribute to the formulation of policies and pro-grammes being developed by economic ministries and financial institutions;

(o) Enact and enforce equal opportunity laws, take positive action and ensure compliance by the public and private sectors through various means;

(p) Use gender-impact analyses in the development of macro and micro-economic and social policies in order to monitor such impact and restructure policies in cases where harmful impact occurs;

(q) Promote gender-sensitive policies and measures to empower women as equal partners with men in technical, managerial and entrepreneurial fields;

(r) Reform laws or enact national policies that support the establishment of labour laws to ensure the protection of all women workers, including safe work practices, the right to organize and access to justice.

Strategic objective F.2. _Facilitate women's equal access to resources, employment, markets and trade_

Actions to be taken

166. By Governments:

(a) Promote and support women's self-employment and the development of small enterprises, and strengthen women's access to credit and capital on appropriate terms equal to those of men through the scaling-up of institutions dedicated to promoting women's entrepreneurship, including, as appropriate, non-traditional and mutual credit schemes, as well as innovative linkages with financial institutions;

(b) Strengthen the incentive role of the State as employer to develop a policy of equal opportunities for women and men;

(c) Enhance, at the national and local levels, rural women's income-generating potential by facilitating their equal access to and control over productive resources, land, credit, capital, property rights, development programmes and cooperative structures;

(d) Promote and strengthen micro-enterprises, new small businesses, cooperative enterprises, expanded markets and other employment opportunities and, where appropriate, facilitate the transition from the informal to the formal sector, especially in rural areas;

(e) Create and modify programmes and policies that recognize and strengthen women's vital role in food security and provide paid and unpaid women producers, especially those involved in food production, such as farming, fishing and aquaculture, as well as urban enterprises, with equal access to appropriate technologies, transportation, extension services, marketing and credit facilities at the local and community levels;

(f) Establish appropriate mechanisms and encourage intersectoral institutions that enable women's cooperatives to optimize access to necessary services;

(g) Increase the proportion of women extension workers and other government personnel who provide technical assistance or administer economic programmes;

(h) Review, reformulate, if necessary, and implement policies, including business, commercial and contract law and government regulations, to ensure that they do not discriminate against micro, small and medium-scale enterprises owned by women in rural and urban areas;

(i) Analyse, advise on, coordinate and implement policies that integrate the needs and interests of employed, self-employed and entrepreneurial women into sectoral and inter-ministerial policies, programmes and budgets;

(j) Ensure equal access for women to effective job training, retraining, counselling and placement services that are not limited to traditional employment areas;

(k) Remove policy and regulatory obstacles faced by women in social and development programmes that discourage private and individual initiative;

(l) Safeguard and promote respect for basic workers' rights, including the prohibition of forced labour and child labour, freedom of association and the right to organize and bargain collectively, equal remuneration for men and women for work of equal value and non-discrimination in employment, fully implementing the conventions of the International Labour Organization in the case of States Parties to those conventions and, taking into account the principles embodied in the case of those countries that are not parties to those conventions in order to achieve truly sustained economic growth and sustainable development.

167. By Governments, central banks and national development banks, and private banking institutions, as appropriate:

(a) Increase the participation of women, including women entrepreneurs, in advisory boards and other forums to enable women entrepreneurs from all sectors and their organizations to contribute to the formulation and review of policies and programmes being developed by economic ministries and banking institutions;

(b) Mobilize the banking sector to increase lending and refinancing through incentives and the development of intermediaries that serve the needs of women entrepreneurs and producers in both rural and urban areas, and include women in their leadership, planning and decision-making;

(c) Structure services to reach rural and urban women involved in micro, small and medium-scale enterprises, with special attention to young women, low-income women, those belonging to ethnic and racial minorities, and indigenous women who lack access to capital and assets; and expand women's access to financial markets by identifying and encouraging financial supervisory and regulatory reforms that support financial institutions' direct and indirect efforts to better meet the credit and other financial needs of the micro, small and medium-scale enterprises of women;

(d) Ensure that women's priorities are included in public investment programmes for economic infrastructure, such as water and sanitation, electrification and energy conservation, transport and road construction; promote greater involvement of women beneficiaries at the project planning and implementation stages to ensure access to jobs and contracts.

168. By Governments and non-governmental organizations:

(a) Pay special attention to women's needs when disseminating market, trade and resource information and provide appropriate training in these fields;

(b) Encourage community economic development strategies that build on partnerships among Governments, and encourage members of civil society to create jobs and address the social circumstances of individuals, families and communities.

169. By multilateral funders and regional development banks, as well as bilateral and private funding agencies, at the international, regional and subregional levels:

(a) Review, where necessary reformulate, and implement policies, programmes and projects, to ensure that a higher proportion of resources reach women in rural and remote areas;

(b) Develop flexible funding arrangements to finance intermediary institutions that target women's economic activities, and promote self-sufficiency and increased capacity in and profitability of women's economic enterprises;

(c) Develop strategies to consolidate and strengthen their assistance to the micro, small and medium-scale enterprise sector, in order to enhance the opportunities for women to participate fully and equally and work together to coordinate and enhance the effectiveness of this sector, drawing upon expertise and financial resources from within their own organizations as well as from bilateral agencies, Governments and non-governmental organizations.

170. By international, multilateral and bilateral development cooperation organizations:

Support, through the provision of capital and/or resources, financial institutions that serve low-income, small and micro-scale women entrepreneurs and producers in both the formal and informal sectors.

171. By Governments and/or multilateral financial institutions:

Review rules and procedures of formal national and international financial institutions that obstruct replication of the Grameen Bank prototype, which provides credit facilities to rural women.

172. By international organizations:

Provide adequate support for programmes and projects designed to promote sustainable and productive entrepreneurial activities among women, in particular the disadvantaged.

Strategic objective F.3. *Provide business services, training and access to markets, information and technology, particularly to low-income women*

Actions to be taken

173. By Governments in cooperation with non-governmental organizations and the private sector:

(a) Provide public infrastructure to ensure equal market access for women and men entrepreneurs;

(b) Develop programmes that provide training and retraining, particularly in new technologies, and affordable services to women in business management, product development, financing, production and quality control, marketing and the legal aspects of business;

(c) Provide outreach programmes to inform low-income and poor women, particularly in rural and remote areas, of opportunities for market and technology access, and provide assistance in taking advantage of such opportunities;

(d) Create non-discriminatory support services, including investment funds for women's businesses, and target women, particularly low-income women, in trade promotion programmes;

(e) Disseminate information about successful women entrepreneurs in both traditional and non-traditional economic activities and the skills necessary to achieve success, and facilitate networking and the exchange of information;

(f) Take measures to ensure equal access of women to ongoing training in the workplace, including unemployed women, single parents, women re-entering the labour market after an extended temporary exit from employment owing to family responsibilities and other causes, and women displaced by new forms of production or by retrenchment, and increase incentives to enterprises to expand the number of vocational and training centres that provide training for women in non-traditional areas;

(g) Provide affordable support services, such as high-quality, flexible and affordable child-care services, that take into account the needs of working men and women.

174. By local, national, regional and international business organizations and non-governmental organizations concerned with women's issues:

Advocate, at all levels, for the promotion and support of women's businesses and enterprises, including those in the informal sector, and the equal access of women to productive resources.

Strategic objective F.4. *Strengthen women's economic capacity and commercial networks*

Actions to be taken

175. By Governments:

(a) Adopt policies that support business organizations, non-governmental organizations, cooperatives, revolving loan funds, credit unions, grass-roots organizations, women's self-help groups and other groups in order to provide services to women entrepreneurs in rural and urban areas;

(b) Integrate a gender perspective into all economic restructuring and structural adjustment policies and design programmes for women who are affected by economic restructuring, including structural adjustment programmes, and for women who work in the informal sector;

(c) Adopt policies that create an enabling environment for women's self-help groups, workers' organizations and cooperatives through non-conventional forms of support and by recognizing the right to freedom of association and the right to organize;

(d) Support programmes that enhance the self-reliance of special groups of women, such as young women, with disabilities, elderly women and women belonging to racial and ethnic minorities;

(e) Promote gender equality through the promotion of women's studies and through the use of the results of studies and gender research in all fields, including the economic, scientific and technological fields;

(f) Support the economic activities of indigenous women, taking into account their traditional knowledge, so as to improve their situation and development;

(g) Adopt policies to extend or maintain the protection of labour laws and social security provisions for those who do paid work in the home;

(h) Recognize and encourage the contribution of research by women scientists and technologists;

(i) Ensure that policies and regulations do not discriminate against micro, small and medium-scale enterprises run by women.

176. By financial intermediaries, national training institutes, credit unions, non-governmental organizations, women's associations, professional organizations and the private sector, as appropriate:

(a) Provide, at the national, regional and international levels, training in a variety of business-related and financial management and technical skills to enable women, especially young women, to participate in economic policy-making at those levels;

(b) Provide business services, including marketing and trade information, product design and innovation, technology transfer and quality, to women's business enterprises, including those in export sectors of the economy;

(c) Promote technical and commercial links and establish joint ventures among women entrepreneurs at the national, regional and international levels to support community-based initiatives;

(d) Strengthen the participation of women, including marginalized women, in production and marketing cooperatives by providing marketing and financial support, especially in rural and remote areas;

(e) Promote and strengthen women's micro-enterprises, new small businesses, cooperative enterprises, expanded markets and other employment opportunities and, where appropriate, facilitate the transition from the informal to the formal sector, in rural and urban areas;

(f) Invest capital and develop investment portfolios to finance women's business enterprises;

(g) Give adequate attention to providing technical assistance, advisory services, training and retraining for women connected with the entry to the market economy;

(h) Support credit networks and innovative ventures, including traditional savings schemes;

(i) Provide networking arrangements for entrepreneurial women, including opportunities for the mentoring of inexperienced women by the more experienced;

(j) Encourage community organizations and public authorities to establish loan pools for women entrepreneurs, drawing on successful small-scale cooperative models.

177. By the private sector, including transnational and national corporations:

(a) Adopt policies and establish mechanisms to grant contracts on a non-discriminatory basis;

(b) Recruit women for leadership, decision-making and management and provide training programmes, all on an equal basis with men;

(c) Observe national labour, environment, consumer, health and safety laws, particularly those that affect women.

Strategic objective F.5. *Eliminate occupational segregation and all forms of employment discrimination*

Actions to be taken

178. By Governments, employers, employees, trade unions and women's organizations:

(a) Implement and enforce laws and regulations and encourage voluntary codes of conduct that ensure that international labour standards, such as International Labour Organization Convention No. 100 on equal pay and workers' rights, apply equally to female and male workers;

(b) Enact and enforce laws and introduce implementing measures, including means of redress and access to justice in cases of non-compliance, to prohibit direct and indirect discrimination on grounds of sex, including by reference to marital or family status, in relation to access to employment, conditions of employment, including training, promotion, health and safety, as well as termination of employment and social security of workers, including legal protection against sexual and racial harassment;

(c) Enact and enforce laws and develop workplace policies against gender discrimination in the labour market, especially considering older women workers, in hiring and promotion, and in the extension of employment benefits and social security, as well as regarding discriminatory working conditions and sexual harassment; mechanisms should be developed for the regular review and monitoring of such laws;

(d) Eliminate discriminatory practices by employers on the basis of women's reproductive roles and functions, including refusal of employment and dismissal of women due to pregnancy and breast-feeding responsibilities;

(e) Develop and promote employment programmes and services for women entering and/or re-entering the labour market, especially poor urban, rural and young women, the self-employed and those negatively affected by structural adjustment;

(f) Implement and monitor positive public- and private-sector employment, equity and positive action programmes to address systemic discrimination against women in the labour force, in particular women with disabilities and women belonging to other disadvantaged groups, with respect to hiring, retention and promotion, and vocational training of women in all sectors;

(g) Eliminate occupational segregation, especially by promoting the equal participation of women in highly skilled jobs and senior management positions, and through other measures, such as counselling and placement, that stimulate their on-the-job career development and upward mobility in the labour market, and by stimulating the diversification of occupational choices by both women and men; encourage women to take up non-traditional jobs, especially in science and technology, and encourage men to seek employment in the social sector;

(h) Recognize collective bargaining as a right and as an important mechanism for eliminating wage inequality for women and to improve working conditions;

(i) Promote the election of women trade union officials and ensure that trade union officials elected to represent women are given job protection and physical security in connection with the discharge of their functions;

(j) Ensure access to and develop special programmes to enable women with disabilities to obtain and retain employment, and ensure access to education and training at all proper levels, in accordance with the Standard Rules on the Equalization of Opportunities for Persons with Disabilities;[30] adjust working conditions, to the extent possible, in order to suit the needs of women with disabilities, who should be assured legal protection against unfounded job loss on account of their disabilities;

(k) Increase efforts to close the gap between women's and men's pay, take steps to implement the principle of equal remuneration for equal work of equal value by strengthening legislation, including compliance with international labour laws and standards, and encourage job evaluation schemes with gender-neutral criteria;

(l) Establish and/or strengthen mechanisms to adjudicate matters relating to wage discrimination;

(m) Set specific target dates for eliminating all forms of child labour that are contrary to accepted international standards and ensure the full enforcement of relevant existing laws and, where appropriate, enact the legislation necessary to implement the Convention on the Rights of the Child and International Labour Organization standards, ensuring the protection of working children, in particular, street children, through the provision of appropriate health, education and other social services;

(n) Ensure that strategies to eliminate child labour also address the excessive demands made on some girls for unpaid work in their household and other households, where applicable;

(o) Review, analyse and, where appropriate, reformulate the wage structures in female-dominated professions, such as teaching, nursing and child care, with a view to raising their low status and earnings;

(p) Facilitate the productive employment of documented migrant women (including women who have been determined refugees according to the 1951 Convention relating to the Status of Refugees) through greater recognition of foreign education and credentials and by adopting an integrated approach to labour market training that incorporates language training.

Strategic objective F.6. *Promote harmonization of work and family respon-sibilities for women and men*

Actions to be taken

179. By Governments:

(a) Adopt policies to ensure the appropriate protection of labour laws and social security benefits for part-time, temporary, seasonal and home-based workers; promote career development based on work conditions that harmo-nize work and family responsibilities;

(b) Ensure that full and part-time work can be freely chosen by women and men on an equal basis, and consider appropriate protection for atypical workers in terms of access to employment, working conditions and social security;

(c) Ensure, through legislation, incentives and/or encouragement, oppor-tunities for women and men to take job-protected parental leave and to have parental benefits; promote the equal sharing of responsibilities for the family by men and women, including through appropriate legislation, incentives and/ or encouragement, and also promote the facilitation of breast-feeding for working mothers;

(d) Develop policies, *inter alia*, in education to change attitudes that rein-force the division of labour based on gender in order to promote the concept of shared family responsibility for work in the home, particularly in relation to children and elder care;

(e) Improve the development of, and access to, technologies that facilitate occupational as well as domestic work, encourage self-support, generate in-come, transform gender-prescribed roles within the productive process and enable women to move out of low-paying jobs;

(f) Examine a range of policies and programmes, including social security legislation and taxation systems, in accordance with national priorities and policies, to determine how to promote gender equality and flexibility in the way people divide their time between and derive benefits from education and training, paid employment, family responsibilities, volunteer activity and other socially useful forms of work, rest and leisure.

180. By Governments, the private sector and non-governmental organiza-tions, trade unions and the United Nations, as appropriate:

(a) Adopt appropriate measures involving relevant governmental bodies and employers' and employees' associations so that women and men are able to take temporary leave from employment, have transferable employment and retirement benefits and make arrangements to modify work hours without sacrificing their prospects for development and advancement at work and in their careers;

(b) Design and provide educational programmes through innovative media campaigns and school and community education programmes to raise aware-ness on gender equality and non-stereotyped gender roles of women and men within the family; provide support services and facilities, such as on-site child care at workplaces and flexible working arrangements;

(c) Enact and enforce laws against sexual and other forms of harassment in all workplaces.

G. Women in power and decision-making

181. The Universal Declaration of Human Rights states that everyone has the right to take part in the Government of his/her country. The empowerment and autonomy of women and the improvement of women's social, economic and political status is essential for the achievement of both transparent and accountable government and administration and sustainable development in all areas of life. The power relations that prevent women from leading fulfilling lives operate at many levels of society, from the most personal to the highly public. Achieving the goal of equal participation of women and men in decision-making will provide a balance that more accurately reflects the composition of society and is needed in order to strengthen democracy and promote its proper functioning. Equality in political decision-making performs a leverage function without which it is highly unlikely that a real integration of the equality dimension in government policy-making is feasible. In this respect, women's equal participation in political life plays a pivotal role in the general process of the advancement of women. Women's equal participation in decision-making is not only a demand for simple justice or democracy but can also be seen as a necessary condition for women's interests to be taken into account. Without the active participation of women and the incorporation of women's perspective at all levels of decision-making, the goals of equality, development and peace cannot be achieved.

182. Despite the widespread movement towards democratization in most countries, women are largely underrepresented at most levels of government, especially in ministerial and other executive bodies, and have made little progress in attaining political power in legislative bodies or in achieving the target endorsed by the Economic and Social Council of having 30 percent women in positions at decision-making levels by 1995. Globally, only 10 percent of the members of legislative bodies and a lower percentage of ministerial positions are now held by women. Indeed, some countries, including those that are undergoing fundamental political, economic and social changes, have seen a significant decrease in the number of women represented in legislative bodies. Although women make up at least half of the electorate in almost all countries and have attained the right to vote and hold office in almost all States Members of the United Nations, women continue to be seriously underrepresented as candidates for public office. The traditional working patterns of many political parties and government structures continue to be barriers to women's participation in public life. Women may be discouraged from seeking political office by discriminatory attitudes and practices, family and child-care responsibilities, and the high cost of seeking and holding public office. Women in politics and decision-making positions in Governments and legislative bodies contribute to redefining political priorities, placing new items on the political agenda that reflect and address women's gender-specific concerns, values and experiences, and providing new perspectives on mainstream political issues.

183. Women have demonstrated considerable leadership in community and informal organizations, as well as in public office. However, socialization and negative stereotyping of women and men, including stereotyping through the media, reinforces the tendency for political decision-making to remain the domain of men. Likewise, the underrepresentation of women in decision-making positions in the areas of art, culture, sports, the media, education, religion and the law have prevented women from having a significant impact on many key institutions.

184. Owing to their limited access to the traditional avenues to power, such as the decision-making bodies of political parties, employer organizations and trade unions, women have gained access to power through alternative structures, particularly in the non-governmental organization sector. Through non-governmental organizations and grass-roots organizations, women have been able to articulate their interests and concerns and have placed women's issues on the national, regional and international agendas.

185. Inequality in the public arena can often start with discriminatory attitudes and practices and unequal power relations between women and men within the family, as defined in paragraph 29 above. The unequal division of labour and responsibilities within households based on unequal power relations also limits women's potential to find the time and develop the skills required for participation in decision-making in wider public forums. A more equal sharing of those responsibilities between women and men not only provides a better quality of life for women and their daughters but also enhances their opportunities to shape and design public policy, practice and expenditure so that their interests may be recognized and addressed. Non-formal networks and patterns of decision-making at the local community level that reflect a dominant male ethos restrict women's ability to participate equally in political, economic and social life.

186. The low proportion of women among economic and political decision makers at the local, national, regional and international levels reflects structural and attitudinal barriers that need to be addressed through positive measures. Governments, transnational and national corporations, the mass media, banks, academic and scientific institutions, and regional and international organizations, including those in the United Nations system, do not make full use of women's talents as top-level managers, policy makers, diplomats and negotiators.

187. The equitable distribution of power and decision-making at all levels is dependent on Governments and other actors undertaking statistical gender analysis and mainstreaming a gender perspective in policy development and the implementation of programmes. Equality in decision-making is essential to the empowerment of women. In some countries, affirmative action has led to 33.3 percent or larger representation in local and national Governments.

188. National, regional and international statistical institutions still have insufficient knowledge of how to present the issues related to the equal treatment of women and men in the economic and social spheres. In particular, there is insufficient use of existing databases and methodologies in the important sphere of decision-making.

189. In addressing the inequality between men and women in the sharing of power and decision-making at all levels, Governments and other actors should promote an active and visible policy of mainstreaming a gender perspective in all policies and programmes so that before decisions are taken, an analysis is made of the effects on women and men, respectively.

Strategic objective G.1. *Take measures to ensure women's equal access to and full participation in power structures and decision-making*

Actions to be taken

190. By Governments:

(a) Commit themselves to establishing the goal of gender balance in governmental bodies and committees, as well as in public administrative entities, and in the judiciary, including, *inter alia*, setting specific targets and implementing measures to substantially increase the number of women with a view to achieving equal representation of women and men, if necessary through positive action, in all governmental and public administration positions;

(b) Take measures, including, where appropriate, in electoral systems that encourage political parties to integrate women in elective and non-elective public positions in the same proportion and at the same levels as men;

(c) Protect and promote the equal rights of women and men to engage in political activities and to freedom of association, including membership in political parties and trade unions;

(d) Review the differential impact of electoral systems on the political representation of women in elected bodies and consider, where appropriate, the adjustment or reform of those systems;

(e) Monitor and evaluate progress in the representation of women through the regular collection, analysis and dissemination of quantitative and qualitative data on women and men at all levels in various decision-making positions in the public and private sectors, and disseminate data on the number of women and men employed at various levels in Governments on a yearly basis; ensure that women and men have equal access to the full range of public appointments and set up mechanisms within governmental structures for monitoring progress in this field;

(f) Support non-governmental organizations and research institutes that conduct studies on women's participation in and impact on decision-making and the decision-making environment;

(g) Encourage greater involvement of indigenous women in decision-making at all levels;

(h) Encourage and, where appropriate, ensure that government-funded organizations adopt non-discriminatory policies and practices in order to increase the number and raise the position of women in their organizations;

(i) Recognize that shared work and parental responsibilities between women and men promote women's increased participation in public life, and take appropriate measures to achieve this, including measures to reconcile family and professional life;

(j) Aim at gender balance in the lists of national candidates nominated for election or appointment to United Nations bodies, specialized agencies and other autonomous organizations of the United Nations system, particularly for posts at the senior level.

191. By political parties:

(a) Consider examining party structures and procedures to remove all barriers that directly or indirectly discriminate against the participation of women;

(b) Consider developing initiatives that allow women to participate fully in all internal policy-making structures and appointive and electoral nominating processes;

(c) Consider incorporating gender issues in their political agenda, taking measures to ensure that women can participate in the leadership of political parties on an equal basis with men.

192. By Governments, national bodies, the private sector, political parties, trade unions, employers' organizations, research and academic institutions, subregional and regional bodies and non-governmental and international organizations:

(a) Take positive action to build a critical mass of women leaders, executives and managers in strategic decision-making positions;

(b) Create or strengthen, as appropriate, mechanisms to monitor women's access to senior levels of decision-making;

(c) Review the criteria for recruitment and appointment to advisory and decision-making bodies and promotion to senior positions to ensure that such criteria are relevant and do not discriminate against women;

(d) Encourage efforts by non-governmental organizations, trade unions and the private sector to achieve equality between women and men in their ranks, including equal participation in their decision-making bodies and in negotiations in all areas and at all levels;

(e) Develop communications strategies to promote public debate on the new roles of men and women in society, and in the family as defined in paragraph 29 above;

(f) Restructure recruitment and career-development programmes to ensure that all women, especially young women, have equal access to managerial, entrepreneurial, technical and leadership training, including on-the-job training;

(g) Develop career advancement programmes for women of all ages that include career planning, tracking, mentoring, coaching, training and retraining;

(h) Encourage and support the participation of women's non-governmental organizations in United Nations conferences and their preparatory processes;

(i) Aim at and support gender balance in the composition of delegations to the United Nations and other international forums.

193. By the United Nations:

(a) Implement existing and adopt new employment policies and measures in order to achieve overall gender equality, particularly at the Professional level and above, by the year 2000, with due regard to the importance of recruiting staff on as wide a geographical basis as possible, in conformity with Article 101, paragraph 3, of the Charter of the United Nations;

(b) Develop mechanisms to nominate women candidates for appointment to senior posts in the United Nations, the specialized agencies and other organizations and bodies of the United Nations system;

(c) Continue to collect and disseminate quantitative and qualitative data on women and men in decision-making and analyse their differential impact on decision-making and monitor progress towards achieving the Secretary-General's target of having women hold 50 percent of managerial and decision-making positions by the year 2000.

194. By women's organizations, non-governmental organizations, trade unions, social partners, producers, and industrial and professional organizations:

(a) Build and strengthen solidarity among women through information, education and sensitization activities;

(b) Advocate at all levels to enable women to influence political, economic and social decisions, processes and systems, and work towards seeking accountability from elected representatives on their commitment to gender concerns;

(c) Establish, consistent with data protection legislation, databases on women and their qualification for use in appointing women to senior decision-making and advisory positions, for dissemination to Governments, regional and international organizations and private enterprise, political parties and other relevant bodies.

Strategic objective G.2. *Increase women's capacity to participate in decision-making and leadership*

Actions to be taken

195. By Governments, national bodies, the private sector, political parties, trade unions, employers' organizations, subregional and regional bodies, non-governmental and international organizations and educational institutions:

(a) Provide leadership and self-esteem training to assist women and girls, particularly those with special needs, women with disabilities and women belonging to racial and ethnic minorities to strengthen their self-esteem and to encourage them to take decision-making positions;

(b) Have transparent criteria for decision-making positions and ensure that the selecting bodies have a gender-balanced composition;

(c) Create a system of mentoring for inexperienced women and, in particular, offer training, including training in leadership and decision-making, public speaking and self-assertion, as well as in political campaigning;

(d) Provide gender-sensitive training for women and men to promote nondiscriminatory working relationships and respect for diversity in work and management styles;

(e) Develop mechanisms and training to encourage women to participate in the electoral process, political activities and other leadership areas.

H. Institutional mechanisms for the advancement of women

196. National machineries for the advancement of women have been established in almost every Member State to, *inter alia*, design, promote the implementation of, execute, monitor, evaluate, advocate and mobilize support for policies that promote the advancement of women. National machineries are diverse in form and uneven in their effectiveness, and in some cases have declined. Often marginalized in national government structures, these mechanisms are frequently hampered by unclear mandates, lack of adequate staff, training, data and sufficient resources, and insufficient support from national political leadership.

197. At the regional and international levels, mechanisms and institutions to promote the advancement of women as an integral part of mainstream political, economic, social and cultural development, and of initiatives on development and human rights, encounter similar problems emanating from a lack of commitment at the highest levels.

198. Successive international conferences have underscored the need to take gender factors into account in policy and programme planning. However, in many instances this has not been done.

199. Regional bodies concerned with the advancement of women have been strengthened, together with international machinery, such as the Commission on the Status of Women and the Committee on the Elimination of Discrimination against Women. However, the limited resources available continue to impede full implementation of their mandates.

200. Methodologies for conducting gender-based analysis in policies and programmes and for dealing with the differential effects of policies on women and men have been developed in many organizations and are available for application but are often not being applied or are not being applied consistently.

201. A national machinery for the advancement of women is the central policy-coordinating unit inside government. Its main task is to support government-wide mainstreaming of a gender-equality perspective in all policy areas. The necessary conditions for an effective functioning of such national machineries include:

(a) Location at the highest possible level in the Government, falling under the responsibility of a Cabinet minister;

(b) Institutional mechanisms or processes that facilitate, as appropriate, decentralized planning, implementation and monitoring with a view to involving non-governmental organizations and community organizations from the grass-roots upwards;

(c) Sufficient resources in terms of budget and professional capacity;

(d) Opportunity to influence development of all government policies.

202. In addressing the issue of mechanisms for promoting the advancement of women, Governments and other actors should promote an active and visible policy of mainstreaming a gender perspective in all policies and programmes so that, before decisions are taken, an analysis is made of the effects on women and men, respectively.

Strategic objective H.1. *Create or strengthen national machineries and other governmental bodies*

Actions to be taken

203. By Governments:

(a) Ensure that responsibility for the advancement of women is vested in the highest possible level of government; in many cases, this could be at the level of a Cabinet minister;

(b) Based on a strong political commitment, create a national machinery, where it does not exist, and strengthen, as appropriate, existing national machineries, for the advancement of women at the highest possible level of government; it should have clearly defined mandates and authority; critical elements would be adequate resources and the ability and competence to influence policy and formulate and review legislation; among other things, it should perform policy analysis, undertake advocacy, communication, coordination and monitoring of implementation;

(c) Provide staff training in designing and analysing data from a gender perspective;

(d) Establish procedures to allow the machinery to gather information on government-wide policy issues at an early stage and continuously use it in the policy development and review process within the Government;

(e) Report, on a regular basis, to legislative bodies on the progress of efforts, as appropriate, to mainstream gender concerns, taking into account the implementation of the Platform for Action;

(f) Encourage and promote the active involvement of the broad and diverse range of institutional actors in the public, private and voluntary sectors to work for equality between women and men.

Strategic objective H.2. *Integrate gender perspectives in legislation, public policies, programmes and projects*

Actions to be taken

204. By Governments:

(a) Seek to ensure that before policy decisions are taken, an analysis of their impact on women and men, respectively, is carried out;

(b) Regularly review national policies, programmes and projects, as well as their implementation, evaluating the impact of employment and income policies in order to guarantee that women are direct beneficiaries of development and that their full contribution to development, both remunerated and unremunerated, is considered in economic policy and planning;

(c) Promote national strategies and aims on equality between women and men in order to eliminate obstacles to the exercise of women's rights and eradicate all forms of discrimination against women;

(d) Work with members of legislative bodies, as appropriate, to promote a gender perspective in all legislation and policies;

(e) Give all ministries the mandate to review policies and programmes from a gender perspective and in the light of the Platform for Action; locate the responsibility for the implementation of that mandate at the highest possible level; establish and/or strengthen an inter-ministerial coordination structure to carry out this mandate, to monitor progress and to network with relevant machineries.

205. By national machinery:

(a) Facilitate the formulation and implementation of government policies on equality between women and men, develop appropriate strategies and methodologies, and promote coordination and cooperation within the central Government in order to ensure mainstreaming of a gender perspective in all policy-making processes;

(b) Promote and establish cooperative relationships with relevant branches of government, centres for women's studies and research, academic and educational institutions, the private sector, the media, non-governmental organizations, especially women's organizations, and all other actors of civil society;

(c) Undertake activities focusing on legal reform with regard, *inter alia*, to the family, conditions of employment, social security, income tax, equal opportunity in education, positive measures to promote the advancement of women, and the perception of attitudes and a culture favourable to equality, as well as promote a gender perspective in legal policy and programming reforms;

(d) Promote the increased participation of women as both active agents and beneficiaries of the development process, which would result in an improvement in the quality of life for all;

(e) Establish direct links with national, regional and international bodies dealing with the advancement of women;

(f) Provide training and advisory assistance to government agencies in order to integrate a gender perspective in their policies and programmes.

Strategic objective H.3. *Generate and disseminate gender-disaggregated data and information for planning and evaluation*

Actions to be taken

206. By national, regional and international statistical services and relevant governmental and United Nations agencies, in cooperation with research and documentation organizations, in their respective areas of responsibility:

(a) Ensure that statistics related to individuals are collected, compiled, analysed and presented by sex and age and reflect problems, issues and questions related to women and men in society;

(b) Collect, compile, analyse and present on a regular basis data disaggregated by age, sex, socio-economic and other relevant indicators, including number of dependants, for utilization in policy and programme planning and implementation;

(c) Involve centres for women's studies and research organizations in developing and testing appropriate indicators and research methodologies to strengthen gender analysis, as well as in monitoring and evaluating the implementation of the goals of the Platform for Action;

(d) Designate or appoint staff to strengthen gender-statistics programmes and ensure coordination, monitoring and linkage to all fields of statistical work, and prepare output that integrates statistics from the various subject areas;

(e) Improve data collection on the full contribution of women and men to the economy, including their participation in the informal sector(s);

(f) Develop a more comprehensive knowledge of all forms of work and employment by:

(i) Improving data collection on the unremunerated work which is already included in the United Nations System of National Accounts, such as in agriculture, particularly subsistence agriculture, and other types of non-market production activities;

(ii) Improving measurements that at present underestimate women's unemployment and underemployment in the labour market;

(iii) Developing methods, in the appropriate forums, for assessing the value, in quantitative terms, of unremunerated work that is outside national accounts, such as caring for dependants and preparing food, for possible reflection in satellite or other official accounts that may be produced separately from but are consistent with core national accounts, with a view to recognizing the economic contribution of women and making visible the unequal distribution of remunerated and unremunerated work between women and men;

(g) Develop an international classification of activities for time-use statistics that is sensitive to the differences between women and men in remunerated and unremunerated work, and collect data disaggregated by sex. At the national level, subject to national constraints:

(i) Conduct regular time-use studies to measure, in quantitative terms, unremunerated work, including recording those activities that are performed simultaneously with remunerated or other unremunerated activities;

(ii) Measure, in quantitative terms, unremunerated work that is outside national accounts and work to improve methods to assess and accurately reflect its value in satellite or other official accounts that are separate from but consistent with core national accounts;

(h) Improve concepts and methods of data collection on the measurement of poverty among women and men, including their access to resources;

(i) Strengthen vital statistical systems and incorporate gender analysis into publications and research; give priority to gender differences in research design and in data collection and analysis in order to improve data on morbidity; and improve data collection on access to health services, including access to comprehensive sexual and reproductive health services, maternal care and family planning, with special priority for adolescent mothers and for elder care;

(j) Develop improved gender-disaggregated and age-specific data on the victims and perpetrators of all forms of violence against women, such as domestic violence, sexual harassment, rape, incest and sexual abuse, and trafficking in women and girls, as well as on violence by agents of the State;

(k) Improve concepts and methods of data collection on the participation of women and men with disabilities, including their access to resources.

207. By Governments:

(a) Ensure the regular production of a statistical publication on gender that presents and interprets topical data on women and men in a form suitable for a wide range of non-technical users;

(b) Ensure that producers and users of statistics in each country regularly review the adequacy of the official statistical system and its coverage of gender issues, and prepare a plan for needed improvements, where necessary;

(c) Develop and encourage the development of quantitative and qualitative studies by research organizations, trade unions, employers, the private sector and non-governmental organizations on the sharing of power and influence in society, including the number of women and men in senior decision-making positions in both the public and private sectors;

(d) Use more gender-sensitive data in the formulation of policy and implementation of programmes and projects.

208. By the United Nations:

(a) Promote the development of methods to find better ways to collect, collate and analyse data that may relate to the human rights of women, including violence against women, for use by all relevant United Nations bodies;

(b) Promote the further development of statistical methods to improve data that relate to women in economic, social, cultural and political development;

(c) Prepare a new issue of *The World's Women* at regular five-year intervals and distribute it widely;

(d) Assist countries, upon request, in the development of gender policies and programmes;

(e) Ensure that the relevant reports, data and publications of the Statistical Division of the United Nations Secretariat and the International Research and Training Institute for the Advancement of Women on progress at the national and international levels are transmitted to the Commission on the Status of Women in a regular and coordinated fashion.

209. By multilateral development institutions and bilateral donors:

Encourage and support the development of national capacity in developing countries and in countries with economies in transition by providing resources and technical assistance so that countries can fully measure the work done by women and men, including both remunerated and unremunerated work, and, where appropriate, use satellite or other official accounts for unremunerated work.

I. Human rights of women

210. Human rights and fundamental freedoms are the birthright of all human beings; their protection and promotion is the first responsibility of Governments.

211. The World Conference on Human Rights reaffirmed the solemn commitment of all States to fulfil their obligation to promote universal respect for, and observance and protection of, all human rights and fundamental freedoms for all, in accordance with the Charter of the United Nations, other instruments relating to human rights, and international law. The universal nature of these rights and freedoms is beyond question.

212. The promotion and protection of all human rights and fundamental freedoms must be considered as a priority objective of the United Nations, in accordance with its purposes and principles, in particular with the purpose of international cooperation. In the framework of these purposes and principles, the promotion and protection of all human rights is a legitimate concern of the international community. The international community must treat human rights globally, in a fair and equal manner, on the same footing, and with the same emphasis. The Platform for Action reaffirms the importance of ensuring the universality, objectivity and non-selectivity of the consideration of human rights issues.

213. The Platform for Action reaffirms that all human rights—civil, cultural, economic, political and social, including the right to development—are universal, indivisible, interdependent and interrelated, as expressed in the Vienna Declaration and Programme of Action adopted by the World Conference on Human Rights. The Conference reaffirmed that the human rights of women and the girl child are an inalienable, integral and indivisible part of universal human rights. The full and equal enjoyment of all human rights and fundamental freedoms by women and girls is a priority for Governments and the United Nations and is essential for the advancement of women.

214. Equal rights of men and women are explicitly mentioned in the Preamble to the Charter of the United Nations. All the major international human rights instruments include sex as one of the grounds upon which States may not discriminate.

215. Governments must not only refrain from violating the human rights of all women, but must work actively to promote and protect these rights. Recognition of the importance of the human rights of women is reflected in the fact that three quarters of the States Members of the United Nations have become parties to the Convention on the Elimination of All Forms of Discrimination against Women.

216. The World Conference on Human Rights reaffirmed clearly that the human rights of women throughout the life cycle are an inalienable, integral and indivisible part of universal human rights. The International Conference on Population and Development reaffirmed women's reproductive rights and the right to development. Both the Declaration of the Rights of the Child[31] and the Convention on the Rights of the Child[11] guarantee children's rights and uphold the principle of non-discrimination on the grounds of gender.

217. The gap between the existence of rights and their effective enjoyment derives from a lack of commitment by Governments to promoting and protecting those rights and the failure of Governments to inform women and men alike about them. The lack of appropriate recourse mechanisms at the national and international levels, and inadequate resources at both levels, compound the problem. In most countries, steps have been taken to reflect the rights guaranteed by the Convention on the Elimination of All Forms of Discrimination against Women in national law. A number of countries have established mechanisms to strengthen women's ability to exercise their rights.

218. In order to protect the human rights of women, it is necessary to avoid, as far as possible, resorting to reservations and to ensure that no reservation is incompatible with the object and purpose of the Convention or is otherwise incompatible with international treaty law. Unless the human rights of women, as defined by international human rights instruments, are fully recognized and effectively protected, applied, implemented and enforced in national law as well as in national practice in family, civil, penal, labour and commercial codes and administrative rules and regulations, they will exist in name only.

219. In those countries that have not yet become parties to the Convention on the Elimination of All Forms of Discrimination against Women and other international human rights instruments, or where reservations that are incompatible with the object or purpose of the Convention have been entered, or where national laws have not yet been revised to implement international norms and standards, women's *de jure* equality is not yet secured. Women's full enjoyment of equal rights is undermined by the discrepancies between some national legislation and international law and international instruments on human rights. Overly complex administrative procedures, lack of awareness within the judicial process and inadequate monitoring of the violation of the human rights of all women, coupled with the underrepresentation of women in justice systems, insufficient information on existing rights and persistent attitudes and practices perpetuate women's de facto inequality. De facto inequality is also perpetuated by the lack of enforcement of, *inter alia*, family, civil, penal, labour and commercial laws or codes, or administrative rules and regulations intended to ensure women's full enjoyment of human rights and fundamental freedoms.

220. Every person should be entitled to participate in, contribute to and enjoy cultural, economic, political and social development. In many cases women and girls suffer discrimination in the allocation of economic and social resources. This directly violates their economic, social and cultural rights.

221. The human rights of all women and the girl child must form an integral part of United Nations human rights activities. Intensified efforts are needed to integrate the equal status and the human rights of all women and girls into the mainstream of United Nations system-wide activities and to address these issues regularly and systematically throughout relevant bodies and mechanisms. This requires, *inter alia,* improved cooperation and coordination between the Commission on the Status of Women, the United Nations High Commissioner for Human Rights, the Commission on Human Rights, including its special and thematic rapporteurs, independent experts, working groups and its Subcommission on Prevention of Discrimination and Protection of Minorities, the Commission on Sustainable Development, the Commission for Social Development, the Commission on Crime Prevention and Criminal Justice, and the Committee on the Elimination of Discrimination against Women and other human rights treaty bodies, and all relevant entities of the United Nations system, including the specialized agencies. Cooperation is also needed to strengthen, rationalize and streamline the United Nations human rights system and to promote its effectiveness and efficiency, taking into account the need to avoid unnecessary duplication and overlapping of mandates and tasks.

222. If the goal of full realization of human rights for all is to be achieved, international human rights instruments must be applied in such a way as to take more clearly into consideration the systematic and systemic nature of discrimination against women that gender analysis has clearly indicated.

223. Bearing in mind the Programme of Action of the International Conference on Population and Development[14] and the Vienna Declaration and Programme of Action[2] adopted by the World Conference on Human Rights, the Fourth World Conference on Women reaffirms that reproductive rights rest on the recognition of the basic right of all couples and individuals to decide freely and responsibly the number, spacing and timing of their children and to have the information and means to do so, and the right to attain the highest standard of sexual and reproductive health. It also includes their right to make decisions concerning reproduction free of discrimination, coercion and violence, as expressed in human rights documents.

224. Violence against women both violates and impairs or nullifies the enjoyment by women of human rights and fundamental freedoms. Taking into account the Declaration on the Elimination of Violence against Women and the work of Special Rapporteurs, gender-based violence, such as battering and other domestic violence, sexual abuse, sexual slavery and exploitation, and international trafficking in women and children, forced prostitution and sexual harassment, as well as violence against women, resulting from cultural prejudice, racism and racial discrimination, xenophobia, pornography, ethnic cleansing, armed conflict, foreign occupation, religious and anti-religious extremism and terrorism are incompatible with the dignity and the worth of the human person and must be combated and eliminated. Any harmful aspect of certain traditional, customary or modern practices that violates the rights of women should be prohibited and eliminated. Governments should take urgent action to combat and eliminate all forms of violence against women in private and public life, whether perpetrated or tolerated by the State or private persons.

225. Many women face additional barriers to the enjoyment of their human rights because of such factors as their race, language, ethnicity, culture, religion, disability or socio-economic class or because they are indigenous people, migrants, including women migrant workers, displaced women or refugees. They may also be disadvantaged and marginalized by a general lack of knowledge and recognition of their human rights as well as by the obstacles they meet in gaining access to information and recourse mechanisms in cases of violation of their rights.

226. The factors that cause the flight of refugee women, other displaced women in need of international protection and internally displaced women may be different from those affecting men. These women continue to be vulnerable to abuses of their human rights during and after their flight.

227. While women are increasingly using the legal system to exercise their rights, in many countries lack of awareness of the existence of these rights is an obstacle that prevents women from fully enjoying their human rights and attaining equality. Experience in many countries has shown that women can be empowered and motivated to assert their rights, regardless of their level of education or socio-economic status. Legal literacy programmes and media strategies have been effective in helping women to understand the link between their rights and other aspects of their lives and in demonstrating that cost-effective initiatives can be undertaken to help women obtain those rights. Provision of human rights education is essential for promoting an understanding of the human rights of women, including knowledge of recourse mechanisms to redress violations of their rights. It is necessary for all individuals, especially women in vulnerable circumstances, to have full knowledge of their rights and access to legal recourse against violations of their rights.

228. Women engaged in the defence of human rights must be protected. Governments have a duty to guarantee the full enjoyment of all rights set out in the Universal Declaration of Human Rights, the International Covenant on Civil and Political Rights and the International Covenant on Economic, Social and Cultural Rights by women working peacefully in a personal or organizational capacity for the promotion and protection of human rights. Non-governmental organizations, women's organizations and feminist groups have played a catalytic role in the promotion of the human rights of women through grass-roots activities, networking and advocacy and need encouragement, support and access to information from Governments in order to carry out these activities.

229. In addressing the enjoyment of human rights, Governments and other actors should promote an active and visible policy of mainstreaming a gender perspective in all policies and programmes so that, before decisions are taken, an analysis is made of the effects on women and men, respectively.

Strategic objective I.1. *Promote and protect the human rights of women, through the full implementation of all human rights instruments, especially the Convention on the Elimination of All Forms of Discrimination against Women*

Actions to be taken

230. By Governments:

(a) Work actively towards ratification of or accession to and implement international and regional human rights treaties;

(b) Ratify and accede to and ensure implementation of the Convention on the Elimination of All Forms of Discrimination against Women so that universal ratification of the Convention can be achieved by the year 2000;

(c) Limit the extent of any reservations to the Convention on the Elimination of All Forms of Discrimination against Women; formulate any such reservations as precisely and as narrowly as possible; ensure that no reservations are incompatible with the object and purpose of the Convention or otherwise incompatible with international treaty law and regularly review them with a view to withdrawing them; and withdraw reservations that are contrary to the object and purpose of the Convention on the Elimination of All Forms of Discrimination against Women or which are otherwise incompatible with international treaty law;

(d) Consider drawing up national action plans identifying steps to improve the promotion and protection of human rights, including the human rights of women, as recommended by the World Conference on Human Rights;

(e) Create or strengthen independent national institutions for the protection and promotion of these rights, including the human rights of women, as recommended by the World Conference on Human Rights;

(f) Develop a comprehensive human rights education programme to raise awareness among women of their human rights and raise awareness among others of the human rights of women;

(g) If they are States parties, implement the Convention by reviewing all national laws, policies, practices and procedures to ensure that they meet the obligations set out in the Convention; all States should undertake a review of all national laws, policies, practices and procedures to ensure that they meet international human rights obligations in this matter;

(h) Include gender aspects in reporting under all other human rights conventions and instruments, including ILO conventions, to ensure analysis and review of the human rights of women;

(i) Report on schedule to the Committee on the Elimination of Discrimination against Women regarding the implementation of the Convention, following fully the guidelines established by the Committee and involving non-governmental organizations, where appropriate, or taking into account their contributions in the preparation of the report;

(j) Enable the Committee on the Elimination of Discrimination against Women fully to discharge its mandate by allowing for adequate meeting time through broad ratification of the revision adopted by the States parties to the

Convention on the Elimination of All Forms of Discrimination against Women on 22 May 1995 relative to article 20, paragraph 1,[32] and by promoting efficient working methods;

(k) Support the process initiated by the Commission on the Status of Women with a view to elaborating a draft optional protocol to the Convention on the Elimination of All Forms of Discrimination against Women that could enter into force as soon as possible on a right of petition procedure, taking into consideration the Secretary-General's report on the optional protocol, including those views related to its feasibility;

(l) Take urgent measures to achieve universal ratification of or accession to the Convention on the Rights of the Child before the end of 1995 and full implementation of the Convention in order to ensure equal rights for girls and boys; those that have not already done so are urged to become parties in order to realize universal implementation of the Convention on the Rights of the Child by the year 2000;

(m) Address the acute problems of children, *inter alia*, by supporting efforts in the context of the United Nations system aimed at adopting efficient international measures for the prevention and eradication of female infanticide, harmful child labour, the sale of children and their organs, child prostitution, child pornography and other forms of sexual abuse and consider contributing to the drafting of an optional protocol to the Convention on the Rights of the Child;

(n) Strengthen the implementation of all relevant human rights instruments in order to combat and eliminate, including through international cooperation, organized and other forms of trafficking in women and children, including trafficking for the purposes of sexual exploitation, pornography, prostitution and sex tourism, and provide legal and social services to the victims; this should include provisions for international cooperation to prosecute and punish those responsible for organized exploitation of women and children;

(o) Taking into account the need to ensure full respect for the human rights of indigenous women, consider a declaration on the rights of indigenous people for adoption by the General Assembly within the International Decade of the World's Indigenous People and encourage the participation of indigenous women in the working group elaborating the draft declaration, in accordance with the provisions for the participation of organizations of indigenous people.

231. By relevant organs, bodies and agencies of the United Nations system, all human rights bodies of the United Nations system, as well as the United Nations High Commissioner for Human Rights and the United Nations High Commissioner for Refugees, while promoting greater efficiency and effectiveness through better coordination of the various bodies, mechanisms and procedures, taking into account the need to avoid unnecessary duplication and overlapping of their mandates and tasks:

(a) Give full, equal and sustained attention to the human rights of women in the exercise of their respective mandates to promote universal respect for and protection of all human rights—civil, cultural, economic, political and social rights, including the right to development;

(b) Ensure the implementation of the recommendations of the World Conference on Human Rights for the full integration and mainstreaming of the human rights of women;

(c) Develop a comprehensive policy programme for mainstreaming the human rights of women throughout the United Nations system, including activities with regard to advisory services, technical assistance, reporting methodology, gender-impact assessments, coordination, public information and human rights education, and play an active role in the implementation of the programme;

(d) Ensure the integration and full participation of women as both agents and beneficiaries in the development process and reiterate the objectives established for global action for women towards sustainable and equitable development set forth in the Rio Declaration on Environment and Development;[18]

(e) Include information on gender-based human rights violations in their activities and integrate the findings into all of their programmes and activities;

(f) Ensure that there is collaboration and coordination of the work of all human rights bodies and mechanisms to ensure that the human rights of women are respected;

(g) Strengthen cooperation and coordination between the Commission on the Status of Women, the Commission on Human Rights, the Commission for Social Development, the Commission on Sustainable Development, the Commission on Crime Prevention and Criminal Justice, the United Nations human rights treaty monitoring bodies, including the Committee on the Elimination of Discrimination against Women, and the United Nations Development Fund for Women, the International Research and Training Institute for the Advancement of Women, the United Nations Development Programme, the United Nations Children's Fund and other organizations of the United Nations system, acting within their mandates, in the promotion of the human rights of women, and improve cooperation between the Division for the Advancement of Women and the Centre for Human Rights;

(h) Establish effective cooperation between the United Nations High Commissioner for Human Rights and the United Nations High Commissioner for Refugees and other relevant bodies, within their respective mandates, taking into account the close link between massive violations of human rights, especially in the form of genocide, ethnic cleansing, systematic rape of women in war situations and refugee flows and other displacements, and the fact that refugee, displaced and returnee women may be subject to particular human rights abuse;

(i) Encourage incorporation of a gender perspective in national programmes of action and in human rights and national institutions, within the context of human rights advisory services programmes;

(j) Provide training in the human rights of women for all United Nations personnel and officials, especially those in human rights and humanitarian relief activities, and promote their understanding of the human rights of women so that they recognize and deal with violations of the human rights of women and can fully take into account the gender aspect of their work;

(k) In reviewing the implementation of the plan of action for the United Nations Decade for Human Rights Education (1995–2004), take into account the results of the Fourth World Conference on Women.

Strategic objective I.2. *Ensure equality and nondiscrimination under the law and in practice*

Actions to be taken

232. By Governments:

(a) Give priority to promoting and protecting the full and equal enjoyment by women and men of all human rights and fundamental freedoms without distinction of any kind as to race, colour, sex, language, religion, political or other opinions, national or social origins, property, birth or other status;

(b) Provide constitutional guarantees and/or enact appropriate legislation to prohibit discrimination on the basis of sex for all women and girls of all ages and assure women of all ages equal rights and their full enjoyment;

(c) Embody the principle of the equality of men and women in their legislation and ensure, through law and other appropriate means, the practical realization of this principle;

(d) Review national laws, including customary laws and legal practices in the areas of family, civil, penal, labour and commercial law in order to ensure the implementation of the principles and procedures of all relevant international human rights instruments by means of national legislation, revoke any remaining laws that discriminate on the basis of sex and remove gender bias in the administration of justice;

(e) Strengthen and encourage the development of programmes to protect the human rights of women in the national institutions on human rights that carry out programmes, such as human rights commissions or ombudspersons, according them appropriate status, resources and access to the Government to assist individuals, in particular women, and ensure that these institutions pay adequate attention to problems involving the violation of the human rights of women;

(f) Take action to ensure that the human rights of women, including the rights referred to in paragraphs 94 to 96 above, are fully respected and protected;

(g) Take urgent action to combat and eliminate violence against women, which is a human rights violation, resulting from harmful traditional or customary practices, cultural prejudices and extremism;

(h) Prohibit female genital mutilation wherever it exists and give vigorous support to efforts among non-governmental and community organizations and religious institutions to eliminate such practices;

(i) Provide gender-sensitive human rights education and training to public officials, including, *inter alia*, police and military personnel, corrections officers, health and medical personnel, and social workers, including people who deal with migration and refugee issues, and teachers at all levels of the educational system, and make available such education and training also to the judiciary and members of parliament in order to enable them to better exercise their public responsibilities;

(j) Promote the equal right of women to be members of trade unions and other professional and social organizations;

(k) Establish effective mechanisms for investigating violations of the human rights of women perpetrated by any public official and take the necessary punitive legal measures in accordance with national laws;

(l) Review and amend criminal laws and procedures, as necessary, to elimi-nate any discrimination against women in order to ensure that criminal law and procedures guarantee women effective protection against, and prosecu-tion of, crimes directed at or disproportionately affecting women, regardless of the relationship between the perpetrator and the victim, and ensure that women defendants, victims and/or witnesses are not revictimized or discrimi-nated against in the investigation and prosecution of crimes;

(m) Ensure that women have the same right as men to be judges, advocates or other officers of the court, as well as police officers and prison and detention officers, among other things;

(n) Strengthen existing or establish readily available and free or affordable alternative administrative mechanisms and legal aid programmes to assist disadvantaged women seeking redress for violations of their rights;

(o) Ensure that all women and non-governmental organizations and their members in the field of protection and promotion of all human rights—civil, cultural, economic, political and social rights, including the right to development—enjoy fully all human rights and freedoms in accordance with the Universal Declaration of Human Rights and all other human rights instru-ments and the protection of national laws;

(p) Strengthen and encourage the implementation of the recommendations contained in the Standard Rules on the Equalization of Opportunities for Persons with Disabilities,[30] paying special attention to ensure non-discrim-ination and equal enjoyment of all human rights and fundamental freedoms by women and girls with disabilities, including their access to information and services in the field of violence against women, as well as their active participa-tion in and economic contribution to all aspects of society;

(q) Encourage the development of gender-sensitive human rights programmes.

Strategic objective I.3. *Achieve legal literacy*

Actions to be taken

233. By Governments and non-governmental organizations, the United Nations and other international organizations, as appropriate:

(a) Translate, whenever possible, into local and indigenous languages and into alternative formats appropriate for persons with disabilities and persons at lower levels of literacy, publicize and disseminate laws and information relating to the equal status and human rights of all women, including the Universal Declaration of Human Rights, the International Covenant on Civil and Political Rights, the International Covenant on Economic, Social and Cultural Rights, the Convention on the Elimination of All Forms of Discrimination against Women, the International Convention on the Elimination of All Forms of Racial Discrimination,[33] the Convention on the Rights of the Child, the Convention against Torture and Other Cruel, Inhuman or Degrading Treatment or Punishment, the Declaration on the Right to Development [34] and the Declaration on the Elimination of Violence against Women, as well as the outcomes of relevant United Nations conferences and summits and national reports to the Committee on the Elimination of Discrimination against Women;

(b) Publicize and disseminate such information in easily understandable formats and alternative formats appropriate for persons with disabilities, and persons at low levels of literacy;

(c) Disseminate information on national legislation and its impact on women, including easily accessible guidelines on how to use a justice system to exercise one's rights;

(d) Include information about international and regional instruments and standards in their public information and human rights education activities and in adult education and training programmes, particularly for groups such as the military, the police and other law enforcement personnel, the judiciary, and legal and health professionals to ensure that human rights are effectively protected;

(e) Make widely available and fully publicize information on the existence of national, regional and international mechanisms for seeking redress when the human rights of women are violated;

(f) Encourage, coordinate and cooperate with local and regional women's groups, relevant non-governmental organizations, educators and the media, to implement programmes in human rights education to make women aware of their human rights;

(g) Promote education on the human and legal rights of women in school curricula at all levels of education and undertake public campaigns, including in the most widely used languages of the country, on the equality of women and men in public and private life, including their rights within the family and relevant human rights instruments under national and international law;

(h) Promote education in all countries in human rights and international humanitarian law for members of the national security and armed forces, including those assigned to United Nations peace-keeping operations, on a routine and continuing basis, reminding them and sensitizing them to the fact that they should respect the rights of women at all times, both on and off duty, giving special attention to the rules on the protection of women and children and to the protection of human rights in situations of armed conflict;

(i) Take appropriate measures to ensure that refugee and displaced women, migrant women and women migrant workers are made aware of their human rights and of the recourse mechanisms available to them.

J. Women and the media

234. During the past decade, advances in information technology have facilitated a global communications network that transcends national boundaries and has an impact on public policy, private attitudes and behaviour, especially of children and young adults. Everywhere the potential exists for the media to make a far greater contribution to the advancement of women.

235. More women are involved in careers in the communications sector, but few have attained positions at the decision-making level or serve on governing boards and bodies that influence media policy. The lack of gender sensitivity in the media is evidenced by the failure to eliminate the gender-based stereotyping that can be found in public and private local, national and international media organizations.

236. The continued projection of negative and degrading images of women in media communications—electronic, print, visual and audio—must be changed. Print and electronic media in most countries do not provide a balanced picture of women's diverse lives and contributions to society in a changing world. In addition, violent and degrading or pornographic media products are also negatively affecting women and their participation in society. Programming that reinforces women's traditional roles can be equally limiting. The world-wide trend towards consumerism has created a climate in which advertisements and commercial messages often portray women primarily as consumers and target girls and women of all ages inappropriately.

237. Women should be empowered by enhancing their skills, knowledge and access to information technology. This will strengthen their ability to combat negative portrayals of women internationally and to challenge instances of abuse of the power of an increasingly important industry. Self-regulatory mechanisms for the media need to be created and strengthened and approaches developed to eliminate gender-biased programming. Most women, especially in developing countries, are not able to access effectively the expanding electronic information highways and therefore cannot establish networks that will provide them with alternative sources of information. Women therefore need to be involved in decision-making regarding the development of the new technologies in order to participate fully in their growth and impact.

238. In addressing the issue of the mobilization of the media, Governments and other actors should promote an active and visible policy of mainstreaming a gender perspective in policies and programmes.

Strategic objective J.1. *Increase the participation and access of women to expression and decision-making in and through the media and new technologies of communication*

Actions to be taken

239. By Governments:

(a) Support women's education, training and employment to promote and ensure women's equal access to all areas and levels of the media;

(b) Support research into all aspects of women and the media so as to define areas needing attention and action and review existing media policies with a view to integrating a gender perspective;

(c) Promote women's full and equal participation in the media, including management, programming, education, training and research;

(d) Aim at gender balance in the appointment of women and men to all advisory, management, regulatory or monitoring bodies, including those connected to the private and State or public media;

(e) Encourage, to the extent consistent with freedom of expression, these bodies to increase the number of programmes for and by women to see to it that women's needs and concerns are properly addressed;

(f) Encourage and recognize women's media networks, including electronic networks and other new technologies of communication, as a means for the dissemination of information and the exchange of views, including at the international level, and support women's groups active in all media work and systems of communications to that end;

(g) Encourage and provide the means or incentives for the creative use of programmes in the national media for the dissemination of information on various cultural forms of indigenous people and the development of social and educational issues in this regard within the framework of national law;

(h) Guarantee the freedom of the media and its subsequent protection within the framework of national law and encourage, consistent with freedom of expression, the positive involvement of the media in development and social issues.

240. By national and international media systems:

Develop, consistent with freedom of expression, regulatory mechanisms, including voluntary ones, that promote balanced and diverse portrayals of women by the media and international communication systems and that promote increased participation by women and men in production and decision-making.

241. By Governments, as appropriate, or national machinery for the advancement of women:

(a) Encourage the development of educational and training programmes for women in order to produce information for the mass media, including funding of experimental efforts, and the use of the new technologies of communication, cybernetics space and satellite, whether public or private;

(b) Encourage the use of communication systems, including new technologies, as a means of strengthening women's participation in democratic processes;

(c) Facilitate the compilation of a directory of women media experts;

(d) Encourage the participation of women in the development of professional guidelines and codes of conduct or other appropriate self-regulatory mechanisms to promote balanced and non-stereotyped portrayals of women by the media.

242. By non-governmental organizations and media professional associations:

(a) Encourage the establishment of media watch groups that can monitor the media and consult with the media to ensure that women's needs and concerns are properly reflected;

(b) Train women to make greater use of information technology for communication and the media, including at the international level;

(c) Create networks among and develop information programmes for non-governmental organizations, women's organizations and professional media organizations in order to recognize the specific needs of women in the media, and facilitate the increased participation of women in communication, in particular at the international level, in support of South-South and North-South dialogue among and between these organizations, *inter alia*, to promote the human rights of women and equality between women and men;

(d) Encourage the media industry and education and media training institutions to develop, in appropriate languages, traditional, indigenous and other ethnic forms of media, such as story-telling, drama, poetry and song, reflecting their cultures, and utilize these forms of communication to disseminate information on development and social issues.

Strategic objective J.2. *Promote a balanced and non-stereotyped portrayal of women in the media*

Actions to be taken

243. By Governments and international organizations, to the extent consistent with freedom of expression:

(a) Promote research and implementation of a strategy of information, education and communication aimed at promoting a balanced portrayal of women and girls and their multiple roles;

(b) Encourage the media and advertising agencies to develop specific programmes to raise awareness of the Platform for Action;

(c) Encourage gender-sensitive training for media professionals, including media owners and managers, to encourage the creation and use of non-stereotyped, balanced and diverse images of women in the media;

(d) Encourage the media to refrain from presenting women as inferior beings and exploiting them as sexual objects and commodities, rather than presenting them as creative human beings, key actors and contributors to and beneficiaries of the process of development;

(e) Promote the concept that the sexist stereotypes displayed in the media are gender discriminatory, degrading in nature and offensive;

(f) Take effective measures or institute such measures, including appropriate legislation against pornography and the projection of violence against women and children in the media.

244. By the mass media and advertising organizations:

(a) Develop, consistent with freedom of expression, professional guidelines and codes of conduct and other forms of self-regulation to promote the presentation of non-stereotyped images of women;

(b) Establish, consistent with freedom of expression, professional guidelines and codes of conduct that address violent, degrading or pornographic materials concerning women in the media, including advertising;

(c) Develop a gender perspective on all issues of concern to communities, consumers and civil society;

(d) Increase women's participation in decision-making at all levels of the media.

245. By the media, non-governmental organizations and the private sector, in collaboration, as appropriate, with national machinery for the advancement of women:

(a) Promote the equal sharing of family responsibilities through media campaigns that emphasize gender equality and non-stereotyped gender roles of women and men within the family and that disseminate information aimed at eliminating spousal and child abuse and all forms of violence against women, including domestic violence;

(b) Produce and/or disseminate media materials on women leaders, *inter alia*, as leaders who bring to their positions of leadership many different life experiences, including but not limited to their experiences in balancing work and family responsibilities, as mothers, as professionals, as managers and as entrepreneurs, to provide role models, particularly to young women;

(c) Promote extensive campaigns, making use of public and private educational programmes, to disseminate information about and increase awareness of the human rights of women;

(d) Support the development of and finance, as appropriate, alternative media and the use of all means of communication to disseminate information to and about women and their concerns;

(e) Develop approaches and train experts to apply gender analysis with regard to media programmes.

K. Women and the environment

246. Human beings are at the centre of concern for sustainable development. They are entitled to a healthy and productive life in harmony with nature. Women have an essential role to play in the development of sustainable and ecologically sound consumption and production patterns and approaches to natural resource management, as was recognized at the United Nations Conference on Environment and Development and the International

Conference on Population and Development and reflected throughout Agenda 21. Awareness of resource depletion, the degradation of natural systems and the dangers of polluting substances has increased markedly in the past decade. These worsening conditions are destroying fragile ecosystems and displacing communities, especially women, from productive activities and are an increasing threat to a safe and healthy environment. Poverty and environmental degradation are closely interrelated. While poverty results in certain kinds of environmental stress, the major cause of the continued deterioration of the global environment is the unsustainable pattern of consumption and production, particularly in industrialized countries, which is a matter of grave concern, aggravating poverty and imbalances. Rising sea levels as a result of global warming cause a grave and immediate threat to people living in island countries and coastal areas. The use of ozone-depleting substances, such as products with chlorofluorocarbons, halons and methyl bromides (from which plastics and foams are made), are severely affecting the atmosphere, thus allowing excessive levels of harmful ultraviolet rays to reach the Earth's surface. This has severe effects on people's health such as higher rates of skin cancer, eye damage and weakened immune systems. It also has severe effects on the environment, including harm to crops and ocean life.

247. All States and all people shall cooperate in the essential task of eradicating poverty as an indispensable requirement for sustainable development, in order to decrease the disparities in standards of living and better meet the needs of the majority of the people of the world. Hurricanes, typhoons and other natural disasters and, in addition, the destruction of resources, violence, displacements and other effects associated with war, armed and other conflicts, the use and testing of nuclear weaponry, and foreign occupation can also contribute to environmental degradation. The deterioration of natural resources displaces communities, especially women, from income-generating activities while greatly adding to unremunerated work. In both urban and rural areas, environmental degradation results in negative effects on the health, well-being and quality of life of the population at large, especially girls and women of all ages. Particular attention and recognition should be given to the role and special situation of women living in rural areas and those working in the agricultural sector, where access to training, land, natural and productive resources, credit, development programmes and cooperative structures can help them increase their participation in sustainable development. Environmental risks in the home and workplace may have a disproportionate impact on women's health because of women's different susceptibilities to the toxic effects of various chemicals. These risks to women's health are particularly high in urban areas, as well as in low-income areas where there is a high concentration of polluting industrial facilities.

248. Through their management and use of natural resources, women provide sustenance to their families and communities. As consumers and producers, caretakers of their families and educators, women play an important role in promoting sustainable development through their concern for the

quality and sustainability of life for present and future generations. Governments have expressed their commitment to creating a new development
paradigm that integrates environmental sustainability with gender equality
and justice within and between generations as contained in chapter 24 of
Agenda 21.[19]

249. Women remain largely absent at all levels of policy formulation and
decision-making in natural resource and environmental management, conservation, protection and rehabilitation, and their experience and skills in advocacy for and monitoring of proper natural resource management too often
remain marginalized in policy-making and decision-making bodies, as well as
in educational institutions and environment-related agencies at the managerial level. Women are rarely trained as professional natural resource managers with policy-making capacities, such as land-use planners,
agriculturalists, foresters, marine scientists and environmental lawyers. Even
in cases where women are trained as professional natural resource managers,
they are often underrepresented in formal institutions with policy-making
capacities at the national, regional and international levels. Often women are
not equal participants in the management of financial and corporate institutions whose decision-making most significantly affects environmental quality.
Furthermore, there are institutional weaknesses in coordination between
women's non-governmental organizations and national institutions dealing
with environmental issues, despite the recent rapid growth and visibility of
women's non-governmental organizations working on these issues at all levels.

250. Women have often played leadership roles or taken the lead in promoting an environmental ethic, reducing resource use, and reusing and recycling
resources to minimize waste and excessive consumption. Women can have a
particularly powerful role in influencing sustainable consumption decisions.
In addition, women's contributions to environmental management, including
through grass-roots and youth campaigns to protect the environment, have
often taken place at the local level, where decentralized action on environmental issues is most needed and decisive. Women, especially indigenous
women, have particular knowledge of ecological linkages and fragile ecosys-
tem management. Women in many communities provide the main labour
force for subsistence production, including production of seafood; hence,
their role is crucial to the provision of food and nutrition, the enhancement of
the subsistence and informal sectors and the preservation of the environment.
In certain regions, women are generally the most stable members of the
community, as men often pursue work in distant locations, leaving women to
safeguard the natural environment and ensure adequate and sustainable
resource allocation within the household and the community.

251. The strategic actions needed for sound environmental management
require a holistic, multidisciplinary and intersectoral approach. Women's
participation and leadership are essential to every aspect of that approach.
The recent United Nations global conferences on development, as well as
regional preparatory conferences for the Fourth World Conference on
Women, have all acknowledged that sustainable development policies that do

not involve women and men alike will not succeed in the long run. They have called for the effective participation of women in the generation of knowledge and environmental education in decision-making and management at all levels. Women's experiences and contributions to an ecologically sound environment must therefore be central to the agenda for the twenty-first century. Sustainable development will be an elusive goal unless women's contribution to environmental management is recognized and supported.

252. In addressing the lack of adequate recognition and support for women's contribution to conservation and management of natural resources and safeguarding the environment, Governments and other actors should promote an active and visible policy of mainstreaming a gender perspective in all policies and programmes, including, as appropriate, an analysis of the effects on women and men, respectively, before decisions are taken.

Strategic objective K.1. *Involve women actively in environmental decision-making at all levels*

Actions to be taken

253. By Governments, at all levels, including municipal authorities, as appropriate:

(a) Ensure opportunities for women, including indigenous women, to participate in environmental decision-making at all levels, including as managers, designers and planners, and as implementers and evaluators of environmental projects;

(b) Facilitate and increase women's access to information and education, including in the areas of science, technology and economics, thus enhancing their knowledge, skills and opportunities for participation in environmental decisions;

(c) Encourage, subject to national legislation and consistent with the Convention on Biological Diversity,[35] the effective protection and use of the knowledge, innovations and practices of women of indigenous and local communities, including practices relating to traditional medicines, biodiversity and indigenous technologies, and endeavour to ensure that these are respected, maintained, promoted and preserved in an ecologically sustainable manner, and promote their wider application with the approval and involvement of the holders of such knowledge; in addition, safeguard the existing intellectual property rights of these women as protected under national and international law; work actively, where necessary, to find additional ways and means for the effective protection and use of such knowledge, innovations and practices, subject to national legislation and consistent with the Convention on Biological Diversity and relevant international law, and encourage fair and equitable sharing of benefits arising from the utilization of such knowledge, innovation and practices;

(d) Take appropriate measures to reduce risks to women from identified environmental hazards at home, at work and in other environments, including appropriate application of clean technologies, taking into account the precautionary approach agreed to in the Rio Declaration on Environment and Development;[18]

(e) Take measures to integrate a gender perspective in the design and implementation of, among other things, environmentally sound and sustainable resource management mechanisms, production techniques and infrastructure development in rural and urban areas;

(f) Take measures to empower women as producers and consumers so that they can take effective environmental actions, along with men, in their homes, communities and workplaces;

(g) Promote the participation of local communities, particularly women, in identification of public service needs, spatial planning and the provision and design of urban infrastructure.

254. By Governments and international organizations and private sector institutions, as appropriate:

(a) Take gender impact into consideration in the work of the Commission on Sustainable Development and other appropriate United Nations bodies and in the activities of international financial institutions;

(b) Promote the involvement of women and the incorporation of a gender perspective in the design, approval and execution of projects funded under the Global Environment Facility and other appropriate United Nations organizations;

(c) Encourage the design of projects in the areas of concern to the Global Environment Facility that would benefit women and projects managed by women;

(d) Establish strategies and mechanisms to increase the proportion of women, particularly at grass-roots levels, involved as decision makers, planners, managers, scientists and technical advisers and as beneficiaries in the design, development and implementation of policies and programmes for natural resource management and environmental protection and conservation;

(e) Encourage social, economic, political and scientific institutions to address environmental degradation and the resulting impact on women.

255. By non-governmental organizations and the private sector:

(a) Assume advocacy of environmental and natural resource management issues of concern to women and provide information to contribute to resource mobilization for environmental protection and conservation;

(b) Facilitate the access of women agriculturists, fishers and pastoralists to knowledge, skills, marketing services and environmentally sound technologies to support and strengthen their crucial roles and their expertise in resource management and the conservation of biological diversity.

Strategic objective K.2. *Integrate gender concerns and perspectives in policies and programmes for sustainable development*

Actions to be taken

256. By Governments:

(a) Integrate women, including indigenous women, their perspectives and knowledge, on an equal basis with men, in decision-making regarding sustainable resource management and the development of policies and programmes for sustainable development, including in particular those designed to address and prevent environmental degradation of the land;

(b) Evaluate policies and programmes in terms of environmental impact and women's equal access to and use of natural resources;

(c) Ensure adequate research to assess how and to what extent women are particularly susceptible or exposed to environmental degradation and hazards, including, as necessary, research and data collection on specific groups of women, particularly women with low income, indigenous women and women belonging to minorities;

(d) Integrate rural women's traditional knowledge and practices of sustainable resource use and management in the development of environmental management and extension programmes;

(e) Integrate the results of gender-sensitive research into mainstream policies with a view to developing sustainable human settlements;

(f) Promote knowledge of and sponsor research on the role of women, particularly rural and indigenous women, in food gathering and production, soil conservation, irrigation, watershed management, sanitation, coastal zone and marine resource management, integrated pest management, land-use planning, forest conservation and community forestry, fisheries, natural disaster prevention, and new and renewable sources of energy, focusing particularly on indigenous women's knowledge and experience;

(g) Develop a strategy for change to eliminate all obstacles to women's full and equal participation in sustainable development and equal access to and control over resources;

(h) Promote the education of girls and women of all ages in science, technology, economics and other disciplines relating to the natural environment so that they can make informed choices and offer informed input in determining local economic, scientific and environmental priorities for the management and appropriate use of natural and local resources and ecosystems;

(i) Develop programmes to involve female professionals and scientists, as well as technical, administrative and clerical workers, in environmental management, develop training programmes for girls and women in these fields, expand opportunities for the hiring and promotion of women in these fields and implement special measures to advance women's expertise and participation in these activities;

(j) Identify and promote environmentally sound technologies that have been designed, developed and improved in consultation with women and that are appropriate to both women and men;

(k) Support the development of women's equal access to housing infrastructure, safe water, and sustainable and affordable energy technologies, such as wind, solar, biomass and other renewable sources, through participatory needs assessments, energy planning and policy formulation at the local and national levels;

(l) Ensure that clean water is available and accessible to all by the year 2000 and that environmental protection and conservation plans are designed and implemented to restore polluted water systems and rebuild damaged watersheds.

257. By international organizations, non-governmental organizations and private sector institutions:

(a) Involve women in the communication industries in raising awareness regarding environmental issues, especially on the environmental and health impacts of products, technologies and industry processes;

(b) Encourage consumers to use their purchasing power to promote the production of environmentally safe products and encourage investment in environmentally sound and productive agricultural, fisheries, commercial and industrial activities and technologies;

(c) Support women's consumer initiatives by promoting the marketing of organic food and recycling facilities, product information and product labelling, including labelling of toxic chemical and pesticide containers with language and symbols that are understood by consumers, regardless of age and level of literacy.

Strategic objective K.3. *Strengthen or establish mechanisms at the national, regional and international levels to assess the impact of development and environmental policies on women*

Actions to be taken

258. By Governments, regional and international organizations and non-governmental organizations, as appropriate:

(a) Provide technical assistance to women, particularly in developing countries, in the sectors of agriculture, fisheries, small enterprises, trade and industry to ensure the continuing promotion of human resource development and the development of environmentally sound technologies and of women's entrepreneurship;

(b) Develop gender-sensitive databases, information and monitoring systems and participatory action-oriented research, methodologies and policy analyses, with the collaboration of academic institutions and local women researchers, on the following:

(i) Knowledge and experience on the part of women concerning the management and conservation of natural resources for incorporation in the databases and information systems for sustainable development;

(ii) The impact on women of environmental and natural resource degradation, deriving from, *inter alia*, unsustainable production and consumption patterns, drought, poor quality water, global warming, desertification, sealevel rise, hazardous waste, natural disasters, toxic chemicals and pesticide residues, radioactive waste, armed conflicts and its consequences;

(iii) Analysis of the structural links between gender relations, environment and development, with special emphasis on particular sectors, such as agriculture, industry, fisheries, forestry, environmental health, biological diversity, climate, water resources and sanitation;

(iv) Measures to develop and include environmental, economic, cultural, social and gender-sensitive analyses as an essential step in the development and monitoring of programmes and policies;

(v) Programmes to create rural and urban training, research and resource centres that will disseminate environmentally sound technologies to women;

(c) Ensure the full compliance with relevant international obligations, including where relevant, the Basel Convention and other conventions relating to the transboundary movements of hazardous wastes (which include toxic wastes) and the Code of Practice of the International Atomic Energy Agency relating to the movement of radioactive waste; enact and enforce regulations for environmentally sound management related to safe storage and movements; consider taking action towards the prohibition of those movements that are unsafe and insecure; ensure the strict control and management of hazardous wastes and radioactive waste, in accordance with relevant international and regional obligations and eliminate the exportation of such wastes to countries that, individually or through international agreements, prohibit their importation;

(d) Promote coordination within and among institutions to implement the Platform for Action and chapter 24 of Agenda 21 by, *inter alia*, requesting the Commission on Sustainable Development, through the Economic and Social Council, to seek input from the Commission on the Status of Women when reviewing the implementation of Agenda 21 with regard to women and the environment.

L. The girl child

259. The Convention on the Rights of the Child recognizes that "States Parties shall respect and ensure the rights set forth in the present Convention to each child within their jurisdiction without discrimination of any kind, irrespective of the child's or his or her parent's or legal guardian's race, colour, sex, language, religion, political or other opinion, national, ethnic or social origin, property, disability, birth or status" (art. 2, para. 1).[11] However, in many countries available indicators show that the girl child is discriminated against from the earliest stages of life, through her childhood and into adulthood. In some areas of the world, men outnumber women by 5 in every 100. The reasons for the discrepancy include, among other things, harmful attitudes and practices, such as female genital mutilation, son preference—which results in female infanticide and prenatal sex selection—early marriage, including child marriage, violence against women, sexual exploitation, sexual abuse, discrimination against girls in food allocation and other practices related to health and well-being. As a result, fewer girls than boys survive into adulthood.

260. Girls are often treated as inferior and are socialized to put themselves last, thus undermining their self-esteem. Discrimination and neglect in childhood can initiate a lifelong downward spiral of deprivation and exclusion from the social mainstream. Initiatives should be taken to prepare girls to participate actively, effectively and equally with boys at all levels of social, economic, political and cultural leadership.

261. Gender-biased educational processes, including curricula, educational materials and practices, teachers' attitudes and classroom interaction, reinforce existing gender inequalities.

262. Girls and adolescents may receive a variety of conflicting and confusing messages on their gender roles from their parents, teachers, peers and the media. Women and men need to work together with children and youth to break down persistent gender stereotypes, taking into account the rights of the child and the responsibilities, rights and duties of parents as stated in paragraph 267 below.

263. Although the number of educated children has grown in the past 20 years in some countries, boys have proportionately fared much better than girls. In 1990, 130 million children had no access to primary school; of these, 81 million were girls. This can be attributed to such factors as customary attitudes, child labour, early marriages, lack of funds and lack of adequate schooling facilities, teenage pregnancies and gender inequalities in society at large as well as in the family as defined in paragraph 29 above. In some countries the shortage of women teachers can inhibit the enrolment of girls. In many cases, girls start to undertake heavy domestic chores at a very early age and are expected to manage both educational and domestic responsibilities, often resulting in poor scholastic performance and an early dropout from schooling.

264. The percentage of girls enrolled in secondary school remains significantly low in many countries. Girls are often not encouraged or given the opportunity to pursue scientific and technological training and education, which limits the knowledge they require for their daily lives and their employment opportunities.

265. Girls are less encouraged than boys to participate in and learn about the social, economic and political functioning of society, with the result that they are not offered the same opportunities as boys to take part in decision-making processes.

266. Existing discrimination against the girl child in her access to nutrition and physical and mental health services endangers her current and future health. An estimated 450 million adult women in developing countries are stunted as a result of childhood protein-energy malnutrition.

267. The International Conference on Population and Development recognized, in paragraph 7.3 of the Programme of Action,[14] that "full attention should be given to the promotion of mutually respectful and equitable gender relations and particularly to meeting the educational and service needs of adolescents to enable them to deal in a positive and responsible way with their sexuality," taking into account the rights of the child to access to information, privacy, confidentiality, respect and informed consent, as well as the responsibilities, rights and duties of parents and legal guardians to provide, in a manner consistent with the evolving capacities of the child, appropriate direction and guidance in the exercise by the child of the rights recognized in the Convention on the Rights of the Child, and in conformity with the Convention on the Elimination of All Forms of Discrimination against Women. In all actions concerning children, the best interests of the child shall be a primary consideration. Support should be given to integral sexual education for young people with parental support and guidance that stresses the responsibility of males for their own sexuality and fertility and that help them exercise their responsibilities.

268. More than 15 million girls aged 15 to 19 give birth each year. Motherhood at a very young age entails complications during pregnancy and delivery and a risk of maternal death that is much greater than average. The children of young mothers have higher levels of morbidity and mortality. Early childbearing continues to be an impediment to improvements in the educational, economic and social status of women in all parts of the world. Overall, early marriage and early motherhood can severely curtail educational and employment opportunities and are likely to have a long-term adverse impact on their and their children's quality of life.

269. Sexual violence and sexually transmitted diseases, including HIV/AIDS, have a devastating effect on children's health, and girls are more vulnerable than boys to the consequences of unprotected and premature sexual relations. Girls often face pressures to engage in sexual activity. Due to such factors as their youth, social pressures, lack of protective laws, or failure to enforce laws, girls are more vulnerable to all kinds of violence, particularly sexual violence, including rape, sexual abuse, sexual exploitation, trafficking, possibly the sale of their organs and tissues, and forced labour.

270. The girl child with disabilities faces additional barriers and needs to be ensured non-discrimination and equal enjoyment of all human rights and fundamental freedoms in accordance with the Standard Rules on the Equalization of Opportunities for Persons with Disabilities.[30]

271. Some children are particularly vulnerable, especially the abandoned, homeless and displaced, street children, children in areas in conflict, and children who are discriminated against because they belong to an ethnic or racial minority group.

272. All barriers must therefore be eliminated to enable girls without exception to develop their full potential and skills through equal access to education and training, nutrition, physical and mental health care and related information.

273. In addressing issues concerning children and youth, Governments should promote an active and visible policy of mainstreaming a gender perspective into all policies and programmes so that before decisions are taken, an analysis is made of the effects on girls and boys, respectively.

Strategic objective L.1. *Eliminate all forms of discrimination against the girl child*

Actions to be taken

274. By Governments:

(a) By States that have not signed or ratified the Convention on the Rights of the Child, take urgent measures towards signing and ratifying the Convention, bearing in mind the strong exhortation made at the World Conference on Human Rights to sign it before the end of 1995, and by States that have signed and ratified the Convention, ensure its full implementation through the adoption of all necessary legislative, administrative and other measures and by fostering an enabling environment that encourages full respect for the rights of children;

(b) Consistent with article 7 of the Convention on the Rights of the Child,[11] take measures to ensure that a child is registered immediately after birth and has the right from birth to a name, the right to acquire a nationality and, as far as possible, the right to know and be cared for by his or her parents;

(c) Take steps to ensure that children receive appropriate financial support from their parents, by, among other measures, enforcing child-support laws;

(d) Eliminate the injustice and obstacles in relation to inheritance faced by the girl child so that all children may enjoy their rights without discrimination, by, *inter alia*, enacting, as appropriate, and enforcing legislation that guarantees equal right to succession and ensures equal right to inherit, regardless of the sex of the child;

(e) Enact and strictly enforce laws to ensure that marriage is only entered into with the free and full consent of the intending spouses; in addition, enact and strictly enforce laws concerning the minimum legal age of consent and the minimum age for marriage and raise the minimum age for marriage where necessary;

(f) Develop and implement comprehensive policies, plans of action and programmes for the survival, protection, development and advancement of the girl child to promote and protect the full enjoyment of her human rights and to ensure equal opportunities for girls; these plans should form an integral part of the total development process;

(g) Ensure the disaggregation by sex and age of all data related to children in the health, education and other sectors in order to include a gender perspective in planning, implementation and monitoring of such programmes.

275. By Governments and international and non-governmental organizations:

(a) Disaggregate information and data on children by sex and age, undertake research on the situation of girls and integrate, as appropriate, the results in the formulation of policies, programmes and decision-making for the advancement of the girl child;

(b) Generate social support for the enforcement of laws on the minimum legal age for marriage, in particular by providing educational opportunities for girls.

Strategic objective L.2. *Eliminate negative cultural attitudes and practices against girls*

Actions to be taken

276. By Governments:

(a) Encourage and support, as appropriate, non-governmental organizations and community-based organizations in their efforts to promote changes in negative attitudes and practices towards girls;

(b) Set up educational programmes and develop teaching materials and textbooks that will sensitize and inform adults about the harmful effects of certain traditional or customary practices on girl children;

(c) Develop and adopt curricula, teaching materials and textbooks to improve the self-image, lives and work opportunities of girls, particularly in areas where women have traditionally been underrepresented, such as mathematics, science and technology;

(d) Take steps so that tradition and religion and their expressions are not a basis for discrimination against girls.

277. By Governments and, as appropriate, international and non-governmental organizations:

(a) Promote an educational setting that eliminates all barriers that impede the schooling of married and/or pregnant girls and young mothers, including, as appropriate, affordable and physically accessible child-care facilities and parental education to encourage those who have responsibilities for the care of their children and siblings during their school years to return to, or continue with, and complete schooling;

(b) Encourage educational institutions and the media to adopt and project balanced and non-stereotyped images of girls and boys, and work to eliminate child pornography and degrading and violent portrayals of the girl child;

(c) Eliminate all forms of discrimination against the girl child and the root causes of son preference, which result in harmful and unethical practices such as prenatal sex selection and female infanticide; this is often compounded by the increasing use of technologies to determine foetal sex, resulting in abortion of female foetuses;

(d) Develop policies and programmes, giving priority to formal and informal education programmes that support girls and enable them to acquire knowledge, develop self-esteem and take responsibility for their own lives; and place special focus on programmes to educate women and men, especially parents, on the importance of girls' physical and mental health and well-being, including the elimination of discrimination against girls in food allocation, early marriage, violence against girls, female genital mutilation, child prostitution, sexual abuse, rape and incest.

Strategic objective L.3. *Promote and protect the rights of the girl child and increase awareness of her needs and potential*

Actions to be taken

278. By Governments and international and non-governmental organizations:

(a) Generate awareness of the disadvantaged situation of girls among policy makers, planners, administrators and implementors at all levels, as well as within households and communities;

(b) Make the girl child, particularly the girl child in difficult circumstances, aware of her own potential, educate her about the rights guaranteed to her under all international human rights instruments, including the Convention on the Rights of the Child, legislation enacted for her and the various measures undertaken by both governmental and non-governmental organizations working to improve her status;

(c) Educate women, men, girls and boys to promote girls' status and encourage them to work towards mutual respect and equal partnership between girls and boys;

(d) Facilitate the equal provision of appropriate services and devices to girls with disabilities and provide their families with related support services, as appropriate.

Strategic objective L.4. *Eliminate discrimination against girls in education, skills development and training*

Actions to be taken

279. By Governments:

(a) Ensure universal and equal access to and completion of primary education by all children and eliminate the existing gap between girls and boys, as stipulated in article 28 of the Convention on the Rights of the Child;[11] similarly, ensure equal access to secondary education by the year 2005 and equal access to higher education, including vocational and technical education, for all girls and boys, including the disadvantaged and gifted;

(b) Take steps to integrate functional literacy and numeracy programmes, particularly for out-of-school girls in development programmes;

(c) Promote human rights education in educational programmes and include in human rights education the fact that the human rights of women and the girl child are an inalienable, integral and indivisible part of universal human rights;

(d) Increase enrolment and improve retention rates of girls by allocating appropriate budgetary resources and by enlisting the support of the community and parents through campaigns and flexible school schedules, incentives, scholarships, access programmes for out-of-school girls and other measures;

(e) Develop training programmes and materials for teachers and educators, raising awareness about their own role in the educational process, with a view to providing them with effective strategies for gender-sensitive teaching;

(f) Take actions to ensure that female teachers and professors have the same possibilities and status as male teachers and professors.

280. By Governments and international and non-governmental organizations:

(a) Provide education and skills training to increase girls' opportunities for employment and access to decision-making processes;

(b) Provide education to increase girls' knowledge and skills related to the functioning of economic, financial and political systems;

(c) Ensure access to appropriate education and skills-training for girl children with disabilities for their full participation in life;

(d) Promote the full and equal participation of girls in extracurricular activities, such as sports, drama and cultural activities.

Strategic objective L.5. *Eliminate discrimination against girls in health and nutrition*

Actions to be taken

281. By Governments and international and non-governmental organizations:

(a) Provide public information on the removal of discriminatory practices against girls in food allocation, nutrition and access to health services;

(b) Sensitize the girl child, parents, teachers and society concerning good general health and nutrition and raise awareness of the health dangers and other problems connected with early pregnancies;

(c) Strengthen and reorient health education and health services, particularly primary health care programmes, including sexual and reproductive health, and design quality health programmes that meet the physical and mental needs of girls and that attend to the needs of young, expectant and nursing mothers;

(d) Establish peer education and outreach programmes with a view to strengthening individual and collective action to reduce the vulnerability of girls to HIV/AIDS and other sexually transmitted diseases, as agreed to in the Programme of Action of the International Conference on Population and Development and as established in the report of that Conference, recognizing the parental roles referred to in paragraph 267 of the present Platform for Action;

(e) Ensure education and dissemination of information to girls, especially adolescent girls, regarding the physiology of reproduction, reproductive and sexual health, as agreed to in the Programme of Action of the International Conference on Population and Development and as established in the report of that Conference, responsible family planning practice, family life, reproductive health, sexually transmitted diseases, AIDS infection and AIDS prevention, recognizing the parental roles referred to in paragraph 267;

(f) Include health and nutritional training as an integral part of literacy programmes and school curricula starting at the primary level for the benefit of the girl child;

(g) Emphasize the role and responsibility of adolescents in sexual and reproductive health and behaviour through the provision of appropriate services and counselling, as discussed in paragraph 267;

(h) Develop information and training programmes for health planners and implementors on the special health needs of the girl child;

(i) Take all the appropriate measures with a view to abolishing traditional practices prejudicial to the health of children, as stipulated in article 24 of the Convention on the Rights of the Child.[11]

Strategic objective L.6. *Eliminate the economic exploitation of child labour and protect young girls at work*

Actions to be taken

282. By Governments:

(a) In conformity with article 32 of the Convention on the Rights of the Child,[11] protect children from economic exploitation and from performing any work that is likely to be hazardous or to interfere with the child's education, or to be harmful to the child's health or physical, mental, spiritual, moral or social development;

(b) Define a minimum age for a child's admission to employment in national legislation, in conformity with existing international labour standards and the Convention on the Rights of the Child, including girls in all sectors of activity;

(c) Protect young girls at work, *inter alia*, through:

(i) A minimum age or ages for admission to employment;

(ii) Strict monitoring of work conditions (respect for work time, prohibition of work by children not provided for by national legislation, and monitoring of hygiene and health conditions at work);

(iii) Application of social security coverage;

(iv) Establishment of continuous training and education;

(d) Strengthen, where necessary, legislation governing the work of children and provide for appropriate penalties or other sanctions to ensure effective enforcement of the legislation;

(e) Use existing international labour standards, including, as appropriate, ILO standards for the protection of working children, to guide the formulation of national labour legislation and policies.

Strategic objective L.7. *Eradicate violence against the girl child*

Actions to be taken

283. By Governments and, as appropriate, international and non-governmental organizations:

(a) Take effective actions and measures to enact and enforce legislation to protect the safety and security of girls from all forms of violence at work, including training programmes and support programmes, and take measures to eliminate incidents of sexual harassment of girls in educational and other institutions;

(b) Take appropriate legislative, administrative, social and educational measures to protect the girl child, in the household and in society, from all forms of physical or mental violence, injury or abuse, neglect or negligent treatment, maltreatment or exploitation, including sexual abuse;

(c) Undertake gender sensitization training for those involved in healing and rehabilitation and other assistance programmes for girls who are victims of violence and promote programmes of information, support and training for such girls;

(d) Enact and enforce legislation protecting girls from all forms of violence, including female infanticide and prenatal sex selection, genital mutilation, incest, sexual abuse, sexual exploitation, child prostitution and child pornography, and develop age-appropriate safe and confidential programmes and medical, social and psychological support services to assist girls who are subjected to violence.

Strategic objective L.8. *Promote the girl child's awareness of and participation in social, economic and political life*

Actions to be taken

284. By Governments and international and non-governmental organizations:

(a) Provide access for girls to training, information and the media on social, cultural, economic and political issues and enable them to articulate their views;

(b) Support non-governmental organizations, in particular youth non-governmental organizations, in their efforts to promote the equality and participation of girls in society.

Strategic objective L.9. *Strengthen the role of the family in improving the status of the girl child*

Actions to be taken

285. By Governments, in cooperation with non-governmental organizations:

(a) Formulate policies and programmes to help the family, as defined in paragraph 29 above, in its supporting, educating and nurturing roles, with particular emphasis on the elimination of intra-family discrimination against the girl child;

(b) Provide an environment conducive to the strengthening of the family, as defined in paragraph 29 above, with a view to providing supportive and preventive measures which protect, respect and promote the potential of the girl child;

(c) Educate and encourage parents and caregivers to treat girls and boys equally and to ensure shared responsibilities between girls and boys in the family, as defined in paragraph 29 above.

Chapter V

INSTITUTIONAL ARRANGEMENTS

286. The Platform for Action establishes a set of actions that should lead to fundamental change. Immediate action and accountability are essential if the targets are to be met by the year 2000. Implementation is primarily the responsibility of Governments, but is also dependent on a wide range of institutions in the public, private and non-governmental sectors at the community, national, subregional/regional and international levels.

287. During the United Nations Decade for Women (1976–1985), many institutions specifically devoted to the advancement of women were established at the national, regional and international levels. At the international level, the International Research and Training Institute for the Advancement of Women (INSTRAW), the United Nations Development Fund for Women (UNIFEM), and the Committee to monitor the Convention on the Elimination of All Forms of Discrimination against Women were established. These entities, along with the Commission on the Status of Women and its secretariat, the Division for the Advancement of Women, became the main institutions in the United Nations specifically devoted to women's advancement globally. At the national level, a number of countries established or strengthened national mechanisms to plan, advocate for and monitor progress in the advancement of women.

288. Implementation of the Platform for Action by national, subregional/regional and international institutions, both public and private, would be facilitated by transparency, by increased linkages between networks and organizations and by a consistent flow of information among all concerned. Clear objectives and accountability mechanisms are also required. Links with other institutions at the national, subregional/regional and international levels and with networks and organizations devoted to the advancement of women are needed.

289. Non-governmental and grass-roots organizations have a specific role to play in creating a social, economic, political and intellectual climate based on equality between women and men. Women should be actively involved in the implementation and monitoring of the Platform for Action.

290. Effective implementation of the Platform will also require changes in the internal dynamics of institutions and organizations, including values, behaviour, rules and procedures that are inimical to the advancement of women. Sexual harassment should be eliminated.

291. National, subregional/regional and international institutions should have strong and clear mandates and the authority, resources and accountability mechanisms needed for the tasks set out in the Platform for Action. Their methods of operation should ensure efficient and effective implementation of the Platform. There should be a clear commitment to international norms and standards of equality between women and men as a basis for all actions.

292. To ensure effective implementation of the Platform for Action and to enhance the work for the advancement of women at the national, subregional/ regional and international levels, Governments, the United Nations system and all other relevant organizations should promote an active and visible policy of mainstreaming a gender perspective, *inter alia*, in the monitoring and evaluation of all policies and programmes.

A. National level

293. Governments have the primary responsibility for implementing the Platform for Action. Commitment at the highest political level is essential to its implementation, and Governments should take a leading role in coordinating, monitoring and assessing progress in the advancement of women. The Fourth World Conference on Women is a conference of national and international commitment and action. This requires commitment from Governments and the international community. The Platform for Action is part of a continuing process and has a catalytic effect as it will contribute to programmes and practical outcomes for girls and women of all ages. States and the international community are encouraged to respond to this challenge by making commitments for action. As part of this process, many States have made commitments for action as reflected, *inter alia*, in their national statements.

294. National mechanisms and institutions for the advancement of women should participate in public policy formulation and encourage the implementation of the Platform for Action through various bodies and institutions, including the private sector, and, where necessary, should act as a catalyst in developing new programmes by the year 2000 in areas that are not covered by existing institutions.

295. The active support and participation of a broad and diverse range of other institutional actors should be encouraged, including legislative bodies, academic and research institutions, professional associations, trade unions, cooperatives, local community groups, non-governmental organizations, including women's organizations and feminist groups, the media, religious groups, youth organizations and cultural groups, as well as financial and non-profit organizations.

296. In order for the Platform for Action to be implemented, it will be necessary for Governments to establish or improve the effectiveness of national machineries for the advancement of women at the highest political level, appropriate intra- and inter-ministerial procedures and staffing, and other institutions with the mandate and capacity to broaden women's participation and integrate gender analysis into policies and programmes. The first step in this process for all institutions should be to review their objectives, programmes and operational procedures in terms of the actions called for in the Platform. A key activity should be to promote public awareness and support for the goals of the Platform for Action, *inter alia*, through the mass media and public education.

297. As soon as possible, preferably by the end of 1995, Governments, in consultation with relevant institutions and non-governmental organizations, should begin to develop implementation strategies for the Platform and, preferably by the end of 1996, should have developed their strategies or plans of action. This planning process should draw upon persons at the highest level of authority in government and relevant actors in civil society. These implementation strategies should be comprehensive, have time-bound targets and benchmarks for monitoring, and include proposals for allocating or reallocating resources for implementation. Where necessary, the support of the international community could be enlisted, including resources.

298. Non-governmental organizations should be encouraged to contribute to the design and implementation of these strategies or national plans of action. They should also be encouraged to develop their own programmes to complement government efforts. Women's organizations and feminist groups, in collaboration with other non-governmental organizations, should be encouraged to organize networks, as necessary, and to advocate for and support the implementation of the Platform for Action by Governments and regional and international bodies.

299. Governments should commit themselves to gender balance, *inter alia*, through the creation of special mechanisms, in all government-appointed committees, boards and other relevant official bodies, as appropriate, as well as in all international bodies, institutions and organizations, notably by presenting and promoting more women candidates.

300. Regional and international organizations, in particular development institutions, especially INSTRAW, UNIFEM and bilateral donors, should provide financial and advisory assistance to national machinery in order to increase its ability to gather information, develop networks and carry out its mandate, in addition to strengthening international mechanisms to promote the advancement of women through their respective mandates, in cooperation with Governments.

B. Subregional/regional level

301. The regional commissions of the United Nations and other subregional/regional structures should promote and assist the pertinent national institutions in monitoring and implementing the global Platform for Action within their mandates. This should be done in coordination with the implementation of the respective regional platforms or plans of action and in close collaboration with the Commission on the Status of Women, taking into account the need for a coordinated follow-up to United Nations conferences in the economic, social, human rights and related fields.

302. In order to facilitate the regional implementation, monitoring and evaluation process, the Economic and Social Council should consider reviewing the institutional capacity of the United Nations regional commissions within their mandates, including their women's units/focal points, to deal with gender issues in the light of the Platform for Action, as well as the regional platforms and plans of action. Consideration should be given, *inter alia*, and, where appropriate, to strengthening capacity in this respect.

303. Within their existing mandates and activities, the regional commissions should mainstream women's issues and gender perspectives and should also consider the establishment of mechanisms and processes to ensure the implementation and monitoring of both the Platform for Action and the regional platforms and plans of action. The regional commissions should, within their mandates, collaborate on gender issues with other regional intergovernmental organizations, non-governmental organizations, financial and research institutions and the private sector.

304. Regional offices of the specialized agencies of the United Nations system should, as appropriate, develop and publicize a plan of action for implementing the Platform for Action, including the identification of time-frames and resources. Technical assistance and operational activities at the regional level should establish well-identified targets for the advancement of women. To this end, regular coordination should be undertaken among United Nations bodies and agencies.

305. Non-governmental organizations within the region should be supported in their efforts to develop networks to coordinate advocacy and dissemination of information about the global Platform for Action and the respective regional platforms or plans of action.

C. International level

1. United Nations

306. The Platform for Action needs to be implemented through the work of all of the bodies and organizations of the United Nations system during the period 1995–2000, specifically and as an integral part of wider programming. An enhanced framework for international cooperation for gender issues must be developed during the period 1995–2000 in order to ensure the integrated and comprehensive implementation, follow-up and assessment of the Platform for Action, taking into account the results of global United Nations summits and conferences. The fact that at all of these summits and conferences, Governments have committed themselves to the empowerment of women in different areas, makes coordination crucial to the follow-up strategies for this Platform for Action. The Agenda for Development and the Agenda for Peace should take into account the Platform for Action of the Fourth World Conference on Women.

307. The institutional capacity of the United Nations system to carry out and coordinate its responsibility for implementing the Platform for Action, as well as its expertise and working methods to promote the advancement of women, should be improved.

308. Responsibility for ensuring the implementation of the Platform for Action and the integration of a gender perspective into all policies and programmes of the United Nations system must rest at the highest levels.

309. To improve the system's efficiency and effectiveness in providing support for equality and women's empowerment at the national level and to enhance its capacity to achieve the objectives of the Platform for Action, there is a need to renew, reform and revitalize various parts of the United Nations system. This would include reviewing and strengthening the strategies and working methods of different United Nations mechanisms for the advancement of women with a view to rationalizing and, as appropriate, strengthening their advisory, catalytic and monitoring functions in relation to mainstream bodies and agencies. Women/gender units are important for effective mainstreaming, but strategies must be further developed to prevent inadvertent marginalization as opposed to mainstreaming of the gender dimension throughout all operations.

310. In following up the Fourth World Conference on Women, all entities of the United Nations system focusing on the advancement of women should have the necessary resources and support to carry out follow-up activities. The efforts of gender focal points within organizations should be well integrated into overall policy, planning, programming and budgeting.

311. Action must be taken by the United Nations and other international organizations to eliminate barriers to the advancement of women within their organizations in accordance with the Platform for Action.

General Assembly

312. The General Assembly, as the highest intergovernmental body in the United Nations, is the principal policy-making and appraisal organ on matters relating to the follow-up to the Conference, and as such, should integrate gender issues throughout its work. It should appraise progress in the effective implementation of the Platform for Action, recognizing that these issues cut across social, political and economic policy. At its fiftieth session, in 1995, the General Assembly will have before it the report of the Fourth World Conference on Women. In accordance with its resolution 49/161, it will also examine a report of the Secretary-General on the follow-up to the Conference, taking into account the recommendations of the Conference. The General Assembly should include the follow-up to the Conference as part of its continuing work on the advancement of women. In 1996, 1998 and 2000, it should review the implementation of the Platform for Action.

Economic and Social Council

313. The Economic and Social Council, in the context of its role under the Charter of the United Nations and in accordance with General Assembly resolutions 45/264, 46/235 and 48/162, would oversee system-wide coordination in the implementation of the Platform for Action and make recommendations in this regard. The Council should be invited to review the implementation of the Platform for Action, giving due consideration to the reports of the Commission on the Status of Women. As coordinating body, the Council should be invited to review the mandate of the Commission on the

Status of Women, taking into account the need for effective coordination with other related commissions and Conference follow-up. The Council should incorporate gender issues into its discussion of all policy questions, giving due consideration to recommendations prepared by the Commission. It should consider dedicating at least one high-level segment before the year 2000 to the advancement of women and implementation of the Platform for Action with the active involvement and participation, *inter alia*, of the specialized agencies, including the World Bank and IMF.

314. The Council should consider dedicating at least one coordination segment before the year 2000 to coordination of the advancement of women, based on the revised system-wide medium-term plan for the advancement of women.

315. The Council should consider dedicating at least one operational activities segment before the year 2000 to the coordination of development activities related to gender, based on the revised system-wide medium-term plan for the advancement of women, with a view to instituting guidelines and procedures for implementation of the Platform for Action by the funds and programmes of the United Nations system.

316. The Administrative Committee on Coordination (ACC) should consider how its participating entities might best coordinate their activities, *inter alia*, through existing procedures at the inter-agency level for ensuring system-wide coordination to implement and help follow up the objectives of the Platform for Action.

Commission on the Status of Women

317. The General Assembly and the Economic and Social Council, in accordance with their respective mandates, are invited to review and strengthen the mandate of the Commission on the Status of Women, taking into account the Platform for Action as well as the need for synergy with other related commissions and Conference follow-up, and for a system-wide approach to its implementation.

318. As a functional commission assisting the Economic and Social Council, the Commission on the Status of Women should have a central role in monitoring, within the United Nations system, the implementation of the Platform for Action and advising the Council thereon. It should have a clear mandate with sufficient human and financial resources, through the reallocation of resources within the regular budget of the United Nations to carry the mandate out.

319. The Commission on the Status of Women should assist the Economic and Social Council in its coordination of the reporting on the implementation of the Platform for Action with the relevant organizations of the United Nations system. The Commission should draw upon inputs from other organizations of the United Nations system and other sources, as appropriate.

320. The Commission on the Status of Women, in developing its work programme for the period 1996–2000, should review the critical areas of concern in the Platform for Action and consider how to integrate in its agenda the follow-up to the World Conference on Women. In this context, the Commission on the Status of Women could consider how it could further develop its catalytic role in mainstreaming a gender perspective in United Nations activities.

Other functional commissions

321. Within their mandates, other functional commissions of the Economic and Social Council should also take due account of the Platform for Action and ensure the integration of gender aspects in their respective work.

Committee on the Elimination of Discrimination against Women and other treaty bodies

322. The Committee on the Elimination of Discrimination against Women, in implementing its responsibilities under the Convention on the Elimination of All Forms of Discrimination against Women, should, within its mandate, take into account the Platform for Action when considering the reports submitted by States parties.

323. States parties to the Convention on the Elimination of All Forms of Discrimination against Women are invited, when reporting under article 18 of the Convention, to include information on measures taken to implement the Platform for Action in order to facilitate the Committee on the Elimination of Discrimination against Women in monitoring effectively women's ability to enjoy the rights guaranteed by the Convention.

324. The ability of the Committee on the Elimination of Discrimination against Women to monitor implementation of the Convention should be strengthened through the provision of human and financial resources within the regular budget of the United Nations, including expert legal assistance and, in accordance with General Assembly resolution 49/164 and the decision made by the meeting of States parties to the Convention held in May 1995, sufficient meeting time for the Committee. The Committee should increase its coordination with other human rights treaty bodies, taking into account the recommendations in the Vienna Declaration and Programme of Action.

325. Within their mandate, other treaty bodies should also take due account of the implementation of the Platform for Action and ensure the integration of the equal status and human rights of women in their work.

United Nations Secretariat

Office of the Secretary-General

326. The Secretary-General is requested to assume responsibility for coordination of policy within the United Nations for the implementation of the Platform for Action and for the mainstreaming of a system-wide gender perspective in all activities of the United Nations, taking into account the mandates of the bodies concerned. The Secretary-General should consider specific measures for ensuring effective coordination in the implementation of these objectives. To this end, the Secretary-General is invited to establish a high-level post in the office of the Secretary-General, using existing human and financial resources, to act as the Secretary-General's adviser on gender issues and to help ensure system-wide implementation of the Platform for Action in close cooperation with the Division for the Advancement of Women.

Division for the Advancement of Women

327. The primary function of the Division for the Advancement of Women of the Department for Policy Coordination and Sustainable Development is to provide substantive servicing to the Commission on the Status of Women and other intergovernmental bodies when they are concerned with the advancement of women, as well as to the Committee on the Elimination of Discrimination against Women. It has been designated a focal point for the implementation of the Nairobi Forward-looking Strategies for the Advancement of Women. In the light of the review of the mandate of the Commission on the Status of Women, as set out in paragraph 313 above, the functions of the Division for the Advancement of Women will also need to be assessed. The Secretary-General is requested to ensure more effective functioning of the Division by, *inter alia*, providing sufficient human and financial resources within the regular budget of the United Nations.

328. The Division should examine the obstacles to the advancement of women through the application of gender-impact analysis in policy studies for the Commission on the Status of Women and through support to other subsidiary bodies. After the Fourth World Conference on Women it should play a coordinating role in preparing the revision of the system-wide medium-term plan for the advancement of women for the period 1996–2001 and should continue serving as the secretariat for inter-agency coordination for the advancement of women. It should continue to maintain a flow of information with national commissions, national institutions for the advancement of women and non-governmental organizations with regard to implementation of the Platform for Action.

Other units of the United Nations Secretariat

329. The various units of the United Nations Secretariat should examine their programmes to determine how they can best contribute to the coordinated implementation of the Platform for Action. Proposals for implementation of the Platform need to be reflected in the revision of the system-wide medium-term plan for the advancement of women for the period 1996–2001, as well as in the proposed United Nations medium-term plan for the period 1998–2002. The content of the actions will depend on the mandates of the bodies concerned.

330. Existing and new linkages should be developed throughout the Secretariat in order to ensure that the gender perspective is introduced as a central dimension in all activities of the Secretariat.

331. The Office of Human Resources Management should, in collaboration with programme managers world wide, and in accordance with the strategic plan of action for the improvement of the status of women in the Secretariat (1995–2000), continue to accord priority to the recruitment and promotion of women in posts subject to geographical distribution, particularly in senior policy-level and decision-making posts, in order to achieve the goals set out in General Assembly resolutions 45/125 and 45/23920C and reaffirmed in General Assembly resolutions 46/100, 47/93, 48/106 and 49/167. The training service should design and conduct regular gender-sensitivity training or include gender-sensitivity training in all of its activities.

332. The Department of Public Information should seek to integrate a gender perspective in its general information activities and, within existing resources, strengthen and improve its programmes on women and the girl child. To this end, the Department should formulate a multimedia communications strategy to support the implementation of the Platform for Action, taking new technology fully into account. Regular outputs of the Department should promote the goals of the Platform, particularly in developing countries.

333. The Statistical Division of the Department for Economic and Social Information and Policy Analysis should have an important coordinating role in international work in statistics, as described above in chapter IV, strategic objective H.3.

International Research and Training Institute for the Advancement of Women

334. INSTRAW has a mandate to promote research and training on women's situation and development. In the light of the Platform for Action, INSTRAW should review its work programme and develop a programme for implementing those aspects of the Platform for Action that fall within its mandate. It should identify those types of research and research methodologies to be given priority, strengthen national capacities to carry out women's studies and gender research, including that on the status of the girl child, and develop networks of research institutions that can be mobilized for that purpose. It should also identify those types of education and training that can be effectively supported and promoted by the Institute.

United Nations Development Fund for Women

335. UNIFEM has the mandate to increase options and opportunities for women's economic and social development in developing countries by providing technical and financial assistance to incorporate the women's dimension into development at all levels. Therefore, UNIFEM should review and strengthen, as appropriate, its work programme in the light of the Platform for Action, focusing on women's political and economic empowerment. Its advocacy role should concentrate on fostering a multilateral policy dialogue on women's empowerment. Adequate resources for carrying out its functions should be made available.

Specialized agencies and other organizations of the United Nations system

336. To strengthen their support for actions at the national level and to enhance their contributions to coordinated follow-up by the United Nations, each organization should set out the specific actions they will undertake, including goals and targets to realign priorities and redirect resources to meet the global priorities identified in the Platform for Action. There should be a clear delineation of responsibility and accountability. These proposals should in turn be reflected in the system-wide medium-term plan for the advancement of women for the period 1996–2001.

337. Each organization should commit itself at the highest level and, in pursuing its targets, should take steps to enhance and support the roles and responsibilities of its focal points on women's issues.

338. In addition, specialized agencies with mandates to provide technical assistance in developing countries, particularly in Africa and the least developed countries, should cooperate more to ensure the continuing promotion of the advancement of women.

339. The United Nations system should consider and provide appropriate technical assistance and other forms of assistance to the countries with economies in transition in order to facilitate solution of their specific problems regarding the advancement of women.

340. Each organization should accord greater priority to the recruitment and promotion of women at the Professional level to achieve gender balance, particularly at decision-making levels. The paramount consideration in the employment of the staff and in the determination of the conditions of service should be the necessity of securing the highest standards of efficiency, competence and integrity. Due regard should be paid to the importance of recruiting the staff on as wide a geographical basis as possible. Organizations should report regularly to their governing bodies on progress towards this goal.

341. Coordination of United Nations operational activities for development at the country level should be improved through the resident coordinator system in accordance with relevant resolutions of the General Assembly, in particular General Assembly resolution 47/199, to take full account of the Platform for Action.

2. Other international institutions and organizations

342. In implementing the Platform for Action, international financial institutions are encouraged to review and revise policies, procedures and staffing to ensure that investments and programmes benefit women and thus contribute to sustainable development. They are also encouraged to increase the number of women in high-level positions, increase staff training in gender analysis and institute policies and guidelines to ensure full consideration of the differential impact of lending programmes and other activities on women and men. In this regard, the Bretton Woods institutions, the United Nations, as well as its funds and programmes and the specialized agencies, should establish regular and substantive dialogue, including dialogue at the field level, for more efficient and effective coordination of their assistance in order to strengthen the effectiveness of their programmes for the benefit of women and their families.

343. The General Assembly should give consideration to inviting the World Trade Organization to consider how it might contribute to the implementation of the Platform for Action, including activities in cooperation with the United Nations system.

344. International non-governmental organizations have an important role to play in implementing the Platform for Action. Consideration should be given to establishing a mechanism for collaborating with non-governmental organizations to promote the implementation of the Platform at various levels.

Chapter VI

FINANCIAL ARRANGEMENTS

345. Financial and human resources have generally been insufficient for the advancement of women. This has contributed to the slow progress to date in implementing the Nairobi Forward-looking Strategies for the Advancement of Women. Full and effective implementation of the Platform for Action, including the relevant commitments made at previous United Nations summits and conferences, will require a political commitment to make available human and financial resources for the empowerment of women. This will require the integration of a gender perspective in budgetary decisions on policies and programmes, as well as the adequate financing of specific programmes for securing equality between women and men. To implement the Platform for Action, funding will need to be identified and mobilized from all sources and across all sectors. The reformulation of policies and reallocation of resources may be needed within and among programmes, but some policy changes may not necessarily have financial implications. Mobilization of additional resources, both public and private, including resources from innovative sources of funding, may also be necessary.

A. National level

346. The primary responsibility for implementing the strategic objectives of the Platform for Action rests with Governments. To achieve these objectives, Governments should make efforts to systematically review how women benefit from public sector expenditures; adjust budgets to ensure equality of access to public sector expenditures, both for enhancing productive capacity and for meeting social needs; and achieve the gender-related commitments made in other United Nations summits and conferences. To develop successful national implementation strategies for the Platform for Action, Governments should allocate sufficient resources, including resources for undertaking gender-impact analysis. Governments should also encourage non-governmental organizations and private-sector and other institutions to mobilize additional resources.

347. Sufficient resources should be allocated to national machineries for the advancement of women as well as to all institutions, as appropriate, that can contribute to the implementation and monitoring of the Platform for Action.

348. Where national machineries for the advancement of women do not yet exist or where they have not yet been established on a permanent basis, Governments should strive to make available sufficient and continuing resources for such machineries.

349. To facilitate the implementation of the Platform for Action, Governments should reduce, as appropriate, excessive military expenditures and investments for arms production and acquisition, consistent with national security requirements.

350. Non-governmental organizations, the private sector and other actors of civil society should be encouraged to consider allocating the resources necessary for the implementation of the Platform for Action. Governments should create a supportive environment for the mobilization of resources by non-governmental organizations, particularly women's organizations and networks, feminist groups, the private sector and other actors of civil society, to enable them to contribute towards this end. The capacity of non-governmental organizations in this regard should be strengthened and enhanced.

B. Regional level

351. Regional development banks, regional business associations and other regional institutions should be invited to contribute to and help mobilize resources in their lending and other activities for the implementation of the Platform for Action. They should also be encouraged to take account of the Platform for Action in their policies and funding modalities.

352. The subregional and regional organizations and the United Nations regional commissions should, where appropriate and within their existing mandates, assist in the mobilization of funds for the implementation of the Platform for Action.

C. International level

353. Adequate financial resources should be committed at the international level for the implementation of the Platform for Action in the developing countries, particularly in Africa and the least developed countries. Strengthening national capacities in developing countries to implement the Platform for Action will require striving for the fulfilment of the agreed target of 0.7 percent of the gross national product of developed countries for overall official development assistance as soon as possible, as well as increasing the share of funding for activities designed to implement the Platform for Action. Furthermore, countries involved in development cooperation should conduct a critical analysis of their assistance programmes so as to improve the quality and effectiveness of aid through the integration of a gender approach.

354. International financial institutions, including the World Bank, the International Monetary Fund, the International Fund for Agricultural Development and the regional development banks, should be invited to examine their grants and lending and to allocate loans and grants to programmes for implementing the Platform for Action in developing countries, especially in Africa and the least developed countries.

355. The United Nations system should provide technical cooperation and other forms of assistance to the developing countries, in particular in Africa and the least developed countries, in implementing the Platform for Action.

356. Implementation of the Platform for Action in the countries with economies in transition will require continued international cooperation and assistance. The organizations and bodies of the United Nations system, including the technical and sectoral agencies, should facilitate the efforts of those countries in designing and implementing policies and programmes for the advancement of women. To this end, the International Monetary Fund and the World Bank should be invited to assist those efforts.

357. The outcome of the World Summit for Social Development regarding debt management and reduction as well as other United Nations world summits and conferences should be implemented in order to facilitate the realization of the objectives of the Platform for Action.

358. To facilitate implementation of the Platform for Action, interested developed and developing country partners, agreeing on a mutual commitment to allocate, on average, 20 percent of official development assistance and 20 percent of the national budget to basic social programmes should take into account a gender perspective.

359. Development funds and programmes of the United Nations system should undertake an immediate analysis of the extent to which their programmes and projects are directed to implementing the Platform for Action and, for the next programming cycle, should ensure the adequacy of resources targeted towards eliminating disparities between women and men in their technical assistance and funding activities.

360. Recognizing the roles of United Nations funds, programmes and specialized agencies, in particular the special roles of UNIFEM and INSTRAW, in the promotion of the empowerment of women, and therefore in the implementation of the Platform for Action within their respective mandates, *inter alia*, in research, training and information activities for the advancement of women as well as technical and financial assistance to incorporate a gender perspective in development efforts, the resources provided by the international community need to be sufficient and should be maintained at an adequate level.

361. To improve the efficiency and effectiveness of the United Nations system in its efforts to promote the advancement of women and to enhance its capacity to further the objectives of the Platform for Action, there is a need to renew, reform and revitalize various parts of the United Nations system, especially the Division for the Advancement of Women of the United Nations Secretariat, as well as other units and subsidiary bodies that have a specific mandate to promote the advancement of women. In this regard, relevant governing bodies within the United Nations system are encouraged to give special consideration to the effective implementation of the Platform for Action and to review their policies, programmes, budgets and activities in order to achieve the most effective and efficient use of funds to this end. Allocation of additional resources from within the United Nations regular budget in order to implement the Platform for Action will also be necessary.

NOTES

1. *Report of the World Conference to Review and Appraise the Achievements of the United Nations Decade for Women: Equality, Development and Peace, Nairobi, 15–26 July 1985* (United Nations publication, Sales No. E.85.IV.10), chap. I, sect. A.
2. *Report of the World Conference on Human Rights, Vienna, 14–25 June 1993* (A/CONF.157/24 (Part I)), chap. III.
3. General Assembly resolution 34/180, annex.
4. General Assembly resolution 45/164.
5. General Assembly resolution 44/82.
6. General Assembly resolution 48/126.
7. A/47/308-E/1992/97, annex.
8. General Assembly resolution 48/104.
9. Vienna Declaration and Programme of Action, *Report of the World Conference on Human Rights . . .*, chap. III, para. 5.
10. See *The Results of the Uruguay Round of Multilateral Trade Negotiations: The Legal Texts* (Geneva, GATT secretariat, 1994).
11. General Assembly resolution 44/25, annex.
12. *Final Report of the World Conference on Education for All: Meeting Basic Learning Needs, Jomtien, Thailand, 5–9 March 1990*, Inter-Agency Commission (UNDP, UNESCO, UNICEF, World Bank) for the World Conference on Education for All, New York, 1990, appendix 1.
13. General Assembly resolution 2200 A (XXI), annex.
14. *Report of the International Conference on Population and Development, Cairo, 5–13 September 1994* (United Nations publication, Sales No. E.95.XIII.18), chap. I, resolution 1, annex.
15. *Report of the World Summit for Social Development, Copenhagen, 6–12 March 1995* (A/CONF.166/9), chap. I, resolution 1, annexes I and II.
16. Unsafe abortion is defined as a procedure for terminating an unwanted pregnancy either by persons lacking the necessary skills or in an environment lacking the minimal medical standards or both (based on World Health Organization, *The Prevention and Management of Unsafe Abortion*, Report of a Technical Working Group, Geneva, April 1992 (WHO/MSM/92.5)).
17. *Final Report of the International Conference on Nutrition, Rome, 5–11 December 1992* (Rome, Food and Agriculture Organization of the United Nations, 1993), Part II.
18. *Report of the United Nations Conference on Environment and Development, Rio de Janeiro, 3–14 June 1992*, vol. I, *Resolutions Adopted by the Conference* (United Nations publication, Sales No. E.93.I.8 and corrigenda), resolution 1, annex I.
19. Ibid., resolution 1, annex II.
20. General Assembly resolution 317 (IV), annex.
21. General Assembly resolution 217 A (III).
22. General Assembly resolution 39/46, annex.

23. *Official Records of the General Assembly, Forty-seventh Session, Supplement No. 38* (A/47/38), chap. I.
24. United Nations, *Treaty Series*, vol. 75, No. 973, p. 287.
25. *Report of the World Conference on Human Rights* . . . , chap. III, sect. II, para. 38.
26. See *The United Nations Disarmament Yearbook*, vol. 5: 1980 (United Nations publication, Sales No. E.81.IX.4), appendix VII.
27. General Assembly resolution 260 A (III), annex.
28. United Nations, *Treaty Series*, vol. 189, No. 2545.
29. Ibid., vol. 606, No. 8791.
30. General Assembly resolution 48/96, annex.
31. General Assembly resolution 1386 (XIV).
32. See CEDAW/SP/1995/2.
33. General Assembly resolution 2106 A (XX), annex.
34. General Assembly resolution 41/128, annex.
35. United Nations Environment Programme, *Convention on Biological Diversity* (Environmental Law and Institutions Programme Activity Centre), June 1992.

The Platform for Action was originally disseminated by The United Nations Department for Policy Coordination and Sustainable Development (DPCSD). Reproduction and dissemination of this document, in print or electronic format, is encouraged.

A Review of Resource Volumes Prepared for the United Nations Fourth World Conference on Women

Mariam K. Chamberlain

The widespread recognition of the importance of the Beijing conference is confirmed by the wealth of studies and reports that were prepared by way of background. While the central document was the draft Platform for Action, several major volumes relating to the conference were published. They are the subject of this review. In some cases the reports were published as part of the observance of the fiftieth anniversary of the establishment of the United Nations. In one case, the *Human Development Report 1995*, prepared by the United Nations Development Programme (UNDP) primarily as the basic document for the World Summit for Social Development held in Copenhagen before the Beijing conference in March, was intended also as a contribution to Beijing.

This review covers the foremost volumes prepared for Beijing, both inside and outside the United Nations system. Additional reports and studies may be found listed in *United Nations Publications, Catalogue 1995–1996*, Special 50th Anniversary Issue, and also in *Catalogue of Publications for the Fourth World Conference on Women*. The latter includes publications of the United Nations and several of its related agencies and intergovernmental organizations, such as the International Labor Office (ILO), United Nations Educational, Scientific, and Cultural Organization (UNESCO), and the World Health Organization (WHO). Reports that are primarily regional or specific to topics such as health, literacy, or the media are not included in this review. They are available through the United Nations or directly from the specialized agencies. In any event, their main points are covered in the comprehensive volume *The World's Women, 1995*, described below.

United Nations Publications

Five of the background volumes were published by the United Nations itself. Two are of particular interest. *The United Nations and the Advancement of Women, 1945–1995* is a record of the entire history of United

Nations efforts on behalf of women, beginning with the statement on gender equality in the UN Charter. The charter affirms the equal rights of men and women and specifies that the work of the United Nations must be conducted without distinction as to race, sex, language, or religion. The volume consists of two parts. The first is a lengthy introduction (sixty-five pages) by UN Secretary General Boutros Boutros-Ghali, who describes with great eloquence the evolution of the various phases of the UN campaign for women.

According to the secretary general's report, four phases are discernible in the UN effort. During the initial period, from 1945 to 1962, the United Nations worked to secure women's legal equality. This included equality in laws and customs concerning marriage and the family, access to education, elimination of barriers to employment, and prevention of denial of voting rights. To codify the legal rights of women, the UN adopted the Universal Declaration of Human Rights in 1948. The secretary general sees the second period, from 1963 to 1975, as one in which more and more governments responded to the declaration by adopting laws and programs to protect women's rights. Meanwhile, the UN broadened its focus on equality of rights under the law to encompass the economic and social realities of women's lives, particularly in development assistance programs. This led to the third period, the Decade for Women, 1976–85, a period that generated a series of action programs recognizing the important role of women in economic development. During this period the UN expanded its working relationship with nongovernmental organizations (NGOs) working on behalf of women. It was during this period also that the 1979 Convention on the Elimination of All Forms of Discrimination Against Women (CEDAW) was adopted by the General Assembly of the UN. The secretary general identifies the post-Nairobi period, from 1986 to the present, as "an era of new and more complex challenges, in which the political and economic empowerment of women is the key not only to ending gender discrimination, but to eradicating poverty, enhancing productive employment and ending social disintegration" (p. 7).

The second section of this volume presents a chronology of events and United Nations conferences and provides the texts of relevant documents. The documents reproduced, 126 in all, include resolutions of the General Assembly and the Economic and Social Council, texts of international conventions, reports of the World Conferences on Women, reports of the Commission on the Status of Women, and reports by the secretary general. The volume, nearly seven hundred pages in all, is a valuable historical and documentary resource and reference volume.

A second valuable resource is the United Nations publication, *The World's Women, 1995*. This is an update of the earlier volume, *The World's Women, 1970–1990*, and is an official document of the Beijing conference. As a statistical sourcebook, it is the result of a monumental effort carried out under the direction of Robert Johnson and Joann Vanek of the Statistical Division, Department for Economic and Social Information and Policy Analysis of the UN Secretariat. Eleven UN agencies collaborated on the project.

The volume presents statistics with accompanying analyses in formats and nontechnical language, readily understandable by non-specialists. Data are presented on population, households and families, migration, health, education and training, work, and power and influence. Differences among countries and regions are emphasized. For example, charts and text make clear that while literacy rates for women have increased in recent decades, illiteracy remains high in much of Africa and parts of Asia. A number of regional trends are highlighted. In Latin America and the Caribbean, fertility has declined significantly, dropping 40 percent or more over the past two decades in thirteen of the region's thirty-three countries, but adolescent fertility remains high. In sub-Saharan Africa only minimal progress can be documented in such basic social and economic indicators as health, and gains in education have faltered in the face of economic crises and civil strife. Many countries in Northern Africa and Western Asia have invested in girls' education, but illiteracy remains high and women's labor force participation rates, while rising, are among the lowest in the world. In Southern Asia many health and education indicators remain low. In Eastern and Southeastern Asia, infant mortality has declined significantly over the past two decades; literacy is nearly universal; adolescent marriage rates in Eastern Asia are among the lowest in the world; fertility has declined dramatically; and women's labor force participation is as high as in developed regions— approximately 55 percent. In the West, basic health and education data indicate high levels of well-being, but in Eastern Europe there are signs of deterioration. Labor force participation has increased significantly for regions outside Eastern Europe, but women continue to earn less than men. Overall, the statistics indicate that, although the status and condition of women have improved over the last twenty years, women still lag far behind men in opportunity, wealth, and power. This volume is an unparalleled source of information on the world's women. A third major United Nations volume, *From Nairobi to Beijing: Second Review and Appraisal of the Nairobi Forward-Looking Strategies for the Advancement of Women*, addresses the extent to which the strategies adopted at the United Nations Third World Conference on Women in Nairobi in 1985 have been implemented and with what success. This second review was prepared by the Division for the Advancement of Women of the United Nations Secretariat, the first having been conducted in 1990 as a five-year review. The second review and appraisal provided the basis for the determination of the critical areas of concern identified by the Commission on the Status of Women and embodied in the Platform for Action prepared for discussion and adoption at Beijing. These critical areas of concern are, of course, the persistent and growing burden of poverty on women; inequality in access to education and training; inequality in access to health and related services; violence against women; effects of armed conflict on women; inequality in economic opportunity and in political participation; insufficient mechanisms to promote the advancement of women; lack of awareness of and commitment to women's human rights; insufficient use of mass media to promote positive images of women and their contributions to society; and lack of adequate recognition and support for women's role in safeguarding the environment.

While drawing on a variety of sources of information, the report relies mainly on a review of national reports prepared by more than a hundred countries, including transitional countries of Eastern Europe and the former Soviet Union. The national reports were prepared under government auspices on the issues raised in the Forward-Looking Strategies. The volume provides exhaustive information relating to government actions taken to address the critical areas of concern. Indeed, the most distinctive contribution of this volume may well be the information and analysis of the structure, role, and activities of national machineries to promote the advancement of women. National machineries were established during the Decade for Women to monitor and improve the status of women. Some countries have cabinet-level ministries for women's affairs, while others have advisory groups on women's issues or structures located in the ministry of labor. Also included in this volume is a view of actions taken by international and intergovernmental agencies, such as the United Nations Institute for Research and Training for the Advancement of Women (INSTRAW) and the United Nations Development Fund for Women (UNIFEM). In addition, the volume provides an overview of trends in the global economy and economic restructuring as they affect the implementation of the Nairobi Forward-Looking Strategies.

A fourth United Nations volume published in conjunction with the Beijing conference is *Women: Looking Beyond 2000*. It was prepared by the United Nations Department of Public Information with the cooperation of other agencies and offices of the United Nations system as part of a worldwide educational campaign to increase public awareness of the challenges and obstacles to the advancement of women described in the draft Platform for Action. Intended for the general public rather than the specialist, the book provides background information and case studies relating to the critical areas of concern cited in the Platform. With illustrations and firsthand accounts, it explains the need for action in the areas of reproductive health; violence against women; neglect and overwork of the girl child in many parts of the world; problems of women in the workplace and recognition of women's unpaid labor; and women's access to the media. The book presents examples of successful program initiatives and possibilities for future action programs. In addition, it includes short essays by international experts on key issues: Bella Abzug of the Women's Environment and Development Organization (WEDO) on women and the environment; Margaret Gallagher, freelance consultant on mass communication, on women and the media; Ama Ata Adoo, writer, teacher, and former minister of education in Ghana, on African women; Anita Anand, director of Women's Feature Service, India, on grassroots women's movements; Martha Chen of the Harvard Institute of International Development (HIID) on widowhood; and Mahbub ul Haq, special adviser to the United Nations Development Programme (UNDP) and former minister of finance and planning of Pakistan, on equalizing gender opportunities. The volume concludes with a contribution by Gertrude Mongella, secretary general of the Fourth World Conference on Women, calling for commitments to action following Beijing. This volume will be of interest primarily to those who are not already actively involved in UN activities on behalf of women, especially to those outside the process who wish to know what the Beijing conference was all about.

The fifth volume is the 1994 World Survey on the Role of Women in Development, published under the title *Women in a Changing Global Economy.* The World Survey is the third in a series, which is now issued every five years in connection with the periodic review and appraisal of the Nairobi Forward-Looking Strategies. Like its predecessors, the survey is a team effort involving the staff of the United Nations Secretariat and colleagues from the cognizant specialized agencies. Each survey has had a different point of departure. The first, issued in 1986, immediately following the Nairobi conference, focused on women as participants in development. The second, issued in 1989, explored women's participation in the global adjustment process. The 1994 Survey examines the effects of the restructuring process and the emerging role of women in the global economy. It is one of the basic documents of the Beijing conference.

The 1994 Survey analyzes three development issues—poverty, productive employment, and economic decision making—from a gender perspective. That is, it looks at the situation of women relative to that of men rather than the situation of women only. With regard to poverty, the survey provides data to show that despite worldwide economic growth, the number of people living in poverty, in both urban and rural areas, has increased in developing and developed regions alike. The study further indicates that men and women experience poverty differently. At the household level the burden of coping with poverty falls disproportionately on women and, of course, the situation is particularly severe in the case of female-headed households. Economic restructuring and the globalization of the economy have a differential impact on various countries and on men and women in those countries. In some cases, new job opportunities become available to women in export-oriented industries, but they tend to be low-wage work relative to that of male employment. With regard to women in decision making, the survey shows some improvement in the economic sphere, but the gender gap remains large, especially in the top levels of decision making. This publication is useful as an overview of global economic trends and of national and regional differences with regard to women's economic lives.

Human Development Report, 1995

The *Human Development Report* is a publication that has been produced annually since 1990 to provide an assessment of global development not only in terms of economic growth but also in terms of human well-being. On that basis, successive reports have expressed concern that the rapid growth in economic development in recent decades has been accompanied by rising disparities within and between nations. Issues of equity and poverty are central to the human development assessment. The 1995 report focuses specifically on gender disparities and was produced both as the basic document for the World Summit for Social Development held in Copenhagen in March, before the Beijing conference, and as a contribution to the World Conference on Women in Beijing. It was published for the United Nations Development Programme (UNDP) by Oxford University Press. Unlike publications issued by the United Nations itself, the *Human Development Report* provides the names of the contributors to the volume, an impressive team of eminent economists and development professionals, including leading feminist scholars in the field. The principal coordinator of the report was Mahbub ul Haq as special adviser to the UNDP, working with a UNDP team under the direction of Inge Paul. The panel of consultants for the report includes, among others, Amrita Basu, Mayra Buvinic, Margaret Schuler, Amartya Sen, and Kathleen Staudt. The external advisory panel includes Bella Abzug, Nancy Barry, Nancy Birdsall, Lincoln Chen, Sumiko Iwao, Wangari Maathai, Lucille Mair, Vina Mazumdar, Gertrude Mongella, and Joann Vanek. An interesting feature of the report is a series of special contributions by seven women heads of state in 1995—Khaleda Zia of Bangladesh, Mary Robinson of Ireland, Violetta Barrios de Chamorro of Nicaragua, Gro Harlem Brundtland of Norway, Benazir Bhutto of Pakistan, Chandrika Bandaranaike Kumaratunga of Sri Lanka, and Tanzu Ciller of Turkey.

Over the years the *Human Development Report* has ranked countries on the basis of a Human Development Index (HDI), a simple composite index that includes three indicators—life expectancy, educational attainment, and Gross Domestic Product. In 1995 the report added a new concept to take account of gender differences. The gender-related development index (GDI) is based on the same three variables as the HDI is. The methodology used imposes a penalty for inequality such that the GDI for a country falls when the achievement levels of both women and men go down or when the disparity between their achievement increases.

Estimates of the gender-related development index have been prepared for 130 countries. On this basis the top-ranking countries fall in the Nordic belt, but no society treats its women as well as its men. On the GDI scale, the United States ranks fifth from the top, just behind the Nordic countries. The lowest countries on the scale are Afghanistan, Sierra Leone, Mali, and Niger. One of the conclusions of the report is that gender equality does not depend on the income level of a society. Comparing the GDI ranks of countries with their income levels confirms that removing gender inequality is not dependent on having a high income. For example, Thailand outranks Spain on the GDI index even though its real per capita income is less than half of Spain's. Another conclusion of the report is that although there is still a long way to go, significant progress has been achieved over the last two decades. The GDI values of all countries have improved between 1970 and 1992 but at different rates.

Another innovation in the 1995 report is the Gender Empowerment Index (GEM), which looks at women's representation in parliaments, women's share of positions classified as managerial and professional, women's participation in the active labor force, and their share of national income. It ranks 116 countries on this basis, with the Nordic countries again leading the world. The gendered analysis of human development that has been introduced in the 1995 report will be continued and refined in future reports. It is a highly promising approach as a way to measure progress toward gender equality.

Related Publications

Two other publications prepared in anticipation of the Beijing conference are worthy of note. One is *The Challenge of Local Feminisms*, a work commissioned by the Ford Foundation that provides a portrait of women's movements around the world. It consists of contributed essays on indigenous women's movements in seventeen countries, with particular attention to non-Western countries. The countries represented include China, India, Bangladesh, and the Philippines in Asia; South Africa, Namibia, Kenya, Nigeria, and the Occupied Territories of the Gaza and West Bank in Africa and the Middle East; and Peru, Chile, Brazil, and Mexico in Latin America. For the Europe and North America region, there are four essays—on Russia, post-Communist Central Europe, Western Europe, and the United States. The editor of the volume is Amrita Basu, professor of political science and women's and gender studies at Amherst College.

In her introductory essay, Basu notes the similarities of this volume to Robin Morgan's *Sisterhood Is Global*, published more than ten years earlier, in 1984. The formats of the two books are parallel: both include national studies contributed by scholars, activists, and policy-makers, reflecting the diversity of the women's movement around the world. *The Challenge of Local Feminisms* reflects the changes that have taken place during the intervening period as new nation-states have been formed in Africa and as the collapse of communism in the former Soviet Union and Eastern Europe made possible the rise of independent women's movements. Among the more illuminating essays in the book is one that traces the course of the women's movement in China against the background of historical and political changes and contemporary economic reforms. This volume provides ample evidence, if such is needed, that, as of 1995, the women's movement is alive and well and spreading rapidly across the globe.

Also pertaining to the Beijing conference is the volume *A Rising Public Voice*, a compendium of original essays, profiles, and interviews chiefly by women just in or out of office, edited by Alida Brill, a feminist author, political scientist, and activist. The book is supported in part by the United Nations Office of Public Information and published by the Feminist Press. Given the priority attached to women in political life and the slow progress in this area, this highly readable book makes an important contribution by serving as an inspiration and guide for young women and others to follow. Among others, the book touches on the lives of Hanan Ashwari, official spokesperson for the Palestinian delegation to the Middle East peace talks; Maria de Lourdes Pintasilgo, first woman prime minister of Portugal; Diane Abbott, the first Black woman in the British Parliament; and Barbara Jordan, congresswoman of the United States, renowned for the power of her oratory.

All of the books described above provide resources not only for action programs to implement the Beijing Platform for Action but also for the growing number of women's studies programs around the world. They also provide useful resource material for the media.

BOOKS REVIEWED

Basu, Amrita, ed. *The Challenge of Local Feminisms: Women's Movements in Global Perspective.* Boulder, Col.: Westview Press, 1995. 493 pp. $19.95.

Brill, Alida, ed. *A Rising Public Voice: Women in Politics Worldwide.* New York: Feminist Press at the City University of New York, 1995. 284 pp. $17.95.

From Nairobi to Beijing. Second Review and Appraisal of the Implementation of the Nairobi Forward-Looking Strategies for the Advancement of Women, Report of the Secretary General. New York: United Nations, 1995. 366 pp. $25.00.

Human Development Report, 1995. Published for the United Nations Development Programme (UNDP). New York: Oxford University Press, 1995. 230 pp. $18.95.

The United Nations and the Advancement of Women, 1945–1995. New York: United Nations Department of Public Information, 1995. 689 pp. $29.95.

Women in a Changing Global Economy: 1994 World Survey on the Role of Women in Development. New York: United Nations Department for Policy Coordination and Sustainable Development, 1995. 105 pp. $9.95.

Women: Looking Beyond 2000. New York: United Nations, 1995. 126 pp. $14.95.

The World's Women, 1995: Trends and Statistics, Social Statistics and Indicators, Series K, No. 12. New York: United Nations, 1995. 188 pp. $15.95.

Mariam K. Chamberlain is founding president of the National Council for Research on Women.

Women's Studies in Germany

Tobe Levin

It is commonly supposed that contemporary German feminism descended from the ivory tower; the first activists were academics. Still unclear, however, is the hour of its birth. Can the movement be dated from that tomato thrown in 1968 at a male SDS speaker in Frankfurt? Or will those partial to Berlin claim the "committee for women's emancipation" that arose in that divided city in 1968 as the cradle of it all? Whichever we choose, both correctly emphasize the alliance between activists and educators, whose history goes back to the first feminist wave.

In 1908 German women finally won admittance to university study, but they were among the last in Europe to do so, a fact that seems relevant even today, because, despite constant feminist incursions over the last twenty years, Germany trails the majority of European nations in representation of faculty women. Only 5.5 percent of C-3 and C-4 professors (associate and full rank), or 2.6 percent in the top category, are female (based on the total number of professors in all departments at German universities) (Gerhard 1995; Bock 1993b Frauenforschungsprofessuren (FFP):24; latest available figures from the Statistiches Bundesamt [Federal Office of Statistics] November 1993). Viewed another way, 50 percent of students are female, but only 28.5 percent of the Ph.D. pool are women, which narrows to 12.3 percent of candidates for the second doctorate, or *Habilitation*, required for associate professor status; and at the top, fewer than 3 percent, as we have seen (Baume and Felber 1995:18).

What accounts for this dismal statistical portrait? In addition to cyclic fiscal restraints (shrinking budgets for higher education and reduction of faculty), resistance to women themselves and disparagement of feminist perspectives in the various disciplines represent the most serious structural impediments to women's studies in Germany and have led to a double-pronged strategy: first, reform efforts within the academy and, second, the founding of autonomous institutions.

Note: A version of this article, by Tobe Levin and Sabine Bröck, "Seit 20 Jahren am Anfang: Women's Studies in the Bundesrepublik," was first published in *Konkret* 2 (June 1994): 6–8. All translations from the German are by Tobe Levin.

The following discussion will highlight the background, hurdles, and tactics that feminists employ both within and outside academe in their efforts to ensure a fertile terrain for the field of women's studies.

Background and Obstacles

At the University of Bochum in 1995, an international, interdisciplinary guest professor's chair was named to honor Marie Jahoda, an Austrian Jewish socialist historian forced into exile by the Nazis, whose work on unemployment featured gender analysis in 1933. In fact, the roots of contemporary German women's studies ascend from the older feminist wave. In 1908, for instance, Alice Salomon launched a college for women in social work; in 1924 and 1929, Bertha Pappenheim, founder of the German Jewish Women's Movement, wrote a remarkable study, *Sisyphus-Arbeit* on Jewish women as opponents and victims of the "white" slave trade. These are two examples among many that illustrate the historical links between activism and feminist research, which still obtain today. National socialist dementia, of course, caused a break, but the fifties, despite little expression of feminist consciousness, produced isolated research in the form of doctoral dissertations and monographs on topics that we now recognize as women's studies, including some astonishing work on equal rights and women in politics. "These theses tended to look back to the pioneering efforts of the twenties," Ute Gerhard (1995) noted in a recent interview.

"With the new women's movement, however, a vehemence entered the picture," she continued, "for, compared to the USA, German tradition in higher learning has been virulent in its hostility to women." "Why?" I asked. "I think it goes back to the function of a highly selective university in the nineteenth century," Gerhard responded. As a *Berechtigungssystem* (system of legitimation), higher education validated male entry into liberal professions, a bourgeois tier, it should be underscored, open to men only. At the top, an exclusionary climate remains to this day, with power held by an almost exclusively male elite whose status is far higher than U.S. professors enjoy. As Ann Taylor Allen (1994) confirms: "Access to professorships [is] much more difficult in the German than in the American system. Not simply the highest rung on a career ladder, . . . German full professorships usually require a special appointment that must be approved by the state education ministry as well as faculty recruitment committees. Appointments to such positions, which carry prestige, high pay, and power, often involve heated political controversies in which women, as a minority group with little influence, [are] seldom in a position to prevail" (Allen:13, citing Brigitte Rauschenbach).

Now, the *Hochschulrahmengesetz* (university bylaws) have begun to recognize women's disadvantage, although educational rulings lie within the purview of states and therefore differ among them. Still, even when favoring greater parity for women, rhetoric is often contradicted by policy tied to cutting costs. For instance, financial considerations dictate limiting the number of years an individual may remain at any given career step, a greater hardship for women than for men, since the former more frequently devote time to family. Yet, Gudrun Werner-Hervieu (1992) asserts: "The only realistic professional path has a woman earning the first degree (*Diplom* or *Staatsexamen*) [M.A. or federal qualifying exam] at age twenty-four, receiving the doctorate at twenty-eight, and completing her postdoctoral work, the *Habilitation*, at thirty-one in order to accede to the professorship at thirty-five. Then she might think about children" (91).

Once she has them, another peculiar aspect of German culture compromises her career aspirations. Uta Enders-Dragässer (1988) explains: "A new slice of life begins for mothers when their children start school [for someone must] monitor homework in a competitive educational system which varies from the international standard in offering classes only in the mornings. As a result, afternoons find the children at home with schoolwork needing supervision. . . . In other words, actual lessons take place outside the framework of government financed schooling; they have been privatized. This obviously saves the state a great deal of money for teaching positions while also placing responsibility for academic success squarely on the 'parents' which means the mothers. . . . Dividing school work into the publicly financed and the privatized actually disguises a hidden full-time school day based on the school's exploitation of mothers who, given their differing backgrounds and the degree and kind of homework, cannot help but contribute to the maintenance of class, sex, and race discrimination." Clearly, the abbreviated school day affects women, resonating throughout society. In fact, schools presuppose this non–wage-earning parent. If a teacher is ill, for instance, no substitute is called. Instead, in most cases, children are sent home! Although Germany has the lowest birth rate in the world, enough German women are mothers to make this a problem of the utmost gravity. This is merely one aspect of the dilemma that German women face when aspiring to both careers (including desire for the professorate) and parenthood. Another to which German critics often point can be summed up as the masculine curriculum vitae. Ingrid Lehmann (1994), representing the

German Association of Women in the Natural Sciences and Technology (NUT) at the ECE UN Regional Meeting in Vienna, elaborates this concept in relation to expectations of scientists, whose professional requirements discriminate by failing to take into account what sociologist Ulrike Prokop called in 1975 the context of women's lives (*weibliche Lebenszusammenhang*). Lehmann notes that the job description for engineers presupposes a typical man's career track. From him (gender intended) are expected constant availability, willingness to work full time, not to mention overtime, and to relocate. This is true for the university as well.

And as the (West) German structure of higher education takes over in the former East, it reproduces the old hierarchies that have always been unfriendly to women, including chairs at the top and this masculine career profile. A regular rout of (East) German female academics, twice as likely as their male colleagues to be retired early or made redundant, has resulted. In this regard, the West's failure to learn from the East, where far more women had been engaged in scientific and technical fields, appears particularly regrettable.

Increasing the Number of Academic Women

Helga Schuchard, minister of education in Lower Saxony, contends that "without outside pressure, the universities on their own are not willing to improve women's situation" (quoted in Dickhoven 1994:BW6). She has therefore published a report by the Commission for Women's Research that makes three important recommendations. First, because the *Habilitation* would appear to work as a ceiling barring women's ascent, authorities should consider abolishing it as a career requirement—a controversial stance. Second, not only should more women be promoted but also feminist perspectives should be integrated across the board. The commission report speaks specifically of *Frauenstudien* (women's studies) as offering resonant critiques of traditional fields and methodologies whose broad diffusion would democratize the university structure. A third recommendation supports founding a women's university. These last two points will be developed more fully later in this essay.

Minister Schuchard elaborated on these points in a talk titled "Reform of Higher Education Through the Promotion of Women" at a high-level conference sponsored by the Berlin government on 27–28 June 1995 and attended by three hundred university women, politicians, and *Gleichstellungsbeauftragte* (affirmative action officers)—government or university employees charged since the early eighties with overseeing increased representation of women in academe. Wissenschaft als Arbeit/Arbeit als Wissenschaftlerin (Academic Labor/Academic Women) in Berlin, organized by the Sozialpädagogisches Institut Berlin (SPI) (Pedagogical Institute) addressed the fact that, as we have seen, despite the clear increase in the number of women students and lower-ranking faculty, no corresponding growth in professorial posts awarded to women can be discerned. In fact, the group of experts asked why, instead, they perceived an abyss between accelerating feminist efforts and achievement, with events since reunification marking a "professional fiasco" for female academics in the East, which, as we have noted, imported West German exclusionary mechanisms into its higher-education reform. Many felt as though a watershed had been reached—if not a breakthrough, then a backlash. Speakers' comments summarized the obstacles. Dr. Helga Engel of Berlin's Technical College (FHTW) saw in the gravity of discrimination in the natural sciences a "conspiracy of male civilization" (Baume and Felber 1995:18). Dr. Heide Pfarr, former minister of education in the state of Hesse, warned that a type of strategy may itself prove a barrier: measures to facilitate women's reentry into university life after the family phase could backfire in that they relieve men of their responsibilities and reify the feminine part of an unfair division of labor. Federal Minister for Education, Science, Research, and Technology Helga Ebeling found inadequate the attempts already made to assure a next generation of women scholars. Monika Klinkhammer spoke for many in insisting that opposition to quotas to achieve parity must be confronted. The call for quotas has resonated throughout German discussions of means, and many political allies have been found. On 17 October 1995, however, the all-male European Court of Justice meeting in Luxembourg banned quotas for women as an affirmative action strategy throughout the European Union. Among others, the German government protested, but it is too soon to know precisely what ramifications will follow (*Financial Times*, 23 October 1995, p. 8). Yet despite this major setback, quotas will remain a favored strategy of European women's studies advocates, who also emphasize women's networking on a national and international level to urge implementation of specific parity standards. Summarizing the conference findings, Brita Baume and Christina Felber (1995) write: "The exclusion of women from universities and independent research institutes has many causes: male dominance of all committees and boards with decision-making and financial power, and especially those that call individuals to assume professorial chairs; the male definition of 'qualification' including the legitimation of research themes (which favor

men's preferences and suppress women's); the social background of
gender relations which makes housekeeping and child-rearing women's business; universities taking for granted the male curriculum
vitae; lack of female professors as role models; in general, the conflict
between career and motherhood which, instead of alleviating, the
university aggravates" (20).

Summarizing many of the obstacles detailed so far are the ideals
and aims put forward by the Gesellschaft Deutscher Akademikerinnen e.V. (GDA) [Society of German Women Academics], born on 5 July
1992. This association publishes an informative newsletter, *Neue Impulse*, and, with representatives in fifty-three German cities, acts to (1)
promote women to higher professorial positions, especially in the new
states, (2) accelerate the rise of qualified women [toward] parity with
men, (3) overcome barriers to women's advancement, (4) mentor female students, and (5) monitor the application of EU equal opportunity laws.

Integrating Women's Studies Content

Just as women themselves have encountered formidable gatekeepers,
so too has women's studies been unwelcome. I have been discussing
the general position of women in higher education. Turning now to
the women's studies field, as of December 1993—according to the
latest available figures (Bock 1995)—seventy-six women's studies positions had been assigned or planned at German universities and
Hochschulen (college-level institutions) (excluding *Fachhochschulen*
[colleges specializing in a limited number of disciplines]), all in the
old German states plus Berlin and Brandenburg, and with the exception of one women's studies post in Potsdam, no plans are being made
to increase representation in the field in the new states. Now, this
number represents an even sadder situation once we note that, of ten
thousand full professorships (C-4) in Germany, women's studies accounts for only eighteen, that is, 0.2 percent of the total (Bock
1993b:24), a figure that, in Ulla Bock's view, "reveals the low esteem in
which the field is held in academia" (Bock 1993b:11).

In the seventies, the initial emphatic response of intellectual feminists led to a debate pitting institutionalization against autonomy.
Some left the university altogether, founding independent institutions. Others began offering classes in the *Volkshochschulen* (VHS) (people's high schools or community colleges), well-attended non-degree-
granting institutions for adult learners that charge nominal fees and
are found even in villages; they offer a vast number of courses,

including consciousness-raising groups for women and a broad range of feminist classes. These schools provide a particularly fertile ground for women's lifelong education. As for those who stayed in academia proper, Ute Gerhard notes that they could perform as feminist scholars only outside normal channels, without research grants or institutional backing. The earlier feminist dissertations were often written by women lacking official status, considered "merely" housewives if accepting a husband's support and raising children. Their work would then have to overcome professorial opposition, to be "smuggled in" (Ute Gerhard's term), an exceptional approach that worked but was accompanied by unpleasantness and the need, each time a women's studies topic was treated, to plead for an exception to policy. Only toward the beginning of the eighties did the situation ease, with institutional acceptance beginning and, from the mid-eighties, allowing posts that integrate women's studies content to appear fairly secure, though still exceedingly rare. One of the most troubling challenges to conservative minds has been the claim of women's studies to boundary transgression, resisted with vehemence by the traditional, discipline-oriented institution. Of course, women staff in the middle ranks have been offering feminist perspectives on prescribed material or placing new items on the agenda. But their limited contracts and isolation have made this situation less than ideal, and arguments concerning it as a desirable option have accompanied the discussion of women's studies since the early 1970s. Scholars who want women's studies departments to anchor the gains of the field have been arguing with others for whom integration of feminist perspectives in all disciplines seems the better move. In fact, both strategies have been fruitfully employed. For instance, Bielefeld University's Interdisciplinäre Forschungsgruppe Frauenforschung (IFF) [Interdisciplinary Research Group for Women's Studies], launched in 1983, became the first "department" that inaugurates and directs graduate research. In Dortmund the first graduate school for women's studies in sociology, financed by the Deutsche Forschungsgemeinschaft (German Research Association), began its three-year cycle of fellowships in October 1992. Called "Geschlechterverhältnis und sozialer Wandel. Handlungsspielräume und Definitionsmacht von Frauen" (Gender and the Transformation of Society: Parameters for Women's Action and Their Power to Define) the program supports eight doctoral candidates and one postdoctoral candidate with stipends awarded by the interinstitutional consortium behind the initiative—the Universities of Bielefeld, Bochum, Essen, and Dortmund. According to a 1992 press release, supporters expect the initiative to have a significant "resonance not only in the state but in the nation." The graduate school complements an already existing network of women's studies professorships in North Rhine–Westphalia, where feminist education minister Anke Brunn has assured that her state leads all others in this domain, with forty women's studies professorships (eleven C-4, twenty-eight C-3, one C-2, including those projected). To compare: Berlin has thirteen, Hesse six, Bremen and Lower Saxony five each; Baden-Württemberg and Rheinland-Pfalz two each; Saarland, Hamburg, and Brandenburg one each (Bock 1995).

Thus, despite formidable obstacles, recognition of women's studies is growing, if slowly. The DFG's (German Research Association) commission, for instance, has begun awarding fellowships and supporting projects. "Yes, scepticism still exists, with certain fields not yet having budged an inch," Gerhard concedes. Nonetheless, Gerhard's Lilac Chair in the department of social sciences in Frankfurt may serve as a model of interdisciplinarity and structural innovation: women can earn normal sociology degrees while choosing to study and be tested on specific women's studies themes (i.e., the diploma makes its owner a sociologist; the major, however, is in women's studies).

Even more sanguine about women's studies energy in Germany is Gudrun Werner-Hervieu. "Today at all (West) German universities [plus Potsdam and Humboldt in Berlin], women's studies—broadly viewed to include a wide range of activities—has found a more or less secure reception," she asserts. "The menu ranges from women's studies proper—study groups, [de facto] women-only seminars, lectures and lecture series—to women's representatives as part of democratic student organizations, women's archives, and female meeting places, women's cafés and 'male-free zones' " (Werner-Hervieu 1992:89). Indeed, institutes like the Zentraleinrichtung zur Förderung von Frauenstudien und Frauenforschung (University Center for the Promotion of Women's Studies and Research) at the Free University of Berlin encourage integrating women's studies into existing courses, identifying dozens of feminist-inspired classes that count toward degrees in "normal" disciplines. Berlin's Technical and Free Universities, for instance, listed ninety electives in women's studies in academic year 1989–90, and Frankfurt regularly offers as many as seventy.

Regarding the themes that characterize German women's studies, their multiplicity discourages generalization, yet several stand out: the early years debated Paragraph 218 (concerning abortion) and other issues of women's health. I fondly remember the auburn, fawn, cocoa, and tawny heads—about fifty of us—in a pioneering seminar on

Marxism and feminism in academic year 1975–76, taught by Ingrid Schmidt-Harzbach at the Free University of Berlin. Ute Gerhard also points to a myriad of studies "focused on historical development of mutations in women's work. . . or on housework in relation to wage labor" (1992:101). The eighties have witnessed the preference for "gender studies" clearly emerging in Germany as the topics to which feminists attend range from the critique of science and feminist epistemology to the controversy surrounding a "feminist" ethics, the equality and/or difference debate, and poststructuralism. U.S. feminism, in particular the work of Judith Butler and Seyla Benhabib, has had a profound impact. Berliner Christina Thurmer-Rohr has also proved to be highly influential, along with Maria Mies, whose "postulates" published in 1978 in "Towards a Methodology for Feminist Research" continue to guide women's studies thinking. Mies proposed that the feminist researcher needs to enlist both empathy (*Betroffenheit*) and engagement (*Parteilichkeit*) to transcend the hierarchical and destructive power relationship between the investigator and her object. Since Mies came to her position through experience in the developing world, she has influenced an increasing focus on differences among women.

German women's studies needs to carry on with its concern for racism and integrating the interests of immigrant, refugee. and other minority women into its agenda. Dagmar Schultz (1992) has called for increased outreach of white German women to immigrants working in projects limited to their own groups. Activist leaders, Schultz feels, should be welcomed to teaching positions and actively recruited. In her words:

> As I came to see the absence of immigrants, Blacks and Jews from the German women's movement as neither a transitory nor accidental phenomenon but rather as the result of a certain systemic problem linked to that movement's developing self-image, I felt increasingly ill at ease. . . . [Women's studies'] concentration on issues of local significance and its failure to measure political principles or strategies against global realities and consequences for women elsewhere seemed not only limiting but downright dangerous. Moreover, women's projects of primary relevance to immigrants remained side issues for the German women's movement, a situation women's studies mirrored—research by and about immigrant women was linked to social work but was not integrated into feminist theory.
>
> (Schultz 1992)

Schultz introduced African-American women's literature into her course at the Institute for North American Studies at the Free University of Berlin. Guest professor Audre Lorde initiated contact with Afro-German women, which led to publication of the groundbreaking *Showing Our Colors: Afro-German Women Speak Out* and, in effect, both launched a movement of German women of African origin and helped legitimate interest in African-American studies by German women Americanists.

Unification has made attention to issues of race and nationality even more pressing, although the response of German women's studies dates from at least the early eighties. Gudrun Werner-Hervieu (1992) traces this history. Beginning with the Congress for Foreign and German Women held in Frankfurt in 1984, university seminars addressing racism continued. For a mere eighteen-month period we can list the Bremer Frauenwoche (Bremen Women's Week) against racism and sexism in October 1989; Frauen gegen Nationalismus, Rassismus/ Antisemitismus und Sexismus (Women Against Nationalism, Racism/ Antisemitism and Sexism) in November 1990 in Cologne, organized by Sozialwissenschaftliche Forschung und Praxis für Frauen (Social Science Research and Practice for Women); Jüdische Kultur und Weiblichkeit in der Moderne (Jewish Culture and Femininity in Modernism), sponsored by the Kulturwissenschaftliches Institut Essen (Cultural and Scientific Institute), 11–16 December 1990; and at the University of Mainz, a weekend seminar in June 1991 confronting issues raised by the German peace movement in its relation to Arab and Jewish women. "Interethnic escalation in Germany has challenged the women's movement and its counterparts in academia to give priority in the immediate future to questions of racism, nationalism, and ethnocentricity," Werner-Hervieu concludes (96).

And the future? The women's caucus in American studies at the University of Frankfurt, for instance, has applied for a professorship in English literature and culture with special emphasis on women's studies/gender studies at the Institut für England und Amerikastudien and has won the support of Dr. Evelies Mayer, minister of arts and sciences of the State of Hesse (1994). Elsewhere, too, attempts to set up women's studies professorships and departments continue. To illustrate, the Interdisciplinary Caucus for Women's Studies (1992) at the Johannes-Gutenberg University of Mainz published its proposal for an interdisciplinary women's studies center at the university (Institutionalisierung 88), underscoring the inadequate mentoring of women students and urging institutional support for approaches that cross disciplines: "If women's studies remains limited to isolated chairs in separate departments, the meaning of the field is marginalized and distorts feminist researchers' primary goal: interdisciplinarity and challenge to hegemonic patterns of thought" (89). The institute, to date, has not been won, caucus member Carmen Birkle told me on 24 April 1995; yet the women attained a chair in sociology. Thus, some lobbying efforts pay off. Ulla Bock (1993b) comments:

> It appears that the setting up of chairs has gained greater acceptance on the political level than have women's studies among (male) colleagues. Thus, governmental commissions such as "Education 2000" are not satisfied with a mere network of "Coordinating Posts for Women's Studies and Feminist Research in Institutions of Higher Learning," but urge more, the institutional anchoring of women's studies in curricula and examination schedules, as well as the development of majors and the founding of specialized women's studies professorships. The recommendations of the Westdeutschen Rektorenkonferenz (the [West] German Union of Rectors) and the Federal-State Commission for Research and the Promotion of Education (Bund-Länder-Kommission für Bildungsforschung und Forschungsförderung) move clearly in this direction.
>
> (Bock 1993a:9–10)

Although no national women's studies association unites German feminist academics, the GDA lobbies for improved representation of women, while those concerned with feminist course content have organized broadly in discipline-specific groups of historians, sociologists, jurists, literary critics, art historians, women in science and technology, and more. Each also has its own newsletter or, in some cases, journal. The latter include *Feministische Studien*, the *beiträge zur feministischen theorie und praxis*, both launched in the eighties, and most recently, *Freiburger Frauen Studien* (Freiburg Women's Studies), an interdisciplinary quarterly that hit the market in 1994.

Moving Beyond Institutional Restraints

The proposal for a women's university has become a major topic among German women's studies advocates. A U.S. reader may easily miss the radical edge to this suggestion, but since all institutions of higher learning in Germany have been coed since women were admitted in 1908, the idea of a self-segregated academy on the landscape of state-supported schools is controversial. Critics, of course, even among feminists, exist. Ute Gerhard, for one, fears a diversion of strong female candidates away from the existing system that is so greatly in need of their expertise. Nonetheless, supporters include a number of highly influential people, such as university president (Gesamthoch-

schule Kassel) Ayla Neusel and professors Sigrid Metz-Göckel of Dortmund and Theresia Sauter-Bailliet of Aachen, who contend that a
women's university would, ideally, "foster a self-confident, critical
female intelligence; open academic avenues and job opportunities for
highly qualified women; help them confidently to assume power and
influence; provide a structure which would allow women to take on
social, political and intellectual responsibilities; and provide a forum
for debating the pressing questions of our world (Sauter-Bailliet
1993:22). Neusel describes the envisioned program of study as geared
to the needs and interests of female students, decentralized, transparent, and flexible, so as to facilitate lateral entries and exits. "At the end
of our decade," Sauter-Bailliet presumes, "Europe will offer a multi-
faceted . . . landscape to 3 million German students: private and state
universities, research and vocation-oriented, with study programmes
of various lengths. A women's university—even more than one—
could be an 'alternative' academic institution of feminist scholarship,
one of the answers to the demands for reforming a stagnant university
system" (Sauter-Bailliet 1993:23).

In fact, after a ten-year preparatory period, October 1993 witnessed
the launch of the Förderverein Virginia Woolf–Frauenuniversität
(Backer of the Virginia Woolf Women's University), which targets the
year 2000 for realization of its dream. As Dr. Erika Riemer-Noltenius
(1995), chair of the planning committee, contends, "Virginia Woolf"
would offer a laudatory alternative to traditional universities not only
by bringing the benefits that U.S. women's education is known for—
more professional women graduates more frequently specializing in
technical and scientific fields—but also by enlarging occupational
opportunities for female professors. Riemer-Noltenius sees the institution as a model for Europe, with its potential home in any country.
Its particular relevance to Germany, however, lies in its promise of
dealing directly with the specific obstacles detailed above. Angelika
Köster-Lossack, MdB (Member of Parliament) (Greens, Baden-
Württemberg) (1995) further confirms the growing appeal of this
project:

> In North Rhine–Westphalia a nonpartisan group of women has
> expressed its support . . . as a result of such enormous difficulties
> facing those attempting to place women's studies professorships
> within universities. Integrating feminist content into existing
> programs sometimes seems quite hopeless. Were the context right,
> this would be the better strategy, but in the present case, it leads
> to relativizing feminist theory and research. Sadly, many feel

we've reached a point of stagnation in the discussion of institutionalization.

This suggests why universities are not the only women's studies sites. I have already mentioned the ire that spawned a network of autonomous institutions—a major accomplishment in Germany. One such initiative, the Frauenschule in Frankfurt, is dear to my heart. "Do You Speak Feminist English?" was my regular course listing from 1986 to 1992, meeting Friday nights concurrently with other groups devoted to creative writing, variations of the mother-daughter theme, or poststructuralism, to name but a few. More than one hundred women enrolled regularly each semester, meeting weeknights or weekends. The Saturday-Sunday or weeklong formats—ones I remember include reading the Austrian writer Elfriede Jelinek, discussing the U.S. women's movement, or focusing on Jewish women—often had a special status: participants could be accorded *Bildungsurlaub*—German employees' entitlement to a week of paid vacation time devoted to learning, and governments have given many women's studies courses their approval. To be perfectly clear about this fruitful invention: *Bildungsurlaub* not only continues the employee's salary but also pays course fees.

A second autonomous women's studies project merits honorable mention: the Frauenbildungszentrum Denk(t)räume Bibliothek und Archiv in Hamburg (Women's Educational Center, Library and Archive, whose name makes a pun on Thinking and Daydreaming Rooms) hosted the third "Symposium on Lesbian Studies in German-Speaking Countries," 29 September–1 October 1995. The agenda was shaped by the conference subtitle: "The Last Sex." Looking back over the past twenty years of thought-work in Germany, the more than 120 participants, primarily in literary studies and the social sciences, debated the continued usefulness of the label "lesbian" and worried about its potential essentializing drift. Considered, too, was the influence of U.S. theorizing imposed upon an inappropriate context. As Claudia Koltzenburg notes, "In Germany . . . the situation of lesbians and women of color is radically different from [that in North America]," and she calls for grounding theory "in what real bodies experience as life" (Lesbian Division Newsclip 1995:19). Papers from the previous symposium have already appeared (Marti et al. 1994).

A third exemplary institution representing the network outside universities is Berlin's FFBIZ (Frauenforschungs-, bildungs-, und Informationszentrum) (Women's Research, Education, and Information Center), born in 1978. Its founders rejected university control and demanded autonomy. Center employees need not have earned degrees if they can show experience and dedication within projects interdisciplinary in scope whose purpose is to educate and train women. As Werner-Hervieu notes: "The FFBIZ underwrites analysis of particular women-focused questions and organizes courses, fills auditoriums, schedules congresses, runs exhibitions, and edits publications. It also catalogs women's literature for its own archive and library" (1992:93).

FFBIZ, in turn, is just one among many independent academies that, in 1992, joined to found the Federal Union of Autonomous Women's Studies Institutes (Bundesvereinigung Autonomer Frauenforschungseinrichtungen—BAFF), which aims to promote cooperation among feminist researchers both within and outside higher education institutions, a significant development given the historical debate separating these two groups of women's studies advocates. Werner-Hervieu reminds us of the goals of the secessionists: "self-determination of research topics and self-identification of problem areas; novel forms of communication and cooperation, erasing the hierarchical frontier between the student and the studied and . . . blurring the division of labor" (92). In some cases feminist research in autonomous centers pioneered women's studies perspectives that then moved inside long-established institutions (for instance, with regard to violence against women). BAFF now includes the Archiv der deutschen Frauenbewegung (Archive of the German Women's Movement) in Kassell; the Autonomes Frauenarchiv Wiesbaden (Autonomous Women's Archive) in Wiesbaden; Berliner Institut für Sozialforschung und Sozialwissenschaftliche Praxis (BIS) (Berlin's Institute for Sociological Research and Social Science Practice); Feministisches Informations-, Bildungs-, und Dokumentationszentrum (FiBiDoZ) (Feminist Center for Information, Education, and Documentation) in Nürnberg; Feministische Organisation von Planung und Architektur (FIF) (Feminist Organization for Planning and Architecture); Frauenakademie München (FAM) (Women's Academy, Munich); Frauenforschungs-, bildungs-, und -Informationszentrum (FFBIZ); and associated members Bildungszentrum und Archiv zur Frauengeschichte Baden-Württemberg (Educational Center and Archive for German Women's History in the state of Baden-Württemberg); Rhein-Ruhr Institut für Frauenforschung (Rhine-Ruhr Institute for Women's Studies); and the Stiftung Frauen-Literatur-Forschung, Bremen (Fund for Women's Literary Studies, Bremen). Coordinating is the Archiv der Deutschen Frauenbewegung (Archive of the Women's Movement), which also documents the older women's movement.

Archives represent a final feminist educational institution outside the establishment, and Germany is home to several. On 26 August 1994, the largest and oldest, sponsored by the Jan Phillip Reemtsma Foundation during the eighties, settled into the renovated Bayen Tower, constructed between 1180 and 1250 and renamed Frauen-MediaTurm (Women's Media Tower), in Cologne. The impetus behind the project has been Alice Schwarzer, with co-director Ursula Scheu. They understand the library as more than a repository for documents, as also an arm of both the women's movement and women's studies. It presently houses 25,000 documents, including feminist-inspired M.A. and Ph.D. theses from German universities that may be consulted on-site. Its staff supply journalists with data on the women's movement; it has compiled a feminist thesaurus, and it is gradually going on-line. In this linkage with the globe lies the future.

Moving On in German Women's Studies

In conclusion, Ulla Bock of the Central Coordinating Unit for Women's Studies and Research (Zentraleinrichtung zur Förderung von Frauenstudien und Frauenforschung) at the Free University of Berlin outlines the aims of German women's studies in terms of both course content and institutional anchoring. She would like to see women's studies become a major discipline, develop feminist theory, anchor research in teaching, integrate women's studies in testing and degree requirements, and interact constructively with other disciplines (Bock 1993a:13).

Equally important are efforts to increase the number of academic women and the level of their prestige. Present guidelines urge the promotion of women, but these often remain unenforced (and unenforceable), given their voluntary basis and lack of structural and budgetary backing. And although affirmative action officers, mandated to look after women's interests, are now to be found on most faculties, their effectiveness is minimized by meager finances. Thus, pessimists insist, we shouldn't be misled by cosmetic improvements and paper projects: with few exceptions, the progress of women's studies in Germany has happened not in or with the institution, but against the apparatus, and the field at this writing is still a precarious outsider. The autonomous academies also depend on governmental grace for their existence, threatened in times of fiscal restraint. For instance, the Frankfurter Frauenschule has had to reduce its staff by 50 percent and its course offerings even more dramatically.

Critics tend to be cynical even about successes, Sabine Bröck (1995) reminds me, contending that women's studies posts merely appease feminists and marginalize them within the university. Indeed, as we have seen, there can be no doubt about the weight of academic opposition to the new field. A measure of this is the fact that the first women's studies chair, Ute Gerhard's "Lila-Lehrstühl" (Lilac Chair) in sociology at the University of Frankfurt, was approved in 1986 but demanded since 1974. Gerhard herself (1995) feels a sense of urgency, noting that within the next five to ten years 50 percent of professorial positions will be liberated by retirements. She urges women to complete their *Habilitationen* as quickly as possible in order to join the candidate pool for these posts.

REFERENCES

Allen, Ann Taylor. 1994. "Women's Studies as Cultural Movement and Academic Discipline in the United States and West Germany: The Early Phase, 1966–1982." In *Women in German Yearbook*, 9:1–23, edited by J. Clausen and S. Friedrichsmeyer. Lincoln: University of Nebraska Press.

Baume, Brita, and Christina Felber. 1995. "Wissenschaft als Arbeit, Arbeit als Wissenschaftlerin. Berliner Dialog zu Ergebnissen der Frauenförderung in der Wissenschaft. Ein Kongreß der Berliner Senatsverwaltung für Arbeit und Frauen 27. und 28. 6. 1995" *Neue Impulse* 5: 18–20.

Birkle, Carmen. 1995. Telephone interview, 24 April.

Bock, Ulla. 1993a. "Frauenforschungsprofessuren an deutschen Universitäten/Gesamthochschulen und Hochschulen [ausgenommen Fachhochschulen], Zweite ergänzte und aktualisierte Auflage." *Extra-Info* (December): 15.

———. 1993b. "Die Zeit verändert die Knoten im Netz. Wege der Institutionalisierung von Frauenforschung an bundesdeutschen Hochschulen." In *Die Institutionalisierung von Frauenforschung und Frauenförderung in Deutschland, Europa, und den USA*, 3:66–83, edited by Universität of Mainz. Mainz: Interdisziplinärer Arbeitskreis Frauenforschung Mainz.

———. 1995. Telephone interview, 25 April.

Bröck, Sabine. 1995. Telephone interview, 21 October.

Dickhoven, Ruth. "Frauenforschung für alle Fächer gefordert." *Die Welt*, 12 March 1994.

Enders-Dragässer, Uta. 1988. "Motherlove and Women's Work in Childcare." Unpublished manuscript. Translated by Tobe Levin.

Gerhard, Ute. 1995. Telephone interview, 19 October.

———. "German Women's Studies and the Women's Movement: A Portrait of Themes." Trans. Tobe Levin. *Women's Studies Quarterly*. XX 3&4, Fall/Winter 1992. 98-111.

Köster-Lossack, Angelika, MdB. 1995. Telephone interview, 24 April.

Lehmann, Ingrid. 1994. "Accomplishments and Future for Women in the Natural Sciences and Technology." Unpublished manuscript.

"Lesbian Division Newsclip." 1995. *WISE Women's News*, edited by Tobe Levin and Erna Kas. 5:3–19.

Marti, Madeleine, et al., eds. 1994. *Querfeldein. Beiträge zur Lesbenforschung.* Switzerland: eFeF-Verlag.

Mayer, Dr. Evelies. Minister of Arts and Sciences of the State of Hesse. 16 August 1994. Document No. Az. WI5-907/57-S1-.

Mies, Maria. 1984. "Towards a Methodology for Feminist Research." In *German Feminism: Readings in Politics and Literature,* edited by E. H. Altbach, J. Classen, D. Schultz, and N. Stehan. Albany: State University of New York Press.

Opitz, May, Kathaxina Oguntoye, and Dagmar Schultz, eds. 1992. *Showing Our Colors: Afro-German Women Speak Out.* Translated by Anne Adams. Amherst: University of Massachusetts Press.

Riemer-Noltenius, Erika. 1995. Fax, 24 April.

Sauter-Bailliet, Theresia. 1993. "Frauenuniversität: A Feminist Vision." *WISE Women's News* 2: 22–23. Translation/summary of Neusel, Ayla. 1990. "Die Frauenuniversität." In *Was eine Frau umtreibt. Frauenbewegung— Frauenforschung—Frauenpolitik,* edited by Anne Schluter, Christine Roloff, and Maria Anna Kreienbaum, pp. 65–71. Pfaffenweiler: Centaurus.

Schultz, Dagmar. 1992. "Anti-Racism: The Challenge to Women's Studies." Translated by Tobe Levin. *WISE Women's News* 4: 36–44.

Werner-Hervieu, Gudrun. 1992. "Women's Studies and Feminist Research in the Federal Republic of Germany and Berlin (West)." Translated by Tobe Levin. *Women's Studies Quarterly* 20, nos. 3 and 4 (Fall/Winter): 85–97.

"Vorschlag zur Einrichtung eines Institutes für Interdisziplinäre Frauen-forschung der Johannes Gutenberg-Universität Mainz (Dezember 1992)." 1993. In *Die Institutionalisierung von Frauenforschung und Frauenförderung in Deutschland, Europa, und den USA,* 3:88–91. Mainz: Interdisziplinärer Arbe-itskreis Frauenforschung, Hrsg. Universität Mainz.

After completing a University of Paris maîtrise in 1974 and earning a doctorate from Cornell University in comparative literature in 1979, Tobe Levin joined the English department at the University of Maryland, European Division, and in 1986 began teaching U.S. minority women's literature and women's holocaust memoirs at J. W. Goethe University, Frankfurt am Main, Germany. A cofounder of WISE, she has been coediting the association's bilingual newsletter and has published articles on anti-Semitism, racism, and African-American, African, German, Austrian, and Jewish women's writings.

APPENDIX

Addresses

Archiv der Deutschen Frauenbewegung [Archive of the Women's Movement], Sommerweg lb, 34125 Kassel, Germany.

Commission Report, Niedersächsische Ministerium für Wissenschaft und Kultur, Referat Presse und Öffentlichkeitsarbeit, Postfach 261, 30002 Hannover, Germany.

Das Feministische Archiv / FrauenMediaTurm Bayenturm, 50678 Köln, Germany.

Gesellschaft Deutscher Akademikerinnen e.V. (GDA), Dr. Ingeborg Aumüller, Pfauengasse 10, 93047 Regensburg, Germany. Telephone 0941 5 59 22. Fax 56 34 17.

Sozialpädagogisches Institut Berlin (SPI), Boppstr 10, 10967 Berlin, Germany. Telephone 030 69 00 85-19. Fax 69 00 85-85.

Virginia Woolf Frauenuniversität: Dr. Erika Riemer-Noltenius, Horner Heerstr. 24, 28359 Bremen, Germany. Telephone 0421 · 239753. Fax 0421 · 231955.

Women's Studies in Korea

Chang Pilwha

Women's studies as an academic subject in Korea came into being in the middle of the 1970s. In the course of the last twenty years remarkable progress has been achieved. The first master's and Ph.D. courses in women's studies in Asia have been developed, and most of the more than one hundred universities and colleges in Korea have come to include various women's studies courses in their general curricula. My intention in this paper is not to give a comprehensive statistical description but to draw an overall picture of the development of women's studies in Korea.

To make a national report of any subject intelligible, we need to understand the context in which the subject matter is situated. This point is particularly relevant for women's studies, since its possibilities and limitations are closely linked to the cultural heritage and the degree of openness of the society. For women's studies carries in its core critical approaches toward the given culture, and yet it is subject to the constraints of academic institutions and resources.

The Korean Patriarchy, Educational System, and Labor Market

Scholars generally assume the existence of close links among women's studies, feminism, and women's movements. Less well recognized and usually overlooked is the connection between the beginnings of women's education and the rise of feminism and women's movements. In the case of Korea, this omission is related not only to male centrism with regard to education but also to cultural imperialism, which is experienced by other non-Western nations as well. I use the theoretical concept of cultural imperialism here to denote several interrelated phenomena. First, the early development of "modernity" includes a package of Western "models," among them industrialization and such social projects as educational programs. Second, during the temporal

This essay was originally a paper presented at the "National Reports of Women's Studies Begun in the 1970s" NGO Forum, Beijing 1995, Women's Studies International, 5 September 1995, Huairou, China.

process of "development," the powerful presents its models as superior and imposes them on the less powerful; the less powerful becomes
a collaborator by superimposing the models onto an indigenous way of
life, adapting and imitating them. Third, the success of sustaining a
critical stance on the process or resisting the process depends largely
on the power dynamics of spiritual, ideological, economic, and political elements in the indigenous culture. The use of economic, political,
and military power makes the process an imperialist one rather than a
neutral cultural interaction. Finally, it is important to note that, when
one looks at the long span of history, one finds that the superiority of
one culture over another cannot be sustained forever. It is also particularly important for feminists to see cultural imperialism against the
background of the long history of patriarchy and the universal nature
of male cultural imperialism.

While I will limit the discussion to the areas of education and
feminism, even then I will be able to cover only a small patch of the
field. My intention is motivated less by an urge to condemn cultural
imperialism than by my desire to understand how such complex social
phenomena as the rise of feminisms, women's education, and women's
movements occur indigenously and how they travel internationally.

Surveying Korean history from the third century to the end of the
nineteenth, we observe a gradual systematization of one of the most
ideal types of patriarchy in the world. By the end of the sixteenth
century, the state managed to complete a patriarchal system by implementing Confucian ideology of gender hierarchy and sex segregation
through a sexual division of labor and class divisions that upheld
patriarchal family in strict observance of patrilineage, patrimony, and
patrilocality. Women had to be strong to prove themselves to have
some worth as mothers producing sons to continue the family line and
producing food and clothing to survive in a woman-hostile environment. However strong and capable women were, they were not allowed
to participate in activities outside the close confines of home, and
education was strictly prohibited.

Only in the national crisis at the end of the nineteenth century,
when Korea's sovereignty was threatened by foreign powers, were
there some possibilities of cracking this rigidity. The crisis situation
made proper observation of rites difficult. It also created a space for
critical reflection on the traditional ways of life. Within this space,
criticism of the position of women began. Women's social participation had to be accepted, even if reluctantly, if it was seen as contributing to the national cause. Discourse on the necessity of educating
women centered on its instrumental value—to make good mothers

and wives—rather than on recognition of women's human right to education.

In the last hundred years, Koreans have experienced crisis after crisis: Japanese occupation, the World Wars, the division of the country into North and South, the Korean War, and the industrial war to get into the world capitalist system. These crises valorized efficiency and expediency and justified the sacrifice of individual human rights for the sake of growth and stability. In this context, it was easy to brush aside women's claim for human rights as a luxury, and so the tradition of utilizing women's instrumental values persisted. At the same time, such crises opened some windows of opportunity for women to participate in social activities. It is also true that the models of the "developed" world gave a positive stimulus for women's rights.

Women's suffrage was included in the first modern constitution, in 1947, and primary education became compulsory for girls as well as for boys. In the last few decades, Korea has managed to achieve the appearance of "modernity." Despite the appearance and changes in patriarchal families, however, the underlying assumptions continue to be patriarchal, with the view that a woman's identity is primarily familial.

The resistance to women's studies ought to be analyzed against this background. It is regarded as subversive activity that attempts to uproot Korean tradition. But, of course, no single social group can be accused of responsibility, since the tradition is already in a state of demise as a result of the massive social change brought about by rapid industrialization. Women are an easy target for such accusations partly because we are seen as weak and inferior, but ironically, they are in fact also the strong force maintaining the tradition of everyday life. Women's studies practitioners and feminists have often been snubbed as mindless puppets under the Western influence. At the same time, there is a growing expectation that women's studies could offer prescriptions for many ills of today's "Westernized" industrial society from which more and more members of society suffer.

In Korea, as elsewhere in the world, women's studies is an academic subject and practice centered in academic institutions. In Korea and East Asia, education is highly revered both as desirable in itself and as an instrument for social advancement.

In the last few decades, universities in this part of the world have had to struggle with the multiple tasks of incorporating Western models of higher education and making ends meet within their limited resources and external administrative regulations. The Korean educational system is characterized by its high level of competition, in which entrance exams are most significant, rather than by its curriculum. The status of a university is dependent on its ability to attract the students who have passed the most competitive examinations. While this phenomenon may be argued as a universal tendency, this is exacerbated by the close link between the status of the university and its graduates' employment opportunities. Big companies with superior working conditions exhibit their preference/prejudice with regard to such labels quite openly. The high degree of competition in the educational system produces various private institutions that organize tutoring of schoolchildren by teachers, university students, or graduates. One estimate even suggests that the total sum of such private cost of education surpasses that of public expenditure on education.

The labor market discrimination against women makes the position of women students in higher education something of an anomaly. Regardless of academic performance and even the university label they might have earned, women as a class face discrimination when seeking primary jobs. While there is little direct discrimination on entry to universities, the discrimination in the labor market is both direct and systematic. Thus the financial and social costs of women's higher education have a lower rate of return as a result of gender discrimination in the labor market. (This is, of course, excluding other forms of return, such as their higher quality of unpaid work in childrearing.)

Regardless of the differences between the socioeconomic and the cultural contexts, women's studies is deeply contentious for several reasons: its critical (radical) approach, its affinity for the women's (social) movement, and its demand for social change. The critical approach carries radical implications and challenges in the most fundamental areas, such as the family, work, and sexuality, in a way that no previous public discourse or academic disciplines have addressed. These elements, combined with misogynous attitudes, contribute to the tendency of devaluing women's studies as being beneath the standard of a "proper" academic pursuit. There is some fear that women's studies is a threat to the stability of the family and the status quo of society in general.

Women's Studies and Women's Education
at Ewha Womans University

Ewha Womans University[1] offers a very interesting case study for many core issues in women's studies. It is an example of groundbreaking effort for women's education where no precedents existed. It also shows the difficulties and potentials of women-only organizations that have to operate in a rapidly changing male-centered society. There are many challenging questions related to the tension between ideals and survival. The fact that this university has pioneered the field of women's studies in Korea is deeply related to the above issues. The seed for Ewha Womans University, the largest women's university in the world, was sown in 1886 when the sex segregation rule prohibited women from leaving their homes. The first school for women was built by Ms. Mary Scranton, an American Methodist missionary, and the first students were social outcasts who were more free from the dominant code of society than other women were. It took more than ten years for Korean women to organize themselves to petition King Kojong to establish girls' schools. Some of the pioneers opened a school at the end of the 1890s with their own resources, but it survived only a few years. The first public school for girls was opened in 1906, twenty years after Ewha had opened.

Even before such organized efforts, women must have asked the most elementary questions, such as "Why are we confined at home?" "Why am I not allowed to go to school?" "Why am I told that as a woman I am inferior?" These questions must have occurred to most women from the earliest times. The fact that history shows no record of such questions does not mean that women did not ask them. Either their voices were erased or they did not have enough power to persist. All we can say now is that no organized effort strong enough to communicate and acknowledge the common questions shared by all women allowed them until now to act to change the situation of oppression.

In this sense, the beginning of women's education itself is a landmark of women's studies and feminist endeavors. In other words, the conscious effort to enable women's enlightenment through education cannot be understood except as a feminist movement. Through education, particularly at Ewha since 1886, the first women leaders and professionals in the country were produced—the first woman ever to hold a doctorate degree, the first medical doctor, lawyer, and numerous leaders of national movements as well as women's movements. Women's education enabled women to gain the confidence that women can do as well as, or even better than, men if they are given the opportunity. Gaining confidence in one's ability and worth is one of the most important achievements of education.

In 1975 Ewha Womans University launched one of the most exciting projects in its history, the first Women's Studies Research Project, as a team effort. More than a dozen professors, both women and men, all of

whom were eminent in their respective fields of study, gathered together to engage in an interdisciplinary research project in women's
studies. Each member of the group presented papers reinterpreting
intellectual history in relation to women: religious views on women;
literary traditions in which women had been obscured despite their
most critical contributions, which enabled Korean literature to survive
at all; the economic and legal status of women; and various other
aspects that affect the quality of life of women in contemporary
society. These presentations were followed by heated discussions, not
always reaching agreement on many issues of feminism. There were
many skeptical people, some inside and many more outside the walls
of our campus. However, we knew that we were pioneering something
that was going to be of great importance in the future. Based on the
research, which was enriched by numerous sessions of public and
private discussions, the research team published the first textbook in
women's studies.[2] The new subject was christened with a new name,
"Yeosunghak" (*Yeo-sung* means "women" and *hak* means "a discipline"). Its aim was agreed upon as "to raise consciousness and women's leadership as well as acquaint the undergraduate student with
the broad issues facing the women's movement today and to create new
values in a changing society."[3]

The task of creating new values included a fundamental project.
"Until the present, women have demanded that only what men ascribe
to themselves be applied equally to women. However, if women are to
succeed in their struggle against their derivative status, then they have
to construct their own perception of reality and definitions, instead of
being dependent upon men's perceptions and definitions."[4]

With fresh enthusiasm, the textbook's authors devised experimental
teaching methods. They gave lectures as a team, and students were
then divided into small groups to discuss the subject matter with
teaching assistants. When the first course was given in 1977, after two
years of research and preparation, it was overwhelmingly popular. On
the registration day, students started to line up from five o'clock in the
morning in order to get admitted to the limited-enrollment class. At
the end of the course, an extensive evaluation session was carried out.
The result was indeed very positive.

One of the pioneers of the project wrote in the middle of 1970s as
follows:

> Ewha's first program defined a set of principles and set a precedent
> not only in purpose and method, but in defining the role of a
> women's university in women's movement. The Women's Studies

project demanded a rethinking of some fundamental issues: how to bring the women's movement back to university students, how to translate the Women's Studies paradigm to Korean culture, how to confront problems of personal change in student consciousness-raising, and a questioning of the basic assumptions about the old women's liberation.[5]

Some of the claims proved to be true through subsequent development in the following decade. The deepening need for further research, as well as the popular welcome by the students, encouraged us to take a step forward. The Department of Women's Studies was created in the graduate school of Ewha University in 1982, awarding master's degrees. Since 1990 the department has offered Ph.D. degree courses as well. More recently, women's studies programs for undergraduates have expanded greatly, offering a score of options, from introductory courses to more specialized topics—for example, "Seminar on Feminism," "Sexuality in Korean Culture," "Women and Environment," "Feminist Philosophy," "Feminist Art Criticism," "Women and Social Policy," and "Women and Science," to name just a few.

The Social Impact

The Korean Association of Women's Studies was created in 1984 and has published journals of academic distinction. Other women's universities, Sook-Myung Women's University and Seoul Women's University, were quick to develop their own programs. The number of women's studies courses increased rapidly throughout the nation in the late eighties, and now almost all universities and colleges offer one or more women's studies courses for both women and men students. The number of male students has increased. Adult education programs in women's studies also have multiplied.

One of the remarkable achievements of women's studies education is that it has produced many of the leaders in the women's movements. The rapid spread of women's studies across the nation is partly attributable to the availability of specialists. This, in turn, contributed to encouraging women's movements and produced practical results for Korean society. Those who benefited from the courses have put their skills into practice on what they have learned to identify as being in need of change. They have been instrumental in achieving legal reforms, such as the family law, the equal opportunity law, and the law on sexual violence. Particularly noteworthy is that women's studies research is responsible for raising the issue of sexual violence as a social issue and for providing a theoretical framework for legislating a special amendment in relation to sexual violence.

New organizations were created as a direct result of women's studies education, to activate the women's movement with various emphases: a women's weekly paper, a women's hot line, a sexual violence relief center, and so on. Many of our graduates are currently working in the mass media and in publishing companies, leading public opinion on gender issues. In general, women's consciousness was raised across the board; women were voted in as trade union leaders, and some successful candidates began to appear in local governments, even though their proportion is still one of the lowest in the world.

Such educational efforts have contributed to building women's confidence. The remaining question is how this confidence can be kept up in reality. We have yet a long way to go to achieve equality of opportunity, and even further to enjoy practical equality with men. However, the goal is not simply to achieve equality with men; it is not our goal to excel like men in a war of aggression and greed, domineering, subjugating, and oppressing less powerful people who have fewer worldly possessions. If equality is a goal, it is in order to enable women as full members of society with equal rights and obligations to determine the course and direction that the society is taking. Women have to be empowered in order to make their own experiences and insights more meaningful to and useful for their society.

Theory and Practice of Women's Studies Practitioners

One of the most important observations that I want to share from the experiences of women's studies is related to the theme of "theory and practice." This theme is closely connected with the feminist viewpoint that "the personal is [the] political." One of the starting points of women's studies is the critical examination of patriarchal culture and patriarchal social systems, including educational systems. In critical examinations, the agendas for social change are always implied implicitly or stated explicitly. The agenda for social change is always guided by some kind of value, and in the case of women's studies, the value is a synthesis of equality, freedom, justice, and the welfare of all members of the community. While women's studies practitioners do not hide the fact that the research and teaching they do are guided by these values, the mainstream academic environment, still hanging on to the misguided notion of "value neutrality," criticizes feminist scholarship as value-laden ideology rather than academic endeavor.

Also unlike other "traditional" disciplines, research and theories of women's studies cover the most personal and private issues, such as intimate, everyday dealings of domestic labor of both a material and an emotional nature, sexuality, marital relationships, and so on. This aspect also allows conventional academics to trivialize women's studies. All these characteristics of women's studies make the lives of its practitioners different from those of many other "traditional" academics. If you are in women's studies, whether you give a lecture or engage in a discussion or do research, you are constantly required to defend your discipline, asked to provide an alternative to what you are criticizing, and most disturbingly, scrutinized to see whether you practice what you are preaching. Although this is a great challenge for women's studies practitioners, this very aspect has helped women's studies survive. Practitioners are making public the questions women want to ask, and as they strive to find alternatives, they invite all women and men, and the community, to participate in the process of change. We need to view this activity against the background of Asian universities, which are typically underfunded and overburdened with undergraduate education. A critic suggests that Asian universities are losing community confidence and failing to respond to the crisis primarily because of their "aloofness ... from their environment" and "false starts, false pretences, a self-deceptive nominalism" of excellence that are increasingly apparent to the authorities and the public.[6] If we agree with at least some of this criticism, we might also see that women's studies has the potential to transform the universities. No universities anywhere have ever existed in a socioeconomic and cultural vacuum; they become increasingly dependent on the demands of their students, which are largely determined by prospects in the labor market, led by market forces. In this complex situation, we need to unravel some of the interlocking threads and focus our attention on some very critical questions: Have we, as feminist scholars, envisioned alternative perspectives for the future of education in general and the university as an institution in particular? If we do, how different should our practices be, given the constraints imposed on us?

NOTES

1. Ewha Womans University (instead of Ewha Women's University) is the official English spelling.
2. The English translation of the textbook was published as *Challenges for Women; Women's Studies in Korea*, ed. Chung Sei-wha and trans. Shin

Chang-hyun et al. Korean Women's Institute Series (Seoul: Ewha Womans University Press, 1986).

3. Yoon Soon Young, "Women's Studies—Is It Relevant?" in *Role of the University in the Women's Movement*, ed. Eva Shipstone and Norah Shipstone (Lucknow: Asian Women's Institute, 1979), p. 54.

4. Chang Sang, "Role of the University in the Women's Movement," in *Role of the University in the Women's Movement*, p. 12.

5. Yoon Soon Young, "Women's Studies," p. 53.

6. G. W. Wang, "Universities in Transition in Asia," *Oxford Review of Education* 24 (1992): 17–27, cited in Albert H. Yee, ed., *East Asian Higher Education: Traditions and Transformations* (New York: Pergamon, 1995).

Chang Pilwha *is associate professor of women's studies at Ewha Womans University, Republic of Korea and director of the Asian Center for Women's Studies.*

Women's Studies in the Netherlands

Willy Jansen

In the last twenty years, women's studies has taken an impressive flight in the Netherlands. How can this be understood, given the relatively low representation of women in universities among both students and staff? What are the characteristics of Dutch women's studies? What have been the problems and the dilemmas confronted and the strategies used to acquire this place?

Academic Context

There are thirteen universities in the Netherlands that prepare students for independent scholarly work in an academic or professional setting.[1] Despite Dutch pretensions that theirs is an emancipated country, the representation of women in academe is far from impressive. At the universities the number of female students has increased gradually over the last decades, but in 1993, of the total number of 186,000 students, only 45 percent were female. The distribution of women according to the type of study, moreover, reflects traditional gender divisions; women are underrepresented in disciplines like technology or economics and overrepresented in the humanities and social sciences, fields with unfavorable employment prospects.

Among university employees, 32 percent are female, but this includes administrative personnel. Women's representation in the scientific positions is much lower: despite affirmative action schemes the share of women in the academic staff amounts to little more than 13 percent, while women make up a mere 3.6 percent of the professors (Noordenbos 1994). An international survey on women in academia showed that the Netherlands ranked far behind countries like Turkey, Russia, China, and Botswana with respect to the number of women teaching in universities (Noordenbos 1995). Arab countries like Alge-

With special thanks to José van Alst and Margit van der Steen, who made important contributions. This article is partly based on the papers I presented at the SIGMA Conference, 15–16 June 1995, in Coimbra, Portugal, and at the NGO Forum on Women, Beijing, September 1995.

ria, Egypt, and Saudi Arabia have nearly twice as large a share of women teaching in universities as the Netherlands does (Jansen 1990, 1993). This low participation of women in scholarly occupations is part of a wider pattern of a relatively low participation rate of women in the workforce in the Netherlands.

Women's Studies in the Universities

In the early 1970s the first women's studies or gender studies courses were given, at the initiative of students and staff, on topics relevant to the feminist movement. The established powers thought it would be a passing fashion, that investments in women's studies would be only temporary because the women's movement would soon be over. But contrary to expectations, women's studies had come to stay. In an earlier article in *Women's Studies Quarterly*, Brouns (1992) described four stages in the emergence of women's studies in the Netherlands: after a period in which the contents and methods of the sciences were critically examined for their sexism (1974–77), a period followed in which alternative research methods were proposed and the field's frontiers were explored (1977–81). In the third stage (1981–85) the monolithic oppression theory was abandoned and women's studies's content and themes shifted to make room for complexity and diversity. Since 1986 the theoretical divergence has led to an increasingly controversial profile.

The "Double Track" as Problem and Solution

For an understanding of the specific problems encountered in the development of Dutch women's studies, and the particular strategies that have been applied, the general characteristics of Dutch women's studies mentioned by Brouns (1992) need to be recapitulated. A number of typical characteristics of contemporary Dutch women's studies can be mentioned: a high degree of institutionalization of women's studies, financial support by the government, a wide diversity of theoretical perspectives and a multidisciplinary approach, and an international orientation of women's studies scholars. In all these respects the same dilemma has recurred: how and why to choose between integration or autonomy. The following suggests that often the choice was refused because both were wanted.

Institutionalization

From the early 1980s on, special units or departments were set up in women's studies. To meet the demand on the side of the students, the part-time and temporary staff of the early period expanded. A recent survey by the Dutch Association of Women's Studies shows that more than 260 different courses were taught in 1994–95. Eight universities offer more than five courses in women's studies, and four offer a degree based on a recognized three-year graduate program specializing in women's studies within the social sciences or the humanities. Some 200 women teach women's studies courses at the universities, and 300 do research, with an overlap of 150 who both teach and do research (Lasthuizen 1995).

With the financial support of the Dutch Ministry of Education, women's studies teachers and coordinators were appointed in almost all universities. A hard battle was fought to get tenured positions and professors. With the appointment of seventeen full professors in women's studies plus a number of professors in other disciplines actively devoted to women's studies, women's studies gained not only respectability but also the power to apply for funds within and outside the universities and to set up teaching and research programs. A professorate is needed to accept Ph.D. students and train them for a degree. Nationwide cooperation has made it possible to offer a full Ph.D. curriculum in women's studies at the Netherlands School of Research. During the spring of 1995 this research school was given official recognition by the Netherlands Royal Academy of Science. Between 1990 and 1994, thirty-nine women's studies theses (some interdisciplinary) were successfully defended.

At the eleven women's studies units with one or more chairs, academic work is combined with many other activities. Students can do applied research at the community level or on demand for women's groups. Information and gender assessment instruments are provided to policymakers (cf. van Lenning, Brouns, and de Bruijn 1995; Verloo and Heijmans 1995). Refresher courses are given for professional groups. Documentation centers have been set up, and these centers have cooperated to compose a Women's Thesaurus for retrieving information on women and women's studies. Lectures are given to the general public. Large interdisciplinary international and national conferences have been organized, and their results published (e.g., Angerman 1989; Bertels et al. 1989; Davis, Leijenaar, and Oldersma 1991; Hermsen and van Lenning 1991; Brügmann 1993; Bal and Pattynama 1993; Ras and Lunenberg 1993; Bouw, de Bruijn, and van der Heiden 1994). Evaluative studies have been written (Brouns and Harbers 1994; de Bruijn 1993), and general introductory texts have been produced (e.g., Poldervaart 1983; Brouns, Verloo, and Grünell 1995; Buikema and Smelik 1993).

The trend toward institutionalization of women's studies in academia and its development as a discipline was supported by the establishment of professional organizations: smaller ones related to disciplines like history, anthropology, or theology, and one large association on an interdisciplinary base, the Dutch Association for Women's Studies. Women's studies also gained formal representation in the main Dutch scientific research funding agency, the Netherlands Foundation for Scientific Research (NWO), as well as the Association of Dutch Universities (VSNU). Institutionalization was also visible in the founding of professional journals, such as the *Tijdschrift voor Vrouwenstudies* and the *European Journal of Women's Studies* (Vansuyt 1990).

In retrospect, the development of women's studies might seem linear in development, yet in practice it was not. As the growth was based not on coordinated action but on a variety of initiatives taken in different contexts, the outcomes were very diverse. Active individuals, supportive boards, and timely demands all influenced what form women's studies in specific disciplines and institutions would take. Some disciplines were quick to integrate new concepts and theories about gender, and this was reflected in their personnel policy, such as the social and cultural sciences, but also theology, philosophy, or history. Others, however, despite the urgency of gender in their field, were slower to follow up; these include the political and policy sciences, law, agriculture, and medical sciences. Some disciplines proved to be infertile ground, either because no female staff (or interested male staff) were available to carry initiatives further—in biology or the technical sciences, for example—or because the connection with gender was less direct—for example, in physics, mathematics, dentistry, or astronomy. Also the timing of the demand for institutionalization at the university level proved important. At some universities research and teaching in women's studies flourished for a while, thanks to a temporary financial input, but shrank again when that was not followed up with formal institutionalization or the appointment of senior staff or professors. Much of the early development was shouldered by temporary, part-time teaching staff, who as a result of university budget cuts all but disappeared in the 1980s (Parel and van de Wouw 1988). Only where tenured senior staff were appointed could women's studies in the long term prove itself as a viable discipline that studied and taught about an important, pervasive, and often problematic social topic.

During the institutionalization process, units were confronted with the dilemma of integration versus autonomy. Again and again they found themselves in situations requiring a choice between equally undesirable alternatives. Integration would mean invisibility and becoming subject to automatic loss of positions resulting from the frequent reorganizations that plagued the universities. To choose autonomy for an emerging discipline in this setting carried the risk of being not strong enough to survive. This dilemma on the organizational level would repeat itself on the theoretical level and on the level of individual identity. What would serve the development of women's studies and its participants better: to support the teaching of women's studies in the disciplines or to create an independent institute for women's studies? to introduce a feminist perspective in the existing disciplinary theories or to develop interdisciplinary gender theories? to remain a psychologist, linguist, or anthropologist or to become a women's studies expert?

Most units continue to react to this dilemma by balancing somewhere between the two extremes and using the best of both. This careful balancing has been named a "double track policy." Experience has shown that organizationally a double track policy, despite the cost of tremendous amounts of time, energy and knowledge, has definitely been essential to the survival of women's studies in the universities. This becomes all the more clear when the universities are compared with the vocational colleges. At these colleges the path of integration was chosen. Individual female staff members were very successful in integrating a women's and emancipatory perspective in existing study programs. Yet unfortunately, many of the courses disappeared when the staff member left. The professional colleges lacked recognizable units, headed by a chair, that could maintain and defend positions or programs, or keep records of women's studies courses taught and women staff interested in this topic. The tremendous input of women's work had little permanent effect and easily slipped out of sight and out of the collective memory. On the other hand, the few units who placed their emphasis on autonomy also have had a difficult time, as their student numbers are not sufficient to maintain a viable unit. Most students want to combine their interest in women's studies with work toward a regular degree. The fact that there is not yet a word for the professional practitioner of women's studies is indicative of the dilemma for students as well as for teachers of women's studies.

Government Funding

Higher education is funded by the Ministry of Education in the form of a lump sum given to the universities and based mainly on the number of graduates. Institutions are allowed to formulate their own policies. Sixty-five percent of the cost of research activities is funded from this central grant that universities receive from the government (direct government funding), 10 percent is provided by the Netherlands Organization for Scientific Research (indirect government funding) and about 25 percent comes from research contracts (contract funding by third parties).

Finances for women's studies have always run far short of the demand. The first source, via the universities, was rather late in providing for women's studies. The first women's studies courses were taught by sitting staff on their own initiative and often in their spare time. Temporary, part-time appointments had to be fought hard for, and many qualified personnel were lost in the beginning due to non-renewal because of lack of funds. When the universities themselves made little room for women's studies, the second and third sources were actively approached. A large stimulus came from extra government support through the STEO (Promotion Committee for Emancipation Research). Funds were obtained not only for research but also for the appointment of coordinators and professors. In 1995 the Dutch Association of Women's Studies obtained funds for an Expert Centre. Moreover, in the wake of this impetus, universities have started to appoint tenured staff in women's studies, partly because of student and staff pressure, but occasionally also to stave off a total loss of female staff. As in other countries, Dutch universities suffered from the tightening of budgets for higher education. During reorganizations, university staff were laid off on the basis of "last come first out." This rule hit women harder than men. Departments had tried to hire more women over the last decade, but these newcomers suffered most. Moreover, women had not yet managed to reach the highest positions, which were better protected. As a result, the already small number of female teaching and research staff was approaching zero in many departments. The establishment of women's studies centers and the creation of women's studies chairs (often part-time and/or temporary) enabled the universities to save face and keep their best female employees. Also women's studies units used the diminishing female staff in general as an argument to gain or maintain a place at the university. This partly explains the curious situation mentioned above that the Netherlands belongs to the countries with the lowest percentage of female university staff in general but nevertheless has a fair number of women's studies posts. For instance, of all the professors at the university, women make up only 3.6 percent. But of the 148 female professors in the Netherlands in 1995, 17 are in women's studies, that is, 11.5

percent. Not bad for a new discipline, but we would prefer a fair representation of women in the highest echelons in all disciplines, not just women's studies.

The large financial injection by the Ministry of Education in the early 1980s to boost women's studies research at the University of Amsterdam did not lead to a concentration of women's studies in one university but rather set off competitive action at the other universities. Most women's studies units managed to obtain indirect government funds for independent research as well as funds for contract research from various government departments and agencies (den Dekker 1993). The three sources were mined to forge viable units. Here again the double track was taken: money was obtained for interdisciplinary women's studies research, and at the same time funds were acquired for research proposals that were sent through traditional disciplinary channels.

The prospects for the future are not optimistic. Another cut in the budgets of the universities has been announced, which will affect all departments, including women's studies. It will again affect the youngest staff members, among whom most of the remaining women can be found. Moreover, a large number of women's studies courses are given as optional courses, and these are likely to be first among the courses that are canceled when a planned reduction of study length and thus compression of curricula are implemented. Support through the research funds also seems to be drying up, because many considered it to be a temporary stimulation but not a structural provision. Despite the level of institutionalization, many units continue to face the problem that their funding is not structural. Moreover, the Netherlands Organisation for Scientific Research no longer will allow for an independent position of women's studies and expects us to join with other disciplines.

Women's Studies International's discussion at the NGO Forum on Women in China showed that acquiring structural and permanent funding is a problem that women's studies in many countries has to cope with. To find the funds necessary to start up a women's studies program is easier than to get it structurally financed. To maintain the high level of women's studies in the Netherlands will therefore require continuous attention. Moreover, the strategy to approach all possible sources of funding at the same time remains even more necessary when some sources seem to be drying up.

Theoretical Diversity and Pluriformity

Dutch women's studies shows pluriformity not only in organization and funding but also in content. This is in the first place attributable to

the variety of disciplines in which women's studies originated, which
resulted in the elaboration of discipline-specific theories. An indication of this spread over the disciplines is given in the *Dutch Women's
Studies Guide 1994-1995*. Of the 279 courses offered for the year
1994-95 at Dutch universities, 40 percent are provided in the social
sciences, 13 percent in the arts and literature, and 20 percent in
theology; up to now, women's studies are underdeveloped in geography, communications, and ethnic studies, and in "hard" disciplines
like biology and technology. In detail:

general theory women's studies	10
feminist classics	5
interdisciplinary, thematic women's studies	1
women's studies philosophy	12
feminist theology	39
women's studies literature and arts	26
women's history	15
law and women	14
political and policy sciences	16
sociological, educational, and psychological sciences	67
gender and communication	4
gender and ethnicity	5
anthropology of women	9
physical planning, human geography and gender	3
women and economics	12
gender in sciences and technology	7
women and medical sciences, health sciences	13
women and agriculture	8
lesbian and gay studies	11
women and musicology	2

Total   279

This list indicates how the field of women's studies has spread over the
disciplines and also how difficult it is for it to exist independently of
the established disciplines. Must the question of the organization of
the sexes always be subsidiary to other questions, or has it sufficient
social and scientific relevance of its own to merit a separate discipline?

Those who would answer yes to the last question would prefer to
make the other disciplines subsidiary to women's studies. When doing
so they opt for an interdisciplinary or multidisciplinary orientation.

Most women's studies institutes are multidisciplinary, yet they vary to the degree in which they succeed in bringing an interdisciplinary perspective to their work. In teaching this is done in problem-oriented or feminist classics courses. Or it may be accomplished by setting up a coherent multidisciplinary curriculum in women's studies. Although women's studies is not yet formally recognized as a discipline, students in Nijmegen, Amsterdam, Utrecht, and Leiden can follow a recognized three-year graduate program specializing in women's studies within the social sciences or the humanities. These graduates will find women's studies officially mentioned on their graduation certificate.

The interdisciplinary approach is also favored in research cooperation. Researchers from many disciplines participate in the five research lines of the Netherlands Research School of Women's Studies. The success in getting this research school recognized by the Royal Dutch Academy of Science was another step forward in the acknowledgment of interdisciplinary women's studies. Moreover, it offers a program for the training of Ph.D. students in women's studies. The theses coming out of this school are good examples of the fruitfulness of interdisciplinary cooperation and supervision. At the same time, the problems related to interdisciplinary work and to joint supervision by professors from different disciplines, should not be underestimated. Interdisciplinary work is time-consuming, as in-depth knowledge of more than one field is required. In addition, professors in women's studies who negotiate joint supervision with professors from other disciplines tend to find themselves in an unequal power position. Contractual agreements about duties and rights before starting interdisciplinary projects have proved helpful and effective.

While the above list of courses suggests that, in teaching, integration is somewhat more pronounced, while the Netherlands Research School of Women's Studies indicates that in research more effort is given to autonomy. The use of integration means that gender is integrated into the theories of sociology, law, medicine, literature, theology, economics, etc. The effort demonstrates that work relations, disease patterns, or church attendance cannot be properly understood without reference to gender. Integration, however, can be carried along only by developing an independent body of theory on gender and gender relations from an interdisciplinary perspective. Here gender relations themselves become the focus of study. Here the main question is what the division of labor and property, the reproductive body, or religious ideologies do to women and to women's relations with men, instead of the other way around. The two tracks are intricately bound together, and it would be a theoretical loss if we pursue only one of them.

Internationalization

As citizens of a small trading nation, the Dutch have of old paid much attention to what happened on the other side of their borders. Women's studies scholars have also followed this trend. Theoretically this can be seen in the attention to both Anglo-Saxon feminism and theoretical discussions and the French philosophical tradition. Dutch women's studies representatives were also quick to take advantage of the opportunities for internationalization. At the University of Nijmegen a special fund was called to life to encourage female Ph.D. students to travel and study abroad. In the European context, two Erasmus programs were set up, Wings and NOI♀SE, which organize the exchange of about forty students per year, with a modest staff exchange at their side. The curriculum was adapted to integrate foreign students, for instance, by teaching a number of classes in English, but also by working more from a multicultural perspective. Many topics concerning women, like the feminization of poverty, the rising number of female-headed households, the misogyny of religious fundamentalisms, the feminization of subsistence agriculture, the rising crime rate among women, the resistance to sharing the work of informal care, are all global phenomena that can be understood, in their complexity and contradictions, only from a comparative international perspective. At the Ph.D. level, international summer schools for Ph.D. students were initiated.

The international orientation of women's studies scholars is visible in other aspects as well. Many books or theses are published in English or another European language; the main Dutch review journal of women's studies literature, *Lover*, regularly reviews women's studies journals from the surrounding European countries and beyond; international conferences on women's studies issues are organized and attended. Dutch scholars have played an important role in the internationalization of contacts, journals, and scientific organizations. In 1990 the Dutch Association for Women's Studies took the initiative for a European professional organization called WISE (Women's International Studies Europe), which publishes *WISE Women's News* and the *European Women's Studies Guide*, organizes conferences, and recently gained funds for a European Expert Centre for Women's Studies, and in 1994 started the *European Journal of Women's Studies* (SAGE), with six hundred subscribers. In 1995, during the NGO Forum in Beijing, WISE initiated a federation of women's studies associations worldwide.

This international orientation has posed another dilemma, however. Lately the demand to be international has become so strong that publications in the mother tongue, however interesting they may be, are no longer considered important scientific publications. At the same time, funds for training scientists to write in English, to translate or edit their works, or to finance conference attendance are hardly available. Moreover, taking a multicultural perspective and using a comparative approach are hampered by the lack of adequate teaching materials. This means that women's studies units must spend their own resources to meet the demands for internationalization—resources that they often do not have. Moreover, they find much of their work that focuses on Dutch women or that has direct social relevance, including applied research for local groups or the government, degraded and no longer considered scientific for the mere reason that the publications are written in Dutch. To choose internationalization often implies stepping away from the needs of Dutch women.

Conclusion

The "double track policy" that most women's studies units in the Netherlands have chosen has turned out to be a problem as well as an effective strategy. The double track requires vast investments of time and energy and continuous attention as strong forces tend to push women's studies organizationally and theoretically back into the one track of integration. External factors, such as budget cuts, put pressure on women's studies units to merge with the traditional disciplines. Internal divisions stemming from unequal opportunities or individual status preoccupations prompt women to turn away from gender problems or leave women out of the titles of their publications. The lower status of women and women's studies is sometimes shared by the students and staff involved: it is often more attractive to graduate or teach in, say, sociology or physics than in women's studies, so women find it hard to choose autonomy. In this situation it is best to aim for integration but from an independent position.

The choice for the double track has brought women's studies in the Netherlands visibility, recognition, and influence. The foundation of women's studies units that were integrative and independent at the same time has proved to be essential for survival. Because of such units, women's studies now has a distinctive domain of research, a

teaching curriculum, a history of conceptual and theoretical developments, including internal theoretical differentiation and diversification, professional organizations, and journals. The dilemma has not
been solved—a lot more balancing will have to be done in the future—
but women's studies has managed to become recognized as a discipline in its own right and as a power not to be ignored.

NOTES

1. There are also seventy-eight colleges of higher vocational education, which
concentrate on applied science and prepare students for specific professions. They have integrated women's studies in their curriculum but have
not set up specific women's studies units. I will not explicitly deal with them
here.

REFERENCES

Angerman, A. et al. 1989. *Current Issues in Women's History*. London and New
York: Routledge.

Bal, M., and P. Pattynama. 1993. *Psychoanalyse en feminisme*. Amsterdam: Amsterdam University Press.

Bertels, R., et al. 1989. *Over grenzen: Vrouwen and wetenschappelijke innovaties*.
Groningen: Interfacultaire Werkgroep Emancipatie Vraagstukken/
Vrouwenstudies.

Bouw, C., J. de Bruijn, and D. van der Heiden. 1994. *Van alle markten thuis:
Vrouwen-en genderstudies in Nederland*. Amsterdam: Babylon-de Geus.

Brandt E. 1995. "De Alma Pater." *De Groene Amsterdammer* 119, no. 38: 20–24.

Brouns, M. 1988. *Veertien jaar vrouwenstudies in Nederland: Een overzicht*. Zoeter-
meer: Ministerie van Onderwijs en Wetenschappen.

———. 1992. "The Dutch Development: Women's Studies in the Netherlands.
Women's Studies Quarterly 20, nos. 3 and 4: 44–57.

Brouns, M., and H. Harbers. 1994. *Kwaliteit in meervoud: Reflectie op de
kwaliteiten van vrouwenstudies in Nederland*. Den Haag: VUGA.

Brouns, M., M. Verloo, and M. Grünell, eds. 1995. *Vrouwenstudies in de jaren
negentig: Een kennismaking vanuit de verschillende disciplines*. Bussum:
Coutinho.

Brügmann, M., et al., eds. 1993. *Who's Afraid of Femininity? Questions of Identity*.
Amsterdam and Atlanta: Rodopi.

Bruijn, J. de, et al., eds. 1993. *The Women's Movement: History and Theory*.
Aldershot: Avebury.

Buikema, R., and A. Smelik, eds. 1993. *Vrouwenstudies in de cultuurwetenschap-
pen*. Muiderberg: Coutinho.

Davis, K., M. Leijenaar, and J. Oldersma, eds. 1991. *The Gender of Power*.
London: Sage Publications.

Dekker, K. den. 1993. *Vrouwenstudies in de tweede geldstroom: Groei, kwaliteits- en
vernieuwingseffecten van financiering van vrouwenstudies en emancipatieonderzoek
door de Nederlandse Organisatie voor Wetenschappelijk Onderzoek*. Den Haag.

Hermsen, J., and A. van Lenning. 1991. *Sharing the Difference: Feminist Debates in Holland.* London and New York: Routledge.

Jansen, W. 1990. "Vrouwen in het hoger onderwijs in Jordanië." *Tijdschrift voor Vrouwenstudies* 11, no. 4: 410–19.

———. 1993. *Mythen van het fundament.* Nijmegen: SUN.

Lasthuizen, K. 1995. *Onderzoekers vrouwenstudies in Nederland: Een voerzicht* (Scholars in women's studies in the Netherlands: A survey). Utrecht: Nederlands Genootschap Vrouwenstudies.

Lenning, A. van, M. Brouns, and J. de Bruijn. 1995. *Inzichten uit vrouwenstudies: Uitdagingen voor beleidmakers.* Ministerie van Sociale Zaken en Werkgelegenheid. Den Haag: VUGA.

Lie, S. S., L. Malik, and D. Harris, eds. 1994. *The Gender Gap in Higher Education: World Yearbook of Education.* London.

Noordenbos, G. 1994. "Dat was niet voorzien: Consequenties van universitaire reorganisaties voor de man/vrouw-verdeling." *Universiteit en Hogeschool.* *Themanummer "In dienst van Alma Mater" of "Hoe aantrekkelijk is de universiteit als werkgever"* 40, no. 3: 118–24.

———. 1995. " 'Gender gap in Academe': De positie van vrouwen aan de universiteit in internationaal perspectief." *Universiteit en Hogeschool* 41, no. 3: 105–20.

Parel, G., and M. van de Wouw. 1988. *Kortom . . . men was zeer betrokken: Het ontstaan en de ontwikkeling van vrouwenstudies aan de Nederlandse universiteiten 1974–1981.* Utrecht.

Poldervaart, S. 1983. *Vrouwenstudies: Een inleiding.* Nijmegen: SUN.

Ras, M. de, and M. Lunenberg. 1993. *Girls, Girlhood, and Girls' Studies in Transition.* Amsterdam: Het Spinhuis.

Vansuyt, C. 1990. *"Een koekoeksjong in het wetenschapsnest": De institutionalisering van vrouwenstudies aan Nederlandse universiteiten.* Amsterdam: Vakgroep Wetenschapsdynamica, Universiteit van Amsterdam.

Verloo, M., and E. Heijmans. 1995. *Kwaliteit van onderzoek: Inzichten uit vrouwenstudies voor toegepast onderzoek.* Ministerie van Sociale Zaken en Werkgelegenheid. Den Haag: VUGA.

Willie Jansen is a professor at the University of Nijmegen and a coordinator for Women's Interdisciplinary Network on Gender and Society (WINGS).

APPENDIX
Addresses

Women's Studies Departments and Units at Universities

Women's Studies, University of Groningen
Nieuwe Kijk in 't Jatstr. 70, 9712 SK Groningen, Netherlands

Women's Studies, University of Rotterdam
Postbus 1738, 3000 DR Rotterdam, Netherlands

Women's Studies, University of Nijmegen
Postbus 9104, 6500 HE Nijmegen, Netherlands

Women's Studies Social Sciences, University of Utrecht
Heidelberglaan 2, 3584 CS Utrecht, Netherlands

Women's Studies Humanities, University of Utrecht
Kromme Nieuwegracht 29, 3512 HD Utrecht, Netherlands

Women's Studies, University of Leiden
Wassenaarseweg 52, 2333 AK Leiden, Netherlands

Women's Studies, Polytechnics Enschede
Postbus 217, 7500 AE Enschede, Netherlands

Women's Studies, University of Limburg
Postbus 616, 6200 MD Maastricht, Netherlands

Women's Studies, Polytechnics Eindhoven
Postbus 513, 5600 MB Eindhoven, Netherlands

Women's Studies in Agriculture, University of Agriculture Wageningen
Hollandseweg 1, 6706 KN Wageningen, Netherlands

Women's Studies, University of Amsterdam
O.Z. Achterburgwal 237, 1012 DC Amsterdam, Netherlands

Women's Studies, Free University of Amsterdam
Koningslaan 31-33, 1075 AB Amsterdam, Netherlands

Women's Studies, University of Brabant
Postbus 90153, 5000 LE Tilburg, Netherlands

Nationwide University Organizations of Women's Studies

Nederlands Genootschap Vrouwenstudies/Dutch Association of
    Women's Studies
Heidelberglaan 2, 3584 CS Utrecht, Netherlands
Telephone: -31-30-531881/531857, Fax: -31-30-531619

Nederlandse Onderzoekschool Vrouwenstudies/ Netherlands Research
    School of Women's Studies

Lucas Bolwerk 5, 3512 EG Utrecht, Netherlands
Telephone: -31-30-536001, Fax: -31-30-536695

Interdisciplinaire Commissie Vrouwenstudies (ICV-VSNU)/Interdisciplinary
    Committee Women's Studies of the Association of Universities
    in the Netherlands
Postbus 19270, 3501 DG Utrecht, Netherlands
Telephone: -31-30-363888, Fax: -31-30-333540

Internationaal Informatiecentrum en Archief voor de Vrouwenbeweging
(IIAV)/International Information Center and Archives for the
    Women's Movement
Obiplein 4, 1094 RB Amsterdam, Netherlands
Telephone: -31-20-6244268, Fax: -31-20-6233855

Werkgemeenschap Vrouwenstudies en Emancipatie-onderzoek (WVEO)/
    Section Women's Studies of Netherlands Foundation of Scientific
Research
Postbus 93120, 2509 AC Den Haag, Netherlands
Telephone: -31-70-3440835/3440859, Fax: -31-70-3850971

European Networks

NOI♀SE
Network of Interdisciplinary Women's Studies in Europe
Coordination: Prof. Dr. Rosi Braidotti and Dr. Christine Rammrath
Kromme Nieuwegracht 29, 3512 HD Utrecht, Netherlands
Telephone: -31-30-536013, Fax: -31-30-536695

WINGS
Women's Interdisciplinary Network on Gender and Society
Coordination: Drs. José van Alst, Prof. Dr. Willy Jansen
Center for Women's Studies, University of Nijmegen
Postbus 9104, 6500 HE Nijmegen, Netherlands
Telephone: - 31-24-3613069/2339, Fax: - 31-24-3611881

WISE
Women's International Studies Europe
Heidelberglaan 2, 3584 CS Utrecht, Netherlands
Telephone: -31-30-531881/531857, Fax: -31-30-531619

Women and Management
Coordination: Joke van Antwerpen and Tootje Meppelink
Hogeschool van Amsterdam, Expertisecentrum Vrouw en Management
Singel 132-134, 1015 AG Amsterdam, Netherlands
Telephone: -31-20-5240323, Fax: -31-20-6382949

Women's Studies and Educational Science
Coordination: Dr. Margreet Wegelin and drs. Iet Guinee
Faculty of Educational Science, University of Amsterdam
Prinsengracht 227, 1075 VX Amsterdam, Netherlands
Telephone: - 31-20-5703551,

Women's Studies in Norway

Tove Beate Pedersen

The Pioneering Years: Allies Inside the Establishment

Women's studies in Norway, as in the other Nordic countries, began as part of the students' and women's revolts at the end of 1960s and the beginning of the 1970s. Students, particularly in the humanities, social sciences, and law, plus a few established female intellectuals, worked together to build up what has subsequently made an important contribution to Norwegian scholarship. Within the social sciences, however, women's studies had strong roots in the gender role research of the 1950s and 1960s. What was new about the 1970s was the close cooperation with the women's movement. Research became empirical and pragmatic; documentation and action were the most important elements.

Other factors also contributed to the blossoming of women's studies during these years. The period provides evidence of scholars' enthusiasm, endurance, and interdisciplinary cooperation. Furthermore, individuals and institutions outside academia offered support, as did the women's movement, with some sustainers providing economic and moral assistance from within the establishment. One such body was the Norwegian Research Council for Science and the Humanities (NAVF). Through its scholarship program for women's studies in the humanities in the late 1970s and the establishment of its Secretariat for Women and Research in the Social Sciences in 1977, NAVF has played a central role in recruiting increasing numbers of women as researchers and in encouraging expansion of the field. Several programs were launched at the end of the 1980s, financed by Norwegian research councils. Moreover, throughout these two decades we have had allies in government ministries and political circles, who have provided resources, established a demand for the results of women's studies, and used these data in political debates.

The positive attitude to women's studies also stems from success in the campaign for equal rights. Support for women's equal status in research and the need for women's studies has been clearly underlined in a number of official documents in Norway. Since the end of the 1980s, especially, this policy has been followed up by the

Norwegian Ministry of Church, Education, and Research, which has requested research councils, institutes, universities, and colleges to prepare action schemes for women's equal status, including measures to strengthen women's research. Of course, these often ambitious statements and plans have not always been put into practice. Even so, they have been useful references during the fight for resources and funding.

Norwegian International Characteristics Relevant for Development of Women's Studies

Two particularly Norwegian phenomena have played an important role in the development of women's studies. These are the NAVF Secretariat for Women and Research and independent research institutes in the social sciences. The Secretariat, a central and public agency with national responsibility, has built networks, provided funds for meetings, arranged seminars and conferences, and indicated new research projects. It has also been a lobbying agency, supported publishing activities, and issued its own journal and news bulletin, *Kvinneforskning* (Feminist Research), earlier *Nytt om kvinneforskning* (News in Feminist Research). The Secretariat became interdisciplinary in 1982, and this allowed the recruitment of women to medicine, the natural sciences, and technology, among other fields. Since 1991 the Secretariat has acquired permanent status and has since August 1992 been part of the Research Council of Norway, a new organization consisting of the previously established five Norwegian research councils.

In a Nordic context the significance of the large Norwegian "institute sector" should be emphasized. Instead of placing applied research and development work inside the universities, the tendency in Norway has been to establish institutes of applied research outside these institutions. Women researchers in the social sciences with funding from the research council or ministries have been affiliated with these institutions to a greater extent than with the universities. In Norway there are still relatively few women in tenured university positions (a total of around 20 percent) and as a consequence also few women's studies scholars. What is special about Norway then, is that women's studies for a long time has had an institutional base in settings other than the universities.

When we talk about women's studies in Norway, we use the word *kvinneforskning*, which, directly translated into English, means "women's research." This reflects the fact that teaching women's studies in for-credit courses at the university is a recent phenomenon. Until the last few years women's research has been taught only in noncredit courses and seminars. The reason was a specific academic policy saying that no centers, only departments, are allowed to give for-credit courses. In Norway the course of study is organized by faculties and disciplines. Currently this principle is being watered down, and some of the centers for women's studies at the universities are now developing for-credit courses.

Generally speaking, Norwegian feminist scholars have been extremely active and have published a great deal. Substantial efforts at larger theoretical contributions are, however, only of more recent origin. We believe that this is largely attributable to the conditions under which these scholars have been working, often with short-term research contracts, usually within the institutes; they have had insecure terms of appointment and have not received much support from their respective academic milieus. Furthermore, the institute sector does not undertake postsecondary-level teaching. In addition, there is an obvious lack of qualified instruction in women's studies among the university's tenured staff.

As a consequence, the danger exists that, first, we will have an insufficient number of new recruits to women's studies, since researchers in this field rarely teach students. Second is the attendant risk that theory may be neglected, because short-term contract research does not allow time for its development. Neither has contact across disciplinary boundaries been all that efficient; there has been little cooperation between researchers in the humanities and those in the social sciences. During the last few years, however, some positive developments in interfaculty cooperation and more basic research have emerged. These activities have been strengthened in particular by the centers for women's studies established at universities starting in the mid-1980s. At the University of Bergen, a Centre for Women's Studies in the Humanities was established on a trial basis in 1985 and has since been made permanent. The interdisciplinary centers at the University of Oslo and Trondheim were set up for a trial period in 1987 and 1990, respectively. The Oslo center has been continued until 1997, while the center in Trondheim is secure for the rest of this millennium. The last acquisition to the field is a permanent interdisciplinary center for women's studies and female researchers established in 1995 at the University of Troms.

Most women's studies courses today give no credit. A few credit courses are to be found, but it is still impossible to get a degree in women's studies at any level. The four centers for women's studies, however, now agree on giving priority to developing basic for-credit courses in women's studies. This is also seen as a strategy toward integration of the gender perspective into the various disciplines, the argument being that when the students are offered this perspective in a women's studies course early in their studies, they will later insist on it in the disciplines they go into. At present, the centers for women's studies have no plans to develop full degree programs in women's studies.

Developments in and Between Disciplines

The development of women's perspectives within the different academic disciplines varies a great deal. Both the existence of researchers active in an academic milieu and the characteristics of any particular discipline have had a vital impact on opportunities to develop women's research. In the field of history, the problem of justifying the perspective has been relatively small. A general and basic principle in historical investigation is that surveying and understanding the past can help you discover your identity. Because of the nature of sociology, justifying women's studies in relation to the established body of knowledge has also been relatively unproblematic. In other disciplines, however, such as philosophy, political science, and economics, feminist scholars have had difficulty finding acceptance. In the legal field, in contrast, the Faculty of Law set up a special course in women's law as early as 1974 and, in 1978, the Department of Public Law at the University of Oslo set up a special section for women's jurisprudence. By applying a systematic women's perspective to the legal system in relationship to women's realities and needs, women's studies has had an important impact on Norwegian politics. Today the Institute of Women's Law at the University of Oslo is involved in a regional women's law program for Southern and Eastern Africa, based at the University of Zimbabwe. Important research topics in women's law include equality and labor law, international women's law, child protection and justice. Women's law in Norway has come a long way in terms of theoretical developments and has attracted widespread international attention.

The humanities have witnessed a marked change in the direction of research, moving from a focus on women as objects toward more complicated and challenging projects, with interaction and conflicts between the sexes and between women having become central themes in many disciplines.

Within the natural sciences and some medical specialties, considerable resistance to the construction of women's and gender perspectives has been noted. However, international debate concerning women's point of view within these disciplines has led to an increasing interest in these issues in Norway. It looks as if the new generation of women scholars in the natural sciences is more receptive to debate. Of course, problems specific to women have long been the focus of such disciplines as psychiatry, gynecology, and social and general medicine. In recent years a network of women physicians concerned with female perspectives and feminist research has been formed. In 1990 NAVF even launched a research program for women's studies in medicine.

There is today a growing interest in "new" women's illnesses, such as fibromyalgy and osteoporosis. In addition, interesting research is going on in sports medicine: studies of the damaging effects of top sports on women's bodies and health, as well as medical research on the effects of violence against women.

A Norwegian Picture: Contributions from Researchers in a Nordic Welfare State

From the very beginning, women's studies in Norway has been empirical and pragmatic, and the research topics undertaken have been characterized by their closeness to women's lives. Directions and developments may be explained partly by the characteristic already mentioned: research within the so-called "applied" social sciences has in large part been done in independent social research institutes, instead of within the universities. This has contributed to close relationships and cooperation between women researchers, women bureaucrats, women in the research councils, and women in politics.

In the early phase, in the 1970s and early 1980s, documentation and action in favor of women's rights and equal opportunities were important elements in Norwegian women's studies. The field was closely tied to Norwegian everyday reality and characterized by a braiding of problem-oriented empiricism, critical discipline, and interdisciplinary feminism. From the beginning, researchers in women's studies have taken part in the discussions going on internationally, as is demonstrated by the growing interest in differences between women and conflicts of interests between women. In addition to the many ways in which the development of Norwegian women's studies parallels developments internationally, we can also identify a Norwegian profile, which is most obvious in the social sciences.

The effects of the significant changes in our society over the past thirty years—with women being educated and working full time (or double or triple time), and the consequences of those changes on women's everyday practice—are highly visible on the research agenda. Women's entry into the labor market, the rapid increase of the dual-earner family, and the high representation of women in politics and in public life, as well as the ambitious equal-status policy all raise new questions concerning the significance of gender in the family and society. Central research topics include gender as both a cultural and a social phenomenon; the importance of gender as a basis in conflicts of interests, value orientations, and behavior; the gendered division of labor that we still face; and gender relations in politics and public life. Research concerning changes in the family with regard to care and economic provisions, new ways of combining work and family life, "the organization of everyday life," and the relationship between state and family are characteristic topics for Norwegian women's studies. This includes projects, discussing different divisions of labor between men and women, differences between formal and informal care, including discourse about the meaning and content of terms like *care, caring,* and *care-giving work.*

The point of departure for these studies is that gender typing of caring still constitutes an important aspect of the divisions of labor in our society. The relationship between the welfare state and women has been, and still is, thoroughly discussed: Is Norway a patriarchal state or is the relationship better understood as an alliance or partnership? The interplay between working life and the family is a central theme. Employed mothers are wage-workers, caregivers as well as citizens of the welfare state. The significance of wage work in women's lives in relation to their family roles is an area of study. Time use and time conflicts are important issues in studies of daily lives as well as labor market participation. The representation of women in national political forums, in Norway and in the Nordic countries, is unique in an international context, and questions concerning the integration of women in politics and public life and the impact of the representation of women for political priorities have been central. But the still (to a large extent) traditional patterns in choice of education and occupation, as well as resistant wage differences between men and women, are also the objects of important research nowadays.

The fact that Norway's advanced status regarding women's social position has influenced women's studies will hardly surprise anyone. It may, though, be a surprise that Norway also has a need for comprehensive and sophisticated research on violence against women. In international contexts I have often come across researchers who assume that there is no such thing as violence against women in "a country like ours." Violence against women is studied by researchers from different backgrounds, mainly psychology, sociology, criminology, and medicine.

Aspects of violence toward women that have been studied include, for example, how institutions like the police and the church understand and react to rape and wife battering, how we can better understand and help the woman who stays in an abusive relationship, and how the abusive man perceives what is going on.

Norwegian criminologists have done groundbreaking studies of prostitution, perceiving prostitution as violence against women. Some of these studies have focused on the customers, with qualitative interviews, in order to describe who the customers are and their perceptions of buying sex.

Norway is a country with significant differences between urban and rural areas. In recent years, researchers at our northernmost university and regional college have published important studies on women and regional development. Particularly interesting are studies of the role of women in the fisheries and in our coastal culture.

Since Norway is a country that contributes substantially to development aid, authorities seem now to be reaching an understanding of the need for research that incorporates women's perspectives, to be able to plan for good strategies for adequate and relevant help.

Where Do We Go from Here? Problems and Challenges: Two Sides to the Same Coin!

Since the early 1990s, as the field has become increasingly institutionalized through the centers for women's studies and the Secretariat for Women and Research , more scholars in women's research have gradually been appointed to tenured positions. Their research also finds its way into the disciplines. Its conquered place is, however, marginal and vulnerable.

A feminist theory of science has captured the interest of some scholars in the natural sciences and medicine. To nurture and support such processes is one of the new challenges. Research on gender as a principle by which society is organized has made some headway. Furthermore, problems concerning the relationship between production and reproduction have started to attract attention, and this is undoubtedly a field where the need for interdisciplinary research will be increasingly felt. Women scholars from different disciplines are working together on theories of power and theories of gender, while others have become involved in men's studies.

Male colleagues in particular have shown women's studies scholars both resistance and indifference, the latter reflected in the absence of book reviews, academic debates, and invitations to participate in projects and seminars. Few men include women's research texts on their reading lists and in their teaching. They are obviously considering this new knowledge irrelevant to them and their work, viewing women's studies as a special-interest area.

Women's research texts are only beginning to be integrated into some traditional academic disciplines, for example, social anthropology, sociology, psychology, history, and literature. To further these developments and to integrate women's perspectives into the research and teaching in the established disciplines is at present an acute and difficult challenge.

If, however, we look at the "result" of women's studies from another perspective—as members of public councils and committees within and outside the research system, and its influence on political decision-making processes—the picture is altogether different. Here, the competence and expertise of women's studies scholars are considered scarce resources and the demand is much greater than the supply. All in all, we can say that feminist researchers and their competence are sought as "wares" in Norway—particularly outside academia—but that they are gradually also being accepted into the academic world.

To secure our gains as well as further resources, our experience so far points to the strategy most likely to succeed: we must strengthen and nurture our relationships to our sisters at the student level and inside the research and state bureaucracies, as well as in politics.

Tove Beate Pedersen is the director of the Secretariat for Women and Research, the Research Council of Norway.

Women's Studies in China

Tao Jie

For almost thirty years after the founding of the People's Republic in China in 1949, Chinese women assumed with great pride that they were fully emancipated and had achieved true equality with men. To them, the best proof of their liberation was that they enjoyed equal job opportunity and equal pay for equal work with men. They would also enumerate the measures taken by the government to protect their rights and interests. In the early 1950s, the government adopted the marriage law, which prohibited arranged marriage, rescued many women from misery, and gave them the freedom to choose their spouses. It was the government that encouraged women to be trained as tractor drivers, airline pilots, electricians, or engineers—trades that used to be considered men's fields only. It was the government that gave girls and women the opportunity of education, of going to illiteracy classes, primary schools, middle schools, even colleges, free of charge. In 1958, during the Big Leap Forward, it was again the government that called upon women to leave their households to participate in productive labor. And in the early 1960s, Mao Zedong, then the highest authority in the whole nation, praised women for being "an important force in production, holding up half the sky."

Because of such slogans and government policies, Chinese women never suspected that there was any prejudice against women in their society. They firmly believed that they were enjoying much greater freedom than did women in other countries, even those in the West. In those days, if anyone had talked about women's liberation movements or women's rights, she would have been frowned upon or considered crazy.

If we explore more closely the situation of women during those thirty years, however, we will discover that women were considered in the same category as children. The protection provided to women was the sort provided by the strong, the man, to the weak, the woman. The effort to achieve women's emancipation seemed to be focused only on providing women with jobs. Very little was done to raise their own self-awareness, to improve their abilities, or to cultivate their confidence. As a matter of fact, the consciousness of women was not enhanced during that period, which ultimately has caused more problems today, in the era of reform. For instance, while women make up 48.67 percent of the total population, according to the third population census, and women with jobs are 43.69 percent of the total number of employed people, 45.20 percent of the country's illiterates and semi-illiterates age twelve and above are women. If we disregard those born before 1949, the percentage of women illiterates and semi-illiterates born after liberation is 40.31 percent among those aged thirty to thirty-five and 43.48 percent among those aged thirty-five to forty. As to school-age girls who have not yet enrolled, the figure is 40.8 percent for the seven-year-olds, 19.2 percent for the eight-year-olds, 30.7 percent for the thirteen-year-olds, and as high as 43.9 percent for the fourteen-year-olds. It is inconceivable that these girls with little education and very low self-awareness will become the competitive equals of men in a market-oriented economy.

Chinese women's complacency began to break down in the late 1970s when China entered its era of reform and opening up. For once, China ended its state of self-enclosure. In its eagerness to modernize the country, the Chinese government began to send people abroad to study and began to invite foreigners to teach and work in China. The returned students and the foreign experts brought new ideas and new theories into China that opened people's eyes to their own shortcomings and forced them to engage in serious reflection. For instance, they came to understand that the women's liberation movement in the United States has not been about bra burning or man hating. Its chief purpose was to cultivate women's self-awareness and foster the confidence of women so as to allow them to compete with men as equals. And this was exactly what women in China had neglected to do. They had depended too much on the government to give them equal status with men.

Another factor that disturbed Chinese women's peace of mind was that because of the reform and the open-door policy, the country's news media had become more open in exposing the malaise of society, including not only prejudice against women but also injustices done to women. For instance, one statistic revealed that, in 1986, in a small county in Sichuan Province, 323 women were cheated out of their houses and sold to men in places thousands of miles away. Another statistic showed that, in 1989, women made up only 33.7 percent of the total enrollment of students at colleges and universities and as few as 9.2 percent of the professors were women. On the other end of the scale, however, 70 percent of those waiting for employment were women. Such statistics speak eloquently about the prejudice against women.

A third important factor is the competitive system that emerged along with the policy of a market-oriented economy. The low cultural and educational level of a large number of women placed them at a disadvantage in competing with men. For instance, a common way for factories to become more efficient and to cut down their expenses is to reduce the number of workers. Very often, then, women are considered surplus labor force and thus become the first to lose their jobs. The low education of women also gives people with male chauvinist ideas a pretext for excluding women from their institutions. It is a well-known fact nowadays that women college graduates have more difficulty than men in finding jobs. The irony is that many institutions reject better-qualified women, even those who have distinguished themselves in colleges or graduate schools, in order to hire a man who is not as well qualified. In 1987, the National Trade Union surveyed 660 leaders of different enterprises in eleven provinces and autonomous regions about their preference in employment. Of the group, 30.4 percent responded that they favored hiring men rather than women. Only 5.3 percent showed an interest in hiring women. Even in the textile industry, which has always been considered a women's field, only 25 percent of the 89 leaders interviewed expressed any interest in hiring women, while 37.5 percent preferred to have male workers. For a period of time in the mid-1980s, the demand that women go back to their homes was supported by men and even by women themselves. Even today, in some places, women are made to stay at home after pregnancy or birth-delivery for as long as six years, under the pretext that their husbands would like them to be more comfortable. The pity is that there are women who are thankful for such "thoughtfulness from men" and never think about the loss of their careers or their ability to compete with men when they want to resume their work. All this has made some Chinese women acutely aware of prejudice against women in their society. They have come to realize that there is a long road ahead if women are to achieve real equality with men.

What has been done in this era of reform and competition to raise women's consciousness and to do away with the prejudice against women? In the past, the women's movement was often started by the government rather than out of women's own need. This time, I would say, it is a kind of joint effort carried out by both government organizations and women themselves.

The Chinese government, in its effort to improve women's opportunities, has passed several laws in recent years: the new Marriage Law in 1980, the Law for Marriage Registration in 1985, and of course, the most important one—the Law of the People's Republic of China on the

Protection of the Rights and Interests of Women, which was adopted in 1990. To enforce this law, commissions have been set up in provinces and cities to supervise and coordinate work that guarantees women's rights and interests. Special mention should also be made of the All-China Women's Federation, which is the only formally established institution in China that deals with women's issues. It has local branches at the grassroots level all over the country. It is this organization that has been carrying out the publicizing of the laws that protect women's rights and interests. It is also this organization that deals with everyday matters in safeguarding women's rights and interests. In the new era of reform and opening up, the Women's Federation has come to realize that it needs to be better qualified for its work, armed especially with new ideas and new theories. Since 1984, it has created short-term and long-term programs, even institutes at all levels, to train their cadres in theories of women's studies. In 1988, a college for women cadres was formally set up in Beijing. So far, it has three departments: women's rights, law, and preschool education. Its students are women working for the Women's Federation, women who are directors of day care centers, and women cadres of governmental institutions, schools at different levels, as well as factories and business enterprises. Participants must be under forty years of age, with five years of working experience and a high school education. After one year of schooling at this college, they return to the place from which they came and are assigned jobs related to women and their welfare. It is evident that such programs are set up to enable women cadres to do their work better.

To broaden the minds of the students and the cadres, these institutes often invite Chinese and foreign scholars to lecture on such topics as "Differences in Psychology Between Men and Women," "Gender Discrimination: A Universal Issue," "Tradition, Scientific Progress, and Changes in Chinese Families," "Women, Marriage, Psychology, Culture," as well as others, like "Christianity and Western Women," "Confucianism and Its Impact on Women in China," and "Women and Folk Tradition." One most impressive event was a conference jointly held in 1991 by the All-China Women's Federation and Global Interactions, Inc., of the United States. About 250 Americans and 200 Chinese participated in this conference. Its topics covered career and employment, health and lifestyle, family planning, child care, job training, and health care. It was at this conference that Chinese officials such as Luo Qiong, a former vice chairman of the Women's Federation, openly admitted that there are invisible barriers in China with regard to women's job opportunities and career advancement and that discrimination against women still exists in Chinese society.

In addition to such efforts, the Women's Federation has also carried out investigations at the grassroots level, even in remote and backward regions, of women's social status, their difficulties, and aspirations. Such surveys have provided data for scholars of women's studies and frames of reference for the government to work out measures to protect women's rights and interests.

In the meantime, newspapers and magazines have begun to help promote women's studies. In the thirty years from 1949 to 1979, there was only one magazine for women—*Women in China.* Now there are about a dozen journals, including one newspaper, aimed at women readers, with such names as *Women's Friends, Life and Marriage, Women's Health, Marriage and Family.* They are a little bit like *Better Homes and Gardens* or *Good Housekeeping* in the United States and may not always give good advice to women. In addition, there are also more serious journals, such as *Gender Studies, Women's Forum,* and *Women's Movement in China,* that carry articles about theories on women's studies, analyses of surveys about psychological obstacles to women's advancement, the causes of girls' quitting school, modern women's aesthetics, and the remnant feudalistic ideas in people's minds. Books by famous women leaders in foreign countries have also been translated into Chinese. It is no exaggeration to say that Chinese women now have more access than ever before to the latest theories on women's issues and to what is going on in women's movements outside China.

What has been mentioned above is actually work done by the government. Since the late 1970s, more and more Chinese women have come together in an attempt to raise women's consciousness and to find ways for women to achieve genuine equality with men. One important form that these efforts take is the women's studies group, which has been emerging rapidly in many places, especially in cities and very often among women scholars in universities or research institutes. It is estimated that there are now about two thousand women's studies groups or centers of different levels and forms all over China, including those organized by the Women's Federation and others formed by women themselves on a voluntary or informal basis. For instance, in 1987, a group of women, both Chinese and foreign, got together at the Beijing Foreign Studies University to start such a group. They meet regularly every other week and hold discussions about topics related to women's issues, ranging from the role of women in history to the pressure and challenges that women have to confront nowadays to books about women and work that should be undertaken to raise the social status of women.

In addition to such informal groups, women's studies centers are springing up in China. The first was founded in 1984 in Zhengzhou University, Henan Province, by Li Xiaojiang. This center has done some pioneering work in women's studies by holding regular national symposiums and publishing books on new theories of women's studies, the history of women in Chinese society, women's movements abroad, and women's issues in China and their possible solutions. It has also made a great effort to set up a women's museum and is carrying on fieldwork among women in local rural areas. It is no exaggeration to say that this center heralded a new era of the women's movement in China.

As an illustration of activities carried out by women themselves, I will describe the evolution of the Women's Studies Center at my university. Peking University was founded in 1898 as the Metropolitan University of the Qing Dynasty and has always been in the forefront of the women's movement in China. It was the first university in Chinese history to open its doors to women, early in this century. As early as 19 May 1919, Deng Chunlan, a young woman from Gansu Province, wrote to Cai Yuanpei, then president of Peking University, requesting that women be allowed to enter the university. Also in the spring of 1919, Li Dazhao and a number of other professors wrote to newspapers, advocating coeducation. In his article, "The Women's Rights Movement in Modern Times," Li Dazhao remarked, "The 20th century is an age in which women will find themselves and one in which men will come to see the importance of women." Later, on 1 January 1920, in an interview with a journalist of *New China Daily*, Cai Yuanpei made public the decision of Peking University to enroll women students. From then on, this university trained many distinguished women scholars and women activists. After liberation, Peking University went through the 1952 campaign to reorganize and reregulate universities and departments and became a comprehensive university with departments of both sciences and liberal arts focused mainly on teaching and research in fundamental disciplines. At present, there are 29 departments, 86 undergraduate programs, 132 M.A. programs and 90 Ph.D. programs. The enrollment has reached 12,000, with more than 500 foreign students from more than 60 countries and regions. It is one of the most important and one of the largest universities in China.

The Women's Studies Center at Peking University has gone through three stages in its development. The first stage began in the mid-1980s, when the English department took the lead in offering such courses related to women as "American Women's Literature," "Victorian Women Novelists," and "British and American Women Writers." Some of its women professors got together to form a loosely organized, informal forum that met every other week. Very quickly, women from other departments, especially from the departments of history and Chinese, joined in to form a study group made up of professors, graduate students of history, Chinese, English, and sociology, with women from other institutions like the Academy of Sciences or the Party School in Beijing joining as well. Some foreign experts and foreign students on the campus also came to these discussions, although they were conducted in Chinese.

At this stage, we invited people who were engaged in jobs relating to women, such as reporters from women's magazines, professors from the College of Women Cadres, or cadres working for the Women's Federation. They told us about the "new women" in villages, who were taking a significant lead in reform movements or in village and county enterprises and about women who still suffer from arranged marriages or who are abused by their husbands. We also learned about women criminals, discrimination against women in job opportunities or in promotion, and the trend of retrogression back into old traditions and old ideas among men as well as among women themselves. Foreign students and teachers were invited to talk about the situation of women in such countries as Japan, Thailand, West Germany, and the United States.

For academics, somewhat isolated from the outside world, such talks and discussions broadened our views and helped us to see things as they really were outside the campus. We came to see that the achievements of Chinese women were relatively small. Compared with the situation before 1949, the lives of women in China had been much improved, but it was evident that Chinese women had lagged behind in their effort for real emancipation as compared with women in other countries. There was still much room for improvement and a long and difficult way to go to achieve true equality with men. We also came to realize that, although it was important for the government to take measures to protect the rights and interests of women, it was even more important for women themselves to work together and raise their own self-awareness. Inequality exists in Chinese society not only because there is discrimination on the part of men but because women, influenced by centuries of feudalistic ideas and codes of behavior, often look down upon themselves.

The second stage in the development of our center started around 1989. After three years of meetings and discussions, we became dissatisfied with this passive form of activity and felt strongly that we must do more effective and more productive work. As professors, we naturally thought of integrating women's studies with our teaching. Following the lead of the English department, professors in the history department and the Chinese department began to offer courses on women. Professors of the Population Research Institute and the sociology department began to focus their research on women's issues. Courses such as "Women in Chinese History," "Women at Home and Abroad," and "Feminist Literary Criticism" were quite popular not only among female but also male students. The success of these courses has taught us that teaching women's studies is a good way to help the younger generation to see problems concerning women in our society and to recognize the necessity for a women's movement. It is also an effective way to attract, organize, and train more dedicated activists who are interested in women's issues. By 1992, members of the center teaching in different departments had encouraged their master's students to work on theses related to women's studies, and we believe that in the foreseeable future there will be Ph.D. candidates writing their dissertations on women's issues at Peking University.

In order to intensify our influence on campus, we also organized a series of lectures on women's studies, not only on theories but also on women's history, women's writings, and current issues that are concerns of most people. In order to carry out more activities and to offer more courses to students in general, we applied to the university authorities to be formally acknowledged as a working organization. In October 1990, a Women's Studies Center was finally established at Peking University. Actually, at that time. it was only a nominal center, as we had no budget, no working staff, not even an office of our own. We were, however, greatly encouraged, for the recognition meant that our influence was already felt not only by the students but also by university authorities.

Since the center was formally founded, we have continued to offer women's studies courses in different departments of the social sciences and humanities, but we have also had many exchanges with women's organizations at home and abroad, as we believe it is important to learn from others and to share our vision with others. We have held three symposiums on such topics as "Traditional Culture and Chinese Women" and "Chinese Women in the Age of Reform," and we also hosted three international conferences on women's issues, in 1992, 1993, and 1994, as well as an international symposium on women and literature in June 1995. Some of our members have also been abroad to attend women's conferences in Japan, Britain, Canada,

France, Korea, and the United States. In the meantime, theses written by members of the center began to appear in different women's magazines and to be presented at conferences of all kinds.

In October 1992 we were recognized as a fully empowered organization, and appointments of a director, an executive director, two deputy directors, and a secretary general were made at a meeting of university presidents. We were even given an office and a telephone to help us carry on our work. This success of the center was truly a great moment for the work of the women's movement on our campus. With the formal establishment of the center, we entered the third stage of the center's development—not confining ourselves to teaching or research within the campus but combining academic research with actual fieldwork in areas where much has to be done to promote the status of women.

The revival of the women's movement in recent years is an outcome of social changes in Chinese society and a necessity felt by women themselves. Therefore, the main task of women's studies should be closely linked with issues confronting Chinese women today. Women's studies should be able to find ways to solve problems and to help women raise their own awareness and improve their self-image so as to enable them to make greater contributions to the transformation of society. While it took us some time to discover this direction, the process that we went through has been characteristic of most women's studies centers in research institutes or institutions of higher learning.

So far, we had focused our efforts mainly in teaching and research, especially in the fields of history and literature. While there was nothing wrong with our work, it was rather divorced from what was actually going on outside the university. In the past, we had also placed too much emphasis on the division of labor, believing that, as a center at a university, our job was teaching and research and that it was the task of the Women's Federation to solve everyday problems. After exchanging experiences with other women's centers in China and abroad, after much discussion and serious consideration, we decided that, in addition to teaching and research, we should have closer links with society and reality, and thus we began the immediate preparation for the 1995 World Conference on Women.

What Did We Do for the Fourth World Conference on Women?

We decided on the following five tasks as our main concerns in preparation for the conference:

1. We were to collaborate with Ningxia Educational Institute in carrying out an in-depth investigation of more than seven thousand seven- to fifteen-year-old girls in the four provinces or autonomous regions of Ningxia, Guizhou, Gangsu, and Qinghai and in carrying out a three-year experimentation program among forty-eight village schools, ten minority communities, and twenty poverty-stricken counties in these four provinces or autonomous regions in order to improve the environment for the education of girls and to solve in an effective way the difficulties facing girls who want to go to school.

2. With women professors and women students of Peking University as our main targets of investigation, we were to carry out a project surveying the different roads taken by women intellectuals in the past fifty years and more. The main object was to discover changes in women's outlook, the choices made by different generations of women, and the causes of their successes or failures. It was our hope that the experience of these women intellectuals would help to stimulate more women of the younger generation to take the road to success.

3. We were to combine women's studies with actual work among women in order to suggest feasible ways for improving the lives of women. The subjects included, among others, the drafting of the Law on the Protection of the Rights and Interests of Women, and the problems in its enforcement; the living environment and psychology of old women in rural areas; women and folk customs; the history and current situation of Miao women; the reproductive health of women in rural areas. It was emphasized that the process of completing these projects will be a process of research and investigation. This procedure will, in turn, be a process of helping to find the right solutions to those problems under investigation. The results were to be summarized in a book, to be dedicated to the 1995 World Conference on Women.

4. We were to set up a Women's Studies Library and Resource Center at Peking University. The Peking University Library holds more than four million volumes, a large number of which are about women and women's issues. Unfortunately, they have been little used and are little known to women scholars in China, as no systematic catalog has been made of the holdings. What is more, not one library in China is able to provide the badly needed resources for women's studies scholars in China and from abroad. We feel it is our duty to make good use of the Peking University Library and to set up a resource center for women's studies. Of course, in order to build up the library's current limited holdings into a comprehensive collection, we will still need to continue purchasing more titles from among the many that are being published almost every day inside and outside China. It is our sincere hope that we will obtain support from women's studies scholars all over the world in the course of developing this Women's Studies Library into a national clearinghouse and resource center for Chinese and foreign researchers in this field.

5. We were to prepare for the Women and Culture Forum at the 1995 Fourth World Conference on Women. We were privileged to be entrusted with this NGO Forum, and we believe it will be a good opportunity for us to learn from other NGOs all over the world.

In preparation for the Fourth World Conference on Women, we held two international symposiums in order to give our members some information about the NGO Forum and to select the best papers for the NGO workshop on traditional culture and women. We planned books on eight topics, including women and psychology, the population issue, the divorce phenomenon, the influences of traditional customs and habits, some ethnic minorities, and the life experience of a number of successful women at the university. We also recorded two books of oral history: for one of them, some female educated youth spoke of their lives in the countryside and their struggle for success after they returned to the city, and in the other, people in the three remote northwestern regions told stories. We also edited a book on women and women's studies outside China. These books, published by the end of July and distributed at Huairou during the NGO Forum, were highly acclaimed by scholars and others.

During the NGO Forum, more than fifty women professors were involved in different workshops, and five of them chaired sessions on traditional culture and women, women and literature, women and environment, women and education, and women professors and women college students. Peking University may well have been the institution with the greatest number of participants at the NGO Forum. Altogether, there were seventy Chinese observers to the UN Conference, among whom only four were university professors. Peking University Women's Studies Center was one of the two universities honored to have two such observers.

Frankly speaking, we were not too sure of ourselves when we were preparing for our workshops, especially those on traditional culture and women's literature. Other people had criticized us for being too academic or too divorced from reality. We were surprised to see so many people crowding into the meeting place, and we were deeply moved by their interest in our discussions. We were greatly encouraged by the understanding and support of our audience.

What are we going to do beyond the UN Fourth World Conference on Women?

It is still too early to have a detailed plan for our future work. But we believe we must make good use of the opportunity that we had of having the Fourth World Conference on Women convened in China.

This narrative has chronicled the development of our center from an informal and loosely organized study group, to a well-organized institution formally recognized by the authorities, to an organization that is not self-contained but that has broken out of the confines of university campus walls and is doing actual fieldwork in addition to teaching and research. Such a process of development is typical of most women's studies centers in China.

What are the benefits of being a well-organized, formally recognized institution? First of all, it is now easier to do what we want, since we have the support of the authorities. When we were an informal group, things were much more difficult. For instance, we discovered that some people were reluctant to come and talk to a group of women that got together informally. To do away with their suspicion, we had to look for a connection, a kind of mutual friend, to persuade them to come. Nowadays, they think it a great honor to be invited by the Women's Studies Center at Peking University. Second, being institutionalized, our center has been able to make more contact with other women's organizations in China and abroad. In the past, people did not know how to reach us even if they were interested in working with us. Now, they can just write to the center. Through correspondence we have learned about conferences or activities concerning women and are able to send people to attend them. It is even easier for us to look for funding since we are now a well-organized institution.

It is certain that we will do better once we go out into the real world and work with women in backward areas, where they are still kept at very low social status. It is an undeniable fact that the women's movement in China is being carried on mainly by educated women. To help more women to develop their self-awareness, it is important for educated women to go among the broad masses of women, especially those at the grassroots level, and work with them. As individuals, we can hardly do that. Now that we are an institution, it is easier for us to make arrangements with local authorities and be welcomed. This might have something to do with the situation and the general practice in China.

What about the disadvantages of being institutionalized? Have we lost the kind of freedom we enjoyed as an informal group? To me, it is still too early to predict, just as we are not sure what our fourth stage will be. One thing, however, is quite certain. We will move ahead in our commitment even though there will be difficulties.

We are now more confident of ourselves and believe that we should keep the research-oriented characteristics of our center and continue our research by making full use of the interdisciplinary resources of the university, as well as the many projects concerning practical matters. The Program for the Development of Chinese Women adopted by the State Council of Chinese Government states that the social environment for women's development should be improved. We believe that theory and scientific research will be very important in reaching this goal. It is necessary to examine in a scientific way the negative influences of traditional culture, the prejudice against women and the different expressions of it, and especially the kind of laws or social structures that might help raise women's self-consciousness. Our center may play a significant role in all these respects.

What is more, we plan to persuade the university to agree to the founding of a graduate program in women's studies and to undertake some curricular reform. We've been thinking of organizing a graduate program for several years but have never succeeded. Because of our success in the NGO Forum, the university presidents have agreed to think about our request and have told us to write a proposal. It is important to train young women's studies scholars to carry on our work. It is not enough to offer haphazard courses on women writers or women's history. We should start from the teaching of basic theories in women's studies and train scholars who not only know how to carry on fieldwork but also know the right theory to guide their work.

If we succeed in obtaining approval to establish the graduate program, we will immediately face the big problem of funding. But we are sure that there will be ways of solving this problem, though we may not know what they are at this moment. So far, we have succeeded without much financial help. We will succeed again if we persist, as we always have.

Tao Jie is a professor of English and deputy director of the Women's Studies Center at Peking University, China. She is president of the Society for the Study of Women's Literature and has translated several English works into Chinese including Alice Walker, Charles Chesnutt, and William Faulkner.

Gender Studies in Peru

Narda Henríquez

During the 1970s, Peru stood out among Latin American countries for the intensity and variety of its women's movements. It was not until the 1990s, however, that gender studies gained legitimacy in the academic community. Both the feminist movement and gender studies are part of an international step that questions the discrimination that permeates women's daily lives, as well as the creation of a body of knowledge in which women are invisible. Simply to explain the practices and experiences of women and the evolution of gender studies in these terms is insufficient. As we shall see, issues raised by women's movements and once viewed as marginal have recently emerged to become part of national policy, claiming the attention of politicians and economists.

In the first half of this century, Peru went through a process of modernization and urbanization, sustained by economic growth and by the reforms of President Juan Velasco Alvarado (1968–75). As a result, there was an expansion of the middle class and of the educational system. These developments represented a significant change in the lives and status of women, who entered various spheres of political and social life at a massive rate. The urban working classes—and, within these, women—became significant pressure groups in the society. The emergence of the women's movements of the 1970s and of the first nongovernmental development organizations (NGOs) is, in a way, the legacy of two generations of popular women leaders and professionals who emerged as part of this process.

Since the 1970s, various efforts had been made to bring the condition of women to the forefront, but it was not until the end of the 1980s and beginning of the 1990s that people became conscious of the relevance to society as a whole of women's experience, women's status, and women's knowledge. This timing is not merely coincidental. Peru began this decade in the midst of the most profound political and economic crisis of this century. The nation faced an accumulation of long unresolved historical and structural problems; in addition, it was a time of instability and terrorism.

On the other hand, following a period of authoritarianism in the 1980s, the central axis of the intellectual debate in Latin America swung in the direction of democracy. This shift introduced new perspectives into the theoretical and political debate. Women's organizing work, as well as gender studies, contributed to the new outlook—not only by raising practical issues but also by placing the "personal" at the center of political and theoretical debate. During this time, working-class women continued to strengthen their networks. As a result, they would play a central role in the reconstruction of the society.

Taking these premises into account, this piece will discuss women's movements and gender studies in Peru, commenting on the following topics:

- The complex and fragmentary nature of women's movements and the role of feminists as a pressure group
- The educative role of NGOs through their women's programs
- The path traced by gender studies at universities
- The state of the education system, and the current agenda.

Women in a Multicultural Society

Peru is a multicultural society, characterized by contrasting geography and uneven development. Tradition and modernity are combined within a predominantly *mestizo* population, which experiences with great hope, but also with great anxiety, the challenges of national integration. The everyday lives of men and women are marked by poverty, social inequality, and regional and ethnic differences.

Despite such difficulties, the expansion of the education system allowed important advances to take place in the direction of democracy: the spread of the middle classes, the training of professionals, and in particular, the improvement of women's access to education.

Between 1940 and 1990 illiteracy fell from 60.3 percent to 17.4 percent among women, while among men it dropped from 45 percent to 4 percent. (In Peru, a person is considered illiterate if he or she cannot read or write in Spanish, even though he or she may maintain a large part of the oral tradition in Quechua and Aymara, the native languages of the country.) It is also worthwhile to note that by the 1980s and 1990s most of the illiterate women in Peru were adults (Centro 1993).

According to a recent survey, the most significant changes in women's level of education have occurred in the last twenty years. Twenty-five years ago, 19 percent of women aged twenty to twenty-four did not attend school, while today this figure is a mere 2 percent. Twenty-five years ago, 15 percent of women between the ages of twenty and thirty-four had attained levels of higher education; today, the figure is 36 percent.

During the last twenty-five years, the proportion of women active in the workforce increased from 20 percent to 40 percent. These figures are an indication that, despite the fluctuations resulting from economic adjustments, women's entry into the labor market continues, particularly in urban areas. Rural women's work is often underestimated in censuses and surveys; however, the last few years have seen an expansion of small businesses and enterprises that rely on family labor (such as handicrafts, and street vendoring), adding to women's employment in the informal sector.

Finally, more than 100,000 women are joined in activities such as "community kitchens" (*comedores*) and "glass of milk" committees for daily meal distribution to their communities.[1] Many of these women spend more than eight hours every day carrying out voluntary activities for these organizations. In 1989 there were four thousand community kitchens and more than seven thousand glass-of-milk committees in Peru.

As for women's participation in politics, their presence as a group with shared interests was articulated only in the 1980s. Although women had acquired the right to vote in the 1950s (a decision made by the president in power at the time), it was really the promulgation of the 1979 Constitution, the concession of the vote to illiterates, and the convocation of municipal elections that opened up new channels of political expression to women as well as the peasant population.

Although a mere 10 percent of political officials are women, from the 1970s onward there has been a rising tide of women who participate in the political and social life of the country. These consist of intermediate-level women leaders in unions, neighborhood groups, political parties or cultural organizations (Henríquez 1994). (In the last few years, the achievements of these women have been threatened by the economic crisis and by terrorism, as various popular leaders have been attacked or assassinated).

The most outstanding feature of the women's movement since the 1970s has been the massive drive toward organization, which has found expression in a variety of ways. In addition to the traditional union and professional organizations, there were neighborhood organizations and self-help groups, the latter consisting mainly of women. In addition, there was an emergence of organized discussion groups and workshops on the condition of women, out of which emerged feminist organizations with their own systems of coordination and centralization. Finally, women involved mainly in leftist political parties introduced matters related to everyday life into the political debate. Because of this great variety of activities, the women's movement of the 1970s is usually identified as having three branches: the popular, the feminist, and the political. Little by little, these branches of the movement have transcended the personal arena, and carried the debate beyond the women's arena. Examples of this process include a proposal for a community kitchen law, which would offer a subsidy for the kitchens' food supply. This law, developed by a group of leaders and professionals, was passed in December 1991 but is yet to be implemented. In addition, a domestic violence law proposal, propelled by the feminist movement, was presented to Congress by members of various political parties.

While self-help organizations made gains in empowering women for public participation on a massive scale, thus contributing to the valuing of domestic work and to the uniting and strengthening of human rights and women's rights organizations, feminist organizations made gains in terms of public debate, becoming part of an active current of opinion that has helped to sensitize the media.

Itineraries of Knowledge

Initially, women's studies research was geared toward the practical support of popular, feminist, political, and social activities. Nongovernmental organizations, as well as some research centers, afforded a sort of "accompaniment" to the social movements, providing a foundation for their demands. With the exception of some pioneer works, it is only since 1985 that a sustained effort at research has been observable among both academic and feminist institutions.

From the 1970s to the 1990s research has shifted from research on women to research on gender. Ruiz-Bravo (1995) identifies three stages in this process. The first stage was characterized by the predominance of research carried out by NGOs with the aim of making women's lives and status visible. The second stage occurred in the 1980s, a time of violence and economic crisis, when attention was focused on women in popular organizations. In the third stage, which occurred in the 1990s, research was focused on gender as a social construction. This is also the period of the institutionalization of gender studies. The following pages aim to outline this shift, discussing the issues, and the debates on women and gender studies among NGOs and at universities.

The Educative Work of NGOs

During the last fifteen years, NGOs in Peru have grown rapidly. Before 1975, their activities were restricted and specialized, but now these activities are diverse. The period between 1975 and 1980 is especially significant for the creation of many NGOs working with or financially supporting women's projects. Some of these organizations defined themselves as feminist institutions from the beginning, but work with women was not restricted to feminist NGOs. In practice, most NGOs in Lima and other Peruvian provinces worked on behalf of women, even when promoting women was not specifically mentioned in their programs.

More recently, institutions have made a considerable effort to coordinate projects, to initiate evaluations, and to systematize their experiences. NGOs working with women have significantly provided a space for resocialization and for the raising of self-esteem, as well as for attending to such specific demands as health, sexuality, and technical training. It is estimated that these activities reach 5 to 10 percent of women in local sectors of Lima (Montero 1990). Although they do not constitute an alternative to the official education system, these projects reach those adult women who want an education, which not only raises their opportunities for work and social improvement but also serves as a means for dialogue and autonomy and teaches them how to defend their rights.

During the last few years, the number of NGOs with programs that help start up and give credit to small enterprises has multiplied. This reflects a greater availability of resources, but it also is an indication of women's rising expectations about getting involved in productive activities and small businesses.

At the same time, NGOs working with women have created networks and forums that have increased their capacity to make political proposals. For example, Foro Mujer (Women's Forum) emerged as an interinstitutional initiative that worked to make political proposals. The Red Nacional de la Mujer (National Women's Network) emerged as part of an effort to create a National Women's Plan solicited by the government in 1990. This proposal was never made official, but it did bring together many institutions and individuals, who later joined the National Women's Network. NGOs have also produced many journals and publications reporting on their broad experiences of working with women, but reports of systematic research are still lacking.

Universities and Professions

Since the 1970s, universities in Peru have experienced serious problems. A lack of interest from the government has added to their structural weaknesses, including insufficient resources to serve a rapidly expanding student population (a consequence of demographic growth and of the democratization of the education system). In the 1980s, universities reached "rock bottom" (Portocarrero 1993), when the stereotype of the university student became that of a "potential terrorist," and the institutions were even more neglected by the state. Unlike the rest of Latin America, which has given priority to higher education, the Peruvian government devoted only 20 percent of its budget to education as a whole. This crisis was accompanied by a proliferation of private universities, technical institutions, and pre-university preparatory colleges.

According to available sources, Peruvian universities fulfill a mere 10 percent of the potential demand (Centro 1993). According to the same sources, women represented 50.9 percent of the total number of non-university higher education graduates in Lima in 1981. On the other hand, the percentage of women in the universities increased from 27 percent in 1960 to 39 percent in 1990.

A division between the sexes persists in the choice of university professions. Women predominate in social service, education, and obstetrics. Recently, however, women have also begun to enter into law, engineering, and media studies in much greater numbers than before. In the technical institutions, computer science has been added to the traditionally female careers of accounting and nursing.

Regarding women in the academic community, although female professors continue to constitute a small percentage, their numbers have increased rapidly in a short period of time. Between 1982 and 1987, the overall number of university teachers increased from three thousand to five thousand. During this period, the number of female teachers increased by more than 66 percent, while the number of male teachers increased by a mere 2.5 percent.

Universities and Gender Studies

The development of women's studies and of a gendered perspective has fed on intellectual streams originating both in Latin America and in other latitudes. However, the creation of knowledge, like all intellectual activities, is also the result of self-reflection. The latter is especially relevant in Peru, a country going through tremendous stress and change. For this same reason—and in the case of gender, even more than in others—the relationships between the subject and the object of study are exposed to many pressures. Traditionally, studies dealing with family and women's issues have been rare in academic research and came about mainly as a result of individual efforts. It is only in the 1990s that a gendered perspective has gained legitimate academic status and become institutionalized.

The 1970s produced various debates on the condition of women, which drew upon three principal sources—Latin American networks, feminist networks, and national debates—within a social context that included the development of the social sciences. The Latin American academic community, and in particular the Latin American Commission for the Social Sciences (CLACSO), assumed an active role with the creation of the Research Program on Women and Society (Programa de Investigaciones sobre Mujer y Sociedad). Here, the work of M. C. Feijoo and T. de Barbieri deserves particular mention. The international networks, which elicited the active participation of feminist organizations, also were important. The work of Kate Young, Charlotte Bunch, Jane Jacquette, and later Caroline Moser influenced not only the feminist movement but also the programs of NGOs working with women.

The third source was tied to the national social and political process and found expression in the debates of the 1970s and 1980s. The first of these debates was on feminism and social class. In Peru—unlike Chile, where there was a recognized distance between feminists and party politics—the feminist movement was marked by a double militancy among its members, many of whom were also linked to leftist parties (Barrig 1988). A second debate, on which there exists a vast body of literature, revolved around women's self-help organizations and the growing efforts to keep women in domestic work. The debate polarized NGOs that worked with popular and feminist organizations, since the latter considered self-help activities to be a continuation of domestic work. In the course of the last decade, women have demonstrated that they value their organizations not only as educational centers but also as avenues through which to propose public policy. Nevertheless, there remains much debate about the relationship between these organizations and the state in the management of assistance programs.

In the 1990s, in the midst of the political violence sweeping the country, women's issues found a place on the public agenda. There was much preoccupation with national identity, gender identity, the relationship between gender and ethnicity, and the generation gap. The terms of discussion of the Researchers Workshop organized by

FOMCIENCIAS (Mannarelli 1990) and in the research topics of the Gender Program of the Universidad Católica (Fuller 1993; Rivera 1993)
reflected this focus.

At the academic level, Violeta Sara-Lafosse's course on the sociology
of the family, held at the Universidad Católica since 1969, deserves
special mention, as does the Workshop on Women's Studies that took
place at the Universidad Católica in 1978, organized by the Instituto
Nacional de Cultura (National Cultural Institute) and sponsored by the
Institute of International Studies at the Hague. Under the initiative of
Virginia Vargas, women such as Vicky Mennen, Virginia Guzmán,
Narda Henríquez, Roxana Carrillo, Kate Young, Magdalena León de
Leal, and Concepción Dumois contributed to this workshop.

Among the opportunities for intellectual and research exchanges,
the Meeting of Latin American Women, organized by the Centre Flora
Tristán in 1985, also deserves mention, as does the Congress on
Women's Research in the Andean Region, organized by Perú Mujer at
the Universidad Católica in 1982, an effort of Jeanine Anderson,
among others, that brought together a considerable number of Peruvian women who were working on various topics.

Toward the end of the 1980s, significant research and publication
carried out by NGOs (Flora Tristán, ADEC-ATC and the Instituto de
Estudios Peruanos) came to the forefront. But it was FOMCIENCIAS that
generated a seminar on gender studies (1988), promoting the work of
specialists in various disciplines. Another interinstitutional program,
SUMBI, aimed to analyze and develop urban policies with a gender
perspective, promoting critical reflections of a wider scope, through
interdisciplinary dialogue.

Themes relating to the condition of women, discrimination, and
gender relations did not traditionally have priority in the content of
curriculum or research topics in Peruvian universities. By the 1970s,
some interest in these themes could be noted at the Universidad of San
Marcos and the Universidad Católica through the appearance of relevant theses in social science fields. But the acceptance of topics relating to the family and women's education employment as part of the
curriculum did not occur until the nineties. Although at the Universidad Católica the departments of psychology, social work, and sociology offered such courses as "Sexuality and Sexual Roles," "Women
and Social Welfare," "Sociology of the Family," and "Women, Social
Movements, and Feminism," the program in gender studies was not
created until 1990 within the faculty of social sciences. Recently, some
public universities, such as Federico Villarreal in Lima and San
Agustín de Arequipa, have also been attempting to change their

curricula to include gender issues. At the same time, some private universities are making efforts in this direction in the areas of public and business administration (Universidad del Pacífico) and in the fields of medicine and psychology (Universidad Cayetano Heredia).

Gender studies has moved beyond the pioneer works, which viewed women's experience as a contribution to the production of knowledge, to analyze gender as a dimension of social processes. This shift illuminates the fact that women's issues have become a part of mainstream theoretical thought, albeit in only a partial and symbolic manner. The contributions made by gender studies can be summed up by the following theoretical and practical points:

■ The epistemological value of the female experience. In its first stages, this knowledge has been particularly relevant to militant and academic feminists. More recently, it has been recognized by male colleagues who have also pursued this line of thought.

■ The demand for information disaggregated by sex. This has contributed to research as well as to the formulation of development plans and public policies. This demand has grown as a result of economic adjustments, the consequent state assistance programs, and the interests of organizations.

■ The analytical value of gender studies. This refers to the relevance of a gendered perspective to an understanding of inequality and existent power relations. This does not mean adding "women" as one more item on the list or, as Ruiz-Bravo (1994) notes, incorporating a "gendered perspective" into development programs as an additional compartment. Rather, it means inquiring about the relevance and absence of this perspective.

■ The political value and utopian dimensions of gender studies. This allows for the expression of such demands as "democracy in the home and in society at large," made by feminists in Peru and Latin America.

When Latin American universities were transformed from elite institutions to massive institutions open to all social classes, their doors also opened to women. This happened in Peru following the sixties. Many more years went by before women became a recognized body of academics, and many more yet passed before some of these (female academics born nonfeminists) began to embody a desire to infuse the curriculum with a gendered perspective. A critical mass of women teachers and researchers is needed to legitimate the study of gender within the academic community and research institutions. But even when this critical mass exists and is willing to take action, it may encounter resistance among authorities.

These academic women face the conflicting traditions of Latin American universities. In addition, very few of them have had the opportunity to do research. Teaching is the only way of earning a living in most universities, yet it is considered a demanding and badly paid job. Despite these restrictions, working on gender issues in universities has its advantages. Gender studies—whether in degree programs or merely independent courses—benefits from debates within open-minded communities.

The Universidad Católica Gender Studies Program emerged as part of the social science faculty and was aimed at filling gaps in the curriculum and creatively organizing a space for critical reflection. In effect, the gender studies teaching team aimed to work with theoretical contributions from feminist academics in diverse disciplines. From the beginning, the program had an interdisciplinary character and benefited from being part of an academic community.

In its first stages (1990–93), the program concentrated on creating a curriculum for a diploma in gender studies, which was first offered in 1991 and which has produced three graduating classes to date. The curriculum consists of some basic new courses and others that were previously offered at the university. The prerequisite for graduation, in addition to thirty-five credits, is an essay based on a piece of research or on a systematic account of professional experiences. In its early years, the research program focused on students' work on the construction of gender identities among women from diverse social backgrounds.

At a later stage (1994–96), the program's focus turned to consolidating the teaching team and encouraging interinstitutional interactions within the country and abroad. The program now aims to offer specific courses for government officials and to contribute to other disciplines and universities. Working plans and publications are being developed for this purpose.

In addition to research in the usual areas of culture, development, and democracy, a special effort has been made, in this later period, to create working groups on reproductive rights and social policies. In addition, conferences on feminist ethics, love, art, masculinity, family, and civil law have been organized.

Finally, today, the program faces other challenges related to the institutionalization process. Gender studies offers a perspective; it is not a discipline. Hence, the degree program is at an experimental stage. Strategies and alternatives need to be considered. The next stages should guarantee continuity but also flexibility. Another challenge is the sustainability of gender studies, since activities and student scholarships have in the past received international funding.

In the recent past some voices have been raised to point out the risks associated with the "institutionalization" of gender studies. One argument states that it could lose both its critical and its creative qualities. There are also demands for research that integrates a gendered perspective into an analysis of class and ethnicity or generational issues (Anderson 1995). In addition, as Martha Lamas pointed out at Mar del Plata (1994), we must be aware of our own prejudices about gender.

As noted by other scholars (Henríquez 1994), the experiences gained at the Universidad Católica drew not only on feminist criticism but also on cultural criticism. The term *cultural criticism* stems from the questioning over the last two decades of the political, social, and intellectual assumptions in Latin America. The feminist critique during this period enriched the reflections of the academic world, providing it with a new dimension of knowledge, exposing its androcentric slant, and making women visible. A gendered perspective is now considered a vital prerequisite for the education of any social researcher, not only for those who specialize in gender.

Gender studies should respond to the warnings of feminist criticism but also to the intellectual demands and challenges associated with contributing to knowledge. In fact, criticism has been a source of creativity in the acquisition of knowledge within the social sciences in Latin America and Peru. Today, however, criticism demands not only deconstruction and revelation but also re-creation and redevelopment at a theoretical and practical level.

Academic life in Latin America is a scarce resource, hence a precious resource. In this sense, academic exchange and networks can be considered a form of solidarity that should be encouraged.

Educational Polices and Gender Studies

Although women and gender studies have contributed to sensitizing various streams of opinion, including those of the public sector, they have barely influenced educational policies. Various reforms of the educational system have been projected in the last few years, but only the 1970 reform paid special attention to the needs of women. At that time a special commission assembled specialists from private and public institutions, and coeducation was promoted. So far, however, it has been implemented in only half of the secondary schools in Lima.

During the last government, a Program on Popular Education was encouraged, but it was discontinued in the first years of the present government. This program incorporated women's topics into the curriculum. Between 1988 and 1989, the program had managed to work on primary education and on the first two years of secondary education. This program has also had the support of many feminist NGOs and family planning institutions. Government commitments made by Peru at the UN Fourth World Conference on Women in Beijing seemed to favor new programs and attitudes in the public sector and the educational system.

With regard to adult schooling, in 1989 the Ministry of Education provided for 5 percent of the national demand at primary school level and 7 percent of the demand at secondary school level. Within the Lima metropolitan area, 61 percent of those enrolled in adult primary education were women and at the secondary school level women represented 43 percent (Centro 1993). Recently the Ministry of Education and the NGO Peru Mujer signed an agreement to produce a series of materials on family and sexuality.

As noted previously, the NGOs working with women and the feminist movement have a long history in the area of adult education, working on innovative teaching approaches and with grass-roots organizations. However, their area of influence is limited and their programs are scattered.

In Peru, as in the rest of Latin America, the gap between men and women with regard to access to education at the primary and secondary levels is slowly diminishing over the long term. It persists in higher education, however, where only sixty women matriculate for every one hundred men, according to 1988 figures. Institutions such as CEPAL and UNESCO have acknowledged the positive contribution that gendered perspectives have made to the education system. They have postulated an integrated approach, with policies that reinforce complementarity and weaken conflict and that allow for development and equity to occur simultaneously. As Maria Luisa Jauregui (1994) points out in a study comparing the principal writings in this area, the education system should incorporate policies that are geared to take action on sociocultural issues, including social relations that perpetuate sexual inequality. Hence, what matters is not only the number of female and male students but also the content of courses and teaching methods (since teaching practices can also be discriminatory against women). At the same time there is a need to improve vocational training and opportunities for women who wish to follow careers in the areas of science and technology.

Despite its adverse economic conditions, Peru has been a favorable arena for achievements in education. Much remains to be done, however, to influence the educational agenda on gender issues, as well as public policies.

NOTE

1. Community kitchens, found in many Latin American countries, are cooperative arrangements in which families in a community pool resources to buy, prepare, and sometimes eat their meals together, often with support from government, local nonprofit, or international organizations.

REFERENCES

Anderson, Jeanine. 1995. "Los estudios de género, las ciencias sociales y el cambio social." In Portocarrero and Valcárcel, eds., *El Perú frente al siglo XXI.*

Backhaus, A. 1988. La dimensión de género en los proyectos de promoción de la mujer. Lima Fundación Nauman.

Barrig, Maruja. 1988. "Democracia emergente y movimiento de mujeres." In E. Ballon, *Movimientos sociales y democracia.* Lima: DESCO.

Centro Mujeres Peruanas. 1993. La mitad de la población del Perú a comienzos de los noventa. Lima: CENTRO.

Fuller, N. 1993. *Dilemas de la femineidad, mujeres de clase media en el Perú.*

Henríquez, N. 1994a. "L'expérience des femmes des querties populaires de Lima." In *Problèmes d'Amérique Latine,* no. 14. Paris.

———. 1994b. "Recursos e instituciones en torno a low estudios de género." Paper presented at a seminar sobre la pruducción de conocimientos y la formulación de políticas públicas: En los estudios de género, Santiago de Chile, CEM, October.

Jauregui, María Luisa. 1994. "La igualdad de oportunidades educativas de las mujeres: Mitos y realidades." UNESCO/CEPAL July. Mimeographed.

Lamas, Martha. 1994. "Usos, dificultades y posibilidades de la categoria género." Ponencia presentada an Mar del Plata, Foro Regional Pre-Beijing, September.

Mannarelli, María E. 1990. "Algunas reflexiones sobre las investigaciones sobre mujer y género en el Perú." Lima: FOMCIENCIAS.

Mariategui, José C. "La mujer y la política" and "Las reivindicaciones feministas." In *Temas de educación.* Lima: Amauta.

Montero, Carmen. 1990. *Le dije lo que quise, la mujer pobladora y el sistema educativo.* Lima: SUMBI.

Portocarrero, G. 1993. "Comentarios." In *Notas para el debate,* no. 10. Lima: GRADE.

Ruiz-Bravo, Patricia. 1995. "Estudios, prácticas y presentationes de género." In *El Perú frente al siglo XXI.* Lima: Universidad Católica.

———. 1994. "Imposición o autonomía, notas sobre la relación entre *ONGs* y agencias de cooperación a propósito de la perspectiva de género." In *Propuestas no. 1 entre mujeres.* Lima: Escuela para el Desarrollo.

Rivera, Cecilia. 1993. *María Marimacha. Los Caminos de la identidad Femenina.* Lima: Universidad Católica.

Sara-Lafosse, Violeta, et al. 1989. *Escuela mixta: Alumnos y maestros la prefieren.* Lima: Universidad Católica.

Schwartzman, Simon. 1993. "La profesión académica en América Latina y politícas de educación superior en América Latina." In *Notas para el debate no. 10.* Lima: GRADE.

Vargas, Virginia. 1989. *El aporte de la rebeldía.* Lima: Flora Tristán.

Narda Henríquez *teaches at Catholic University, Lima, Peru.*

Women's Studies in South Africa

Debby Bonnin

At present South Africa is in transition: the old has not yet been left behind and the new is not yet in place. While a final constitution still has to be negotiated, the interim constitution, which is entrenched in the Constitutional Principles that bind the Constitutional Assembly (South Africa 1994), enshrines the principles of nonsexism and equality for women in the preamble and in chapter 3 ("Fundamental Rights"). The interim constitution also specifically prohibits discrimination on the basis of sexual orientation. New legislation in all spheres is being enacted and women's rights are often specifically mentioned. The space for organizing and mobilizing as women that has been available since the unbanning of the liberation movements is still open and available. Yet despite these advances there is still a long way to go before gender equality becomes reality. South Africa is a very unequal society; its divisions and inequalities are based not only on gender but also on race, class, region, and other categories.

Women's Education and Employment in South Africa: A Brief Background

Before considering women's studies in South Africa, it is important to understand the educational and occupational conditions that have shaped the development and need for women's studies.[1] Thirty percent of the South African population is illiterate; the majority of these are rural Africans, and—although gender statistics are not available—

I would like to thank all those women and men who gave their time to assist me with this project, either through agreeing to be interviewed and/or by making documents available, facilitating interviews with other people, or giving suggestions. A full list of those interviewed appears in the references. In addition, I would like to thank Debbie Budlender and Jenny Radloff. I have not been able to make full use of all the information I collected, particularly with respect to educational policy, and I apologize to all those who might feel slighted. I was not able to deal as extensively with this section as I had anticipated. I would like to thank the Gender Research Fund, University of Natal, and the University of Natal Research Fund for grants that enabled the research to take place. I would also like to thank those who commented on an earlier draft of this paper, in particular Debbie Budlender, Fidela Fouche, Ros Posel, Jenny Robinson, and the referees from Women's Studies International, the Feminist Press.

the regional and occupational distribution of these people indicates that a large portion is likely to be women. Race inequalities, however, further complicate gender inequalities. Education was compulsory only for white and Indian children. And, although there are slightly more girls than boys in school, the pass rate for girls is lower. Gender differences increase as one moves up the educational hierarchy. Women are concentrated in and confined to certain sectors; for example, at the tertiary level, 99 percent of those enrolled in home economics are women, while only 7 percent of engineering students are women.

These inequalities in educational policy have influenced women's occupations. Although the number of economically active women has increased markedly, from 23 percent in 1960 to 41 percent in 1991,[2] South Africa has a highly segmented labor market with a clear horizontal and vertical division of labor. The majority of the employed women are found in service professions, primarily as teachers and nurses, or in clerical and sales positions. Not only is the labor market segmented in terms of gender but it is also segmented by race; for example, within the service sector hairdressers are white women, while cleaners are African women. In an attempt to address past inequalities many companies are implementing affirmative action policies. Very few of these policies, however, specifically mention women as an oppressed group, and even fewer are concerned with job mobility for working-class women.

Given South Africa's apartheid past, many universities were created by the state to serve different "racial" groups. They can be categorized into the historically black universities (HBUs) created by the apartheid government to serve different ethnic groups: University of Western Cape for Coloreds, University of Durban–Westville for Indians, University of Zululand for Zulus, University of the North for Sothos, etc. The historically white universities (HWUs) were divided into the English-speaking campuses (the liberal institutions of University of Witwatersrand (Wits), University of Cape Town, University of Natal, and Rhodes University), and the Afrikaans-speaking campuses (University of Stellenbosh, University of Orange Free State, etc.). During the apartheid years, access to campuses by "other" race groups was strictly controlled. This was eased in the late 1980s. Theoretically all universities are now racially mixed; access, however, is dependent on grades and finances. The historically white universities of Wits, Cape Town, and UNatal are seen as the universities of choice, while, with the exception of University of Western Cape and University of Durban–Westville, the historically black universities are poor in resources and "racially unmixed." Although racial and gender composition of the student body and faculty varies from campus to campus and fluctuates, the faculty at most of the historically white universities is still overwhelmingly white and this influences the racial composition of the student body. During apartheid, the historically black universities were primarily staffed by broederbond members.[3] Today they are staffed by a mixture of black and conservative white professors and academics. Many of the historically white universities have adopted affirmative action policies in an attempt to change the racial composition of their staff. A few policies also include gender (UDUSA 1993).

Women's Studies in South Africa

The material for this study comes from a number of sources. In 1994, *Agenda*, a South African feminist journal that I serve as a member of the editorial collective, commissioned an impact assessment study. As part of this study, and in collaboration with the Equal Opportunities Research Project at the University of Cape Town, a questionnaire was sent to all South African universities. This questionnaire, referred to as the Budlender questionnaire, was designed to glean information on gender policies and women's studies courses at these universities. Twelve of twenty-one universities responded. On the basis of these responses, I selected a number of universities and individuals for more in-depth, open-ended interviews. These interviews and the knowledge that I gained from them form the basis of this essay. I am pleased to have been so intimately involved in much of this history and these events.

Within tertiary institutions, nongovernmental and community-based organizations, and trade unions, numerous courses, seminars, and workshops relating to women and gender exist. Women's studies teaching and research take place in universities, while nonformal educational programs like gender training, adult education courses, and union education seminars take place at a variety of sites. Each of these is a separate area, with its own history and context. To do justice to the history of women's studies in South Africa, each would have to be investigated separately, and the influence and relationships among them explored.

Most of the people I interviewed seemed to view women's studies as part of a tertiary-level course or program. While there was acknowledgment that other, non-university programs have contributed to the advancement of women and that they shaped and were shaped by the women's movement, their work and existence were viewed independently from women's studies at tertiary institutions. Thus, for the purposes of this discussion I am interpreting women's studies as formal academic courses taught at tertiary institutions. In adopting this perspective, however, I do not intend to discount the work being done outside of these institutions, which includes such wide-ranging programs and initiatives as the Gender Trainers Network, gender committees in most of the major trade unions, the gender trainer at the National Land Committee, a woman's desk at the South African Council of Churches, and numerous specific local projects like the Gender Advocacy Project and the Community-Based Development Project.

Early Programs and Initiatives

In 1984 the University of South Africa opened its Women's Studies Center. Despite intense efforts by women academics, they were not allowed to offer a teaching program. The center offers a resource facility, produces a newsletter, runs various seminar series, and since 1995 has offered a Certificate Course in Law (run with private sponsorship). It hopes to offer an honors degree in 1997. In addition, numerous departments within many of the universities have offered courses on women and gender since the early 1980s. These courses cover a wide range, from "Women's Voices in Society," offered by the English department at the University of Natal, to "Women in Ancient Greek Gynaecological Works," offered by the classics department at the University of Natal, to "Normative Theory: Feminism," offered by the politics department at the University of Stellenbosch, to "Nutrition During Pregnancy and Lactation" offered by the dietetics department at the University of Western Cape. Most courses are within the faculties of humanities and social sciences. The University of Natal and the University of the Western Cape offer the widest selection of courses. Overall, sociology seems to be the discipline that takes women's studies most seriously, and most of the universities list courses within their sociology departments (Budlender 1994). Given their status as the elite universities, it is interesting to observe that neither the University of Cape Town nor the University of Witwatersrand responded to the Budlender questionnaire.

In 1989 the first women's studies courses, a master's degree, and a one-semester undergraduate course in women's studies were offered at the University of Natal–Durban.[4] The following year, the Pietermaritzburg campus of the University of Natal offered an honors program in gender studies[5] and then an interdisciplinary undergraduate course. The introduction of these courses was preceded by a module[6] on feminism and philosophy, the favorable response to which encouraged the introduction of the honors course. An attempt to begin a women's studies course at the University of the North foundered in the face of resistance from other academic staff.[7] In 1995 the University of Western Cape (UWC) offered, for the first time, an honors and master's degree in women's studies. The University of Natal's courses differ from those of the Western Cape in that they are hosted by existing academic departments. The University of Transkei, University of Port Elizabeth, and University of Durban-Westville are discussing plans for women's and gender studies programs.

In 1991 the Women's Studies Network was formed in Natal. Meeting quarterly, it sought to involve women from the Pietermaritzburg and Durban campuses of Natal University, the University of Durban-Westville, and the University of Zululand's Ngoya and Umlazi campuses. In reality, however, only the first three universities were consistently involved. In 1993 a Black Women's Research Network formed a national organization with regional structures, but it did not exist for very long. In 1996 the University of Cape Town plans to open a Gender Institute, which will provide nine-month-long research associateships for women from other African countries. In 1995 a limited pilot program is being run (EORP 1994).

Rectifying Sexism on Campus

Besides teaching initiatives, women at many universities have become concerned with the conditions affecting women staff as well as with issues affecting both staff and students, such as sexual harassment. Associations were formed at a number of universities to organize around these issues. Some, like the Gender Forum at the Natal University–Durban, the Gender Forum at University of Witwatersrand, the Gender Policy Action Group at Western Cape, the Combined Staff Association (COMSA) Gender Committee at the University of Durban-Westville, and the Women's Forum at the University of South Africa were formed by women staff members (sometimes including students), while at other universities—for example, the University of Cape Town's Equal Opportunity Research Project (EORP), the formation of such associations was an executive initiative.

The University of Western Cape, UOrange Free State, University of South Africa, UNatal, Durban-Westville, and Medunsa have implemented equal opportunity and affirmative action programs that include women as a designated group. UWestern Cape, Natal, Orange Free State, and Medunsa have policies on sexual harassment while Durban-Westville and Port Elizabeth are busy formulating such policies. At all universities, however, benefits still discriminate on the basis of gender (Budlender 1994).

Responses Outside Academe

Since the early 1980s trade unions have set up "women's structures" to respond to gender inequalities. Concerned with the rights of women members, the unions began to address issues like maternity rights and sexual harassment. Trade unions also organized educational work-shops. In the late 1970s and early 1980s a number of community-based women's organizations were formed, most affiliated with the United Democratic Front when it was launched in 1983. In 1982 *SPEAK* magazine, a magazine for working-class women, was founded. While its objective was the emancipation of women, it was not overtly femi-nist. South Africa's first feminist journal, *Agenda*, was launched in September 1987 with the specific aim of bridging the gap between academics and activists. In the early 1990s, the University of Transkei launched its journal *Women's Studies*. It was not until the late 1980s and early 1990s that many more nongovernmental organizations and com-munity organizations began to take up women's issues and to set up separate departments. At that same time the language began to change from that of women to that of gender.

Examining the Current State of Women's Studies

A "landmark" event in South African women's studies was the 1991 Conference on Women and Gender in Southern Africa. The confer-ence organizers described it as follows:

> The first full-blown conference at which "women's studies" took stock of itself, its achievements, and its shortcomings. The size (some 300 delegates), the excitement, and the intensity of debate all joined to an invigorating intellectual energy, and suggested the possibility of even stronger challenges to androcentric dominance in the acad-emy in the 1990s. More significantly, however, the conference is widely recognized as a landmark political event, the implications of which have reverberated not only through women's studies but also through the various organizations and structures that together form the broad "women's movement" in South Africa.
>
> (Bonnin et al. 1993:1)

This conference, its debates, and their ramifications have posed an enormous challenge to women's studies in South Africa (see Letlaka-Rennert 1991, Lund 1991, Robinson 1994). In terms of the development of South African feminism it was a point of no return. The politics of difference, of race, of exclusion, of activism versus academia, of who controls women's studies, and of its relationship to the women's movement were openly inspected and challenged.

Women's studies is often defined as an interdisciplinary project. This seems to suggest that, while women's studies might not be exclusively defined in terms of degree programs, many people do see it that way. The University of South Africa's Women's Studies Center, however, began to explore the idea of an independent center that could coordinate all departments. Its founders argued that the best way to organize an interdisciplinary course was to locate the modules within departments. This model seems a similar to that followed by the Durban and Pietermaritzburg campuses of Natal University and the University of Western Cape. A core program is coordinated by the center and the other modules are offered from different departments that also offer those same courses to their students. However, as Dr. Ros Posel, coordinator of the women's studies program at the University of Natal–Durban, commented, "At the Durban Campus of Natal University this approach was soon abandoned in order to achieve coherent and relevant syllabi appropriate to the women's studies students."

A very useful and wide-ranging definition was given by Jane Barrett of the Equal Opportunities Research Project at the University of Cape Town:

> Women's studies is an interdisciplinary field of scholarship and research which has four or five main goals, including the following items. Firstly it has a archaeological goal and needs to examine those areas which are kept unexamined because of sexism and racism in traditional academia. In other words it needs to recover experiences. Secondly it needs to identify those effects of social experience which can be attributed to the way in which gender is deployed in particular societies. Thirdly it should integrate the analysis of those effects with the analysis of the effects of other systems of social categorization across time and place. Fourthly [it should] challenge the institutional dichotomy between theory and practice, between research and activism, and through this build productive bridges between educational institutions and the projects beyond. And lastly, [it should] develop new tools of philosophy and scholarship in order to better envision a future in which social categorization can't determine human potential.

While Barrett's definition is not explicitly descriptive of any of the present women's studies programs, it provides a useful focus for many different ideas about women's studies and its goals. Dr. Ros Posel has pointed out that while these might not be the stated objectives of any of the programs, in fact, except for the fourth point all programs deal with these issues. South Africa still has much to do in resolving the rift between theory and practice.

Relationship Between Women's Studies and the Women's Movement(s)

In referring to "women's movement(s)" I'm not suggesting that one or even two such organizations exist. Rather I'm using the term in a general way to refer to the large number of women's organizations that address issues of women's inequality. Since the formation of the Women's National Coalition, many of these organizations have affili- ated with this coalition. The relationship between women's studies and the women's movement(s) can probably be summed up by the response of many women working in women's organizations to my request to interview them for this report. Women's studies? they said. What's that got to do with us?

Some have endeavored to map the history of the women's movement and its relationship to the development of academic women's studies (see Dubel 1991). Women who were involved in these events have their own memories, which differ depending on region, generation, race, and political affiliation. Some claim that women's studies has not grown out of a strong women's movement; they don't dispute a rela- tionship between women's studies and a political women's movement, but they reiterate that no strong autonomous women's movement gave birth to women's studies (see Hassim and Walker 1992).

This debate reflects the difference in perspectives and how this difference shapes memory and history. White women were and are active in political groups; many of these same women were influential within women's movements and organizations of the 1970s (for exam- ple, the National Union of South African Students–NUSAS, Rape Crisis, consciousness-raising groups, and feminist reading groups) and also subsequently played a part in the development of women's studies in South Africa. Just as one cannot underestimate the influence of this kind of feminist politics on the development of women's studies courses, so one cannot underestimate its influence on the develop- ment of the reemerging grass-roots women's movement in the 1980s. Dubel (1991) attributes much of the "women under apartheid" litera- ture to white women students, many of whom were politically active in feminist politics.

Although black women had less access to power, they were involved in creating women's studies programs and women's movements. Grass-roots women's organizations (Black Women's Federation, uwco, fedsaw, fedtraw, now),[8] reemerged in the late 1970s and early 1980s. These organizations, made up of older women who had been active in the African National Congress (anc) in the 1950s and younger women "who had been radicalized through student politics, school boycotts and the experience of forced removals" (Dubel 1991:18), addressed apartheid as it affected women (for example, bread-price increases and vigilantes; see Beall et al. 1987). But they also took up the need for "strengthening women's organizational skills and confidence, issues which could be addressed more easily within a women-only environment" (Dubel 1991:18).

Many of the women involved in this nascent women's movement were also involved in other political groups (such as anc, udf, housing groups) and were influential in national politics and the eventual negotiated political settlement (see Kemp et al. 1995). A number of them also located themselves within university teaching departments and brought their feminism, developed in a political and activist context, to their teaching and research work. In particular, they were concerned about the absence of women from the academic curriculum. They waged internal battles within their departments to get women's studies courses taught.

At the same time that these feminist concerns were shaping the internal movement, similar issues were influencing the movement in exile. Women in exile were engaging with feminism and, as Frene Ginwala (a prominent anc member) noted at the 1991 Conference on Women and Gender, they were trying to develop "their own thinking on women's issues and constantly struggling to get women's concerns and the whole question of gender onto the agenda of the National Liberation Movement." In addition, women in exile had access to international feminist movements and events, including the international Decade of Women. Consequently, many of the returning exiles brought back with them their learning and thinking as feminists, and so were critical of what was happening in women's studies. Many of these concerns were expressed at the 1991 conference, especially with reference to questions of representation. In addition, their voices strengthened the work of women active in feminist politics and women's organizations during the 1970s, who had since submerged their feminist thinking in favor of national liberation politics. With the unbanning of political organizations, the return of exiles, and the opening up of political space, these different threads came together, bumping and crashing into each other. Kemp et al. (1995) mark this moment by analyzing the developments since then as "the new South African feminism."

In April 1992 the National Women's Coalition was formed, its objec-tive the drawing up of a Women's Charter for Effective Equality. However, as Frene Ginwala pointed out at the Conference on Women and Gender, the history of apartheid has meant that the people who are in positions of power to chart out the field of women's studies tend to be white women who are informed by Western thinking.

While this is the history (or one version of it) of certain individuals and their position, what about organizational history? At present there is very little direct contact between women's studies and wo-men's organizations. While some women's studies courses give voice to women's organizations (and struggles) they don't relate to them in terms of course content or the priorities that women's organizations have set. Although developing countries are deeply concerned with women's issues, if one examines university curricula, the study of gender and development does not appear to be a priority.

Women's studies programs have little formal contact or relationship with women's organizations. The women's studies programs were not established with the debate, consultation, or discussion of women's organizations. Dr. Ros Posel asserts, however, "This was not how it was envisaged. The important criterion was to ensure and get support of the academic community." Sheila Meintjes from Wits (which doesn't have a women's studies degree program) explains that she perceived the process of establishing women's studies courses to "explore the theoretical exclusions of women." Natasha Primo from Western Cape says that the "discussion was amongst academics on campus. Individ-ual women are involved in both the Gender Equity Unit and [women's] organizations and in that way feed in but we didn't go to organizations as a unit." One exception was the University of the North, which began its planning with a Women's Week, to which women's organizations were invited. The University of Natal–Pietermaritzburg also had a slightly different approach: the course was discussed with members of both Black Sash[9] and Rape Crisis,[10] who gave their written support to initiation of the course. Challenges to the racial exclusiveness of women's studies enable one, with hindsight, to note that both of these organizations are perceived to be white women's organizations. While credit can be given to an initiative to consult organizations outside academe, the race-blindness of the consultation needs to be ques-tioned. The Pietermaritzburg campus also attempted to respond to the academic/activist gap:

> About a year ago we approached women's organizations locally and
> tried to have a practical element in the program. Students would go
> to women's organizations and get a credit. Groups were unsure how
> to respond and how this would work. The response was not negative
> but it was not positive either. There was a perception of the
> academic/activist gap but we were not sure how this should work.

These differing responses to activist and organizational concerns
and their relationship to academe highlight some interesting issues.
One of the major debates and challenges at the Women and Gender
Conference was that of accountability and representation. Despite
having this challenge laid squarely on the table, there is little evidence
(with the exception of representation) that women's studies responded
to it. Second, there is the political project of feminism (the fourth
point in Jane Bennett's definition). In order for women's studies to
have a feminist direction (broadly, the emancipation of women), it is
crucial that links with organizations be established and that the needs
and priorities of the broader feminist political project be kept in
mind.

In mitigation of that position, however, many of the women's studies
initiatives encountered strong opposition from the rest of the academy, primarily on the questioning of its theoretical rigor. "Is there
much to say about this?" is a comment remembered by Sheila Meintjes.
Attempts to consult and draw women's organizations into the planning are likely to enhance these negative perceptions. Yet it is imperative that women's studies finds a way to deal with and respond to these
challenges. Pointing to the associated problems is not an adequate
response. This of course is not meant to disguise the links between
individual women and women's organizations. But once again this is
not sufficient: remove those individuals or replace them with others
who do not have the same beliefs and those links are gone. It is perhaps
precisely because those women are activists that they were involved.

In the postconference period some attempts were made to establish
links. The University of South Africa's Center for Women's Studies
became affiliated with the Women's National Coalition (wnc). The
Gender Research Group, an informal group of academics with an
interest in gender issues from the Durban campus of the University of
Natal, became part of the Southern Natal Women's Charter Alliance
(affiliated with the Women's National Coalition) and the Durban
Women's Forum, a group concerned with local government issues. The
Gender Research Group made policy recommendations around the
constitution and the bill of rights. Individual women from the

University of Natal–Durban were invited to the Unpaid Labor Conference that influenced the development of new, gender-sensitive macroeconomic policy. Similarly, individual women at Wits and from the University of South Africa's Women's Studies Center participated in research that was instrumental in drawing up the Women's Charter. Again, what is interesting is that these are primarily individual initiatives outside of formal programs. None are formal arrangements between women's studies programs and women's organizations. Despite these engagements, which Cherryl Walker (Gender Research Group coordinator at the University of Natal) terms "brief," there "was lots of suspicion of policymakers and academics coming in" and the issue of race was not resolved. Walker makes the point that "individuals were having these links rather than programs or women's studies formally. University of Natal, Durban women's studies didn't see the importance of engaging with these needs. There is a tremendous need on the part of the women's movement for those kinds of resources."

The Major Achievements of Women's Studies

Most people involved in women's studies programs in universities view realizing the establishment of women's studies programs as the major achievement. Reaching this point has meant overcoming many obstacles within the universities, primarily "proving" the academic worthiness of the endeavor. Dr. Ros Posel summed up the feeling: "We've made women's studies a legitimate part of the academic curriculum on this campus."

Women's studies has also contributed to confronting the sexual politics of tertiary institutions. For example, the University of South Africa's Women's Forum, which is tackling the "grass-roots issues" of housing subsidies, medical aid, and sexual harassment, was formed as an offshoot of the Women's Studies Center so that the center would be able to concentrate on "its main task, teaching and research." Meanwhile, at the University of Western Cape, the Gender Policy Action Group (later to become the Gender Equity Unit) began with working conditions and benefits.

There was also a sense that women's studies was more than a teaching program, since on the university campuses such teaching was effecting wider social repercussions. Faculty at different universities have reported "seeing the way in which the course overturns many of the perspectives of students" (Dr. Meintjes, University of Witwatersrand) and the way in which "students started to take their lives into their hands. They were meeting in hostels and dealing with issues.

More rape cases were reported" (Dr. Takalo, former coordinator of the women's studies committee at UNorth). In 1995 at the University of Natal–Pietermaritzburg, for the first time the student orientation program "had a whole day devoted to gender and we [gender studies] ran the workshop. This is a big advance" (Mr Lambert, coordinator of Gender Studies Honors program at the University of Natal–Pietermaritzburg).[11]

Unfinished Business of Women's Studies

While many centers claim that their existence is in itself a major achievement, that existence is marginal and often contested. All programs raised the issues of lack of funds, limited resources for books and library grants, and no staff allocation so that all staff involved in teaching were generally carrying double loads. There was a consensus that universities were taking advantage of the commitment of feminist academics to offer women's studies courses: "The major problem is that we do it out of love and our time is squeezed. We are falling apart" (Interview, UNISA Women's Studies Center)

In addition, very often those who do teach in women's studies are junior, part-time, marginalized members of staff (Interview, University of Natal–Pietermaritzburg). This issue of the marginalization and nonrecognition of women's studies is ironically exacerbated by "[the] degree of rhetoric and formal support (for women's studies) but it's not a priority. The opinion is that women's studies is not a solid and serious contribution to knowledge but it's politically incorrect to take this on" (Interview, Cherryl Walker, University of Natal–Durban). The perception that universities cannot admit that they do not support women's studies is widespread. So is the opinion that universities provide as few resources as possible but publicly lay claim to women's studies' achievements.

Besides material resources, other more weighty issues need to be addressed by women's studies. A theme frequently raised was ghettoization. Those located within women's studies programs were not as concerned with this problem as were those who taught women's studies within departments. The debate centers on women's studies versus gender studies and integration of women's studies into departments versus creation of specific degree structures. Dr. Ros Posel comments:

> When we started women's studies our view was that our primary
> focus was the various issues which pertained to women's lives. This

was important because in various disciplines these issues are neglected or marginalized and we wanted to highlight them. In the
process we realized that we can't understand the lives of women if we
don't understand the lives of men, but we kept the title "women's
studies" because this was our primary interest.

Representatives of the University of Natal–Pietermaritzburg, which
offers a gender studies honors program, said:

[We decided on] gender studies [so as] not to exclude men. Some of
the male philosophy students objected to the term feminism since
they felt that the issues raised were relevant to them as well as to
women. We opted for gender studies because we wanted to reach as
many students as possible. But we are beginning to feel that gender
studies has shunted women's studies [aside]. Lots of work in gender
studies has been taken over by men with all the masses of studies on
masculinities. Some people feel that women's studies must be
restored.

Sheila Meintjes (from Wits) reflects an oft-expressed opinion that it
was easier to get courses on women's studies accepted within departments than to establish new degree programs. She suggests that strategically this might be the place to start, but she was unsure: "I might
have argued differently a few years ago, but now I feel we'll achieve
more by having a broad base within departments." While debate still
needs to run its course, the different approaches complement each
other and are part of building an environment in which gender is an
acceptable unit of analysis in all spheres of academic work.

Another issue raised at the 1991 conference was that of race. This
question has two aspects: representation (who can speak for whom)
and racism (though some might argue that these are the same). The
issue of representation is one that women's studies has attempted to
work on. A number of interesting articles in have appeared in *Agenda*
(see Funani 1992, Thompson 1992, Fouche 1993, Funani 1993, Gouws
1993, Sunde and Bozalek 1993, as well as Robinson 1994), all sparked
by the attendance of white South African women at a conference,
"African Women and the Diaspora," in Nigeria. The main debate was
whether white women have the right to research and write about the
experiences of black women and then present their papers. While
these pieces were very emotional and hurtful, they nevertheless served
a useful purpose in allowing the emotion to be aired. Ultimately black
women called for "their own space to explore their own realities,
before making this space available to others" (Funani 1992). White

women responded by raising a number of issues, the most interesting of which was the need to question the "outsider within" (Robinson 1994). The second issue of racism or racial domination has not really been addressed. It is something everyone is aware of and uncomfortable about, but that is where it stays. Sheila Meintjes related the experience from the University of Witwatersrand: "[We] had an integrated forum [Gender Forum] at one point, then a black women's caucus was established, but this hived off. It was a painful experience because we hoped we could transcend difference." Cherryl Walker mentioned that at UNatal–Durban, "the Gender Research Group remained small; part of this is a racial dynamic." Women's studies needs to deal with race and power on an interpersonal level.

Linked to the question of race is the argument that women's studies is white and Western. Women's studies organizers at the University of Western Cape needed to responded to this belief: "Amongst students there was some resistance and hostility to the program. They said it was divisive and elitist.... Women's studies and feminist issues are Western issues and don't reflect the position of Third World women or black women" (Interview, Primo). Once the program began, however, these opinion-makers were won over. Most women interviewed recognized that this view existed. They felt that it didn't necessarily reflect their opinions and that the debate needed to be qualified. For example, Dr. Teboho Moja, from the department of education, argues that it depends where you are placing it. We do have resistance to women's studies in South Africa, but that doesn't mean that black women are against it. The question is who controls the territory? Women's studies needs to address race, but it tends to focus on gender and puts race at the margin.

The Impact of Women's Studies on the Traditional Curriculum

It is not particularly easy to assess the impact of women's studies on the traditional curriculum. On the one hand, women's studies programs have highlighted the androcentric nature of departments, while, on the other hand, women's studies courses in departments have facilitated the development of women's studies degree programs. This work has mostly been done in the arts and social sciences. In science and engineering much work still must be done.[12]

In most arts and social science disciplines, progressive academics attempt to include gender. According to Cherryl Walker, however, it is "generally an add-on approach. And often we [Gender Research Group,

University of Natal] are picked as the women's voice. I resent this and am irritated by it." Others, like Michelle Friedman, working in a development context, are just as critical: "People that I've worked with who've done courses on women come out into these kinds of jobs [gender-related jobs in NGOS]. They might think about speaking to women separately, but it doesn't transform their thinking. They don't internalize it. Is it a product of problems in teaching or is teaching too separate from politics?"

With respect to academic associations, some have special sessions or working groups for women's studies, while others are very resistant. Even when the atmosphere is sympathetic to women's studies, the conundrum of ghettoization is ever-present. As Cherryl Walker sees it, "The dilemma of a session on women and gender is one of specialized knowledge versus contributing to other sessions. There is an ambivalence amongst feminist academics. We are comfortable with our closed group, but it's problematic because we are not challenged from other literature."

Many women argue that the overwhelming culture of the universities is still masculine and white (in the case of the historically white universities). But a few, like Carla Sutherland, point out that we need to set more manageable goals and that "we don't do enough celebrating. Sometimes we need to say where we were ten years ago."

The Impact of Women's Studies on Educational Policy

Educational policy is in the process of being rewritten. At the top of the government's agenda is the integration of twelve education departments into one and the provision of ten years of free and compulsory schooling. In September 1994 the Ministry of Education released a white paper on education and training. The white paper "acknowledges that education and training is a basic human right and commits itself to the goal of 'life-long learning irrespective of race, class, gender, creed, or age' " (cited in Daniels 1995:49). This has implications for women's access to education and addresses women's needs directly through the Gender Equity Task Team.[13]

But women's studies has not had an organizational impact on primary or secondary education. While individuals might have played a role in formally drafting some of the NEPI documents,[14] there was no interaction or imperative to ensure that policy specifically included gender equity. Nevertheless, a few individuals have made an impact. As Dr. Posel commented, a few women's studies graduates are now primary or secondary school teachers and have been able to implement their new knowledge in their jobs.

The conundrum is that, while educational policy has the potential to address women's needs, in its present form it is gender-blind. The National Qualification Framework (NQF) is the vehicle for access to education. In an interview, Adrienne Bird describes the NQF as a "ladder system made up of levels and pathways." The levels are of different complexity or cognitive difficulty, and entry can take place at any level. The learning outcome is linked to the assessment criteria. This framework is meant to capture learning that takes place not only in schools but also in adult basic education and training (ABET), community colleges, and tertiary institutions. Bird thinks that this system is potentially of great benefit to women:

> It makes learning explicit. It is possible to say we have already learned these things which haven't been given recognition, for example running a household requires "management skills." If learning has been achieved, then you could get credits for it. So it is measuring what people have done against learning outcomes. The question is will these skills be given recognition? And this is a gender struggle.

Daniels, however, is more skeptical (1995:49). She argues that the white paper doesn't recognize that most women are not in a position to upgrade their skills. They are employed in menial jobs, and there is a danger that unless further mechanisms are put in place to ensure that women get access to training and skills-upgrading, the benefits of the National Qualification Framework to the majority of women who are black, working-class, and rural, will be very limited.

Strong organizational and lobbying initiatives could unleash this potential for change. Women's studies could be organizationally significant, but as Daniels outlines, a key obstacle needs to be overcome: "Part of the problem is that centers and research units are disconnected from non-governmental organizations and the political process. We need to create an interactive process so that we can network."

Conclusion

If one were to take Carla Sutherland's advice to celebrate the achievements of women's studies, one could conclude that women's studies in South Africa has moved a long way since the first few courses were taught in the early 1980s. But one should not be too complacent. The suspension of courses at the Durban and Pietermaritzburg campuses of Natal University is a warning of the potential effect on women's studies of cutbacks to university funding. Many of the issues that very emotionally tore the academy apart at the 1991 Conference on Women and Gender still have not been adequately addressed. Most pressing are those of race and the relationship between women's studies and the women's movement(s).

In addition, women's organizations and policymakers have made demands on women's studies that aren't presently being met. As Ms. Govender, member of Parliament and a key initiator of parliamentary policy and debate around gender equity, says: "There is a huge policy need, if only women's studies had developed the policy backup. People in government are looking for policy around women and if it was there they would take it." Dr. Ngato, of the Development Bank of South Africa, has similar views: "If people were exposed to women's studies, our development program would be much more sensitive. We have a range of specialists but no gender specialists."

The challenges are there. The question is, How will women's studies meet them?

NOTES

1. For a more comprehensive account, readers are referred to the 1994 South African government country report on the status of South African women. For the purposes of this report I have restricted the discussion to educational and occupational indicators. Unless otherwise indicated, all references are to South Africa 1994.
2. Please note that these are official figures and exclude women in subsistence agriculture and unpaid labor.
3. The Afrikaner Broederbond was formed in 1918 "to promote the interests of the Afrikaner nation." It became a secret organization in 1921. It laid the foundation for the coming to power of the National Party in 1948. During the apartheid era it acted as a clandestine and highly exclusive Afrikaner nationalist organization which tried to coordinate and direct the policies and activities of all Afrikaner political, cultural, ideological, economic, and religious organizations. Membership is by recruitment and, in many respects, remains a self-chosen elite, which exercises an enormous influence through its network of members, including nearly cabinet ministers and senior civil servants. The 1982 split in the National Party led to a sharp struggle for control of the Broederbond. As a new black elite occupies positions of power it is difficult to gauge the extent of its present influence (Davies, O'Meara, and Dlamini 1984).
4. Because of a lack of resources and the retirement of the coordinator this year (1995), the master's and the undergraduate courses have been suspended, and at this point no other staff member is prepared to take on the large, unpaid task of coordinating the program. As part of the general university restructuring, a small committee is in place to lobby for a gender school, which would encompass both women's studies and a new gender

studies program. Currently, the university is supportive of this initiative and has appointed a full-time coordinator for a two-year period.

5. Because of a lack of resources the honors program is suspended for 1995.

6. Module refers to a smaller course within a semester; a module would consist of several lectures.

7. The issues that allegedly succeeded in scuttling the initiative at the University of the North were who is the coordinator of the program and why is she someone new to the university; what are the criteria for selecting her; why is the committee made up of only unmarried women (who are regarded as not having any direction, since they have no husbands to guide them). Untruthful rumors about the personal lives of the committee were also circulated, in an effort to discredit their integrity.

8. The Black Women's Federation was linked to the Black Consciousness Movement and was banned in 1977. UWCO (United Women's Congress) in the Western Cape, FEDTRAW (Federation of Transvaal Women) in the Transvaal, FEDSAW (Federation of South African Women)—an umbrella body but mainly in the Transvaal, and NOW (Natal Organisation of Women) in Natal were regional women's organizations affiliated with the United Democratic Front (UDF).

9. Black Sash is an organization made up primarily of white women. It was initially set up in the late 1950s to protest the exclusion of colored people from the voters rolls. It has been important in anti-apartheid activities.

10. Rape Crisis assists and counsels rape survivors. It has autonomous branches in different cities. With few exceptions it has failed to gain a membership among black women.

11. Finally, one should not forget the 1991 Conference on Women and Gender organized by the Gender Research Group at the University of Natal, Durban. Despite the controversy surrounding it, it raised debate in a way that has not been repeated. One should also mention some of the other conferences: The Gender Research Group at UNatal-Durban together with the Institute for Democratic Alternatives in South Africa and the Women's National Coalition, organized a Conference on Women in Democratic Government in 1993. UCape Town's Equal Opportunity Research Project organized a conference on Sexual Harassment in 1994. In 1995 there was a Women and Arts Conference organized by UNatal Pietermaritzburg; and the University of South Africa's Women's Studies Center hosts an annual conference, which has a different theme each year.

12. Carla Sutherland did mention that the engineering faculty at UCape Town was becoming aware that "women" were one of the potential growth areas for attracting students.

13. The "Education and Training" white paper in recognition of the specific nature of gender inequality proposes to establish a Commission on Gender Equality. The ministry proposes to appoint a full-time gender equity commissioner (located within the Gender Equity Unit) who will lead a Gender Equity Task Team. The Gender Equity Unit will report directly to

the director general of education and is expected to work closely with the national Commission on Gender Equality.

It is impossible to go into a detailed analysis of the white paper here. Its proposals are wide-ranging and cover curriculum development, teacher training, adult basic education, the National Qualification Framework, and the establishment of a Gender Equity Unit. A provocative critique of this is to be found in Daniels (1995). In this section I address the influence of women's studies on the development of this policy.

14. The National Education Policy Initiative (NEPI) was set up under the auspices of the National Educational Consultative Committee (NECC) to interrogate policy options in all aspects of education. It began its work in December 1990 and concluded in August 1992 and operated within the ideals of the broad democratic movement.

REFERENCES

Documents

Beall, J., M. Friedman, S. Hassim, R. Posel, L. Stiebel, and A. Todes. 1987. "African Women in the Durban Struggle, 1985–1986: Towards a Transformation of Roles?" In G. Moss and I. Obery, eds., *South African Review,* vol. 4. Johannesburg: Ravan.

Bonnin, D., J. Fairbairn, S. Hassim, and C. Walker. 1993. Introduction to "Selected Papers from the Conference on Women and Gender in Southern Africa." Unpublished manuscript.

Budlender, D. 1994. "Preliminary Report on Questionnaire to Universities." *Agenda Evaluation.* Unpublished report.

Daniels, D. 1995. "Gender Gaps in the Education White Paper." *Agenda* 24: 49–53.

Davies, R., D. O'Meara, S. Dlamini. 1982. *The Struggle for South Africa: A Reference Guide to Movements, Organisations and Institutions,* vol. 2. London: Zed Press.

Dubel, I. 1991. "Whither South African Women's Studies." Paper presented to the Conference on Women and Gender in Southern Africa, University of Natal, Durban, January.

Equal Opportunity Research Project. 1994. "A Vision for an Africa-wide Gender Institute: Selected Extracts from the 1994 report of the Equal Opportunities Research Project." EORP, UCTXC. Cape Town.

Fouche, F. 1993. "Nigerian Conference Revisited." *Agenda* 16: 39–41.

Funani, L. 1992. "Nigerian Conference Revisited." *Agenda* 15: 63–68.

———. 1993. "The Great Divide." *Agenda* 17: 55–57.

Gouws, A. 1993. "An Angry Divide." *Agenda* 19: 67–70.

Hassim, S., and C. Walker. 1992. "Women's Studies and the Women's Movement." *Transformation* 18/19: 78–85.

Kemp, A., N. Madlala, A. Moodley, and E. Salo. 1995. "The New South African Feminism." Mimeographed.

Letlaka-Rennert, K. 1991. "Impressions: Conference on Women and Gender in Southern Africa." *Agenda* 9: 20–23.

Lund, F. 1991. "Impressions: Conference on Women and Gender in Southern Africa." *Agenda* 9: 20–23.

Robinson, J. 1994. "White Women Researching/Representing Others: From Anti-Apartheid to Postcolonialism?" In G. Rose and A. Blunt, eds., *Sexual/Textual Colonisations*. London: Guilford.

South Africa. 1994. *Beijing Conference Report: 1994 Country Report on the Status of South African Women.*

Sunde, J., and V. Bozalek. 1993. "(Re)searching Difference." *Agenda* 19: 29–36.

Thompson, E. 1992. "Mad Women in the Tropics." *Agenda* 15: 61–62.

UDUSA. 1993. "Race and Gender Report." Johannesburg.

UNISA Women's Studies Center. 1995. "Report of Coordinator of the Center for Women's Studies for the Year Ending 26 February 1995." Unpublished document. Pretoria.

Interviews

Albertyn, Cathi. 28 March 1995. Gender Project, Center for Applied Legal Studies, University of Witwatersrand.

Bennett, Jane. 11 April 1995. Sexual harassment coordinator, Equal Opportunities Research Project, University of Cape Town.

Bird, Adrienne. 28 March 1995. Metal Training Board.

Daniels, Desiree. 11 April 1995. Education Projects Unit, UDUSA, University of Western Cape.

De la Rey, Cheryl. 7 April 1995. Past UDUSA vice president, Department of Psychology, University of Cape Town.

Fouche, Fidela, and Michael Lambert. 23 March 1995. Past coordinator and coordinator, respectively, Gender Studies Honors Program, University of Natal, Pietermaritzburg.

Friedman, Michelle. 17 March 1995. Gender trainer, National Land Committee.

Govender, Pregs. 11 April 1995. Member of Parliament.

Lemon, Jenny, Department of Communication; Jeanette Malherbe, Department of Philosophy; Maganthri Pillay, Research Assistant; Pamela Ryan, Department of English; Jenny Wilkinson, Department of Philosophy, Center Coordinator. UNISA Women's Studies Center. 27 March 1995.

Meintjes, Sheila. 28 March 1995. Department of Political Studies, Gender Forum, University of Witwatersrand.

Moja, Teboho. 27 March 1995. Ministry of Education.

Pandor, Naledi. 6 April 1995. Member of Parliament, Standing Committee on Education.

Posel, Ros. 4 April 1995. Coordinator, Women's Studies Program, University of Natal, Durban.

Primo, Natasha. 10 April 1995. Coordinator of Women's Studies, Women's Studies Program, University of Western Cape.

Sardien, Tony. 10 April 1995. Anti-Racism and Gender Project, Center for Adult and Continuing Education, University of Western Cape.

Sutherland, Carla. 7 April 1995. Researcher, Equal Opportunities Research Project, University of Cape Town.

Takalo, Ngoato. 27 March 1995. Former coordinator of Women's Studies Committee, University of North. (Currently working at the Development Bank.)

Walker, Cherryl. 22 March 1995. GRG coordinator, Department of Sociology. Gender Research Group, University of Natal, Durban.

Debby Bonnin *is an industrial sociologist, who holds a joint post in the sociology department and the Centre for Industrial, Organisational, and Labour Studies at the University of Natal, Durban. She is a founding editor of* Agenda, *a quarterly South African feminist journal, and is the convener of the women's studies working group for the South African Sociological Association.*

Women's Studies in Turkey

Necla Arat

Women ought to show their faces to the world, and they ought to look
on the world with their own eyes.

Mustafa Kemal Atatürk, 1925

The History of Women's Rights in Turkey

Modern Turkey has inherited a rich history of multinational and
multicultural traditions and is also unique among the Islamic countries because it is a secular state. The status of women in Turkey varies
over an extremely wide range, from the highly educated professional
women in the cities to the majority of women in the urban and rural
areas. There are important differences in lifestyle and social status not
only between urban and rural women but also among women of
different social classes, levels of education, and employment status.
Turkish history often emphasizes that the woman question was an
important part of national reforms and that Turkish women were the
first Islamic women to be granted legal and social rights (Abadan-Unat
1979:291). Kemalists, the founding fathers of the republic, believed
that granting equal rights to women in the political and social arenas
was an integral part of their modernization efforts. Among these
rights, suffrage held special importance. The efforts to integrate women into social and political life as full citizens led to the proliferation
of various women professionals, including academics, since the new
Turkish Republic needed a "new woman who would epitomize its
ideological shift into a secular nation state."

In 1923, Turkey was an underdeveloped agricultural country, in
contrast to industrialized Europe. Women in Turkey still carried the
heavy burden of giving birth to as many children as possible while
working in the fields and doing housework. Nevertheless, at the same
time the Kemalist government was preparing the most radical revolution for women. First of all, women were encouraged to give up
wearing the veil, a symbol of religious and patriarchal oppression. The
leaders of the republic tried to set an example by appearing in public
in the company of unveiled women. Then, in 1926, the Swiss Civil

Code, which introduced civil marriage and divorce and banned polygamy, was adopted.

Through the civil code, women acquired the juridical status of "person," which enabled them to enjoy equal rights with men, and Turkey became the first Islamic country to eliminate the Sharia, the Islamic code that underlies the segregation of sexes and their differential legal treatment. Furthermore, women were enfranchised in time to vote in local elections in 1930, and in 1934 they were given equal political rights for national elections. In the 1934 elections, an informal quota system was implemented by Mustafa Kemal Atatürk, and the number of female deputies reached a peak of 18 among the 395 members of parliament.

Mustafa Kemal was concerned with every aspect of women's lives, including clothing, as well as duties and responsibilities in the society. According to him, the new woman was to take her place in the public life of the republic as an educated social individual. He saw women as "pillars of society" and the "wellspring of the nation." For these reasons women had to become "enlightened, virtuous and dignified in order to educate a strong new generation" (Taşkıran 1976:62–63). His public support for the recognition of equal rights for women was unquestionably rooted in a genuine belief in women's intrinsic equality with men. He wanted neither to demonstrate to the international community that Turkey was becoming a Western nation nor to establish control over gender role definitions within Turkish society (Kardam 1991:19). On the contrary, he declared openly that there would be no difference between men and women. Moreover, he promised that Turkish women would be free, enjoy education, and occupy a position equal to that of men, since they are entitled to equality (Abadan-Unat 1981:11).

He always stressed the importance of women's participation as full members of the society in the building of the nation. For example, in a 1923 speech in Izmir, he stated:

> We have to believe that everything in the world is the result, directly or indirectly, of the work of women. . . . If a society is content that only part of its population move with the times, then more than half of that society is doomed to be weak. . . . The weakness in our society lies in our indifference towards the status of women. . . . If our nation now needs science and knowledge, men and women must share them equally. . . . Domestic duties are not necessarily the most important of a woman's responsibilities.

> (Taşkıran 1976:55–56)

The Status of Women

As early as 1923, Mustafa Kemal had recognized and foreseen the importance of women to the development process. He therefore tried to break down the traditional norms of women's lives and also to overcome the prejudices of male-dominated institutions, including religion. The implementation of an egalitarian gender policy, beginning with the new Latinized alphabet, was the first step (Helvacıoğlu 1994). In the second step, legal reforms and the separation of religion from the state have affected the lives of women in Turkish society. Today, among the professions there is a marked absence of gender-typing, which is thought to be the result of both secular education and the encouragement of women in the republican era. To give an example, today the participation of women among university staff is much higher than the world average. (In the 1991–92 academic year, 32 percent of all teaching staff in higher education were women.)

But because of poor economic conditions, a rapidly growing population, and some prevailing traditional and religious obstacles, the status of the majority of Turkish women appears to have changed little since the beginning of the republican era (*Turkey* 1993:2). Schooling rates and the literacy ratio among women and girls remain far behind the desired levels. In 1990 the rate of illiteracy among women over the age of fifteen was 31 percent. Although the schooling rates for boys and girls at the compulsory primary school level are similar (85.4 percent for girls and 91.1 percent for boys in the 1991–92 academic year), in secondary and higher education institutions, the number of female students drops sharply. For instance, in the 1991–92 academic year, 53.2 percent of girls continued on to the secondary school after completing their primary school education, whereas 72.8 percent of the boys did so. The proportion of women in higher education is 33.05 percent (1991).

In addition to low schooling rates, women have have little access to health care services. The mortality rate in maternal delivery is very high when compared with that in developed countries. For every 100,000 live births, 100 mothers lose their lives. This means that almost 1,500 women lose their lives during pregnancy and delivery and after birth in approximately 1.4 million live births annually. This is half the number of total maternal deaths occurring in all developed countries put together (Ministry of Health 1995:42). The major factors contributing to high maternal mortality rates are frequent and early pregnancies. In rural areas communities still lack the awareness that pregnant women are in need of special care. Abortion is legal in Turkey. A law issued in 1983 requires the consent of both spouses for abortion for married women. Fertility surveys reveal that more than 500,000 abortions occur every year. Although the use of contraceptives has gradually increased since family planning became legal, the high incidence of abortions shows that families are not very successful in avoiding unwanted pregnancies.

Notwithstanding the gender-neutral character of the 1982 Constitution and the 1926 civil code, in a number of areas the legal framework constrains women's full participation. It does not provide full equality for women. For example, articles 151–58 on the family define the husband as the head of household, who determines domicile and whose views prevail on family matters in cases of dispute. While the provisions of the civil code regarding women's issues were progressive at the time of adoption, some have proved to be insufficient for present-day society (*Turkey* 1993:2). Proposals have been submitted since 1984 to declare the insufficient and discriminatory laws obsolete, but the National Assembly has taken no action yet. When we look at women in the labor force, we see that 32.3 percent of all women participate (16.1 percent urban, 50.2 percent rural). Unfortunately, 94 percent of women have no social insurance coverage. In addition to family responsibilities, these women work long hours, frequently unpaid, especially in rural areas. In 1992 65.1 percent of female workers were unpaid. Although universal education has been an important principle of the state since the founding of the republic and although the constitution assures equal educational opportunity for boys and girls, 2.1 million girls of primary and middle school age are not attending school. Particularly in the rural areas, because of limited economic resources and prevailing patriarchal values, the education of girls continues to be problematic. This indicator is certainly the most obvious evidence of gender inequality in Turkey, and we still need to work hard to achieve gender equality both in the family and in the society.

The Relationship Between the Women's Movement and Women's Studies

The history of women's studies as a new area of academic knowledge in Turkey is very brief, although various works on women's rights have been published since the 1970s (for example, Taşkıran 1973 and Afet Inan 1975), research and teaching related to women have emerged and flourished only in the last two decades, in part because of the international women's movement, which succeeded in bringing women to agendas all over the world (Kardam 1991:3, 11).

The first pioneering work on women's issues that compiled research on women was the book *Türk Toplumunda Kadın* (Women in Turkish Society), edited by Nermin Abadan-Unat (1979). This book was a turning point in the study of women in Turkey because it served as a primary reference book to the newcomers to the field in the 1980s (Y. Arat 1993:125). During this time, in some Turkish universities several works on the status of women in the family, at work, and in public life were published (for example, K ray 1979, *Küçük Kasaba Kadınları* (Small-Town Women); Kağıtçıbaşı 1981, *Çocuğun Değeri* (Value of Children); N. Arat 1980, *Kadın Sorunu* (Woman's Question); and Tekeli 1981, *Kadınlar ve Siyasal—Toplumsal Hayat* (Women and Political-Social Life). Many women scholars individually began to teach courses related to women, mainly from disciplines such as philosophy, sociology, economics, and political science. These publications, courses, and public meetings organized by women's groups made their impact on political and intellectual circles. Women's groups increasingly widened their influence in the society throughout the 1980s and encouraged academic research on various questions. The growing public activism of women's groups such as the Women's Circle, the Association in Support of Contemporary Living, and the Association of Turkish Women Jurists has also given the women's struggle for equal rights and liberation a new impetus. As a result of the activity of these organizations, both the media and the general public have become more interested in and knowledgeable about women's issues. These organizations have also grown influential in the setting of social and political agendas on behalf of women. In addition to the activities of the women's groups, the increase in studies on women made women more visible both in society and in the social sciences. In 1986 women's movement activities and women's studies were intertwined and interrelated. For example, Women's Circle took part in organizing a petition signed by seven thousand women demanding the implementation of the United Nations Convention Against Discrimination Against Women.

The following year, a campaign against the battering of women was launched and about three thousand women marched in the streets of Istanbul in protest of domestic violence against women. In 1989 the Association in Support of Contemporary Living organized a two-day international symposium on women's participation in decision making and politics. More than two thousand women attended the symposium and discussed equal rights–equal participation in the society with the leaders of the political parties and academics. During the 1980s different women's groups (for example, Kemalist feminists, socialist feminists, and radical feminists) tried to influence government policy to change discriminatory laws. They launched campaigns against sexual harassment, against article 438 of the penal code, which provided a reduction of two-thirds in the penalty of the rapist if the raped woman was a prostitute. They organized street demonstrations and petition campaigns against violence and fundamentalism. Especially the Kemalist feminists emphasized the maintenance of secularism and the upholding of rights that Atatürk gave women against the onslaught of religious conservatism.

For secularism and democracy women marched in the streets of Istanbul in the tens of thousands. Some results of these activities include the abolition of article 438 by the parliament and the abolition of article 159 of the civil code, which required the husband's permission for a married woman to engage in employment outside the home, by the Constitutional Court. Now women do have the right to work without the permission of their husbands. All of these activities were carried out mostly in urban areas by educated women. These women also demand affirmative action quotas to participate in political life, and they believe that when they succeed in becoming real participants in a participatory democracy, their female identity will transform the society positively with a new and strong balance.

The 1980s in general was a time when feminist publications appeared, ranging from translations of Western classics (for example, J. Mitchell, A. Michel, L. Segal, and A. Oakley) to feminist novels written by Turkish and foreign women writers. There were two magazines published, *Feminist* and the socialist feminist *Kaktüs*, which were run by fairly small groups of women.

December 1989 witnessed the foundation of the first Women's Research and Education Center at the University of Istanbul. The opening announcement was made at the International Symposium of the Association in Support of Contemporary Living. This was the first step toward institutionalizing women's studies in academia. Women academics who also had been active in the Association in Support of Contemporary Living were the pioneers who set up the center, which turned out to be a fruitful effort in many respects. Then came the establishment of the first Women's Library and Information Center (1990), which instantly began to collect valuable material, with the help of academics and other volunteers, in order to offer services for those who need information about Turkish women throughout the ages. The Purple Roof, a private foundation established just after the

Women's Library, offered help to battered women from volunteers among whom are professionals such as lawyers, doctors, and psychologists. In 1993 another Women's Research and Education Center chaired by Professor Ülker Gürkan was established at the University of Ankara, and the Women's Center of Çukurova University (Southern Turkey) chaired by Professor Gaye Erbatur was also established. The first Women's Center at the University of Istanbul chaired by Professor Necla Arat, offered an interdisciplinary women's studies graduate program in the academic year 1990–91.[1] The Middle East Technical University of Ankara also began to offer a program of gender studies in the spring term of 1993.[2] This gender studies program, which is taught in English, is chaired by Professor Feride Acar.

Although the history of women's centers is quite short, their achievements have been considerable and they have become staunch propagators of women's rights in Turkey. For example, the purposes of the Women's Research and Education Center of Istanbul were several: instigating research on issues relating to women's educational, legal, economic, and social rights and status; implementing programs, campaigns, and other activities to enhance public awareness with regard to women's rights and gender equality in general; accelerating administrative measures for eliminating discrimination based on gender; and establishing independent academic programs in women's studies. The Women's Research and Education Center of Istanbul has also undertaken several projects and established close links with non-academic democratic mass organizations and NGOs and cooperated with them to achieve its purposes; in this effort the center also sought the help of the media and was well received and well covered by the daily papers and television. One innovative initiative of the center was the founding of the Association for Women's Studies, with the primary purpose of fundraising for the activities of the center.

From the start, the center has been involved with several women's groups and the related NGOs in Turkey. One of its activities was to hold meetings with these organizations to discuss and disseminate the UN Convention against Discrimination against Women. For example, in February 1991 a special campaign was launched by the center on secularism and women's rights. In November 1991 a two-week campaign against sexual harassment was organized, and the center collected more than 25,000 signatures to be presented to the UN Secretary General asking for an amendment in the UN Declaration of Human Rights in favor of women's rights.

The year 1992 witnessed a truly historic event: at the initiative of the center, more than one hundred thousand signatures were collected petitioning for an amendment of the Turkish civil code, which still contained some nonegalitarian articles (including the one granting the husband a privileged position as head of the family). The signatures were presented to the president of the national parliament by a delegation of some fifty women from various NGOs and democratic mass organizations. In January 1993 the center initiated a mass demonstration in Istanbul to condemn the ongoing brutality and sexual crimes against women in Bosnia-Herzegovina. In April 1993, together with other democratic organizations, the center participated in the mass rally held against the threat of fundamentalism and religious intolerance. The center also took part in the campaign against illiteracy with a poster on 8 March 1993 proclaiming "In Turkey 38 women out of 100 are illiterate." Women's Day has been celebrated by the center since its foundation, and for the last three years was turned into Women's Week, featuring lectures, panel discussions, films, concerts, and plays—all aimed at heightening public consciousness about gender equality and democracy in the society as a whole. An interesting and popular activity in 1994 was the exhibition "Women in Political Life through Caricatures, 1923–1994." In June 1994 the center, together with the Foundation to Develop Human Sources, organized a panel discussion titled "Women, Demography, and Development."

The Major Achievement of Women's Studies Thus Far in Higher Education

While engaging in these lively activities aimed at enhancing public awareness about gender equality, the center never lost sight of its purpose to set up a solid basis for women's studies as an academic area of study. Before 1991, the center offered to graduate students an optional interdisciplinary program that led to the independent M.A. program finally established in the academic year 1993–94. But here it must be mentioned again that in the 1980s there were also individual women's studies courses offered to undergraduate students both in the Bosphorus and in the Middle East technical universities. In the first M.A. program of the University of Istanbul in 1990–91, eleven women's studies courses were offered, all of them interdisciplinary and offered for credit. In this way women's studies and some gender issues have come to be officially integrated in academic curricula for the first time in Turkey.

Some of the important factors that assisted the development of women's studies in higher education were the following: the academic structure facilitating interdisciplinary, interdepartmental, and intercollegiate work; the presence of a significant number of women academics and students; the support of women's groups and other feminists.

Fifty women scholars have been doing research in women's studies, most of them from the social sciences and humanities. They have disseminated the results of their research through both scholarly and popular means—see, for example, Abadan-Unat's (1979), Kandıyotı's (1987), Ecevıt's (1990), and Yesim Arat's (1993) research on women and the effects of migration; Necla Arat's work on women's participation in education (1992), employment, and public life; women and the manufacturing industry; and women and political life. Equally important work was done by Kağıtçıbaşı (1981) and Sırman (1990) on the position of women in the family (a cross-cultural study) and the economic role of rural women in agriculture.

Although institutionalized women's studies in Turkey has had only a short history, we are optimistic about its future, since we have already seen hundreds of graduate and postgraduate theses produced, books published, and articles printed concerning various aspects of women's issues. For example, among the recent publications of the center are books like *Women's Problems in Turkey: New Approaches* (edited by Necla Arat), *Woman and Sexuality* (edited by Necla Arat), and *To Be a Woman in Turkey* (edited by Necla Arat). The Women's Center of Istanbul has also started the publication of a review, containing articles in both Turkish and English, titled *Women's Studies Review.*

To the independent M.A. program in 1993–94, fifteen students (eleven women and four men) were accepted from various academic backgrounds out of fifty applicants. The student interest in the program led the university authorities to raise enrollment from fifteen to twenty students for the next academic year. In the academic year 1994–95, seventy students applied to the master's program, and twenty of them were admitted. This remarkable student interest reflects the increasing concern with women's issues and also the aspirations of the young generation to live and participate in a truly democratic society respectful of citizenship rights and gender equality. The prospect of Turkey's integration with the European Community and the possibility of the emergence of new employment areas in need of a qualified labor force sensitive to gender rights and human rights labor force may also have had some impact upon this interest.

Recently some modifications were made in the program, especially with a view to covering the current problems of Turkish society. The program aims to provide an understanding of feminist theory while linking studies to the specific situation and problems of women living in Turkey. The M.A. in women's studies is highly committed to an interdisciplinary approach, and aims to give students a broad perspective of women's studies while also allowing them to develop special interests. The degree emphasizes the issues and debates within women's studies with the objective of developing a grasp of methods and concepts as well as of knowledge. It is expected that this competency with regard to knowledge and research methods will add considerably to the understanding and analysis of gender relations in Turkish society and consequently help to achieve a change in prevalent traditional sex-role stereotyping. The program requires one whole year (two semesters) of courses and seminars and another year for writing an M.A. thesis.[3]

The Unfinished Business of Women's Studies in Higher Education

The Women's Research and Education Center of the University of Istanbul has been a good model for other universities. Women's research centers have been founded one after another following the Istanbul example as we mentioned above. Now there are centers in Marmara University, in Ankara University, and in Çukurova University. The Middle East Technical University of Ankara also has begun to offer gender studies courses. Soon we will have a network of women's research centers in Turkey, and we will also have different women's studies programs that feature specific curricula responding to regional needs. The unfinished business of women's studies is the gaining of independent women's studies departments that offer complete undergraduate and graduate programs. To award the Ph.D. in women's studies is another important target.

Very recently, we began to analyze sexist teaching materials. We found many stereotypical gender-role and male-centered messages in textbooks, not from the reformist republican era but from the period between 1950 and 1990. We hope that in the years to come women's studies will contribute to the improvement of the curriculum and the reform of textbooks and teacher training programs, including elementary and secondary education.

Conclusion

In Turkish society, Kemalist efforts aimed at integrating women into social and political life as full citizens are still valuable and prevailing ideals to be realized. The great majority of women in Turkey now, from both urban and rural areas, want to look on the world with their very eyes, and they also want their voices to be heard everywhere. We believe that the development and success of women's studies in Turkey will contribute both to this cause and to the creation of a public awareness and sensitivity to gender and women's issues and problems of society.

NOTES

1. Women's studies courses offered at the University of Istanbul (1990–91) include: Sexism in the History of Thought; Women in the Turkish Legal System and Comparative Legislation; Women and Economy; Women, Development, and Demography; Fundamental Concepts and Problems of Feminism; Methodology in Women's Studies; Women and Media; Women's Health and Sexuality Feminist History; Gendered Reading and Writing; Problems of Identity and Women's Autobiographies.

2. Courses offered in the Middle East Technical University Gender Studies Program (1993–94) include: Introduction to Women's Studies; The Women Question in Turkey; Research Methods; Making of Feminist Knowledge; Issues on Family and Women; Women and Law; Women and Development; Sexuality and Society; Gender Issues in Organizations; Problems of Studying Women in Muslim Societies; Issues in Women's Work and Labor; Gender Issues in Class and Patriarchy; Gender in Politics and Political Participation; Psychology of Gender; Psychology of Close Relationships; Women's Experience with Hierarchy and State Along the Silk Road.

3. Current women's studies M.A. program courses at the University of Istanbul include: Introduction to Women's Studies and Fundamental Concepts of Feminism, taught by Prof. Necla Arat; Feminist Theories, taught by Dr. Fatmagül Berktay; Women in International and National Law; taught by Prof. Aysel Çelikel, Dean of the Faculty of Law of Istanbul University; Women, Population, and Development, taught by Prof. Nermin Abadan-Unat; Women and Economy, taught by Prof. Tülay Arın; Women's Health and Sexuality, coordinated by Prof. Türkan Saylan, with guest specialists for each topic; Sexism in the Media, taught by Asst. Prof. Türkel Miniba and Dr. Yazgülü Aldoğan; Women in the Face of Monotheistic Religions, taught by Dr. Fatmagül Berktay; Women in Turkish Literature, taught by Prof. Dilek Dolta; Methodology in Social Sciences and Feminist Methodology, taught by Dr. Serpil Çakır.

REFERENCES

Abadan-Unat, Nermin, ed. 1979. *Türk Toplumunda Kadın*. Ankara: Türk Sosyal Bilimler Derneği.

———. 1981. *Women in Turkish Society*. Leiden: Brill.

Arat, Necla. 1991. "The Evolution of Women's Studies Programs and Research in Turkey." Paper presented at UNESCO International Seminar on Gender Studies, 19–22 November, in Moscow.

———. 1992. "Policies and Strategies Towards Women's Education" in *The First International Council on Education for Women*. Turkish Ministry of Education. Ankara.

Arat, Yeşim. 1993. "Women's Studies in Turkey: From Kemalism to Feminism." *New Perspectives on Turkey* 9: 119–37.

Berktay, Fatmagül. 1991. "Women's Studies in Turkey: 1980–1990," paper presented at *Women's Memory*, proceedings of the International Symposium of Women's Libraries. pp. 271–75. Metis Yayınları. Idst.

Ecevit, Yıldız. 1990. "Kentsel Üretim Sürecinde Kadın Emeğinin Konumu ve Değişen Biçimleri." In *Kadın Bakış Açıs ndan 1980 ler Türkiye'sinde Kadın*, edited by Ş. Tekeli. İletişim Yay. Ist.

Helvacıoğlu. 1994. "Sexist School Books in Elementary and Secondary Schools: 1928–1994." Unpublished M.A. thesis.

Inan, Afet. 1975. *Atatürk ve Türk Kadın Haklarının Kazanılması*. Milli Eğitim Basımevi. Ist.

Jayawardena, Kumari. 1988. *Feminism and Nationalism in the Third World*. Zed Books. London.

Kağıtçıbaşı, Çiğdem. 1981. *Çocuğun Değeri*. Türkiye'de Değerler ve *Doğurganlık*, Boğaziçi Üni. Yay. Ist.

Kandıyotı, Deniz. 1987. "Emancipated But Not Liberated?Reflections on the Turkish Case." *Feminist Studies* 13, no. 2 (Summer).

Kardam, Nüket. 1991. "International Norms, The Turkish State and Women." Working Paper no. 5. G. E. Von Grunebaum Center for Near Eastern Studies, University of California, Los Angeles.

Ministry of Health, General Directorate of MCH/FB. 1995. *Population Issues in the World and Turkey*. Ankara.

Sakaranaho, Tuula. 1993. "Woman Question and Ideologies Represented by Turkish Women." Unpublished doctoral dissertation.

Sırman, Nükhet. 1989. "Feminism In Turkey: A Short History." *New Perspectives on Turkey* 3, no. 1: 1–34.

———. 1990. *"Köy Kadının Aile ve Evlilikte Güçlenme Mücadelesi." Kadın Bakış Açısından 1980'ler Türkiye'sinde Kadın*, edited by Ş. Tekeli. İleşitim Yay. Ist.

The Status of Women in Turkey. 1994. The Turkish National Report to the Fourth World Conference on Women.

Taşkıran, Tezer. 1973. *Cumhuriyet'in 50. Yılında Türk Kadın Hakları*. Ankara.

Turkey: Women In Development. 1993. A World Bank Country Study.

"Women's Studies and the Social Position of Women In Eastern and Western Europe." 1990. European Network for Women's Studies Seminar in The Hague, Netherlands, 22–27 November.

Necla Arat is professor of philosophy at the University of Istanbul. She is also the founder of the first women's research center and women's studies unit in Turkey. She teaches both in the philosophy department and in the master's program in women's studies.

Women's Studies in Ghana

Mansah Prah

The Status of Women in Ghana

Indispensable to the economic development of Ghana, women form 51.3 percent of the population of 15 million. They constitute about 52 percent of the agricultural labor force and produce the bulk of the nation's food crops. They are also heavily represented in agro-industries such as oil palm processing, oil extraction, and fish preservation. Despite their prominent presence in agricultural activities, only 26.1 percent of women are farm owners or managers. Ghanaian women are highly visible in activities involving sales or trading and constitute 89 percent of workers in this sector. Most women are self-employed, and while the proportion of wage workers in the country is low overall, at 16 percent, women constitute an even lower percentage. Only 3.8 percent of women fall in that category of workers (Manuh 1989).

The 1992 Constitution of the Fourth Republic guarantees equal opportunities to all citizens and directs that appropriate measures should be taken to achieve regional and gender balance in recruitment and appointment to public offices. It declares that the state shall take the necessary steps to ensure the full integration of women into the mainstream of the economic development of Ghana (chapter 6, clause 36, section 6).

Ghanaian law recognizes women's rights to their separate property and their freedom to enter into transactions of their own. Yet this de jure equality does not reflect reality for the majority of Ghanaian women. Compared to men, women in Ghana suffer heavier time burdens and enjoy fewer productive resources. According to the *Ghana Living Standards Survey* (Republic of Ghana Statistical Service 1989), only 23 percent of the literate population are women. Because they lack education, training, and skills, the majority of women remain in agriculture and selling. Women in Ghana are disproportionately concentrated in the informal sector of the economy, where they are generally self-employed. Their main activities in this sector are petty trading, food processing, and marketing food crops. About

I am grateful to Boatema Boateng for her useful comments on this paper.

85 percent of traders in the major towns of the southern regions of the country are women. Though this arrangement makes women highly visible, women's businesses tend to be small-scale and loosely structured, with limited management expertise and weak infrastructural support. They tend to be home-based, using simple, labor-intensive technologies. Because of their low levels of literacy and skills, women cannot improve their opportunities within the informal sector or even move into the formal sector. For the same reason, women in the formal sector remain in low-skill, low-status, and low-paid jobs.

Women are dominant in the religious and cultural life of communities as priestesses, spirit mediums, healers, and prophets. In matrilineal communities also, royal women are queen mothers and perform constitutional, political, and ritual functions. In these positions they are held in high esteem by the society, and their gender is almost forgotten (Manuh 1991).

Few women occupy positions of authority in formal power structures, however. Currently, only 8 percent of parliamentarians are women, and less than 8 percent of District Assembly members are women. According to statistics compiled by the National Council for Women and Development (NCWD 1994), women's participation in the power structure of the country stands at about 20 percent.

Women and Education

In Ghana, the sex differential in education is high. With fewer women than men in formal education, the numbers of women decrease drastically as one moves up from primary to secondary and tertiary levels (Prah 1992; Osei 1991). Between 1989 and 1992, for example, the average percentages of all girls enrolled in primary, junior, and senior secondary schools were 44.95 percent, 41.13 percent, and 32.88 percent, respectively. The average percentage of women enrolled in the country's universities during the same period was about 23 percent. As scholars have demonstrated, sociocultural practices, belief systems, poverty, and ignorance are responsible for these statistics (Twumasi 1986; Chinto 1986; Mensah 1992; Sutherland-Addy et al. 1995). Inequitable access to education limits the access of girls and women to employment, especially in administrative, technical, and other areas in the formal sector.

The Relationship Between Women's Studies and Women's Movement Activities

In Ghana a wide range of women's groups aims to improve the situation of women. These include the 31st December Women's Movement, led by First Lady Mrs. Agyeman-Rawlings, the International

Association of Women Lawyers (FIDA), with its affiliate Women in Law and Development in Africa (WILDAF), and church-affiliated groups like the Christian Mothers' Union. The majority of women's groups tend to focus their activities on two main areas: the creation of income-generating projects for women and advocacy for women. The efforts of these groups usually are undertaken independently of each other.

The International Women's Year and Decade helped to raise public awareness of the importance of women's issues and gave an impetus to research on women in Ghana. This set the stage for the development of women's studies. In response to a recommendation by the United Nations to its member states to establish appropriate machinery to accelerate the integration of women in development, the government of Ghana established the National Council on Women and Development (NCWD) in February 1975. The organization's mandate gave it several functions: to advise the government on matters concerning women in development, to conduct research on women, to monitor and evaluate projects affecting women, and to coordinate activities involving women. The establishment of the NCWD and the official attempts to "integrate" women into development created the demand for a body of knowledge on women. The funding possibilities for such research encouraged a favorable environment for the emergence of women's studies as a field of study in Ghana's universities and research institutes.

Manuh (1991) has commented that in spite of these developments, women's studies in Ghana has not fully arrived in many research and academic institutions and is still regarded as a fad, of concern to women only. Further, since many scholars, both male and female, see women's studies as a means for obtaining funding in the continuing credit squeeze in the universities, women's studies has been tolerated (and perhaps respected) only for this reason. While Manuh's point is still valid in 1995, another development has also become clear: a growing number of sensitized academics, researchers, and activists (predominantly women) are either involved in developing women's studies or introducing a gender perspective into their professional activities.

The persistence of an interest and a commitment to the study and analysis of issues that affect women may be a result of the realities for Ghanaian women. Gender inequality, marginalization, unequal access to productive resources, the constraints imposed on women through the economic crisis—all these underscore a need to keep women's studies alive. Because of their general experience of relative deprivation in relation to men, and their exposure to discrimination on the basis of sex, women are more likely to appreciate the relevance of women's studies. That may explain why women's studies is being spearheaded by women.

Women's Studies in Ghana

The main centers for research on women in Ghana are the universities. At the University of Ghana, research institutes such as the Institute of African Studies (IAS), the Institute of Statistical, Social, and Economic Research (ISSER), and the Regional Institute for Population Studies (RIPS) conduct research on women. The departments of sociology, home science, and geography and resource development also are involved in some research on women. This research is done by both staff and students, by the latter often to satisfy the requirements for the award of an undergraduate or higher degree (Manuh 1991).

At the University of Cape Coast, some research and teaching on women are undertaken at the Center for Development Studies, the faculty of education, the department of vocational and technical education, the department of sociology, and the department of English.[1] At the University of Science and Technology, little research has been conducted on women, although the Bureau of Integrated Rural Development (BIRD) has investigated issues concerning women, and students at the faculty of environmental studies and the department of land economy have carried out some research for the purposes of their long essays (Manuh 1991). Since 1994, two new universities have been established in the country, and not much teaching and research on women is done at these institutions.[2]

Currently, the only teaching program that exists in women's studies in Ghana is located within the Development and Women's Studies Program (DAWS) at the Institute of African Studies at the University of Ghana. Established in 1989, DAWS is pioneering women's studies in Ghana through the development of a graduate program in gender studies and is on the verge of opening its doors. DAWS plans to offer two yearlong courses at the graduate level: "Gender Relations in African Societies" and "Gender and Development in Africa: Politics and Practice." Some of the themes studied in "Gender Relations in African Societies" include the development of women's/gender studies and important concepts in the study of gender differences; an introduction to different feminist theories and perspectives and their relevance for gender relations in Africa; historical perspectives on gender relations in Africa; colonialism, the anticolonial struggle, independence and gender relations; the postcolonial state and gender. "Gender and Development in Africa: Politics and Practice" will cover key concepts in gender and will critique state and international policy responses to the gender dimensions of underdevelopment. It will also examine state policy and gender relations. Some of the themes to be included are an introduction to development theories and feminist critiques of development theories and policies; concepts in the feminist critique of development and their application to African societies; the history of state and international responses to gender biases in development; case studies of responses to gender critiques; the history of women's and men's involvement in African politics since independence; women organizing for change; and gender, state policy, and the environment.

At a recent DAWS Interregional Workshop in Accra (February 1995), aptly titled "Enhancing Gender Research and Training," that sought to initiate dialogue among politicians, policymakers, academicians, and nongovernmental organizations, the master's degree program was presented for discussion. The attempt by DAWS to include non-academics in its discussion of the women's studies curriculum indicates an awareness of the need to bridge the gap between theory and practice in women's and gender issues. According to Manuh (1991), who is a founding member of DAWS, the Institute of African Studies, within which DAWS is located, was for many years the locus of much of the research on women, and its biannual journal, *Research Review*, has provided a forum for the publication of research findings on women by institute staff and other scholars. The first issue of its new series in 1985 was devoted to research on Ghanaian women. For Manuh, the setting up of the DAWS program is merely a formalization of an existing tradition. The proposed DAWS master's degree course in gender studies draws on the interdisciplinary expertise of several institute staff, both male and female (Manuh 1991).

At the University of Cape Coast, a women's studies program is in the planning stages. The impetus for it came from a small organization of women faculty members and senior administrative staff who have formed a women's caucus, which among other things organizes lectures, debates, and films that deal with women's issues so that gender sensitization can take place within the campus community and the student body. The University of Cape Coast Women's Caucus (UCCWOC) in March 1995 presented a proposal for the establishment of a women's and gender studies center and program to the vice chancellor, who has set up a committee to draw up a curriculum for an interdisciplinary women's and gender studies program. The gender and women's studies courses at the University of Cape Coast will be at the undergraduate level.

The gender studies committee has recommended that women's studies at the University of Cape Coast should begin as an autonomous unit located within the African and general studies department. It is mandatory for all students to have three credits from this department, and putting women's studies there gives many students the opportunity to choose it as an option in their African and general studies course. It is proposed that the women's studies unit should eventually develop into a full department, which will serve as the university's teaching and research center for women's and gender studies.

The brief description of the development of women's studies in the two universities points to the fact that the move to introduce teaching programs in women's studies in Ghanaian universities seems to depend on an active core of sensitized lecturers taking the initiative to conduct research and teach courses focusing on issues and the position of women. To begin with, women and gender-related courses at the institutions are disparate, scattered among different faculties and departments. The next step is to coordinate all such courses in one program. The University of Cape Coast seems to be heading toward that option, while the DAWS program represents another alternative, in which an institute within the university establishes a full-fledged women's studies program.

Both options (and others) can be initiated only when there are favorable conditions for "airing" women's issues in the society. The internationalization of women's issues that occurred in the wake of the United Nations International Women's Year in 1975 and the following Decade for Women has been a major factor in the creation of a favorable atmosphere. The NCWD, after its establishment in 1975, commissioned a series of papers on the condition of Ghanaian women, and government departments such as the Ministry of Education, the Ministry of Local Government, the Ministry of Agriculture, and the Ministry of Health sponsored or commissioned studies on women to aid the formulation or implementation of policy. The donor community in Ghana, represented through bilateral and multilateral agencies, employs local and foreign consultants to undertake research on the condition and needs of women in Ghana, mainly to increase the efficacy of their development projects.

During the last two decades, a slow but steady growth in levels of gender awareness seems to have taken place, especially among Ghanaian professional women, probably as the result of a combination of factors: the UN International Women's Year and Decade; women's felt need to interpret existing realities; the "acceptance" by the political establishment that women in Ghana do face many constraints in their lives in comparison with men; and finally, the support given to women's issues by the donor community.

The Achievements of Women's Studies at the University Level

While teaching programs in women's studies have not yet formally begun, one can demonstrate that the few women's studies and gender-related courses offered at the universities have made an impact on students. Clearly, the teaching of women's studies courses positively affects students' levels of gender sensitivity. This is especially important in non-Western countries, like Ghana, that have not experienced women's political activism aimed at changing the present inequalities between men and women. Because of the ambivalence toward so-called Western feminist ideas, it may be politically expedient for feminists in non-Western cultures to work toward creating gender consciousness in a nonconfrontational manner. And this is where the teaching of gender-related and women's studies courses can be of importance. (This should not be limited to higher education.) To illustrate the process, I will describe an undergraduate course titled "Women and Society," which I taught at the University of Cape Coast in 1992. The course focused on reasons for the rise of women's issues globally in the twentieth century, introduced students to such concepts as feminism and gender, examined the feminist critiques of the social sciences, and discussed the position of women in African societies in historical perspective. Here are some comments from students:

> The course has made me aware of some of the reasons why, for example, women are somehow considered to be inferior to men.

> Where I come from it is unrealistic to sit in the kitchen to cook food or to assist my wife. Not that I do not want to do so, it is society that has created that role difference in my community, making it necessary for me to behave that way. You can find yourself being mocked at by your friends if they found you in the kitchen with your wife, cooking. However, with this course I am being exposed to new ideas, I hope to be able to rethink my decisions and carry out roles played by my wife and family.

Although the sincerity of such responses from students may be questionable, there is no doubt that women's studies and gender-related subjects do jolt the minds of students and cause them to reflect on their own attitudes toward women.[3]

The achievement of causing students to reflect on their attitudes toward women, although small, is important. Its effect could be multiplied if women's studies programs were established in some form at all levels of the educational system of the country.

The Unfinished Agenda of Women's Studies in Higher Education

The establishment and institutionalization of women's studies in Ghana's tertiary institutions are long overdue. Women have been responsible for the blossoming of interest in women's issues and women's studies in Ghana since 1975. As far as the teaching of this material is concerned, gender issues, gender-related courses, and women's studies are still largely presented as specialty courses taught by women or as a small subsection "added on" to courses that otherwise ignore women and gender/feminist issues altogether. Gender analysis and women's studies as categories in their own right need to be recognized in order that the discipline can be put on a straight course. Imam (1990) has suggested that the status of gender-related studies and courses would be enhanced if those who have ignored the subject would look at it more closely and consider how to rethink their analyses. The involvement of both men and women in understanding the social relations of gender will take us a long way.

Women are still grossly underrepresented in higher education, both as teachers and as students, and there is a need to redress this imbalance. Generally, there is a great need to raise the visibility and status of women in higher education.

The Impact of Women's Studies on the University Curriculum

At the tertiary level, women's studies generally has not yet made any visible impact on the university curriculum. At the University of Cape Coast, there are some discussions among women faculty on the necessity of factoring gender issues into syllabi. But this can hardly materialize without a basis in women's studies.

The Impact of Women's Studies on Elementary and Secondary School Curricula and Public Policies

The impact of women's studies is more evident in elementary and secondary school curricula. Ghana reformed its educational system in

1987. The structure of the new system includes a basic education of six years: three years of Junior Secondary School and three years of Senior Secondary School or Vocational/Technical Institutions. The new system attempts to make the curriculum gender-neutral. Under the new curriculum, all pupils are obliged to take such subjects as technical skills and life skills. Under the old system, subjects like home science, needlework, and cookery were done by girls, while boys did carpentry and technical subjects.

Another measure taken by the Ministry of Education under the 1987 educational reform was to make textbooks gender-sensitive and avoid sex stereotypes. This measure has been put into effect nationwide; its effectiveness has yet to be assessed. A 1994 content analysis of a textbook used in primary school, however, showed that sex stereotypes still exist (Gyamfi 1994). Attention has been given to low levels of female participation in science, technology, and mathematics education (STME). In 1987, a Commonwealth Workshop was held in Accra on the theme "Gender Stereotyping in Science and Technology." Participants from selected African countries were specifically women in science and technology and policymakers. Since that conference, STME clinics have been held for Ghanaian primary and secondary school girls annually (Sutherland-Addy et al. 1995). There is no explicit educational policy on women, although some aspects of the policy positively affect women.

The new educational system appears to be gender-sensitive in scope, and the Ministry of Education is actively taking steps to raise the level of female participation in education in Ghana. The ministry recognizes the need for increasing the status of women in tertiary education, and at the end of 1994 it commissioned a study on developing feasible strategies to increase female participation in tertiary education, especially science and technology. A firm political and financial commitment, however, is necessary in order that the objective of raising the status of women can be fulfilled.

In summary, it is fair to say that only the first steps have been taken to establish women's studies in Ghana at the tertiary level. While a favorable atmosphere among academics and policymakers can sustain the development of women's studies, there is a long road ahead before we will see its establishment and integration into all levels of education.

NOTES

1. This information is based on the results of an informal survey conducted by the Gender Studies Committee, University of Cape Coast, to determine which departments offer gender-related or women's studies courses.

2. The two new universities are the University College of Education (UCE) at Winneba and the University of Development Studies (UDS) at Tamale. UCE's department of social studies has designed a course titled "Women and Development," which has not yet been taught. At the University of Development Studies the faculty of integrated development studies has designed a course titled "Women in Rural Development," which has also not yet been taught (personal communication with the head of the department of social studies, UCE, and the dean of integrated development studies, UDS).

3. Nine out of sixteen students in my "Sociology of Sex Roles and Gender" course (which was offered in 1992 and which introduced students to the background and main trends in the discussion in sociology on sex roles and gender) chose gender-related topics for their "long essays." Long essays are dissertations based on independent research. The long essay is an important part of the undergraduate program in Ghanaian universities. Students generally write this dissertation during their final year. Some of the topics my students offered in 1992 were "The Hidden Curriculum and Gender: Teacher-Student Interaction in the Classroom," "Women and Education in the Keta District, Volta Region, Ghana," and "Television and Gender Messages: A Content Analysis of *By the Fireside*, a Children's Television Program."

The choice of such topics shows that the course stimulated the students enough that they selected gender-related research themes. A colleague in the English department has observed a similar effect among students in her class. Her "Gender and Writing" course "focuses on four women writers whose biographies have little in common except gender: George Eliot, Toni Morrison, Ama Atta Aidoo, and Nadine Gordimer. Attempts will be made to analyze the texts as a thematic unit with overarching feminist concerns" (from the course outline of Jane Opoku-Agyemang, English Department, University of Cape Coast).

REFERENCES

Chinto, Martin Adam. 1986. "Attitudes Towards Formal Education: A Case Study of Northwestern Tamale District." Unpublished long essay presented to the Faculty of Education, University of Cape Coast.

Gyamfi, Anthony Owusu. 1994. "Sex-Role Stereotyping in a Cultural Studies Textbook at Junior Secondary School Level." Unpublished long essay presented to the Faculty of Social Sciences, University of Cape Coast.

Imam, Ayesha. 1990. "Gender Analysis and African Social Sciences in the 1990's." *Africa Development* 15, nos. 3-4: 241-257.

Manuh, Takyiwaa. 1989. "A Study of Selected Voluntary Development Organizations in Ghana." In *Women as Agents and Beneficiaries of Development Assistance*. Dakar: AAWORD Occasional Paper Series no. 4.

———. 1991. "The Status of Research on Women in Ghana." Paper presented to the Women's Caucus of the African Studies Association, 22-23 November 1991, in St. Louis, Missouri.

Mensah, Joseph. 1992. "Attitudes of the Rural Folk Towards Female Education." Unpublished long essay presented to the faculty of social sciences, University of Cape Coast.

National Council for Women and Development (NCWD). 1994. *The Status of Women in Ghana 1985–1994: National Report for the Fourth World Conference on Women.* Accra: NCWD, 1994.

Osei, Juliana. 1991. "Gender Inequalities in Education and Access to the Labour Market in Ghana." Paper presented to HEP Trainees Programme in Educational Planning and Administration, Paris.

Prah, Mansah. 1992. "Women and Education." In *Proceedings of the Workshop on Gender Analysis, Development, and Women's Studies (DAWS).* Institute of African Studies, University of Ghana.

Republic of Ghana Statistical Service. 1989. *Ghana Living Standards Survey.*

Sutherland-Addy, Esi, Boatema Boateng, Juliana Osei, and Mansah Prah. 1995. *Study on Developing Feasible Strategies to Increase Female Participation in Tertiary Education, Particularly in Science and Technology: Interim Report.* Development and Women's Studies, Institute of African Studies, University of Ghana. Commissioned by the Ministry of Education, Accra, March 1995.

Twumasi, P. A. 1986. *Social Research in Rural Communities: The Problem of Fieldwork in Ghana.* Accra: Ghana Universities Press.

Mansah Prah, *a former Fulbright Scholar, is a lecturer in sociology at the University of Cape Coast, Ghana. She is a founding member and the current chair of the University of Cape Coast Women's Caucus. She is the editor of* Women's Studies with a Focus on Ghana: Selected Readings.

Women's Studies in Hungary

Katalin Koncz

Budapest, March 1995

In order to understand the situation of women's studies in Hungary, it is necessary to consider the specific political, social, and economic changes that have occurred since 1989. Before the change of regime that took place in that year, the terms "feminism" and "women's studies" were, for ideological reasons, simply not accepted in Hungary. Today these concepts are being widely discussed, but there is some disagreement on how to define these terms.

"Traditional" and "New" Feminism

In my view, feminists are those who express and protect women's interests. Within this broad definition, there exists a wide variety of feminist theoretical approaches: liberal, Marxist, African-American, socialist, essentialist, psychoanalytic, and lesbian separatist (Rosser 1992), and even existentialist and postmodern (Tong 1992). From another angle, we can also distinguish "academic feminism" (feminist scholarship) from "empirical feminism" (the women's movement), though it is important to build a bridge between the two.

Women's studies is a critical area of knowledge and its criticism has generally taken two forms: the critique of present policies and practices concerning the position of women and the critique of traditional male-centered experiences, epistemologies, and research methodologies. In Hungary, we can distinguish between two feminist approaches, divided more or less along these lines. Before the regime change, feminist institutions and feminist researchers did exist (but a feminist movement did not). The majority of feminist researchers were Marxist or socialist. They believed that gender and class both played a decisive role in any exploration of women's oppression (Tong 1992:39). Liberal feminism also had some influence. The liberal position was to "seek no special privileges for women and simply demand that everyone receive equal consideration without discrimination on the basis of sex" (Tong 1992:45). Since the change of regime, the "traditional" feminists have continued to focus on and project an overall picture of the position of women within present social, political, and economic circumstances. The traditional feminist critique contributes to the perception of female disadvantage in society and to the improvement of the position of women in the short run. Yet these feminist critiques are based on present social conditions in a male-dominated world and on masculine epistemologies and masculine methods.

After 1989, as Hungarian society began to be reshaped politically and economically along Western lines, a more diverse women's movement also emerged. The "new" feminism encompassed a wide range of feminist viewpoints, including those of radical groups. The new feminist approach provides the basis for the transformation of society in the long run to achieve gender equality.

At the present time in Hungary, these two feminist approaches are in conflict. It will be important, in the future, to respect the different kinds of knowledge, the plurality of feminist theories. The collaboration of the two approaches will enrich women's studies. I agree with the new feminists that the traditional feminist approach provides limited insights into society with regard to gender identity, because it does not draw upon feminist epistemologies. Yet the traditional feminist approach yields practical knowledge for improving the position of women within present social conditions. At the Budapest University of Economic Sciences (BUES), the women's studies courses now reflect this dichotomy. Before the regime change, women's studies research was based narrowly on traditional feminists point of view. In my opinion, we have to develop women's studies in two ways: by extending the traditional feminist approach to an interdisciplinary perspective and by integrating the new feminist approach.

Characteristics of the Change of Regime in Hungary

Hungary and the other countries of Eastern and Central Europe face a historically unparalleled task. They have embarked on a radically different course, and changes in the political and economic system are taking place simultaneously, under unfavorable internal conditions and disturbing foreign economic circumstances. The resulting tensions are creating explosive situations in the countries of the area.

In Hungary, this transformation is fundamentally rearranging the political and economic conditions of the country and, with them, the underlying human relations. It is difficult to estimate the effects, of this change—in part because of the complexity, variety, and inextricable interrelations involved and in part because of the often contradictory and limited information available to researchers. One thing, however, can be stated with absolute certainty: these radical changes deeply affect the women's (and men's) public lives, in the labor market, and in family relations. They challenge established social and individual roles, creating uncertainty and vulnerability. Individuals bear such shocks differently, depending on their social position and personality. The winners and losers in this time of change do not separate primarily along gender lines. Yet a few obvious consequences affect men and women differently.

The most important elements of the transformation are the democratization of society, the shift from public to private ownership of property and resources, and the ascendancy of the market economy. The precondition of true democracy is to ensure equal opportunity for all, regardless of gender, and to develop the institutional system needed to achieve that goal. "Democracy without women is only half a democracy" (Leuprecht 1994:2). At the same time, private industry, operating on the profit motive, focuses on the most efficient use of resources. This efficiency leads to the elimination of superfluous resources, including labor resources of below-average market productivity, such as married women with small children. This process can result in even greater differences in concentration by gender in the various branches of industry and the professions. The most important characteristic of the market economy is competition. Although in principle competitive markets are open to men and women alike, women are in fact at a disadvantage because of their social status and their different training and experiences. The rise of the market economy will further weaken their position in the labor market.

These conditions help to determine the social implications of gender and will be decisive in the coming years. The integration of Hungary into the European Community will reinforce the present tendencies. Under these circumstances, the traditional feminist approach is indispensable to the understanding and improvement of women's status in society.

Traditional Feminist Research in the Socialist Period

Before 1989, research on women's issues was limited and one-sided. Most of it focused on one goal: to increase the number of female workers, thereby serving the economic interests of the country. The continuous increase in female employment required the improvement of women's education. At the same time, a widespread system of maternity benefits ensured the reproduction and growth of the population. This required the development of an infrastructure to reconcile the double work of women—in the home and in the workforce.

The two-earner-family model became general, as a result of both the demand for labor and the available supply of it. By the early 1970s, the country had achieved "the socially possible maximum" in women's employment, to use the expression often seen in Hungarian economic literature. Most women who remained at home belonged to the older age group, had a low level of schooling, or lived in scattered settlements.

During this period (1950–89), only a few researchers worked on women's issues. The predominant approaches were economic and statistical. There was very little literature of high intellectual quality. Most publications served the glorification and survival of the socialist system. Books in foreign languages were also not available. During the later part of the period, sociological and interdisciplinary studies appeared, and research on social inequalities came to the fore. Studies were carried out on the division of labor within the family and society, raising new issues of social inequality. Empirical sociological studies and life-course studies were also produced at the time, and some translations of well-known books were published, notably the books of Evelyn Sullerot (1963, 1973).

During this period there was much discussion of the contribution of women to the economy, specifically the GDP (gross domestic product). About 40 percent of women's work is invisible work, in households and in agriculture. Feminists argued that it was necessary to recognize invisible female work in national accounts and to remunerate women for it. Feminists also analyzed the child care system and its conse-quences for the division of labor within the family and the employ-ment of women. It was their conclusion that, contrary to socialist belief and practice, extended employment is not sufficient to ensure the full emancipation of women. The emancipation of women is a broader concept, which involves all aspects of gender roles in society.

Traditional Feminist Research After the Regime Change

The social transformation that began in 1989 affected the impact of gender on all spheres of society—on public policy, on the labor market, and on the family. Feminist research has concentrated on the nature of change and its effects on the position of women, particularly in these three areas. The preparations for the UN Fourth World Confer-ence on Women provided an initiative for studying the social position of women and the role of women in social change. In March 1995 the

Hungarian National Committee was set up. It included representatives from government agencies concerned with women, women's sections of political parties and trade unions, and the women's movement. As a consequence of the Beijing conference, there is a strong possibility that the national institutions will be built for greater participation of women in the political decision-making processes.

Women in Policy

One result of the pluralization and democratization process in Hungary, which may at first seem paradoxical, is that women have been pushed into the background in the political decision-making process. The government has no women's policy or any office responsible for women's issues. However, feminist researchers are examining various forms of political participation—the participation of women in the legislative and executive power structure, in political parties, trade unions, and the development of women's movements. Researchers at the Women's Studies Center at Budapest University of Economic Sciences have engaged in a variety of cross-cultural analyses and comparisons. The findings of these traditional feminist researchers offer a point of departure for improving the position of women in the period of transition to democracy. The political leadership of Hungary is insensitive to the female question of equal opportunity for women. If it deals with this question at all, it does so exclusively for population and family reasons, neglecting the demands, expectations, and possibilities of particular women and the requirements of their human evolution and development. The question of women's equality is increasingly obliterated from the consciousness of most Hungarians, who are shackled by the struggles of everyday life.

The deteriorating economic situation of families and the renewal of the traditional division of labor that binds women again to the home as well as to work make women's lives increasingly more difficult to organize and leave little energy for child care, rest, relaxation, and hobbies. Without the public support needed to reconcile the double burden of women with children, their participation in public life is a mere chimera, an undertaking that inevitably fails. Under these conditions women's movements are still too weak to become a major force in shaping politics and society. In their everyday lives, women face a continuous and drastic rise in the prices of basic products, a steady increase in taxation, and a decrease in support for child care institutions, as well as decaying household machinery and outdated, midcentury methods of housework.

Women in the Labor Market

Traditional feminist research continues to address both the quantitative and the qualitative characteristics of women's presence in the labor market. Under socialism, the very expression "labor market" was forbidden for ideological reasons: the labor force cannot be merchandise in a socialist society where exploitation by capital does not exist. Under the market system, the continuous expansion of employment ceases to exist, and the economy's demand for labor decreases. In Hungary, the labor market conditions have undergone a complete change, manifested by a rapid increase in the rate of unemployment. This lack of labor market equilibrium has led some to suggest that women should be forced back into the home. This view, from the feminist interpretation, is no solution. This idea would crush the accomplishments, thus far, of the emancipation process. According to a 1988 Central Statistical Office (CSO) survey, three-fourths of the women would not stop paid work even if they could afford to (Central Statistical Office 1988:11). Paid work has been built into the value systems of most women, who do not wish to renounce the advantages offered by it, especially the opportunities for higher education.

The lack of part-time employment is a special problem for women in Eastern and Central European countries. In Hungary, among those women who wanted to work, more than four-fifths said they would like the opportunity to work part-time and to work at home. Part-time work can, of course, result in significant loss of income (Central Statistical Office 1988:11). It also should not be overlooked that a number of discriminatory elements can be found in part-time employment. Lower-than-average wages, limited opportunities for promotion, and less employment security are characteristics of part-time employment. The danger will presumably also arise that some of those who undertake part-time jobs will do so not spontaneously but because they have no possibility for full-time jobs. This is a form of hidden unemployment, which primarily affects women. It is best to avoid using part-time employment as a remedy for unemployment, because international experience had not proved this approach to be viable. In Hungary, well-considered measures are needed to eliminate, insofar as possible, the discriminatory elements of the system. A kind of affirmative action (the stimulation of employment) also may become temporarily necessary. The elaboration of specific alternatives requires research specifically organized for this purpose.

Solutions to the inflexibility of employment and the improvement of the labor market's equilibrium are equally important to achieve better living and labor conditions for individuals and families. The traditional feminist researchers propose freer choices for both genders by creating, at the same time, the conditions needed for choosing. It is also important that men and women be able to change to different forms of employment (full-time or part-time) at various stages in their careers, to suit their special needs.

The traditional feminist researchers have also analyzed the process and structure of unemployment. As a result of the economy's decreasing labor demands, unemployment rose at an extraordinarily fast rate in the years following the political and economic change, until the first part of 1993. Then the number of unemployed began to decrease. Everywhere in the world, the real numbers of unemployed are higher than the recorded ones—especially among women. A portion of women are not entitled to unemployment benefits, and therefore they do not even appear to register in the labor offices. Others do not appear because they have no hope that the employment agencies will find an appropriate job for them.

In 1991–95, the proportion of women within the registered unemployed was 42 percent—lower than their proportion within the active earners, 49.5 percent. The feminization of unemployment has not yet appeared in Hungary, as it has in the majority of the developed market economies and in the other Eastern and Central European countries. Female underrepresentation among the unemployed derives from the characteristics of the economic structural reorganization: the employment rate decreased in heavy industry, where the proportion of women is low. The traditional feminist critique points out, however, that in the future, following the reform in public administration and light industry, the numbers of female unemployed will increase. The prevention of the deterioration of female employment requires an effective training project for a better reintegration of women into a changing labor market.

In general, the position of women in the labor market is jointly determined by the preconditions under which they enter the market, by their chances of improvement within the market, and by their ability to protect their interests. According to the traditional feminist critique, women entering the labor market are at a disadvantage. The level of their professional skills is generally below that of men, and because of the double burden deriving from their social position, they sometimes find it difficult to adjust to the requirements of the workplace. For these reasons—and because of the deeply rooted negative attitude towards female labor in the workplace—men have an advantage over women in finding jobs.

The educational level of the female population has lately shown a significant upward trend. In the case of the younger generations, more women than men are completing secondary and higher education. But women's position in the labor market has not improved proportionally. The feminist critique underscores the fact that the labor market does not primarily reward schooling, but rather vocational skills, experience, and practice, and ranks the skills and professions to women's disadvantage. The structure of female schooling, its concentration in certain areas, and the preponderance of women in certain educational institutions contribute to their disadvantageous position in the competition of the labor market.

After the regime change, the private sector began to dominate the labor market. In the private sphere the profit motive has a strong effect on the recruitment and selection of employees. According to certain indications, this weakens the employment opportunities for women in private-sector jobs, which carry higher prestige and income. The lack of equal opportunity for women in Hungary may be seen in the feminization of the state employees, with their lower salary (three-quarters of state employees are women) as well as in the masculine character of the sphere of private ownership (two-thirds of the owners are men).

Several feminist studies relate to the promotion of women. They find that vertical mobility among women—their chances of being promoted and becoming managers—is more limited than among men. Most women remain at the bottom of the employment pyramid, in badly paid, monotonous jobs, in unfavorable conditions, and with little chance of promotion. In the world of blue-collar jobs the majority of women are semi-skilled or unskilled workers. Though the proportion of women among managers rose in the past decade, the underrepresentation of women in such positions is still remarkable. In 1990, 45 percent of men employed in white-collar jobs were in managerial positions, while only 15 percent of women were managers (Central Statistical Office 1992:84–87). Discrimination against women appears to be most conspicuous at the top levels of power.

Wage and income differences also reflect women's disadvantages in the labor market, although their income positions have improved in the past decades. In Hungary, women earned 71 percent of men's gross average income in 1990 (Central Statistical Office 1991:53). The difference is explained partly by objective facts and partly by the consequence of persistent discrimination, which is expressed in nonmeasurable or not-easily-measurable activities. For older women, for example, the wage gap opens as a direct consequence of limited promotions among women. The feminists criticize the wage and income differences and propose to eliminate the objective and discriminatory causes of these gender differences. One feminist study (Koncz 1995) emphasizes how, during the years of the changing political system, the feminization of poverty also came to light.

New Feminist Criticism After the Regime Change

Paralleling the appearance of a pluralistic women's movement in Hungary, the "new feminist" critique has opened up new horizons and brought new angles and feminist perspectives into research. Its epistemological interest is situated in the analysis of women's oppression and discrimination and in the conceptualization of new gender relationships. The new feminist approach discovers new spheres of feminist knowledge and experiences. It criticizes the sexist prejudices that characterize the majority of traditional scientific approaches to knowledge, and it imposes new analytical categories and new concepts and methods on gender relationships. The new feminist approach protests the sexual oppression of women and the mechanisms that perpetuate the patriarchal system and gives great importance to the abortion issue and to violence against women. (A new organization was born to help battered women.) These last issues are neglected in traditional feminist research.

In 1994 an important book, titled *Male Domination* (Hadas 1994), was published. It was the first book in Hungarian offering "new feminist" approaches. The foreign authors (Martha Lampland, Gayle Rubin, bell hooks, Philip Corrigan, and Donna Haraway) represent new voices and new areas of knowledge for Hungarians. Nearly all Hungarian researchers have, until now, based their work on the traditional feminist approaches.

Women's Studies and the Women's Movement

In the Western European countries and in the United States there is a strong relationship between women's studies and the women's movement; women's studies has been greatly influenced by the women's movement. In the Eastern and Central European countries, inversely, the academic world has inspired the development of a women's movement. Women's studies analyzes the social position and the various disadvantages of women, thereby shaping the course of women's political work. However, the cooperation of researchers and women's activists is insufficient. Academic scholarship and the women's movement remain separate from each other. They have a small, productive connection through certain persons, yet only a few experts take part in the women's movement and introduce their research results in practice.

In Hungary, as part of the overall change in the political system, the women's movement has grown more and more pluralized, and the political parties have established their women's sections one after the other. At present, support for the movement is limited. Under the present conditions grass-roots organizing of Hungary's atomized female society can only be a slowly and gradually ripening process.

The Institutionalization of Women's Studies

In Hungary the development of women's studies and its introduction to the universities' curricula is part of the democratization process, which is a very contradictory process. On the one hand, the pluralization of society and of the women's movement has begun, but on the other hand, women have been pushed into the background of the political decision-making process. These circumstances determine the possibilities and raise the obstacles for the development of women's studies.

The development of true democracy requires the elimination of all forms of discrimination. Discrimination against women originates, in part, from traditional attitudes, which can be changed only through the educational system. Therefore, women's studies should be part of all education, and research concerning women's issues serves the future educational process. In the past and today as well, women's studies was initiated and supported by women researchers dealing with women's issues. Many are also active in the women's movement. Research aimed at furthering the principle of equality between men and women is in progress in Hungary within the framework of academic institutes at the universities.[1]

Most of the research concerning women's issues is done by women on their own initiative. Women's studies researchers are in a precarious situation in Hungary. Often they do "double" research. First they do the official and obligatory research for the institute where they are working; then they pursue research in women's studies for their own interests. Often they are volunteers, and their research on women's issues is an addition to their regular work.

The foreign women's studies theories were important sources of inspiration. Hungarian feminist scholars have always been in contact with foreign theories and women's studies organizations (especially American, British, and German). The Women's Studies Center at

Budapest University of Economic Sciences (BUES) has contact with more than fifty women's studies organizations worldwide.

The integration of women's studies at the university level is still not sufficient in Hungary, and the institutionalization of women's studies is limited. Very positive progress has been made in the last few years, however, owing considerably to the initiatives of the European Network on Women's Studies (ENWS). The Women's Studies Center at BUES was officially set up in October 1992. It is the first and only WSC in Hungary.

Our WSC is a formal and officially recognized center for teaching and research on women's studies. It facilitates and promotes the research and teaching of gender issues in various disciplines. According to the conceptional framework of the WSC, gender is the main subject of women's studies; women's studies is an interdisciplinary research movement; and the complex issues of gender cannot be dealt with within the framework of one single scientific discipline or methodological and theoretical approach. Our WSC is an independent organization that integrates the work of the different departments of the university and academic institutes.

The educational reform in progress at BUES, based on Western European practice, makes possible the introduction of new courses or topics and the extension of free choice to students to plan their own curriculum. It was under these circumstances that the university accepted my proposal to set up the WSC. The strategy and mission of the WSC are to introduce gender theory and gender interests into education and research, to integrate gender issues into the social sciences, and to help change, through education and mass media, the way society thinks about gender issues. I work alone with a secretary in the WSC. The center invites people from other departments of the university and academic institutes to teach and do research. The Budapest University of Economic Sciences was always one of the important sources of research concerning women's issues; researchers in various departments—sociology, economics—had previously offered announced courses on women's issues.

At the beginning, the WSC launched women's studies courses in the form of faculty seminars, discussions in small groups at the graduate and postgraduate levels. While no degree is offered in women's studies, any student can choose to take the women's studies courses. Course descriptions are as follows:

- "The Social Position of Women and Men" involves the most important aspects of the social position of women and men. It analyses the biological, psychological, and social differences of gender and the origins of these differences.

■ "The Successful Women" helps students use practical knowledge to be more effective and successful. It uses small-group discussions and role playing. It analyzes the strong and weak points of women, emphasizing the importance of assertiveness and a more dominant attitude for women.

■ "The Social Position of Women from a Historical Point of View" is a sociohistoric analysis of gender roles. It follows the lives of men and women across different historical eras and regimes.

■ "Women in the Labor Market" examines the level and structure of female employment and unemployment in a cross-cultural and historical context. The position of women in the labor market is presented as the consequence of gendered social roles.

■ "Women in the Hierarchy" focuses on the situation of women in political and managerial positions. Broad issues of power, politics, and empowerment are analyzed from diverse historical, cultural, economic, and social perspectives.

The second goal of the WSC is the integration of women's studies into the conventional research programs and the organization of research projects on women's issues. We are taking part in international studies, and we participated in the development of the Hungarian program for the UN Fourth World Conference on Women.

A student research group works at the Women's Studies Center. The common research involves a process of getting students to think in critical ways about gender. Some students study the career motivations, attitudes, and aspirations of female students on the basis of a questionnaire/survey. Twenty students have written studies on a highly scientific level dealing with different women's issues. Two of these students participated in international conferences with their studies. The students' papers will soon be published in the first WSC periodical.

An informal research network was created among the researchers inside and outside the university who deal with women's issues. The WSC has forged links with the other research institutes. There are about twenty-five to thirty people and eight research institutes in Hungary whose research includes some aspects of women's issues. The main focus of the research network is the mutual sharing of information concerning research results and the possibilities for participation in international research projects and conferences. The network also promotes the introduction of gender-based perspectives into other research fields and organizes common interdisciplinary research projects. The coordination of research concerning women's issues is an important part of the work of the Women's Studies Center. Thus far, women's studies has not made a deep impact on Hungarian society. Women's issues are not at the forefront of social interest. Our times are not favorable for the development of new disciplines. An important barrier to the efficient functioning of the WSC is the lack of financial resources—as it is generally in the Eastern and Central European countries. Budapest University has financial difficulties simply in providing for basic education. Under these circumstances, it cannot offer sufficient support for the WSC. It is extremely important, therefore, for the WSC to find other Hungarian and international possibilities for financial support. In 1993, I established, with my own money, the Science for Women Foundation. The British Council contributed to the establishment of a women's studies library, and we now have the largest women's studies collection in the country. The Hungarian Telecommunication Company has financed some students' research. The National Scientific Research Fund has financed an international study on the position of women in policymaking. American Peace Corps volunteers are teaching English for our staff.

The best possible solution to the financial problems may be to make every effort to create an international fund (with the help of international organizations such as the United Nations Organization, the Council of Europe, UNESCO, and other important international institutions) for the establishment of women's studies institutes in Central and Eastern European countries.

NOTE

1. Budapest University of Economic Sciences, Semmelweis University of Medicine, Hungarian Institute for Educational Research, Lóránd Eötvös Science University, Demographic Research Institute, Central Statistical Office, Research Institute of Labor, Research Institute of Sociology.

REFERENCES

Beauvoir, Simone de. 1969. *A második nem* (The second sex). Budapest: Gondolat.
Bureau International du Travail. 1990. "Document technique de base." Paper presented at Colloque tripartit sur l'égalité de chances et de traitment pour les hommes et les femmes en matière d'emploi dans les pays industrialisés, Geneva, 19–23 November 1990 SEEIC.
Central Statistical Office. 1988. *A nők helyzete a munkahelyen és a családban* (The situation of women in the workplace and in families). Budapest: Népesedésstatisztikai Fosztály (Department of Population Statistics).

————. 1991. *Magyar statisztikai évkönyv 1990* (Hungarian Statistical Yearbook 1990). Budapest.

Frey, Mária. 1993. "Nõk a munkaerõpiacon" (Women in the labor market). *Társadalmi Szemle* (Social Review) 3: 26–36.

Hadas, Miklós. 1994. *Férfiuralom: Írások nõkrõl, férfiakról, feminizmusról* (Male domination: Studies on women, on men, on feminism). Budapest: Replika Kör.

H. Sas, Judit. 1993. "Nõies nõk és férfias férfiak. A nõkkel és a férfiakkal kapcsolatos társadalmi sztereotípiák élete és eredete" (Feminine women and masculine men: The origin and life of the social stereotypes concerning women and men). *Tér és Társadalom* (Space and society), nos. 1–2. Budapest: Akadémiai Kiadó.

Hrubos, Ildikó. 1993. "A férfiak és nõk iskolai végzettsége és szakképzettsége" (The educational level and qualifications of men and women). In Hadas 1994, pp. 196–209.

Koncz, Katalin. 1985. *Nõk és férfiak: Hiedelmek, tények.* (Women and men: Myths, facts). Budapest. Kossuth Könyvkiadó.

————. 1987. *Nõk a munkaerõpiacon* (Women in the labor market). Budapest: Közgazdasági és Jogi Könyvkiadó (Publisher of Economics and Law).

————. 1995. "A felsõvezetés véleménye: a nõk helyzetérõl" (Opinion of top leaders on the position of women). Budapest: OTKA (National Scientific Research Fund). Kézírat. Unpublished manuscript.

————. 1995. "A nõk társadalmi helyzete Magyarországon" (The social position of women in Hungary). *Társadalmi Szemle* (Social Review) 3: 14–26.

————. 1995. "Women in Policy: The Hungarian Case." Paper presented at the Fifth World Congress for Central and East European Studies, Warsaw, 6–11 August 1995.

Nagy, Beáta. 1994. "Women in Management." *Sociológiai Szemle/Sociological Review* 2: 95–114.

Nelson, Barbara, and Najma Chowdhury. 1994. *Women in Politics Worldwide.* New Haven and London: Yale University Press.

Pongrácz, Tiborné. 1993. "Párkapcsolat, reprodukció, gazdasági aktivitás kérdései a nõk szempontjából" (Relation of couples, reproduction, economic activity from a feminist perspective). Social Welfare Ministry, Cabinet of Human Policy, Budapest. Unpublished manuscript.

Rosser, Sue V. 1992. "Are the Feminist Methodologies Appropriate for the Natural Sciences and Do They Make a Difference?" *Women's Studies International Forum* 15, nos. 5–6: 535–50.

Sullerot, Evelyn. (1971). *A nõi munka története és szociológiája* (The history and sociology of female work). Budapest: Gondolat Könyvkiadó (Publisher Tought).

————. 1983. *A nõi nem. Tények és kérd jelek.* (The female sex: Facts and marks). Budapest: Gondolat Könyvkiadó (Publisher Tought).

Szegvári, Katalin N. 1981. *Út a nõk egyenjogúságához* (Way to the emancipation of women). Budapest: Kossuth.

Tong, Rosemarie. 1992. *Feminist Thought: A Comprehensive Introduction*. London: Routledge.

Tóth, Olga. 1994. "A nõi életút Magyarországon" (The life-course of women in Hungary). In Hadas 1994, pp. 223–35.

Katalin Koncz *is associate professor at the Budapest University of Economic Sciences. She teaches in the department of human resources and is head of the Women's Studies Centre. Her research interests include employment policy and human resource management on women, women in the labor market, and women in political decision-making processes.*

Women's Studies in Latvia

Irina Novikova

Women are the majority in both of the largest segments of society—ethnic Latvian and ethnic Russian—53 percent of the population. Having Latvian-speaking and Russian-speaking communities of women is a new and specific political, social, and national situation in a country with a very short modern tradition of nation-statehood. As such, the two communities need to be considered by Latvian women's organizations and women researchers in women's and gender studies.

Women's issues were never articulated as important and autonomous during the process of national mobilization for regaining independence in the late 1980s and early 1990s. Fifteen women were elected as representatives of different political parties to the one-hundred-seat national parliament during the first elections after the restoration of political independence. Their representation of different political interests did not, however, allow them to cooperate in the promoting of women's issues and interests during the transitional period. But it is noteworthy that women won two to five in the elections of the local governments in 1994, and this victory may become a significant landmark in the awareness of women of the necessity for active political participation and representation of women's issues in the institutions of political power.

The antipathy of the majority of women to political lobbying of their interests and rights is rooted in many aspects of both historical and present-day reality. Among them, the effects of the past Soviet "sex equality" politics and the "revival-of-old-values" politics in the post-Soviet national state rebuilding are interacting factors that strongly affect women's status in Latvia. Women live and work in the midst of a backlash response to the "double burden" and its everyday stresses under economically aggravated conditions in the USSR of the 1980s. The complex experience of women's emancipation in the Soviet period is interpreted as an exemplary failure of the very principle of gender equality. At the same time, the current neopatriarchal politics of postsocialist nation-state rebuilding in Latvia has been strongly attached to the idea of the return to past traditions, values, and roles. The idea is strengthened through the growing conservative tendencies of church. Today, however, the situation of women in Latvia is different in many respects from that of women in the prewar nation-state before its incorporation into the USSR in 1940, and the politics of returning women to the domestic sphere and to patterns of subordination (vertical and horizontal segregation in the labor market) is part of various mechanisms that stratify today's political-economic hierarchy in ways that are harmful to women individually and collectively. The economic restructuring from command to market economy has also proved deprivileging to the political, social, and reproductive rights of women and to their status as citizens.

Apart from all this, the Western market economy enters the underdeveloped national market in the form of competent and highly competitive intervention and contributes to pushing women to the economic edges of the labor market and the margins of society. Moreover, the process of state rebuilding also signals a threatening division among women across their national-political identities by effecting the citizenship law, which grants the status of citizen to those who lived in Latvia before 1940 and their ancestors and the status of resident to people who settled in the country after 1940 and their ancestors. The political and representational ideology of differences, "citizenshipped" into two large ethnic communities, is a distinctive dimension of patriarchal pressures in Latvian society that blocks in many ways the search for commonalities in the social and economic experiences of women.

This complicated process is also indicative of the tendency toward strengthening the dichotomy of private versus public. Its complex dynamics are constituted, on the one hand, by the reproduction of the "family-state" controversy of the socialist period and, on the other hand, as a symptomatic effect of marketization upon post-Soviet restructuring of gender roles. The relationship between this process and the prevalence of women's representations as mothers and homemakers ("artists of the interior") in the mass media has been obvious. And this process takes place when women are really confused, in the aftermath of rapid changes, about challenges to their notions of women's place and women's bodies in today's symbolic integration, the attempt to become a "cultural fragment" of the West and especially of the United States of America.

Women's Organizations in Latvia

The Council of Latvian Women's Organizations includes the representatives of women's associations, political parties, and unions as well as public or professional women's organizations. Among them, such organizations as the Latvian Women's League and the Latvian Association of Academically Involved Women are the successors to women's organizations that existed in the Republic of Latvia before 1940. The ideologies of existing women's organizations vary. Generally, the goals of many women's organizations in Latvia focus on providing material assistance to impoverished women, including both single and divorced mothers. Such charity organizations are most numerous since women assume that their public duty is to help old people, women, and children. The Latvian Women's League started as a movement of soldiers' mothers to protect their sons from Soviet military service. Currently, its attention is focused on assisting women during this difficult transitional period. Single and divorced mothers are the target groups for another public organization, Initiative-Help-Love, headed by Lubov' Druktein. Only one women's organization deals with women's involvement in politics: the Women's Social Democratic Organization, founded in 1991 and headed by Laila Balga. Its aims include the education of women about their political rights, their struggle for active political participation, and the representation of women on local and national levels. Until recently, there was no feminist and women's independent liberation movement in the country. A small group of women registered as the Feminist Movement of Latvia in the summer of 1994, with Tatyana Skamaranga as president. In many ways the development of women's organizations has been influenced by the fact that the society is divided into two language communities and two collective identities, and Russian-speaking women are not numerous in women's organizations. Existing women's nongovernmental organizations are weak, and they are not experienced in lobbying, networking, and especially working with women divided.

Women's Studies: Questions for Our Future

Women's studies as an interdisciplinary educational practice currently searches for a model in a country in which assuming feminist critical approaches toward existing culture are next to impossible; in which women's studies is viewed negatively as uprooting tradition; and in which a women's independent movement is still invisible. As Slovenka Drakulich argues:

> The limitations of that feminism, when faced with economics of scarcity rather than affluence, are immediately apparent, and an urgent task facing Western feminists is to learn to listen to accounts

of the lives and experiences of women in the East. Fundamental issues about women's relationships to the state and the public world and to the culture, in the most general sense, are all differently constructed if the prevailing social ideology has been one of collectivism rather than individualism. The powerful, informing, and sustaining alliance between Western feminism and Western individualism has had little history in societies in which individuals have been expected to make common sense with the state, and a one-party state at that.

In this context, the task is not only to appropriate new knowledge and to integrate this new knowledge into teaching. It is also to become intellectually and politically empowered through the analysis of women's relationships to the state, to the public world, to the culture, and to learn how to use feminist theoretical frameworks for the analysis of the present-day divided constructions of women's experiences in our bicultural society, thus giving space and historical understanding to women activists.

The perspectives of women's studies have to be viewed also in terms of the problems of women's participation in educational and research structures. Higher educational establishments have traditionally had a high percentage of female students and lecturers. Female students prevail at pedagogical institutions. In the Academy of Culture, established in 1991, 70 percent of the students are female. At the University of Latvia, humanities departments have been traditionally "female." Women have also been a majority among the teaching staffs of schools and other educational institutions. But the "glass ceiling" effect has also been evident in academe. Women have been significantly underrepresented in the decision-making bodies of the University of Latvia and other institutions of higher education.

Today the feminization of secondary and higher education has been viewed as one more indicator of the failed politics of gender equality in the intellectual and educational spheres. A popular opinion among women as well as men is that the so-called crisis of masculinity ("Where have strong men vanished to?") is the combined consequence of the double burden of women in the family (too much involvement of women in the labor market) and the feminization of teaching staff in educational structures. But it is never stressed that the production of knowledge and ideology always remained the patriarchal prerogative of the Soviet order, in which women functioned as both objects and conductors of "sex equality" politics.

Today a woman is expected to reconsider and prioritize her duties in the family, which are claimed as the domain of her real power, although the economic necessity of a woman's involvement in the labor market also insists on her participation in social production. What is important is that her workplace at school or at the university has become the site of the post-Soviet mode of patriarchal interventionist politics. It is here that a woman is pressed into another construction of her secondary position as intellectually devalued Other. No wonder that a woman's consciousness as an intellectual worker-citizen (teacher, lecturer, researcher, etc.) is under direct and indirect attack from biodeterminists in politics, the mass media, and academe and that this situation thus affects the resulting politics of educational and research priorities.

Another side of the problem is that jobs in the system of secondary and higher education are among the lowest paid. Some research structures have simply ceased to exist. As a result, a number of qualified young women researchers have left the academic system for better-paid jobs in the developing private sector. My women colleagues at the university often say bitterly that only "rich" women can afford to work at the university. Many women educators who have other skills (the knowledge of foreign languages, for example) are engaged in additional work for the financial support of the family. Such overwork diverts them from their research interests and careers.

At present, women educators are also confronted with the transformation of students' motivations, interests, and choices, the results of the economic restructuring of a society and social remobilization. The "free market" has affected the supply-and-demand balance in the relationship between educational structures and the labor market, with the growing private sector and the dwindling educational and research network.

The present-day situation is rather discouraging for developing women's and gender studies as interdisciplinary educational and research projects. This field is plagued by misunderstandings about its aims and by misrepresentations of its origins and influences. It is not taken seriously, and it remains not even marginal but nonexistent in the attention of educational authorities. Feminism is regarded as an "imported" jeopardy, an alien colonization of women's minds and souls, tradition, and culture. Feminism, not as an object of research and teaching but as a theory, discourse, and practice, is viewed as contaminating the knowledge-teaching process, since it can generate an autonomous intellectual and ideological discourse and produce alternative frames of reference.

A significant aspect of this problem, in my view, is the appropriation itself of feminist conceptual frameworks as objects, usually described and interpreted within our Eastern European/Baltic/Latvian
cultural models, meanings, and values of womanhood. This is part of
a wider problem of knowledge appropriation and production today,
during the post-Soviet epistemological crisis. What we know and read
and hear (and the access is random) about feminist discourse and
movements is usually labeled as American feminism or, more generally, as Western feminism. Feminism is regarded as an American
invention, a rather negative aspect of American influences upon the
process of national and cultural traditionalization.

Institutionally, women's studies as a teaching project has not yet
been developed either at the level of women's general education or in
higher education establishments. There are no university posts for
women's studies, not a single department or center of women's studies
at either the University of Latvia or other educational institutions.
Researchers of women's issues work primarily in their academic disciplines. They also cooperate with women researchers in their own
fields or in other fields on various research projects. Often women's
issues are merely included as parts of more general research projects.
Ultimately, organizing Latvian research projects in a gender perspective depends upon funding from the state-aided higher educational
institutions. Since the educational system and research institutions
are now in transition, the support must be sought from outside the
country.

Among other problems, we also confront the difficulty of publishing
the results of research on women for a Latvian audience. So far, only
two collections of articles have been published, and they merely outline such problematic processes as women and poverty, women and
migration of the labor force, young women and life options, women
and education. Such difficulties in publishing articles and books occur
also with regard to promoting information about international developments in women's and gender studies and feminist thought. The
work of collecting, coordinating, and disseminating such information
has become the function of the Women's Studies Information Center,
founded in 1993 and directed by Parsla Eglite, now called the Center of
Research on Women. It is a unit under the umbrella of the Institute of
Demography at the Academy of Sciences of Latvia.

The center "collects statistical and scientific survey data, as well as
publications, memoirs, photographs, and other information about the
women of Latvia; ensures that the above-mentioned information is
made available to the public and all persons interested; advises on

various aspects of research in the field of Women's Studies, as well as advises in the sphere of women's rights; organizes group discussions and seminars; prepares statistical and the scientific survey data about the women of Latvia for publication; performs the research for specially initiated projects" (Eglite 1994:202). But, as Inna Zarinya points out, the center "differs from the model spread abroad because in the nearest future the ties with a direct study process have not been envisaged"(Eglite 1994:202).

Apart from the Center of Research on Women, various women scholars from the Academy of Sciences and the University of Latvia are involved in research projects on women's issues. Among them are Dr. Maiya Ashmane (whose topic is "A Woman of Latvia in the Processes of Social Mobility"), Dr. Ilze Trapenciere ("Woman and Family"), Dagmara Beitnere ("Masculinity and Femininity in Latvian Mythology"), and Dr. Maiga Kruzmetra ("Rural Women and Legal Reform in the Transitional Period"). In 1994 Ella Buceniece of the Academy of Sciences and Ausma Cimdinya of the University of Latvia started a joint research project on feminism and Latvian culture. The first results were two articles outlining the history of Western feminism and translations of excerpts from Simone de Beauvoir's *The Second Sex* in the literary monthly *Karogs*.

The experiences of the first women's studies center and of women scholars involved in research on women suggest that women scholars need to understand the significant differences between women's and gender studies as interdisciplinary projects built on feminist conceptual frameworks, on the one hand, and "research on women" in the traditional sense of mainstream academic activities as we had in the Soviet period, on the other. It must be emphasized that our awareness of Western feminist theory and feminist methods is not the question of their transmission or blind adaptation in research and teaching. In our sharply different cultural context we have to develop our consciousness as feminist researchers, educators, and teachers in Latvia.

Second, the development of a woman researcher's consciousness as a feminist is closely related to her awareness of the necessity to raise Latvian women's issues in the context of patriarchal restructurings of the society that are harmful to women's status, self-esteem, and consciousness. Among the issues that should be raised by women researchers on women today and integrated into the programs in women's education and university curricula are the problems of violence and women, of reproductive issues, of nationalism and women, of citizenship and gender identification in a bicultural society.

A very important issue on our agenda is the problem of definition. In the Soviet period we had to deal with the "industrialized" production of knowledge about women. The feminine was obviously confined to the structural position of the object of patriarchal knowledge. This is one of the reasons we feel some confusion about and even resistance to using the term "women's studies." The term, generated in other political and cultural conditions, is often perceived differently in our context. The term "gender studies" suggests a more useful and productive perspective, since it lets us, first, stress the interdependence of the sociocultural variables functioning in the production and reproduction of gender relations and, second, challenge the construction of woman again, but this time as the object of post-Soviet neopatriarchal ideologies.

Another issue related to the introduction of feminist conceptual frameworks is the problem of language. The languages of two large communities, Latvian and Russian, reflect the absence of gender-sensitive awareness among either politicians, mass media people (including women journalists), or educators-researchers. Moreover, the ideas or concepts of women's and gender studies, when introduced in the English language, are sometimes perceived as alien or different by our audience. For example, our audience has various cultural perceptions of the terms "patriarchy," "gender," "politics," or of the dichotomy private/public, etc. On the other hand, the English language remains the only channel through which feminist ideas are now gradually introduced. We are more acquainted with Western, Anglo-American, and French (in English translations) feminisms and less with a wide range of feminist experiences and strategies in various political and cultural contexts of Latin America, Africa, and Asia.

Given all of the above-mentioned problems, the institutionalization of women's studies as a teaching experience is quite a problem for us. Some university women teachers, usually those who have tenured positions in mainstream subjects and departments, integrate feminist issues into their teaching courses and pay particular attention to revising the history and culture of women in Latvia. But they have to face skepticism and irony from their colleagues, both men and women, because feminist studies are treated as culturally hostile and divisive. At present, only a few women scholars of the University of Latvia offer special women-oriented courses for the students of their departments. One of these scholars is Dr. Ausma Cimdinya, who teaches the course for M.A. students called "Feminist Literary Criticism and Latvian Women's Literature," which she developed to address the tradition of Latvian women's writing. I myself have taught several courses in the

department of English and in other universities, such as "Introduction
to Women's Studies"(M.A. students, 1992), "Women's Issues in Post-
Communism" (M.A. students, State University of New York at Albany,
1994), "Gender Issues in Russian Culture" (University of Helsinki,
March 1995), and "Ethnic Women's Literature and Feminism in the
USA" (M.A. students, Spring 1995). In teaching my own courses at the
Faculty of Foreign Languages, I do not have problems with the transla-
tion of Anglo-American sources, since English is the working language
for the students and teaching staff of the department. I usually supply
my students with books (on reserve in the department library) or
copies of the texts. The reading list for the course called "Ethnic
Women's Literature and Feminism" included short stories of Louise
Erdrich, Maria Viramontes, and Alice Walker, and the novels of Zora
Neale Hurston, Gloria Naylor, Sandra Cisneros, and Leslie Marmon
Silko. The articles from *Feminist Studies/Critical Studies*, edited by Ter-
esa de Lauretis, and the anthology of literary theory and criticism
Feminisms, edited by Robyn R. Warhol and Diane Price Herndl, were
used for readings and workshops.

In the spring term Dagmara Beitnere will introduce the course on
feminist history, theory, and practice (in the Latvian language) at the
Private College of Social Workers "Attistiba," which we consider to be
a very important step toward institutionalization of women's and
gender studies as an educational and teaching project.

The discussion of feminist theory and its impact on contemporary
philosophical and sociological thought are parts of general lecture
courses by Skaidrite Lasmane of the faculty of philosophy of the
University of Latvia and Silvia Senykane of the department of sociology. These lecturers, who teach their courses in Latvian, are confronted by the total absence of translations into the Latvian language.
A small part of *The Second Sex* by Simone de Beauvoir has recently been
translated in a monthly literary magazine.

Our teaching experience over the last three years has led to gradually increasing interest of women students in feminist ideas, especially
as they choose topics for term papers and bachelor's papers in cultural, literary, sociological, and psychological studies. Some years ago,
just after the restoration of Latvia's independence, when I initiated a
course called "Introduction to Women's Studies" in the department of
English, the majority of students were quite hostile to feminist ideas.
Today, students seek the course or choose a woman-centered topic for
a term paper because it is something interesting and new and because
the work offers them the opportunity for critical analysis of the
situation of women today. According to my observations, my univer-

sity colleagues have also noted this shift in interest and now tend to broaden the range of topics by including gender-related issues.

On the other hand, the lack of books and other materials and the absence of a teaching-oriented women's studies center are obstacles still to be overcome. These needs have become imperative, since our classrooms today suffer from the randomness of access to information. As a result, we have recently started the Gender Studies Library and Resource Center at the University of Latvia to collect books and journals important for women's and gender studies. We have already received books from the Christina Institute of Women's Studies of the University of Helsinki (Finland) and Network East-West Women (USA). Special attention will be given to providing our students and young women lecturers with information about centers of women's and gender studies in Europe that provide research grants. Research activities resulting from grants as well as the growing participation of Latvian women scholars in international women's studies conferences and seminars have already brought a new and significant dimension into the traditional range of research interests among academic women over the past three years.

The development of international contacts is of particular importance for us as an opportunity for our women researchers engaged in teaching to learn more about how to teach in a feminist perspective in our classrooms. In this respect, the experiences of Nordic academic women with regard to the organization and teaching of women's and gender studies have been extremely useful. Nordic Women's Studies Coordinators has contributed to initiating and promoting cooperation among university women scholars. The Christina Institute of Women's Studies at the University of Helsinki has been very helpful in organizing research grants and annual exchanges of Latvian and Finnish women lecturers in the field of women's studies to the departments of sociology, philosophy, and foreign languages of the University of Latvia. We also expect to initiate cooperation in teaching women's studies with the Belle van Zuylen Institute at the University of Amsterdam.

Our learning, teaching, educating, and disseminating the ideas are of primary concern for feminist intellectuals in Latvia since, in bell hooks's words, there will be "no mass-based feminist movement as long as feminist ideas are understood only by a well-educated few" (hooks 1984).

REFERENCES

Eglite, Parsla, ed. 1994. *Women of Latvija-75: Researches, Statistics, Reminiscences.* Riga: Zvaigzne.

hooks, bell. 1984. *Feminist Theory: From Margin to Center*. Boston: South End Press.

Thorborg, Marina, ed. 1993. *Women Around the Baltic Sea. Part 1: Estonia, Latvia, and Lithuania*. Work Report on Baltic Issues. Lund: Lund University Press.

Tranpenciere, Ilze, and Sandra Kalninya, eds. 1992. *Fragments of Reality: Insights on Women in a Changing Society*. Riga: Vaga Publishers.

Irina Novikova *teaches American women's literature in the English department at the University of Latvia, Riga. In 1994 she was a Fulbright scholar in the women's studies department at the State University of New York, Albany.*

Women's Studies in Uganda

Victoria Miriam Mwaka

Uganda is a landlocked country. It sits astride the equator and borders the Sudan on the north, Kenya on the east, Tanzania on the south, Rwanda on the southwest, and Zaire on the west. Uganda has a total population of 16,671,705, of whom 8,185,747 are male and 8,485,958 are female (Ministry of Finance and Economic Planning 1992). The population of Uganda is characterized by high, fluctuating growth rates and high levels of morbidity and mortality. Fertility stands at 7.4 births per woman of reproductive age. That fact and a young age structure result in a high dependency ratio (Ministry of Health 1989:19). The population is largely rural, with 88.7 percent residing in rural areas. Settlement patterns have been largely influenced by history, infrastructure, terrain, soil fertility, climate, vegetation, water supply, disease agents, and differing land tenure systems. These elements have implications for the status of women in Uganda.

Given the prevailing poverty and poor living conditions in Uganda generally, and because 89 percent of the population lives in rural areas (Kirumira et al. 1993:1), living conditions are of national concern. In rural areas housing is of low quality and short durability. The traditional pattern of scattered homesteads makes it very expensive to procure basic facilities. About 66 percent of the population lives in grass-thatched mud and wattle houses. Only 25 percent of households have access to safe drinking water, and only 5.6 percent have electricity. About 3.5 percent of households in urban areas have no toilet facilities; in rural areas, that figure rises to 24.5 percent. Less than 5 percent of households have rubbish pits, and 91 percent of families scatter refuse within or outside their household compounds. Such poor living conditions have adversely affected women's health and that of their households (Mwaka, Mugyenyi, and Banya 1994:36).

Water quality and availability are other problems faced by women in Uganda. The majority of families, especially in rural areas, fetch water from unhygienic sources, such as unprotected wells, springs, rivers, swamps, and streams, which may contain contaminated water. Second, women lack hygiene education and the resources with which to boil and store water safely. Unhygienic water is one of the major health hazards, particularly in rural areas. Women walk long distances to fetch water, a task that increases their workload and working hours. Food security is threatened by the unpredictable rainfall, since agriculture in Uganda depends entirely on rainfall (UNICEF 1989).

Energy sources in Uganda are mainly firewood (99 percent in rural areas), charcoal, kerosene, and electricity (in a few relatively well-to-do households). Since women are mainly responsible for firewood collection, they are the most seriously affected when forests and bushes are depleted. Presently, women have to walk long distances in search of firewood, which also increases their working hours. In some areas, women are providing fewer and more irregular meals for their households, with negative effects on nutrition and hygiene. For example, women may be unable to boil drinking water and to cook beans enough for meals.

The health of Ugandan women is another cause for special concern. Many women suffer from anemia, HIV/AIDS and other sexually transmitted diseases, as well as such illnesses as malaria, tuberculosis, and hypertension. Morbidity issues include gynecological problems, obstetrics conditions, and general surgical problems affecting women, such as sepsis and hemorrhage. A survey of four districts of Uganda showed in 1993 that the morbidity rate of rural women is alarmingly high, with 76 percent of women reporting sickness in the two weeks prior to the interview (Kirumira et al. 1993). As a result of the strains of repeated childbearing and breast-feeding, combined with poor nutrition and long hours of hard work, women's resistance to disease is low compared to that of their male counterparts.

Acquired Immune Deficiency Syndrome (HIV/AIDS) is an issue of great concern. It is estimated that 6 to 10 percent of the country's population of 16.8 million (1991) are infected with HIV. Of the estimated 1 to 1.6 million people infected with AIDS in Uganda, about a quarter are women of childbearing age, fifteen to forty-nine years. Mother to baby (vertical) transmission among women twenty-five to forty-nine years of age is prevalent, with 25 to 40 percent of the infected children dying in their first year of life. The AIDS scourge has affected women more than men. While more women of reproductive age are reported to suffer from AIDS than men, it is also the women who nurse the sick. Grandmothers, who remain with orphans, have no assistance and no energy to fend for themselves as well as the orphans, some of whom may already be infected with the HIV virus (Kirumira et al. 1993:20).

In the majority of cases, women in Uganda lack control or ownership of the resources of production. For example, only 5 percent of women own land, although they may have access to it through their husbands, brothers, or fathers. Culture dictates that land inheritance is through the male lineage. This practice deprives women of the right to control the land on which they produce and implies that the produce of women's labor belongs to the male landowner. Quite often, women lack security for acquiring credit. Hence, a widow will have to remain within her husband's family in order to continue using the land and looking after her children who bear her husband's lineage. This also explains why women in Uganda do not have custody of their children. Generally, women lack access to available technology, extension services, and information, all of which are available to males whether or not they are heads of households.

Women-headed households tend to be economically vulnerable. First of all, women rarely inherit capital property, and their access to such resources as land and capital is through a male next of kin. Because single women have the lowest incomes, their living standards are poor, and the chances for survival and education of their children are low.

Education, Knowledge, and Skills

Education is a prerequisite to an individual's socioeconomic and political advancement. The importance of women's education is multidimensional because it influences the health and economic welfare of families, the community, and the nation. Education facilitates and improves opportunities for women's participation in the open labor market, in economic production, and in policymaking and decision making, and creates a conducive environment for women's autonomy (Mwaka, Mugyenyi, and Banya 1994:6). The illiteracy rate in Uganda is very high, and women are more likely to be illiterate than men (52 percent of women are illiterate compared with 48 percent of men). Although the enrollment of girls in school is improving (44 percent), the female school dropout rate at higher levels of education is still high, leaving only 26 percent of girls at secondary and 16 percent at postsecondary (including university) levels. Factors responsible for such a trend include poverty, which leads to a scarcity of money for school fees; parental preference for educating boys rather than girls; girls' assignment to domestic duties; early marriages and the need for a bride price for girls; teenage pregnancies; and the lack of practical support and encouragement of girls by the education system.

At Makerere University, the only major government university in the country, the percentage of women students during the years 1989 to 1992 has ranged from a low of 22 percent to a high of 33 percent in 1992. Women's participation in science courses is particularly poor.

Women and Work

Women in general work between fifteen and eighteen hours a day. The domestic division of labor allocates the most tedious and heavy work to women. The daily routine of Ugandan women includes childrearing (90 percent), food preparation (80 percent), fetching water (60 percent) and firewood (70 percent), gardening (70 percent), and cleaning (80 percent) (Mwaka, Mugyenyi, and Banya 1994:8). The heavy workload prevents women from actively participating in functional education and training programs, independent income generation, politics, and leisure. Overwork has a negative effect on women's health as well.

Opportunities for women in employment and managerial positions are limited. According to the public service census of 1987, women accounted for 24 percent of all posts filled in Uganda. Females filled 5.4 percent of the administrative managerial posts, although none were in top management. Women filled 16.2 percent of the professional jobs but 35.5 percent of the technical and semiprofessional and semiskilled jobs. With such small numbers of women in management categories (5.4 percent) and professional jobs (16 percent), we cannot expect many women to have filtered through to top management positions (Mwaka 1994).

Factors that affect women's advancement to employment and management positions include access to higher education in the first place, forms of employment and opportunities available to women, a corporate culture based on male leadership styles and personal traits, lack of self-confidence, other sociocultural and political attitudes and atmospheres, and the general administrative and institutional structure operative in the country, including laws, rules, and regulations that are not in favor of women or sensitive to affirmative action.

**Women in Politics, Decision Making,
and Affirmative Action**

On the other hand, the government of Uganda has recently come out clearly in support of women. Much progress has been made in Uganda toward empowering women and involving them in management, decision making, and political participation. Currently, there is a lot of political goodwill. Uganda is the first African country to have a female vice president, the Hon. Dr. Specioza Wandira Kazibwe, a medical doctor, who also holds the position of minister of gender and community development. There are two female ministers and three ministers of state of various ministries. I was appointed deputy chairperson of the constituent assembly, a body that has worked on the promulgation of the Uganda Constitution. Of a total of 284 constituent assembly delegates, 51 (18 percent) are female. Many women now occupy management positions in various ministries, institutions, commissions, and other government departments.

The present government has initiated policies that encourage women to participate in politics. It has also established institutions that directly affect the political life of women and also allow them access to those structures where political power is seen to be concentrated. In the Resistance Councils (RC) system one position is reserved exclusively for a woman (RC secretary for women). At the national level, one woman representative must be elected in each of the thirty-nine districts to the National Resistance Council (NRC/Parliament). In addition, some women ran for election against men and won on their own merit. Women account for 16 percent of the parliament membership.

The Uganda Constitution of 1995 addressed a number of issues on women in relation to men. On fundamental human rights and freedoms, article 21(1) states that "a person shall not be discriminated against on grounds of sex, race, colour, ethnic origin, tribe, creed or religious or social, economic standing and political opinion or disability." Article 33(1) states that women shall be accorded full and equal dignity of the person with men, and article 33(2) states that the state shall provide the facilities and opportunities necessary to enhance the welfare of women to enable them to realize their full potential and advancement. Article 33(3) states that the state shall protect women and their rights, taking into account their unique status and natural maternal functions in society. Article 33(4) says that women shall have the right to equal treatment with men and that right shall include equal opportunities in political, economic, and social activities. Article 33(5) stipulates that women shall have the right to affirmative action for the purpose of redressing the imbalances created by history, tradition, or customs. Article 33(6) says that cultures, customs, or traditions that harm the dignity, welfare, or interest of women or that undermine their status are prohibited by the constitution. As exemplified by the Uganda Constitution and the formation of a Ministry of Gender and Community Development, women's rights in Uganda are being explicitly addressed at the highest level, as well as at the grassroots level.

The Women's Movements

The history of women's movements in Uganda has not been comprehensively documented. Winfred Brown (1988:4) rightly states, "Largely owing to the political upheavals which Uganda has suffered, the story which I have told of the movement for reform and its achievement is not known in Uganda; very few people are aware of Decree 16 (1973) which provides for the registration of all marriages." She continues, "The reform movement in Uganda has not been widely known outside Uganda. This is probably because those of us who were involved in it were concentrating our attention on the immediate problems as they affected Uganda itself and especially women."

Although traditionally women formed informal groups for coopera-tion during periods of crisis—like heavy workloads, harvesting, and the loss of relatives—more permanent and informal groups came into existence on religious and charitable principles (Kimala 1988:23). Organizations like the Mothers' Union for Protestants, the Uganda Women's Catholic Guild, the Uganda Muslim Women's Association, the Uganda Council of Women, and the Young Christian Association perceive women as mothers, housewives, and housekeepers. Thus their programs are welfare-oriented. The Mothers' Union, formed in 1914, was a Christian-based organization founded by the wife of the headmaster of a school that educated the sons of chiefs (King's College Budo). The first Uganda branch was affiliated to the Mothers' Union in London, and by 1926, there were eighty-eight branches (Brown 1988:5).

Gayaza High School, the first school for girls in Uganda, was started in 1905 by a white woman missionary. Sir Albert Cook wrote: "Even at that very early date, it was recognised that the education of girls, while very backward, was equally important with that of boys" (Cook 1945:208).

As early as 1946, the Uganda government established a women's section in what was then called the Department of Social Welfare, responsible for women's affairs in the country (Tadria 1986:87). Wo-men's organizations were called upon to participate in government programs, partly in response to the increasing number of women's voluntary organizations. The Council for Voluntary Social Services was established in 1953 to register all voluntary organizations and to monitor their activities. In 1957, the Uganda government signed an agreement with UNICEF, under which the latter would provide training for more than 3,500 women's club leaders, who would then work voluntarily in the promotion and extension of the women's clubs movement (Tadria 1986:217–26).

Just before independence in 1962, women's organizations played an important part in the independence campaigns. Early in 1962, the Uganda Council of Women, formed in 1946, spearheaded the women's cause directly by publishing leaflets addressing women's concerns

prior to independence, in conjunction with the Ministry of Information (Kimala 1988:26). Included among these concerns were the needs
for women to have equal opportunities in public life, for girls to have
access to education, for more short-term courses and scholarships for
mature women, for more vocational opportunities for women, and for
more and better hospitals and maternity care (Akello 1982:11).

In 1960, a major conference addressed issues related to bride wealth,
property, and inheritance, rights to succession, marriage laws, women
in public life, and women's right to work. Resolutions passed at the
conference included those on the abolition of the customary payment
of bride price, on the education of women, on women's property rights
and the rights of succession. In one resolution, for example, whether
or not she had children the widow was to receive a substantial share of
her husband's property, including the house and the land attached to
the house, as long as she did not remarry. The government was also
urged to give immediate attention to the creation of facilities for
postprimary and secondary education of girls, especially in those
areas where no such facilities existed. The conference received widespread attention in the press and radio, in both the local language and
English.

By 1965, the achievement of the women's movement could be
summed up in the words of Winfred Brown: "Through their experiences, at the 1960s conference of the Uganda Council of women,
Uganda women demonstrated that they were capable, intelligent and
had a right to be heard. They also discovered that it was possible to
make themselves heard and to move society to change its attitudes"
(1988:24).

In 1975, the United Nations urged its member states to set up
national machineries for women, and in 1979, in response to the UN's
call, the National Council of Women of Uganda was formed under
decree no. 3. The objectives of the council were to provide a national
machinery through which women might communicate in order to
discuss their ideas, coordinate activities, and work for empowerment
through eradicating illiteracy and establishing financial support for
projects. The council was to encourage and facilitate cooperation
among various national and international nongovernmental organizations with similar objectives. The ideology behind these objectives
sought to integrate women into the mainstream of development.

The National Council of Women prepared the Uganda government's official document for the United Nations Third World Conference on Women, held in Nairobi in 1985. It has also been responsible
for training courses, conferences, seminars, and workshops on

women's issues, especially those related to marriage, cultural, and legal rights, opening opportunities for girls' education, and the interpretation of laws relevant to women who speak local languages.

The Development of Women's Studies as an Academic Field

Feminist studies in Uganda was stimulated by the global women's movement and the international development community, particularly after the United Nations Decade for Women, 1975–85, and especially following the Nairobi Forum in 1985. Women's particular concerns, their social and familial positions, the obstacles to their enjoyment of rights and opportunities have become the subject of developmental and academic activities in Uganda. The goal was to organize such studies in a systematic and contextual manner. Women's studies in Uganda is also a product of the Ugandan women's movements. The department of women's studies at Makerere University was created following the efforts of two women's nongovernmental organizations, the Uganda Association of University Women (UAUW) and Action for Development (ACFODE), after the 1985 Nairobi Forum.

Founded in April 1957 and affiliated with the International Federation of University Women, the Uganda Association of University Women (UAUW) has as one of its aims "to provide young graduates with a body of women who could lend moral support to the pioneers in the professions and to offer opportunities for meeting and discussing of problems that are of interest to women in Uganda." The association provides funding for research, seminars, direct assistance to young women (including guidance and counseling), a scholarship fund, and an annual prize for the best women final-year students from each faculty at Makerere University.

Action for Development was founded in 1986 with the aim of uplifting women in all areas. Some of its activities have included workshops and seminars in local communities; research on women's activities; promoting women's participation in politics and decision making; and supporting women's self-help projects. Membership is open to all women, and activities are carried out through a number of committees, including consciousness-raising, and publicity, education, legal and political, research, and finance.

In 1986, a Makerere University committee was set up to review university programs and advise the government accordingly. Female members of the university community under the Association of University Women and Action for Development had already been made aware of problems faced by women in Uganda, the unequal opportunities, especially in education, and the limited information available about women. Some university women had also visited institutions where women's studies existed as an academic program. Hence they proposed the establishment of women's studies at Makerere University. The proposal envisioned the creation of a women's studies program that would educate personnel who might then support the activities of nongovernmental organizations working on behalf of women, as well as the Ministry of Gender and Community Development. The importance of an academic women's studies program was emphasized: it would provide the systematic analysis of gender issues; it would sensitize society about these issues; and, through coordinated research, it would generate valuable data to support policy and other developmental activities.

In July 1987, Makerere University held a donors' conference to solicit help for the rehabilitation and development of the university. At the donors' conference, the proposal to establish a women's studies department at Makerere was discussed. Most of the international donor agencies were aware of the existence of women's studies in other universities, supported the proposal, and pledged financial support. A university committee was set up with a mandate to establish a women's studies department in the faculty of social sciences. The curriculum was drawn up by experts from the United States, Zambia, and Zimbabwe. The department was inaugurated in May 1991, with a core staff of five and thirteen master of arts students. I had the honor of being appointed as the founder head (1990–95) of the new department. The department was expected to produce women and men who could work in the Ministry of Gender and Community Development as well as in other departments and such ministries as health, education, and agriculture, where women predominate and where the focus is on women as participants and beneficiaries (Mwaka 1994:110).

The women's studies department at Makerere University is the first of its kind in Uganda and, more generally, in East Africa. In keeping with Makerere's commitment to build for the future, and to diversify curriculum, the department offers interdisciplinary courses on women and development. The courses introduce key concepts in the analysis of gender relations in different political, economic, and social areas that are currently undergoing transformation, especially with regard to population, reproduction, health, education, family and kinship, rural and urban society, employment, income generation and resource distribution. On completion of the course, candidates are to be able to disseminate the new scholarship on women, stimulate critical approaches to established knowledge, develop practical skills and creative potential, and become role models and advocates for increased opportunities for all women.

As part of its activities, the department trains student leaders from different backgrounds, who might then serve in various ministries, departments, institutions, nongovernmental organizations, or international missions and who would facilitate the integration of women into higher decision making and influence policy decisions on gender issues. The department has worked to revitalize university education, bringing it closer to burning social, economic, and political issues, to working toward their solution, and to producing gender-sensitive persons committed to development activities. The causes, processes, and consequences of gender disparities have been investigated, analyzing structural, cultural, and attitudinal factors that disadvantage women. Men and women have been helped to understand, recognize, and acknowledge the multidimensional lives of women in society—through public lectures, seminars, and the mass media. The department has contributed to the global and national debates on the gender question by linking scholars with activists, extension/field workers, nongovernmental organizations, international concerns, and grassroots women.

Between 1990 and 1995, the M.A. program enrolled fifty-four students, thirteen of whom have graduated. Six of these fifty-four were male. The male candidates are expected to become gender-literate and serve as sensitizers of other men on gender issues. In Uganda currently, the minister of gender and community development is female, while the permanent secretary and the minister of state for gender and community development are male.

The program of study includes course work and a dissertation. The dissertation should make a significant contribution to the knowledge of gender and women in development issues in general. The course work consists of four semesters of classes, followed by a period of field research and submission of an examinable dissertation. Admission requirements include a minimum of a good second class (honors) degree in any discipline from a recognized university. However, applicants with lower qualifications may provide other evidence of academic growth such as research and publications or work in an area relevant to gender/women in development.

The students are expected to complete the following twelve mandatory core courses: "Gender, Population, and Development"; "Feminism, Social Theory, and Social Reform"; "Origins of Sexual Division of Labour and Gender Relations"; "Principles of Development Economies"; "Women and Environment"; "Women and Health"; "Women,

Crime, and Deviance"; "Women's Issues in Rural Development"; "Women in Different Socioeconomic and Political Systems"; "Women, the State, and Policy Formulation in Africa"; "Research Methods and Statistics"; "Project Design, Execution, and Appraisal/Evaluation"; and "Introduction to Computer Use." They are also required to select two of six optional courses: "Internationalization of Capital and Economic Crisis in Africa"; "Women's Question in Underdeveloped Economies"; "Women in Management"; "Women in Science and Technology"; "Gender and the Law"; and "Gender Information and Communication." Seminars, workshops, and conferences are integral parts of the students' programs. Research methodology seminars are held every year for students before they embark on fieldwork in preparation for their dissertations. Seminars are also organized for the dissemination of research results.

In 1991 the department began with one professor as head of the department. By 1995 there were three faculty members with the Ph.D. in gender studies. Two others are halfway through the Ph.D. program. By the year 2000, the program should have six faculty members with doctorates.

Women's Studies Short Courses

The department has been successful in attracting the transfer of the three-month short course "Men, Women, and Development," which was formally offered by the Institute of Development Studies, Brighton, Sussex, to Makerere University. Some Sussex University faculty joined their women's studies counterparts at Makerere University to teach this course. We expect that this three-month course will be offered every year, with funding from the Overseas Development Agency (ODA).

The department has also participated in the course "Women and Human Rights," which was first taught 3–31 July 1995 in Kampala. The course was organized jointly by World University Service Austria, World University Service Uganda, and the faculty of law and women's studies, Makerere University. Participants were drawn from various African countries. Such short courses are intended to sensitize individuals who work in national and international organizations with similar gender-related objectives.

Research, Publications, and Documentation

Research, publications, and documentation are important to women's studies. As part of their training, candidates undertaking the M.A. in

women's studies are expected to submit a field research-based dissertation. The selection of research topics depends on the area of specialization and parent disciplines of the candidates. For example, medical
doctor candidates select topics related to health, while those with
social science backgrounds select social-cultural, economic, political,
and management-based topics.

The department also has a documentation unit with a reasonable
collection of books, journals, periodicals, and monographs. *Research
and Publications on Women in Uganda. An Annotated Bibliography* (Musoke, Mutibwa, and Ddungu 1994) was compiled in collaboration with
UNICEF, the women's studies department of Makerere University, and
the Rural Development Women's Consultancy Group (RUDWOCG). The
overall objective of the bibliography was to bring together all researched work, seminar and workshop papers, and articles on women
in Uganda written since 1985, and thus to provide reference material
for development agencies, donors, researchers, and NGOs within and
outside Uganda (Musoke, Mutibwa, and Ddungu 1994:v).[1]

The bibliography revealed that while certain areas have been well
researched—namely, education, employment, law, health and related
studies—others are underresearched, among them science and technology, environment, the media, housing, water, and sanitation. Further, topics that were emphasized in the World Plan of Action of
1985—namely, female circumcision, prostitution, rape and defile-
ment, domestic violence, water, housing, the girl child—have not been
studied on their own and appear in most cases as parts of studies on
other topics (Musoke, Mutibwa, and Ddungu 1994:ix).

Unfinished Business of Women's Studies in Higher Education

During its first three years, the program devoted itself to postgraduate
studies designed to produce staff for the department of women's
studies and officers for the new Ministry of Gender and Community
Development and for national and international NGOs focusing on
gender-related activities. Because human resources in the new field of
women/gender were scanty, a special effort had to be made to develop
staff. Once staff were in place, the program could embark on undergraduate studies. For that reason, postgraduate and undergraduate
curricula were both designed. The undergraduate curriculum is still
to be approved, however, and implemented in 1996. Right now there is
no provision for a Ph.D. program, but the department should be able
to mount a Ph.D.-level program in the near future.

Impact of Women's Studies on the Traditional Curriculum

Sensitization courses for the university community are yet to be fully implemented. Students in the faculties of agriculture, medicine, veterinary medicine, social sciences, for example, who tend to be recruited into extension services, would greatly benefit from exposure to women's/gender issues. After all, women form the majority of the population in rural areas. It would therefore be legitimate for those who are to work among women in the countryside to be introduced to women's studies. These courses would be voluntary. They would form the basis for courses that would be integrated into the curriculum for the various faculties and at various levels of the education system.

It is with that background that Makerere University has adopted both the "integration" and the "incorporation" models under which undergraduate programs will be pursued. In the integration model, separate disciplinary or interdisciplinary courses in women's studies allow for specialization leading to a degree. The M.A. program adopted this model at the postgraduate level, although we did not expect candidates at the undergraduate level to specialize in women's studies, particularly since relevant job opportunities might be limited.

The women's studies undergraduate course will adopt the incorporation model, however, which attempts to introduce components related to gender/women within already existing syllabi. This will mean developing components of women's studies in history, literature, geography, economics, etc. There is already a gender studies component in the departments of sociology and population studies/demography. Geography is developing a gender-oriented human geography curriculum. This will provide introductory courses in gender/women's studies to interest students in specializing in the study at the postgraduate level. This approach is also cost-effective.

Impact of Women's Studies on National Educational Public Policy

Women's studies/gender analysis is a tool that can be used to guide the inclusion of women's/gender consideration into development policy planning and programming. This tool provides guidelines intended to identify information and issues, especially for gender-sensitive development strategy, action plans, projects, concept papers, and proposals. The impact of women's/gender studies on national educational policy is reflected in the affirmative action programs being implemented in Uganda. The first one is the creation of a fully government-supported women's studies department. Some graduates employed in the Ministry of Gender and Community Development will create a multiplier effect in gender sensitivity. It was women's studies that alerted the government to the need for affirmative action policies.

The government's affirmative action programs for higher education include the weighting of marks/points for women entering the university. Although the weighting system has caused much controversy—it has been charged with perpetuating more marginalization of women and with being unfair to men—it has allowed more women to enter the university. In 1971 women made up 16.5 percent of the student body; in 1985, they were 25.3 percent. In 1989–90, women were only 22 percent of the total but 35 percent in 1990–91, 30 percent in 1991–92 and 33 percent in 1992–93. The attainment of the 30 percent mark during the past three years may be mainly attributed to the recent scheme in which 1.5 bonus points are added to female candidates' scores in the university entrance weighting system.

Conclusion

Women's studies has been recognized as a critical support for policy formulation and as essential to a comprehensive and balanced understanding of social reality. The essential components of women's studies include women's contributions to social processes; women's perceptions of their own lives, their struggles, and aspirations; the roots and structures of inequality that lead to marginalization; and the invisibility and exclusion of women from the scope, approaches, and conceptual frameworks of most intellectual inquiry. Women's studies should therefore be defined not narrowly, as studies about women or information on women, but rather as a critical instrument for social change, economic, political, and academic development and transformation.

The situation of women in Uganda with regard to the availability of and access to basic and strategic needs and resources is not very different from that in economically undeveloped countries characterized by poverty, illiteracy, and high fertility, mortality, and morbidity rates. However, the government of Uganda has been very supportive of the women's cause, as exemplified by the affirmative action outlined earlier in this paper, so far implemented at all levels, and as reflected in the provisions of the new Uganda constitution.

While the integration of gender/women's studies into the curricula of Uganda institutions is timely and although an affirmative action program has been instituted to achieve maximum impact, women's studies should also be integrated into the lower school curricula and upper schools and institutions of higher learning other than Makerere University. Gender studies should be made available to all those concerned with the development of society, namely policymakers, politicians, educators, religious leaders, local and international development workers, grassroots extension workers, and women, men, and youths of all categories.

NOTE

1. Subjects covered include agriculture; bibliographies; children, including child care/survival, and the girl child; culture, including family, marriage, and sexuality; demography and population; directories; economy, including credit, banking, finance, income generation; education; employment, including professions, careers, occupations, and management; empowerment and equality; environment; general studies; health, including HIV/AIDS, reproductive health, and occupational health; housing; land; law, including legal rights, constitution, and crime; management; media and information; prostitution/promiscuity; religion; science and technology; war; water; widows; and women's organizations.

REFERENCES

Akello, Grace. 1982. *Self—Twice Removed*. Uganda Women's Monograph for Change. London.

Brown, W. 1988. *Marriage, Divorce, and Inheritance: The Uganda Council of Women's Movement for Legislative Reform*. Cambridge African Monograph 10.

Cook, Albert. 1945. *Uganda Memories*. Kampala: Uganda Society.

Kimala, Lucia. 1988. "National Machineries for the Integration of Women in Development: An Exploratory Study of the National Machinery for Women in Uganda and the Netherlands." Master's thesis, the IDS-Hague.

Kirumira, E., A. Katahoire, A. Aboda, and A. Karim-Edstrom. 1993. *Study of Sexual and Reproductive Health Among Ugandan Women*. Research report, Child Health and Development Center, Makerere University, Kampala.

Ministry of Finance and Economic Planning, Statistics Department, Government of Uganda. 1992. *1991 Population and Housing Census*. Uganda: Government Printer.

Ministry of Finance and Economic Planning. 1994. Government paper for the population conference in Cairo. Uganda: Government Printer.

Ministry of Health. 1989. *Uganda Demographic and Health Survey Report*. Columbia, Md.: Institute for Resource Development/Macro System, Inc.

———. 1992. *Uganda National Programme of Action for Children*. Uganda: Government Printer.

Musoke, M., O. Mutibwa, Babirye Ddungu. 1994. *Research and Publications on Women in Uganda. An Annotated Bibliography*. Women's Studies Department, Makerere University, SAREC and UNICEF.

Musoke, Maria, ed. 1992. *Development of Academic Courses in Gender Studies in Eastern and Southern Africa*. Proceedings of a workshop organized by the Department of Women's Studies, Makerere University, 3–5 September 1992. Entebbe: Makerere University Printery.

Mwaka, V. M. 1994. *Women in Top Management in Uganda*. Association of Public Administration and Management Research Report.

Mwaka, V. M., M. Mugyenyi, and G. Banya. 1994. *Women in Uganda: A Profile*. Research report sponsored by the Royal Netherlands Embassy, Nairobi, Kenya.

Republic of Uganda. 1995. Constitution of the Republic of Uganda. Uganda: Government Printer.

Tadria, H. M. 1986. "Changes and Continuities in the Position of Women in Uganda." In *Beyond Crisis: Development Issues in Uganda*, edited by D. Wiebe and Cole P. Dodge, pp. 79–90. Makerere Institute of Social Research.

Uganda Constitutional Commission. Draft Constitution of the Republic of Uganda.

***Victoria Miriam Mwaka** is professor of geography and the founder and head chairperson of the women's studies department at Makerere University. She has just been elected president of the International Women's Cross Cultural Exchange Organization and was honored to serve as the deputy chairperson of the Uganda Constituent Assembly from 1994 to 1995.*

Newsbriefs

CONFERENCES

The first **Jean Baker Miller Summer Training Institute,** a post-degree clinical training program on "Relational and Cultural Theory and Applications," will be held at Wellesley College in June. Clinicians and professionals in related fields are invited to attend a first session, 14–18 June 1996. Teachers and supervisors of the relational model, members of Stone Center Study Groups, and those experienced in applying the relational approach are invited to attend a second, advanced session, 21–25 June 1996. For information, contact Helen Matthew at The Stone Center, phone: 617-283-2506; fax: 617-283-3646; E-mail: hmatthew@wellesley.edu.

The Southern Connecticut State University Women's Studies Program will host its Sixth Annual Women's Studies Conference, *Change the Politics: Women Make the Difference,* 5–6 October 1996. The conference will include presentations and panels addressing the current issues and concerns about the role of women in the local, national and international political arenas and the impact of contemporary political forces on women's lives. Fore information on presenting or attending contact Women's Studies, EN 271, 501 Crescent Street, SCSU, New Haven, CT 06515, phone: 203-392-6133; E-mail: griffiths @scsu.ctstateu.edu.

CALLS FOR PAPERS

Frontiers: A Journal of Women Studies welcomes submissions that cross and/or re-examine boundaries, exploring the diversity of women's lives as shaped by a multiplicity of factors, including race, ethnicity, class, sexual orientation, and region. The editors encourage submissions on any topic of interest to women, as well as those addressing the following areas for special upcoming issues: the political and theoretical concept of "frontiers"; intersections between feminism and environmentalism; and Pacific Rim cultures and Asian/Pacific-American women in the U.S. Send submissions to: *Frontiers,* Wilson 12,

Washington State University, Pullman, Washington 99164-4007, phone: 509-335-7268; fax: 509-335-4377; E-mail: frontier@wsu.edu.

The editor of *Feminist Interpretations of Augustine,* a forthcoming book in the *Re-Reading the Canon* series, published by Penn State Press, welcomes entries. This collection will reflect the breadth of Augustine of Hippo's thinking and will include essays from a wide range of feminist approaches. Deadline for submission of completed manuscripts: 15 September 1997. Send inquiries, proposals, and two copies of papers to the editor: Judith C. Stark, Philosophy Dept., Seton Hall University, South Orange, NJ 07079, E-mail: starkjud@lanmail.shu.edu.

FELLOWSHIPS, AWARDS, AND GRANTS

The Women's Research and Education Institute is accepting applications from graduate students for the 1996–1997 Congressional Fellowships on Women and Public Policy. The Fellowship Program places students in congressional offices and on strategic committee staffs to work as legislative aides on policy issues affecting women. For applications: send an SASE to WREI, 1700 18th St., NW, #400, Washington, DC 20009.

The Sociologists for Women in Society has established a scholarship fund for the study of women and breast cancer. The society will award $1,500 to a female doctoral student in the social sciences engaged in a feminist exploration of women's experience of breast cancer. Applications are available from Dr. Rachel Kahn-Hut, The Barbara Rosenblum Scholarship Committee, Department of Sociology, San Francisco State University, 1600 Holloway Avenue, San Francisco, CA 94132.

The Oral History Association invites inquiries regarding its annual contest. Awards will be given for various types of media (film, books, photography). For more information, contact Rebecca Sharpless, Executive Secretary, **Oral History Association**, Baylor University, P.O. Box 97234, Waco, TX 76798-7234; E-mail: OHA_Support@baylor.edu.

The Henry A. Murray Research Center offers several annual awards and grants. The *Radcliffe Research Support Program* offers grants of up to $5,000 for post-doctorate research; the *Jeanne Humphrey Block Dissertation Award Program* offers a grant of $2,500 to a woman doctoral student studying sex and gender differences or a developmental issue of particular concern to girls or women; the *Henry A. Murray Dissertation Award Program* offers grants of $2,500 to doctoral students focusing on issues in human development or personality. For more information, call or write the grants administrator at the **Henry A. Murray Research Center**, 10 Garden Street, Cambridge, MA 02138; phone: 617-495-8140; fax: 617-496-3993.

PUBLICATIONS

The University of Wisconsin System Women's Studies Librarian's Office announces its new Website. Visit their homepage for descriptions of publications and services, tables of contents and articles from *Feminist Collections: A Quarterly of Women's Studies Resources*, full-length bibliographies, core lists of women's studies books, and links to selected other websites on women and gender. URL: http://www.library.wisc.edu/libraries/WomensStudies.

The University of Wisconsin System Women's Studies Librarian's Office has published a special issue (vol. 17, no. 2, 1996) of *Feminist Collections: A Quarterly of Women's Studies Resources*. The issue focuses on "Women's Studies and Information Technology: Reports from the Field." For information, contact UW System Women's Studies Librarian, 430 Memorial Library, 728 State St., Madison, WI 53706; phone: 608-263-5754; E-mail: wiswsl@doit.wisc.edu.

The Network of East-West Women announces the publication of the *NEWW On-Line User's Guide*, an E-mail instruction manual. Topics covered include introductory explanations of E-mail, Internet etiquette, a glossary of computer and E-mail terms, answers to frequently asked questions, Internet service providers in Central and Eastern Europe and the former Soviet Union, and Internet resources for the feminist activist. The 54-page guide is available in English, Russian, and Polish, and costs $15.00. Make checks payable to NEWW and mail to Victoria Vrana, On-Line Program Director, 1601 Connecticut Avenue, NW, Suite 302, Washington, DC 20009; phone: 202-265-3585; fax: 202-265-3508; E-mail: newwdc@igc.apc.org

Education About Asia, a new journal of the **Association for Asian Studies**, is designed to assist secondary, college, and university instructors in teaching about Asia. A resource section includes essays and resources for high school and college classrooms. For information, contact Lucien Ellington, Editor, *Education About Asia*, 314 Hunter Hall, University of Tennessee at Chattanooga, 615 McCallie Avenue, Chattanooga, TN 37403; phone: 423-755-3775 or 423-755-2118 (5* fax/phone); fax: 423-755-4044; E-mail: lellingt @NETFRAME.utc.edu.

Family Care International (FCI) has produced a summary report regarding commitments to sexual and reproductive health and rights for all, made at the FWCW (Beijing), the ICPD (Cairo), and other UN conferences. The document is available in English, French, and Spanish. Contact: fax: 212-941-5563 or E-mail: famcare1@chelsea.ios.com

Alternative Women in Development announces the publication of *Development at the Crossroads: Women at the Center*, including analyses of the current state of global economic development, an exploration of women's role in the global development process, a discussion of various current official women-in-development process, a discussion of various current official women-in-development policy, and outlines of alternative policies. For information, contact the Center of Concern, 3700 13th Street, NE, Washington, DC 20017; phone: 202-635-2757; fax: 202-832-9494.

The Chalice and the Blade in Chinese Culture: Gender Relations and Social Models, by Chinese Partnership Research Group, ed. Prof. Min Jiayin, is a study of Chinese women and gender relations, published in the People's Republic of China. Including a foreword by Riane Eisler, the book incorporates contributions from seventeen scholars in different areas of Chinese history and archaeology and is available in Chinese and English. To order: send $20 for the English or $18 for the Chinese (add an additional $5 for airmail shipment) to Dr. Min Jiayin, Institute of Philosophy, Chinese Academy of Social Sciences, Beijing 100732, P.R. China. For information, write to P. Hosken, Editor, WINN, 187 Grant St., Lexington, MA 02173, U.S.

13th Moon: A Feminist Literary Magazine, edited by Judith Emlyn Johnson, is a magazine committed to celebrating the diversity of literature being produced by women today. For more information, contact the Department of English, University at Albany, SUNY, Albany, NY 12222.

RESOURCES

The National Alliance of Breast Cancer Organizations (NABCO) serves as a non-profit central resource for information about breast cancer and a network of 370 organizations providing detection, treatment, and care. Call NABCO to receive up-to-date information about breast cancer risk, detection, treatment, and research and to order informational publications; phone: 1-800-719-9154.

The American Association of Retired Persons (AARP) urges older women, who are at increased risk of breast cancer, to get screened regularly. Call the Media Relations Dept. at 202-434-2560 for a copy of the AARP Breast Care Campaign media kit. For information about breast cancer and mammograms, send a postcard to: "Chances Are," (D14502), AARP (EE0937), 691 E. St., NW, Washington, DC 20049 or call the National Cancer Institute at 1-800-4-CANCER. (Allow four weeks for delivery.)

The Ohio Lesbian Archives houses books, periodicals, memorabilia, and other aspects of lesbian culture and welcomes visitors on Tuesday & Thursday evenings, 7:00–8:30 P.M.. Volunteers and donations of money and materials are needed. Location: Room 304, The Women's Building, 4039 Hamilton Avenue, Cincinnati, OH 45223; phone: 513-541-1917.

Elaine Prater Hodges Productions announces the release of a new documentary, *Alice Paul: "We Were Arrested of Course!"*. The 28-minute video dramatizes the arrest and imprisonment of Alice Paul and the militant suffragists who were imprisoned for picketing the White House in 1917. For information, contact EPH Productions, Box 1042 Ansonia Station, NY, NY 10023; phone: 212-799-9246.

PROGRAMS

The Institute for Gender and Women's Studies of Aichi Shukutoku University opened formally in April 1995. For information, address inquiries to Junko Kuninobu, Director of Institute for Gender and Women's Studies, Aichi Shukutoku University, 9 Katahira, Nagakute-cho, Aichi-gun, Aichi, 48 0-11 Japan; phone: 0561 2-4111 ext. 498; fax: 0561-63-9308.

The Center for Women's Studies and the College of Law at the University of Cincinnati offer a four-year, joint-degree program combining a juris doctorate and a master of arts in women's studies. For application information, contact the Center for Women's Studies, P.O. Box 210164, Cincinnati, OH 45221-0164; phone: 513-556-6776; fax: 513-556-6771; E-mail: Graduate.Coordinator.WS@UC.Edu or Admissions@Law.UC.Edu

BEIJING FOLLOW-UP

The United Nations Division for the Advancement of Women (DAW) wishes to maintain contact with non-governmental organizations (NGOs) represented at the Fourth World Conference on Women in Beijing. Send updated information on your contact person and organization for DAW's mailing list. Conference documents, press releases, and other information are available through DAW on the Internet: Gopher: gopher://gopher.undp.org:70/11/unconfs/women or www: http://www.undp.org/fwcw/daw1.htm. For information, contact NGO Liaison Officer, DAW, 2 UN Plaza, DC2-12th Fl., NY, NY 10017.

The Honor Roll, one of the key commitments made by the United States government in Beijing, is underway. This calls on the Women's Bureau to "solicit pledges from employers, organizations, and community groups to make systemic changes in policies and practices in the workplace." All kinds of pledges meet the Honor Roll's criteria, from large financial commitments, such as building a new child care center, to simple changes in office policy, like allowing newborns at work. Obtain pledge materials by calling 1-800-827-5385.

The National Council for Research on Women announces the publication of *Issues Quarterly* (vol. 2, no. 1) entitled "A Conference of Commitments: Turning Words into Action." The issue reports on the UN Fourth World Conference on Women and the NGO Forum on Women by examining the impact NGOs had on shaping an international policy agenda for the world's women and girls and tracking efforts to implement the Platform for Action. Articles discuss the Convention on the Elimination of All Forms of Discrimination Against Women, youth at Beijing, the International Women Count Network, "Women's Eyes on the World Bank Campaign," the Global Tribunal on Women's Human Rights, and other major organizing projects. Subscriptions to *Issues Quarterly* are $20 per year, and single copies are available for $5. Contact NCRW, 530 Broadway, 10th Floor, NY, NY 10012-3920; phone: 212 274-0730; fax: 212 274-0821.

ANNOUNCEMENTS

The **Henry A. Murray Research Center** at Radcliffe College has been awarded $1 million in combined grants from the National Science Foundation and the National Institute of Mental Health to collect and make available studies of racial and ethnic minority populations. For the first time, studies with significant samples of African Americans, Asian Americans, Latinos, Native Americans and other underrepresented groups will be archived in one place and made available for new research.

The **Thanks Be to Grandmother Winifred Foundation** of Wainscott New York received 1,447 applications for project support in the three fiscal years between July 1992 and June 1995. The foundation awarded one hundred eight grants totalling $302,169.64, in amounts ranging from $500 to $5,000. Recipients range in age from 54 to 93, and live in thirty-three states, the District of Columbia, and England. For information, write the Thanks Be To Grandmother Winifred Foundation, P.O. Box 1449, Wainscott, NY 11975-1449; phone: 516-725-0323.

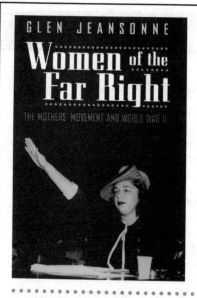

Please Enter My Subscription to the *Women's Studies Quarterly*

	U.S. *1 year*	Outside U.S. *1 year*
Individual	[ ] $30.00	[ ] $40.00
Institution	[ ] $40.00	[ ] $50.00
	3 years	*3 years*
Individual	[ ] $ 70.00	[ ] $100.00
Institution	[ ] $100.00	[ ] $120.00

A charge has been added to foreign subscriptions for surface delivery.

Total enclosed $ _____ .

All orders must be prepaid with checks or money orders payable to The Feminist Press in U.S. dollars drawn on a U.S. bank.

Or charge your VISA / MasterCard *(circle one)*.

Acct # _____   Exp. date _____

Signature _____

Name _____

Institution _____

Address _____

_____

Phone (   ) _____

Mail to: *Women's Studies Quarterly,* The Feminist Press at The City University of New York, 311 East 94th Street, New York, NY 10128.
Tel. (212) 360-5790   Fax (212) 348-1241

NOTICE TO PROSPECTIVE CONTRIBUTORS

Women's Studies Quarterly publishes contributions that introduce new feminist scholarship and theory applied to teaching and the curriculum, original sources and resources of direct use in course and program development, and reflective essays and original creative work on various themes of concern to women's studies practitioners. The intersections of race and class with gender are of special concern, as are the perspectives of members of minority groups within the United States and those of the international community.

Contributions should run from nine to twenty manuscript pages, typed double-spaced throughout, including notes, and are expected to be written in language that is accessible to the nonspecialist. Submissions are reviewed by outside readers in the field. Please send three copies and consult *The Chicago Manual of Style* for manuscript form.

Because many of the issues are planned by guest editors and feature collections of material on specific themes, contributors are urged to consult announcements of upcoming issues in the *Quarterly* and communicate with the guest editors.